The Economics of the Sulphur Industry

The Economics of the Sulphur Industry

Jared E. Hazleton

Published by Resources for the Future, Inc.
Distributed by The Johns Hopkins Press, Baltimore and London

RESOURCES FOR THE FUTURE, INC.
1755 Massachusetts Avenue, N.W., Washington, D.C. 20036

Resources for the Future is a nonprofit corporation for research and education in the development, conservation, and use of natural resources and the improvement of the quality of the environment. It was established in 1952 with the cooperation of the Ford Foundation. Part of the work of Resources for the Future is carried out by its resident staff; part is supported by grants to universities and other nonprofit organizations. Unless otherwise stated, interpretations and conclusions in RFF publications are those of the authors; the organization takes responsibility for the selection of significant subjects for study, the competence of the researchers, and their freedom of inquiry.

This book is one of RFF's resources appraisal studies, which are directed by Hans H. Landsberg. Jared E. Hazleton is a lecturer in economics at the University of Texas at Austin. The charts were drawn by Clare and Frank Ford.

RFF staff editors: Henry Jarrett, Vera W. Dodds, Nora E. Roots, Tadd Fisher.

Manufactured in the United States of America

Library of Congress Catalog Card Number 76–75181

Standard Book Number 8018–1074–4

Price $3.50

Foreword

Unless the next five years produce some unexpected changes, the Paley Commission's 1952 estimate that U.S. sulphur demand in 1975 would be twice that of 1950 will turn out to have been an accurate one. The reason is not hard to find: the use of sulphur has in the past so permeated the economy that the growth of the economy itself has pretty much set the pace of sulphur consumption. And in the past two decades both have grown at about three per cent per year. But, as Jared Hazleton shows, this smooth parallelism has been strained at various times during the twentieth century, with periods of sulphur shortage and glut following one another.

In this study—the revised version of a Ph.D. thesis that was supported by a grant under RFF's Fellowship Program—the author traces the characteristics of the Frasch sulphur industry, which has constituted the largest source of sulphur during this century. For his analysis of the output and price policies followed by the handful of producers that make up the industry, he has drawn upon interviews with industry representatives as well as upon the limited literature and the none-too-satisfactory published statistics.

This may be a particularly good time for such a study. One could make a reasonable guess that the Frasch sulphur industry has reached a turning point. Competing sources of sulphur are continuing to grow and are reducing the dominant role of the Frasch segment in the market. At the same time, the Frasch sulphur companies themselves have begun to diversify into other fields. Finally, we may be on the verge of a massive new source of supply—sulphur or sulphuric acid obtained as a result of pollution-abating practices only now coming into view. What such a development would spell for the conventional producers nobody has yet worked out; but that it would open a wholly new chapter in the life of an ancient industry is certain. In any event, Mr. Hazleton's book is of interest and value as a case study of industrial organization, an analysis of industrial behavior in the presence of great market power, and a contribution to an appraisal of the conditions under which future supplies are likely to become available from both tried and untried sources.

Hans H. Landsberg
Director of Resource Appraisals
Resources for the Future, Inc.

Acknowledgments

This study was first undertaken as a doctoral dissertation prepared for Rice University, under a Natural Resources Fellowship awarded by Resources for the Future. Subsequently, it has been extensively revised, updated, and the chapter on the industry and its resource has been added.

I am indebted to Professor Edward S. Mason of Harvard University for first suggesting to me that the sulphur industry would make an interesting topic for study. Professor Henry Steele, as director of my thesis committee, contributed freely of his time and advice. Professors Gaston Rimlinger and Dwight Brothers read and commented upon various drafts of the manuscript while it was at the dissertation stage.

I owe a special debt of gratitude to Hans H. Landsberg of Resources for the Future, who provided guidance and encouragement in the task of converting the dissertation to its present form. I also wish to thank Professor Lee E. Preston, Associate Dean of the School of Business Administration, University of California at Berkeley, who commented on an earlier draft.

As anyone who has undertaken an industry study realizes, this study could not have been made without the assistance and cooperation of a number of individuals in the sulphur industry, trade associations, and government, who gave freely of their time in providing me with information on the industry. They, of course, bear no responsibility for the conclusions of the study.

My final debt of gratitude is to my wife and family—they also serve who only stand and wait and wait and wait—to whom this book is dedicated.

Jared E. Hazleton

Table of Contents

List of Tables

List of Illustrations

The Economics of the Sulphur Industry

Chapter 1

Introduction

Sulphur is one of the most plentiful of the elements, but twice within the postwar era it has been in tight supply both within the United States and abroad. Sulphur is also one of the most important industrial raw materials, yet it is one of our least known mineral resources.

This study is an economic analysis of the sulphur industry. Its goal is to describe, interpret, and evaluate from the standpoint of public welfare the market structure, behavior, and performance of the domestic sulphur industry. At the same time, economic analysis of the industry should reveal much about the nature of the sulphur resource. In this regard, the study seeks to answer two questions. Does the past pattern of periodic shortage and abundance indicate recurring periods of scarcity in the future? Can the future sulphur requirements of the world be met without significant increases in unit costs?

Description of the Industry

Sulphur is widely distributed in nature, both alone and in combination with other minerals. Although 0.06 per cent of the weight of the earth's crust is believed to consist of sulphur, only an exceedingly small portion of the sulphur occurs in sufficiently concentrated amounts to justify mining. When considered as an industrial raw material, sulphur may be classified into two types. Where not in molecular combination with any other element, sulphur is called "elemental" and, in its natural state, is often termed "brimstone." Sulphur is also classified as elemental where, prior to its use as a raw material, it is separated in pure form from compounds. Sulphur is classified as "nonelemental" where, in molecular combination with some other element, it is used as a raw material without prior separation.

Elemental sulphur is supplied from several sources. Frasch sulphur, which derives its name from the developer of the process by which it is mined, is produced from brimstone deposits found in the salt domes of the United States and Mexican Gulf Coasts. The Frasch process is also used to produce elemental sulphur from non-salt dome deposits in West Texas. In addition, a small quantity of elemental sulphur is mined by conventional methods from sedimentary deposits and surface deposits, and separated from the metal in metallic sulphides. Recovered sulphur is produced from the hydrogen sulphide contained in sour natural or refinery gases.

Nonelemental sulphur is supplied principally as by-product acid from copper and zinc smelters, from gypsum and anhydrite deposits, and from pyrites (metal sulphides), which are burned to produce sulphur dioxide and by-product metallic oxides. A small amount of nonelemental sulphur is produced in the form of hydrogen sulphide by oil refineries and in the form of sulphur dioxide by smelters.

As shown in table 1, domestic production of sulphur in all forms totaled over 9.1 million tons in 1967.[1] Frasch-produced sulphur accounted for 7 million tons, or 75 per cent of total domestic production. Recovered sulphur output of nearly 1.3 million tons accounted for 14 per cent of domestic sulphur production, and various other sources accounted for the remaining 11 per cent. The total value of domestic sulphur shipments in 1967 amounted to about $292.8 million.

Table 1. U.S. Sulphur Production, All Forms, 1967

Source	Net sulphur content
Elemental sulphur:	*long tons*
Frasch process mines	7,014,164
Other mines	284
Recovered	1,267,955
Total elemental sulphur	8,282,403
Nonelemental sulphur:	
Pyrites (including coal brasses)	355,033
By-product	498,675
Total nonelemental sulphur	853,708
Total U.S. sulphur production	9,136,111

SOURCE: U.S. Department of the Interior, Bureau of Mines, *Minerals Yearbook*, 1967.

1. All statistics dealing with physical quantities in the industry will be given in long tons (2,240 pounds) unless otherwise noted.

The Approach

Industry studies by economists have generally been directed toward the analysis of imperfections in the competitive economy, primarily toward the analysis of oligopolistic markets where a few sellers possess varying degrees of market power. Market power exists where at least one firm is of sufficient size relative to the market to influence by its own actions the level of market price and output. The existence of market power results in a situation in which the equilibrium price and output in the industry are indeterminate. Thus, the task of an economic study seeking to analyze an industry of few sellers is to explain why the pattern of price and output behavior observed in the market emerged from the oligopoly being studied, and to provide a full critique of the impact of this behavior on the public welfare.

The sulphur industry is a typical oligopoly in which a few firms have consistently controlled a large share of the market. This study of the sulphur industry is organized along the lines of a number of similar studies of oligopolistic industries. It focuses on the industry's market structure, behavior, and performance.

This approach postulates that definable factors of market structure interact to produce a pattern of market behavior on the part of firms in an industry. This pattern of market behavior in turn provides a basis for evaluating the performance of the industry. The purpose of appraising the performance of the industry is to establish the extent to which firms have used their market power to achieve noncompetitive results. The explanation of market behavior in terms of the market structure of the industry is designed not only to describe how the pattern of market behavior emerged from the industry, but also to identify alternative market structures, obtainable through public policy, which might yield a better pattern of performance for the industry.

The market structure-behavior-performance approach attempts to solve the problem of oligopolistic indeterminacy by introducing additional factors of market structure into the analysis. Thus, structure is defined to include all factors taken into account by the firm in determining its business policies and practices. While the number and relative sizes of the sellers and buyers are an important element in this regard, they represent only one of several aspects of market structure.

Other factors that can be identified as exerting an influence on the firm's behavior include: (1) the geographical distribution of supply and demand; (2) the nature of demand, including the elasticity of demand with respect to both prices and income in the short run as well as in the long run; (3) the organization of the firm, in particular, the marketing and distribution channels used; (4) the nature of costs, including the proportion of fixed costs in the short run, and the ease of exit from the industry; (5) the conditions affecting entry into the industry; (6) the technological environment, i.e., the limitations imposed on the firm's actions by the current state of technology; and (7) the legal setting, including the impact of the patent system, taxation, and other governmental policies and regulations which affect the firm's behavior.[2] While this list is not exhaustive, it summarizes the more important features that lend themselves to empirical analysis.

The oligopolist, operating within an environment defined in terms of these factors of market structure, adopts certain policies in the market where it sells its product. Market behavior is formed by these policies of business firms in determining such factors as prices, outputs, product characteristics, selling expenses, and research expenditures. The importance of market behavior lies in its function as the link between an industry's structure and its performance.

In an oligopolistic industry, market behavior reflects the firm's policies not only toward its product market but also toward the actions taken by its rivals in that market. It is this interreaction of firms in the market that gives oligopolistic industries their unique indeterminateness and makes them an attractive subject for economic analysis. One important set of market behavioral patterns centers on determining oligopolistic prices, i.e., the ways in which firms set their prices and change them in response to others. A second set of policies concerns the product of the oligopolist. Product policies include product differentiation, the level of selling costs, and product quality. The final set includes policies that seek to change the factors of market structure. Coercive practices, for example, seek to drive out weaker rivals, or to reduce the threat of entry. Fear of antitrust litigation may have the opposite effect and result in policies aimed at maintaining the market share of the smaller firms in the industry.

The third element of industry analysis, market performance, is closely related to market behavior.[3] Behavior provides a basis for an evaluation of industry performance in terms of certain economic criteria. These criteria include: (1) cost-price relationships: the extent to which reduc-

2. These factors are summarized from those mentioned by Merton J. Peck, *Competition in the Aluminum Industry* (Cambridge: Harvard University Press, 1961), p. 2; Charles H. Phillips, Jr., *Competition in the Synthetic Rubber Industry* (Chapel Hill: The University of North Carolina Press, 1961), p. 6; and James W. McKie, *Tin Cans and Tin Plate* (Cambridge: Harvard University Press, 1959), p. 5.

3. The term "behavior" is often used to include both the conduct of the firms in the industry and the performance of the industry. It is desirable, however, to distinguish between these two elements because conduct is subject to objective analysis, while performance is substantially a matter of subjective evaluation.

tions in cost are passed on promptly in the form of price reductions; (2) capacity-output relationships: the efficiency of resource use as indicated by the scale and utilization of facilities and the location of production; (3) progressiveness: the extent to which the firms in the industry actively and effectively engage in product and process innovation; and (4) the level of profits: the extent to which profits of firms in the industry (rate of return after taxes on invested capital) exceed or fall short of profits earned by firms in industries exhibiting similar trends in such factors as sales, costs, and innovations.[4]

The purpose of appraising industry performance is to indicate the impact of market power on the public welfare. This impact is usually described in terms of the effectiveness or workability of competition. Economists are in general agreement that perfect competition constitutes neither a normative ideal nor a satisfactory basis for appraising actual market conditions. Therefore, they have sought to derive a "workability criterion," a set of conditions that would be both necessary and sufficient to ensure that market power is used in the public interest.

Unfortunately, it is easier to recognize the need for such normative standards than to provide broadly applicable criteria. At best, the appraisal of the workability of competition in an industry remains a "subjective judgment by a given economist concerning the extent to which he thinks that absence of one or another of the conditions of perfect competition will not prove *unduly* harmful to economic welfare."[5]

An appraisal of workability may lead to one of three conclusions. First, it may be determined that market power is present but has not been used to secure noncompetitive results, and the industry is judged workably competitive. Second, market power may be shown to have produced imperfectly competitive performance which is considered nonetheless workably competitive in light of possible remedial actions available through public policy. Third, market power may be shown to have produced noncompetitive performance that is considered unsatisfactory, and that can be improved through use of public policy. In the latter instance, the industry is considered nonworkably competitive. The key elements in any evaluation of the workability of competition in an industry are, therefore, the degree to which actual performance deviates from desired performance, and the possibility of remedial public action.

4. This list is taken from Edward S. Mason, "The Current Status of the Monopoly Problem," *Harvard Law Review* (June 1949), pp. 1281–82; and Carl Kaysen, *United States v. United Shoe Machinery Corporation* (Cambridge: Harvard University Press, 1956), p. 17.

5. H. H. Liebhafsky, *The Nature of Price Theory* (Homewood, Illinois: The Dorsey Press, Inc., 1963), p. 22.

Application to a Resource Industry

The considerations involved in an industry study described above are particularly suited to an analysis of a resource-based industry such as sulphur. Like other minerals, sulphur is characterized by fixed location, exhaustion of reserves, changing patterns of supply, competition between primary and by-product production, and continuously changing technology. Like other minerals, sulphur has periodically been the subject of public concern because of high prices and inadequate supply.

Harold J. Barnett and Chandler Morse have considered extensively the problem of increasing natural resource scarcity and diminishing returns as reflected in the trend of unit costs of extractive products. They conclude that to a significant degree, the prospect of increasing resource scarcity often generates its own solution in the form of sociotechnical change which results in increasing as opposed to diminishing returns.[6] There is a marked similarity between the argument as advanced by Barnett and Morse and the earlier theory of "creative destruction" developed by Joseph Schumpeter.[7] Both emphasize the dynamic nature of the capitalist economy. Both stress that economic change is embodied in sociological and technological change.

But what is the process through which sociotechnical change occurs? What determines the speed with which advances in technology act to alleviate problems of resource scarcity? How automatic is the process? The fundamental element in the process is, of course, the market, which both signals the need for change and provides the reward which motivates change. New sources of supply, new products and processes, and new forms of organization affect the market structure of an industry. At the same time, they are affected by changes in market structure and by changes in the behavior and performance of the industry.

Thus, a primary goal of this study will be to define the relationship between the sulphur industry and the sulphur resource. In particular, the study will investigate the role of market structure in fostering or hindering extension of the sulphur resource base. Extensions of the resource base will be analyzed to determine if they originated within or without the industry. Their impact on market behavior will be examined. Industry performance will be evaluated not only from the standpoint of

6. Harold J. Barnett and Chandler Morse, *Scarcity and Growth* (Baltimore: The Johns Hopkins Press for Resources for the Future, Inc., 1963). Barnett and Morse first emphasize (p. 7), "Resources can only be defined in terms of known technology." They then conclude (p. 10), "the increasing scarcity of particular resources fosters discovery or development of alternative resources, not only equal in economic quality but often superior to those replaced."

7. Joseph A. Schumpeter, *Capitalism, Socialism, and Democracy* (New York: Harper and Row Publishers, Inc., 1942).

the competitive norm but also in light of the industry's effectiveness in exploiting the sulphur resource.

Plan of This Study

This study is divided into three parts along lines similar to the market structure-behavior-performance approach outlined above. Part I describes the market structure of the sulphur industry. Chapters 2 and 3 deal with the supply aspects and chapter 4 with the demand aspects. Part II analyzes market behavior in the industry. Chapter 5 outlines the behavior of output and prices, while chapter 6 provides a chronological explanation of market behavior from the industry's inception to the present. In Part III, chapter 7 looks at performance from the standpoint of the competitive norm. Chapter 8 appraises the industry's performance with regard to the sulphur resource and presents an evaluation of the outlook for sulphur as a resource. In the final chapter, the major findings of the study are summarized, and the workability of competition in the industry is assessed.

Part I

Market Structure of the Sulphur Industry

Chapter 2

Sources of Supply of Sulphur

Although this study is primarily concerned with the Frasch segment of the domestic sulphur industry, any adequate analysis of the industry must also consider the competitive potential of other sources of supply. This chapter traces the development of the Frasch sulphur industry in both the United States and Mexico, and then describes the recovered sulphur industry which has become an increasingly important source since the Second World War. Other sources of supply which contribute only a small fraction of total sulphur supply are not discussed.

Frasch Sulphur

While sulphur has been known and used since antiquity, it was not until the last decades of the eighteenth century that advances in chemical technology centering around sulphuric acid led to increased demand for sulphur for industrial use. During the early years of the nineteenth century, the world's sulphur needs were supplied by the large volcanic deposits of elemental sulphur in Sicily.[1] The disadvantages of relying on a single source became obvious when the King of Naples granted a monopoly to a French firm for the sale of Sicilian sulphur in 1838, and the company promptly increased the price of sulphur from $25 to $75 per ton, the maximum permitted under its contract. Pressure from foreign purchasers, particularly Great Britain, forced a rescission of the contract in 1840, but by that time an interest in new sources of supply had been aroused. By 1860, Sicily still supplied the bulk of the world's nonacid sulphur needs, but acid manufacturers outside the United States had turned to obtaining sulphur from the roasting of iron pyrites.

1. For a complete description of the geological nature of the Sicilian sulphur deposits, see Walter F. Hunt, "The Origin of the Sulphur Deposits of Sicily," *Economic Geology* (1915), pp. 543–79. The most comprehensive description of the industry in Sicily is found in William Haynes, *The Stone That Burns* (New York: D. Van Nostrand Company, Inc., 1942).

At the turn of the century, American acid manufacturers also switched to iron pyrites. Interestingly enough, this action corresponded with the beginning of the Frasch sulphur industry in the United States.

Description of the Frasch process[2]

The Frasch process generally is applicable to a specific type of sulphur deposit associated with geological formations known as salt domes. In the United States, salt domes occur within a wide belt reaching from Alabama to Texas and extending offshore into the Gulf of Mexico and 75 to 300 miles inland. Outside the United States, salt domes have been discovered in Germany, the Netherlands, Romania, Iran, Russia, and Mexico. Only the U.S. and Mexican deposits have proven amenable to Frasch sulphur mining.

Basically, salt dome formations are pillars of salt extending to great depths and forming a dome-shaped structure in the overlying sediments. The tops of the pillars contain a characteristic series of minerals known collectively as the cap. Cap rock formations, consisting of limestone, gypsum, and anhydrite, differ materially in size, depth, thickness, and configuration, as well as in the relative proportions of the principal and accessory mineral constituents. Within the cap rock, sulphur occurs as well-developed rhombic crystals in the fissures, cracks, and seams of the porous limestone and also in the semicrystalline or massive state as a filling in the openings of formations. In a productive dome, the sulphur-bearing limestone is sealed in by a layer of barren, nonsulphur-bearing limestone above and a layer of equally barren anhydrite or gypsum below. The thickness of the sulphur formation varies widely, though the average is about 100 feet. The average sulphur content in a deposit ranges from 20 to 40 per cent.

The Frasch process for mining sulphur is based on the fact that crystalline sulphur melts at about 116° C. In mining, wells are drilled into the sulphur formation using rotary rigs similar to those employed in the

2. This description of salt dome sulphur deposits and the Frasch process is based on that given by Paul M. Ambrose, "Sulphur and Pyrites," in *Mineral Facts and Problems, 1965 Edition, Bulletin 630*, Bureau of Mines, U.S. Department of the Interior, Washington, D.C., 1965. In addition, for descriptions of salt dome sulphur deposits see: Marcus A. Hanna and Albert G. Wolf, "Texas and Louisiana Salt Dome Cap Rock Minerals," and George Sawtelle, "Salt Dome Statistics," in *Geology of Salt Dome Oil Fields*, ed. Raymond C. Moore (Tulsa, Oklahoma: The American Association of Petroleum Geologists, 1926), pp. 119–32 and 109–18; and W. T. Lundy, "Sulphur and Pyrites," in *Industrial Minerals and Rocks* (2nd ed.; New York: American Institute of Mining and Metallurgical Engineers, 1949). The most complete account of the development of the Frasch process appears in William Haynes, *The Stone That Burns*, pp. 24–45. A good description of the technical aspects of mining sulphur by the Frasch process is given by Will H. Shearon, Jr., and J. H. Pollard, "Modern Sulphur Mining," in *Modern Chemical Processes*, ed. William J. Murphy (vol. 2; New York: Reinhold Publishing Corporation, 1952), pp. 219–29.

petroleum industry. The wells are equipped with a nest of four concentric pipes. A typical well will have an outermost pipe, eight or ten inches in diameter, which extends to the top of the cap rock and lines the well to prevent the sides from caving in. Inside this outer pipe is a six-inch pipe which extends through the sulphur-bearing stratum and rests in the upper portion of the underlying anhydrite or gypsum layer. A three-inch pipe, placed inside the six-inch pipe, reaches nearly to the bottom of the sulphur-bearing rock, but rests on a collar that is set within the six-inch pipe and that seals the annular space between the two. Finally, a one-inch air pipe, inside the three-inch pipe, extends to an area slightly above the collar. The six-inch pipe is perforated at two levels, separated by the collar; the upper set of holes permits the escape of hot water and the lower set the entrance of molten sulphur (see figure 1).

In steaming a well, water is treated to remove scale-forming salts and corrosive substances; heated to 320°–340° F.; pumped, under pressure

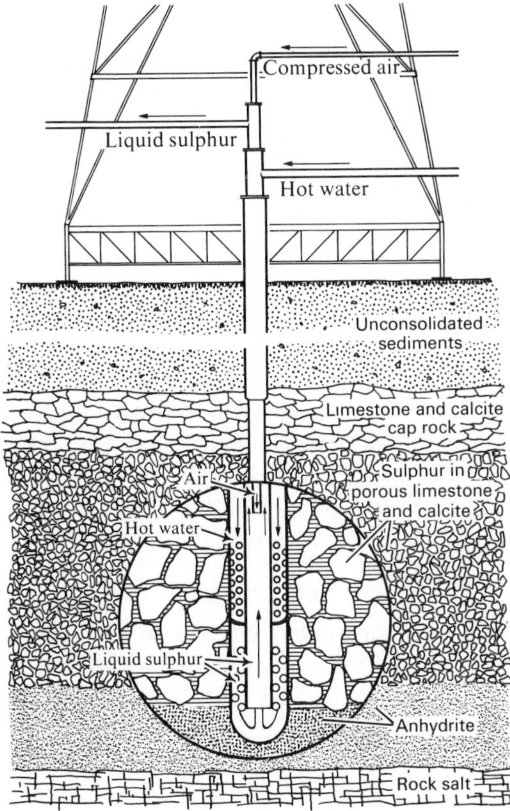

Figure 1. Underground piping arrangement for Frasch mining.

of 100–250 pounds per square inch, down the annular space between the six-inch and three-inch pipe; and discharged into the porous limestone formation through the upper set of perforations in the six-inch pipe. The entire region through which the water circulates is raised to a temperature above the melting point of sulphur. The heated zone formed by the incoming water takes the shape of an inverted cone, whose outer limits remain below the fusion point of sulphur and whose apex is the bottom of the hole. The molten sulphur, being heavier than water, runs within the dome. The amount of water required to recover a ton of sul-Dome pressure forces the sulphur part-way up the three-inch pipe. Compressed air, injected at a pressure of about 500 pounds per square inch through the central one-inch pipe into the molten sulphur, changes the apparent specific gravity of the liquid sulphur and raises it to the surface. Liquid sulphur reaching the surface is discharged into steam-heated tanks. After being metered, the sulphur is pumped through steam-heated lines into vats, where it is stored in either dry or liquid form.

Since each well is able to remove sulphur from only a limited area, the Frasch process requires the constant drilling of new wells. In addition, bleeder wells must be drilled to remove the large volumes of cool water that accumulate within the formation; this makes room for the hot water being pumped into the dome and prevents a buildup of pressure to the bottom of the cone, and forms a pool around the foot of the well. phur varies widely between domes.

The removal of large quantities of sulphur from the cap rock usually affects production in one of two ways. If cavities remain after the sulphur is removed, there is an increase in the water-to-sulphur ratio and, therefore, in the costs of production. To reduce hot-water requirements, the cavities are filled by mudding. If sulphur removal is followed by subsidence, the cavities are often filled and there is no need for mudding, but subsidence often distorts or breaks the strings of pipe in the well and damages surface installations in the immediate area. The defense against subsidence is to drill and equip wells only as needed and to construct power plants and other permanent structures at points beyond the limits of any possible surface subsidence area.

Development of the U.S. Frasch sulphur industry

The birth of the Frasch sulphur industry in the United States can be dated from 1868, when an extensive sulphur deposit was discovered by the Louisiana Petroleum and Coal Oil Company in Calcasieu Parish, Louisiana, about 30 miles inland from the Gulf of Mexico.[3] The firm,

3. This section draws extensively on the descriptions of the U.S. Frasch sulphur industry given by William Haynes in *The Stone That Burns* and in *Brimstone: The Stone That Burns* (Princeton: D. Van Nostrand Company, Inc., 1959).

while prospecting for oil, had discovered a bed of pure sulphur, 108 feet thick, at a depth of about 500 feet. Between 1870 and 1890, several unsuccessful attempts were made to mine this deposit by the conventional means of sinking a shaft to the deposit. Sometime during this period, Herman Frasch, the first research director of the Standard Oil Company, learned of the Louisiana deposit and devised an ingenious system for mining the sulphur. In 1890, Frasch applied for three patents on his now famous hot-water process for mining sulphur, and in the same year he entered into an agreement to develop this process with Frank Rockefeller, brother of John D. Rockefeller, and F. B. Squires, Secretary of the Standard Oil Company. Arrangements were made to obtain the mining rights to the Calcasieu deposit, and late in 1894 the first Frasch sulphur mine was begun. By 1896, the venture showed sufficient promise to cause the parties to incorporate the Union Sulphur Company which acquired title to the land and mineral rights at the sulphur mine and to the Frasch patents. After several delays in bringing the mine into profitable production, output of Frasch sulphur progressed steadily, rising from less than 25,000 tons in 1903 to an average of over 200,000 tons per year between 1905 and 1911.

The expiration of the original Frasch patents in 1908 stimulated competition in the American sulphur market. As early as 1906, the Gulf Development Company had been formed to prospect for sulphur on the Bryan Heights Salt Dome (often called Bryan Mound) in Brazoria County, Texas. In 1912, the Freeport Sulphur Company was incorporated in Texas to mine sulphur from this property using the Frasch process. On 12 November 1912 the first sulphur was mined from Bryan Mound. Efforts by the Union Sulphur Company to contest use of the Frasch process by Freeport on the grounds that such operations infringed on the patent rights of Union were not upheld by the courts.[4]

A second competitor for the Union Sulphur Company developed when Gulf Sulphur Company was organized in 1909 to develop sulphur deposits on the Big Hill Dome, in Matagorda County, Texas. Bernard Baruch, who controlled this firm, delayed development of the deposit because he felt "with both the Union and Freeport sulphur companies in production, there seemed to be no room in the market for a third producer."[5] By 1916, however, the increased demand for sulphur resulting from the war in Europe prompted Baruch to obtain additional capital

4. See *Union v. Freeport*, U.S. District Court, Delaware, In Equity No. 336; and U.S. Circuit Court of Appeals, 3rd Circuit, Nos. 2391 and 2392, October Term, 1918. A summary of the judgment is given in "Frasch Sulphur Mining Process Decision," *The Journal of Industrial and Engineering Chemistry* (April 1919), pp. 374–75.

5. Bernard Baruch, *Baruch, My Own Story* (New York: Henry Holt and Company, 1957), p. 237.

from the Morgan interests, to reorganize the firm as the Texas Gulf Sulphur Company, and to commence development of the property. While the original plan had been to develop the property modestly, the entrance of the United States into the war abruptly changed these plans. The Big Hill mine came on stream early in 1919.

From 1919 to 1924, Texas Gulf and Freeport accounted for between one-half and three-quarters of the total Frasch sulphur output, with Union Sulphur Company providing the remainder. In 1925, Union closed its mine due to depletion, and subsequently—after making several unsuccessful attempts to secure additional reserves and after having sold its aboveground stocks—was forced to leave the industry. Freeport and Texas Gulf were thus the only Frasch producers until the formation of the Duval Texas Sulphur Company in 1928. A fourth company, Jefferson Lake Oil Company (later Jefferson Lake Sulphur Company) entered in 1932. From 1932 until 1966, these four companies controlled virtually the entire output of Frasch sulphur in the United States, with Texas Gulf and Freeport accounting for nearly 90 per cent of total output and Duval and Jefferson Lake sharing the remainder. During this period, there were at least five unsuccessful attempts made to enter the industry.

In response to a growing shortage of sulphur, several firms took steps to enter the Frasch sulphur industry during 1966 and 1967.[6] Union Texas Petroleum Division, a subsidiary of Allied Chemical Corporation, reestablished the original Union mine in Sulphur, Louisiana, beginning production on 18 September 1966. A newly formed company, Phelan Sulphur Company, constructed a $2.5 million plant to produce about 150,000 tons of sulphur per year from the Nash Dome, a mine abandoned in 1956 by Freeport after a little over 150,000 tons had been produced. Hooker Chemical Company built a pilot plant in June 1967 to produce sulphur from Bryan Mound, the initial mine opened by Freeport in 1912 and abandoned in 1935. In 1968, U.S. Oil of Louisiana, Ltd., reopened the Chacahoula Dome. Between 1955 and 1962, Freeport produced about 1.2 million tons from this deposit, which is thought to still hold over 4 million tons.

Table 2 and figure 2 depict the salt domes that have been mined, their location, and the sulphur obtained from each deposit through 1966. It can be seen that in addition to being highly concentrated economically, the Frasch sulphur industry is also very concentrated geographically. Only 27 of the 200-odd salt domes discovered on the Texas and Louisiana Gulf Coasts have been mined, and of these only 10 have produced as much as 5 million tons of sulphur. In 1968, of the 18 mines producing Frasch sulphur in the United States, only three—Grand Isle,

6. See "New Sources of Sulphur Emerge," *Industrial Minerals* (December 1967), pp. 23, 24, 29.

Table 2. Production of Frasch Sulphur in the United States by Mines and Companies, in Chronological Order, 1895 to 1966

Dome	Company	Opened	Closed	Total output
				long tons
Sulphur Mine, La.	Union	12–27–94	12–23–24	9,412,165
Bryan Mound	Freeport	11–12–12	9–30–35	5,001,068
Gulf (Big Hill)	Texas Gulf	3–19–19	8–10–36	12,349,597
Hoskins Mound	Freeport	3–31–23	5–26–55	10,895,090
Big Creek	Union	3– 6–25	2–24–26	1,450
Palangana	Duval	10–27–28	3–10–35	236,662
Boling Dome	Union	11–14–28	8–30–29	9,164
Boling Dome	Texas Gulf	3–19–29	OPEN	61,118,065
Long Point	Texas Gulf	3–19–30	10–19–38	402,105
Lake Peigneur	Jefferson Lake	10–20–32	6– 7–36	430,811
Grande Ecaille	Freeport	12– 8–33	OPEN	30,885,243
Boling Dome	Duval	3–23–35	4–25–40	571,123
Boling Dome	Baker-Williams	6– 2–35	12–18–35	1,435
Clemens Dome	Jefferson Lake	5– 3–37	12–14–60	2,975,828
Orchard Dome	Duval	1–29–38	OPEN	5,149,215
Long Point	Jefferson Lake	6– 7–46	OPEN	4,551,472
Moss Bluff	Texas Gulf	6–24–48	OPEN	5,081,343
Starks Dome	Jefferson Lake	6–15–51	12–13–60	840,249
Spindletop Mine	Texas Lake	5–12–52	OPEN	6,310,721
Bay Ste. Elaine	Freeport	11–19–52	12–29–59	1,131,204
Damon	Standard Sulphur	11–11–53	4–20–57	139,618
Garden Island Bay	Freeport	11–19–53	OPEN	7,006,991
Nash	Freeport	2– 3–54	11–23–56	153,115
Chacahoula	Freeport	2–25–55	9–28–62	1,199,015
Fannett	Texas Gulf	5– 6–58	OPEN	1,773,737
High Island	United States	3–25–60	2– 8–62	36,708
Grand Isle	Freeport	4–17–60	OPEN	4,466,021
Lake Pelto	Freeport	11–26–60	OPEN	2,474,693
Gulf (Big Hill)	Texas Gulf	10– 8–65	OPEN	107,830
Sulphur Mine, La.	Allied Chemical	9–18–66	OPEN	1,447
Nash	Phelan Sulphur Co.	11– 7–66	OPEN	622

SOURCE: Industry data for 1895–1966 compiled by Freeport Sulphur Company.

NOTE: Several mines were opened after 1966. Hooker Chemical operated Bryan Mound from 1967 to 1968, and U.S. Oil of Louisiana, Ltd., began operations at Chacahoula in 1967. In 1968, Freeport began operations at Caminada, Jefferson Lake at Lake Hermitage, and Texas Gulf at Lake Bully Camp.

Grande Ecaille, and Boling—were capable of an output of one million tons per year.

Development of offshore Frasch mining

One of the most interesting developments in the Frasch sulphur industry was the introduction of offshore Frasch operations in the Gulf of Mexico. This development was directly related to the extension of petroleum exploration and production into the coastal waters off Louisiana

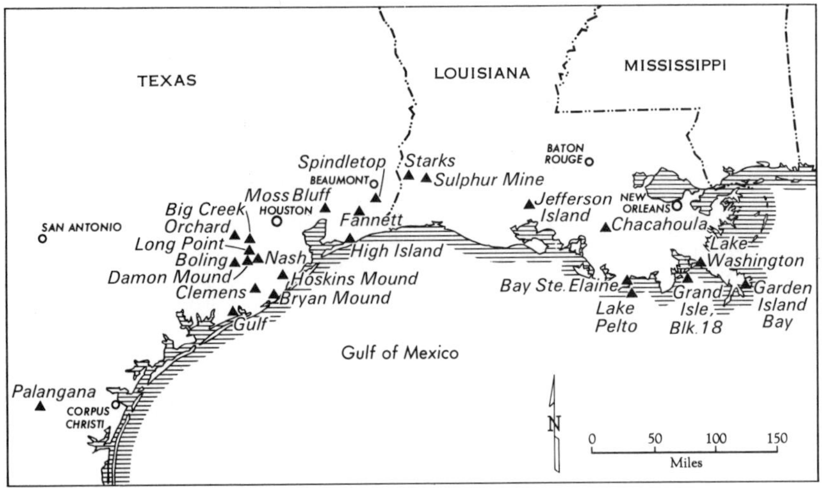

Figure 2. Frasch sulphur mines on Louisiana and Texas salt domes.

and Texas immediately after World War II. The first offshore deposit of sulphur in the Gulf of Mexico was discovered in 1949 by Humble Oil and Refining Company, while drilling for oil on its Grand Isle, Block 16 lease, located in 50 feet of water, 7½ miles off the coast of Jefferson Parish, Louisiana. In 1954, ten sulphur prospect holes were drilled, and sulphur ore was encountered in eight of them. Humble thus established the existence of a major sulphur deposit with estimated reserves of 30–40 million tons.[7] The sulphur rights at Grand Isle were held under leases originally executed by the State of Louisiana and later confirmed by the federal government pursuant to the provisions of the Outer Continental Shelf Lands Act.

Despite the fact that Humble had obtained authorization from its stockholders in October 1954 to expand its activities beyond oil and gas specifically to develop sulphur, two years later it entered into an agreement with Freeport Sulphur Company which gave Freeport the rights to the Grand Isle sulphur deposit and also the sulphur rights on two nearby domes: Grand Isle, Block 16, where a commercially exploitable deposit had been proved; and West Delta, Block 30, where Freeport was to continue prospecting work begun by Humble.

Construction of the Grand Isle plant began in June 1959 and was completed in 1962. The estimated total cost for this first offshore Frasch process plant was $30 million, of which $8 million was reported to rep-

7. C. O. Lee, Z. W. Bartlett, and R. H. Feierabend, "The Grand Isle Mine," *Mining Engineering* (June 1960), p. 578.

resent the additional costs of offshore operations.[8] In 1968, Freeport placed in operation a second offshore Frasch mine on Grand Isle, Block 16, known as Caminada. The $25 million plant is located in 50 feet of water, 6 miles offshore. It mines a sulphur deposit that lies 1,750 feet under sea level.

Several unsuccessful exploration efforts were undertaken on offshore domes by Texas Gulf and Freeport during the mid-fifties. During the decade following there were no additional attempts to seek new sulphur deposits in the offshore waters. For most of this period, sulphur was in surplus and there was little incentive to undergo the costs of offshore exploration. However, in December 1965, following a turn toward tightness in the sulphur market, the Bureau of Land Management of the U.S. Department of the Interior awarded leases to prospect for sulphur on 72,000 acres of the outer continental shelf off the Texas Coast. The tracts leased are located 40–80 miles offshore from the Galveston-Freeport area and lie under 110 to 180 feet of water. Fifty tracts of 1,440 acres each were leased to seven companies or combines for $33.7 million, an average of $468 per acre. This sum represents the highest price ever paid for mineral lease rights in the outer continental shelf area except for certain oil and gas drainage rights. The leases run for ten years with a royalty payment to the federal government of 10 per cent of the gross product or value of sulphur at the wellhead but not less than $2 per long ton.[9]

High costs are a major obstacle to extensive mining of sulphur offshore. The necessity of securing leases from the federal government by competitive bidding greatly increases the initial costs of offshore as compared with onshore exploration.[10] In addition, the costs of exploratory drilling are much higher offshore, as are the costs of building and operating a Frasch plant. The Grand Isle and Caminada mines are located only 6–8 miles offshore. At both mines, sulphur is shipped via a heated underwater pipeline to shore and then transferred by barge to a storage terminal at Port Sulphur. The tracts leased in 1965, however, are located 40–80 miles offshore. Thus, the problems and costs of shipping

8. *Ibid.* Also, see *The Engineering and Mining Journal* (December 1961), p. 137, for details regarding the expansion authorized in 1961 and completed in 1962.

9. U.S. Department of the Interior, Bureau of Land Management, "Interior Leases Sulphur Rights on the Continental Shelf," *News Release*, 21 December 1965.

10. For example, in 1965, in competitive bidding for offshore leases at San Luis Pass, Freeport paid $1.1 million more than the combined bids entered by the other bidders. Similarly, Texas Gulf Sulphur paid $7.1 million for its leases off Galveston Island, while the combined total of all other bids on these leases amounted to only $385,720! Texas Gulf paid $750,000 each for two leases on which it was the only bidder.

sulphur from mines at such locations to an onshore distribution terminal will be much greater than have been faced to date.

Development of the Mexican Frasch sulphur industry[11]

Petroleum exploration disclosed the existence of sulphur in salt dome formations on the Isthmus of Tehuantepec as early as 1902, but for forty years sulphur was of interest only because it indicated the presence of oil. It remained for General Alfredo Breceda, a hero of the Mexican revolution, to capitalize on the results of the early explorations. In 1942, Breceda and his partner, Manuel Urquidi, succeeded in obtaining the first sulphur concession on the Isthmus from the Mexican Ministry of National Economy.

Under Article 27 of the 1917 Constitution, all minerals in Mexico belong to the people of Mexico, regardless of the ownership of the surface land. Legislation passed in 1930 provided for the establishment of national mining reserves and set up the *Comisión de Fomento Minero* (Mining Development Commission), which was empowered to issue concessions within the reserves for the exploration and development of mineral deposits. Sulphur was not included in the national mineral reserves, and the concessions granted to Breceda and Urquidi were therefore based on a regulation issued in 1941 by the Minister of National Economy. However, this regulation established conditions for sulphur concessions which were similar to those for the concessions granted by the *Comisión de Fomento Minero* (the *Fomento*). Breceda and Urquidi received three concessions of 100 hectares each, the maximum size allowable under the mining law.

In 1943, an *acuerdo*, or decree, of President Manuel Avila Camacho placed all unassigned portions of the Tehuantepec area in a *Zona Azufrosa,* a Sulphur Reserve, under the administration of the *Fomento.* The procedures for obtaining rights of exploration and exploitation for sulphur were thereafter defined by the *Fomento*, rather than by the mining law. However, the Breceda and Urquidi concessions remained outside the control of the *Fomento.*[12]

11. This section is based primarily upon Haynes, *Brimstone: The Stone That Burns,* chaps. 1, 14, and 15. Also, see Robert Sheehan, "The 'Little Mothers' and Pan American Sulphur," *Fortune* (July 1960), pp. 96ff.; John H. Kearney, "A New Empire of Frasch Process Sulphur Is Rising from the Jungles of Mexico," *The Engineering and Mining Journal* (January 1955), pp. 72–77; Dale B. Truett, "Sulphur and the Development of a Chemical Fertilizer Industry in Mexico" (Ph.D. dissertation, The University of Texas, 1967); and Miguel S. Wionczek, "Foreign-Owned Export-Oriented Enclave in a Rapidly Industrializing Economy: Sulphur Mining in Mexico," in *El Nacionalismo mexicano y la inversión extranjera* (Siglo XXI Editores, Mexico, 1967).

12. Wionczek, *op. cit.*, states that Breceda suggested this action, the purpose of which was to complicate future possible direct deals between the authorities and foreign companies, namely the two major U.S. Frasch producers, Texas Gulf and Freeport.

Breceda and Urquidi attempted to secure domestic financial backing during the mid-forties. In particular, they sought to join forces with the *Nacional Financiera* (NAFIN), the national industrial development bank. Surface examinations of areas adjacent to their concessions prompted Breceda and Urquidi to apply for additional concessions; however, they withdrew their request when the government indicated its wish to cede these areas to the *Fomento* for exploitation directed by NAFIN and contracted to the Freeport Sulphur Company. The project reportedly fell through when Freeport demanded a contract in which taxes would be frozen at a low level.[13] Subsequently, the President issued a decree (28 April 1944) which directed NAFIN to organize a corporation to develop the Isthmus sulphur deposits. Breceda and Urquidi were furnished with an office by NAFIN from which they organized exploration work under the name Azufres de Tehuantepec. They entered into an agreement with a trio of U.S. wildcat drillers, the Brady brothers, to conduct an exploration program on their initial concessions. When sulphur in commercially minable quantities was proven to exist, Breceda and Urquidi reaffirmed their intention of joining with NAFIN, on NAFIN's terms, to form a national sulphur industry. However, at this point, NAFIN abruptly decided that it was no longer interested in organizing a sulphur operation on the Isthmus.[14] After rejection by NAFIN and several unsuccessful attempts to obtain domestic financing, Breceda and Urquidi assigned their concessions to the Bradys in exchange for a royalty agreement. The Bradys continued exploration on the Isthmus, and their discoveries subsequently led to the formation of three U.S. corporations, each with a subsidiary incorporated in Mexico, to mine sulphur by the Frasch process.

In 1946, the Mexican Gulf Sulphur Company was formed to mine the San Cristobal concession. The plant, financed in part by a loan from the Export-Import Bank, came on stream in 1954, but returns from the wells were irregular, and the output was about half the expected volume. After efforts to expand output and to discover additional reserves proved unsuccessful, Mexican Gulf's plant and equipment were purchased by the *Nacional Financiera* in 1958.

The Mexican Gulf experience points up the uncertain nature of Mexican Frasch operations as compared with the U.S. Gulf Coast. The Texas-Louisiana mines are true salt dome formations, whereas the Isthmus sulphur formations are a combination of domes and anticlines with a salt core apex. The anticlines, folds or ridges of stratified rock, are a less regular formation than a salt plug, and can present very

13. Antonio Acevedo Escobedo, *El azufre en Mexico* (Mexico, D.F.: Editorial Cultura, 1956), p. 185. Also see Wionczek, *op. cit.*

14. It was later established that lack of funds and opposition from U.S. sulphur interests were responsible for NAFIN's withdrawal. Acevedo, *op. cit.*, pp. 188–89.

favorable or almost impossible structures for the operation of the Frasch process. The San Cristobal deposit appeared to be particularly spotty with some very favorable showing mixed with barren holes. Later, other sulphur operations in Mexico were to experience similar difficulties.

The second company established to mine Frasch sulphur on one of the Isthmus concessions, Pan American Sulphur Company (PASCO), fared much better than Mexican Gulf. PASCO was formed in 1947 by a group of Texas oilmen to mine the Jaltipan, Portrerillos, and Teterete domes. PASCO's owners were not initially interested in becoming sulphur producers. Having proved the existence of commercial deposits, they sought to sell their concessions.[15] Only after their attempts to interest Freeport Sulphur Company and Texas Gulf Sulphur Company in purchasing the property were unsuccessful, did PASCO's owners decide to build a plant themselves.[16]

After receiving over $4 million in construction loans from the Export-Import Bank, PASCO brought its plant on stream on 24 September 1954. From the beginning, production proceeded without difficulty. Within eighteen months, the capacity of the plant was expanded by 50 per cent. By 10 December 1956, the company had produced one million tons of sulphur. In the spring of 1955, the Bradys disposed of their stock in PASCO for an estimated $7 million. They retained their royalty interest of $1.00 per ton on sulphur produced from the initial concession and 50 cents per ton on sulphur produced from the concessions acquired in 1950.

In 1951, the Bradys formed a third company, Gulf Sulphur Company, to mine the remaining Breceda-Urquidi concessions on the Mezquital, Soledad, and Salinas domes and part of the Vista Hermosa dome. The company's plant and sulphur mining facilities came on stream on 3 May 1956. Just prior to the commencement of sulphur production from the Salinas dome, Hudson Engineering Company and Baer, Sterns, and Company purchased all the Bradys' Gulf Sulphur stock. Production from the Salinas mine rose slowly from 110,841 tons in 1956 to 373,000 tons in 1962.

Texas Gulf Sulphur Company (TGS) had indicated interest in the sulphur deposits of the Isthmus as early as 1941, and in the fall of 1948 had sent a team of geologists to the Isthmus to survey the deposits there.

15. Drilling undertaken in 1944 and 1945 by the Brady brothers proved that the original concessions obtained by Breceda and Urquidi covered only the fringe of the key salt domes. Subsequently, Breceda and Urquidi, acting on behalf of PASCO, were able to obtain by presidential decree additional concessions of 12,217 hectares in adjacent areas. The areas in question were taken out of the national sulphur reserve. The political factors involved in acquiring these additions to the initial concessions are considered in detail by Wionczek, *op. cit.*

16. Sheehan, *op. cit.*, p. 199.

In 1949, the *Fomento* signed the first direct exploitation contract for sulphur with Compañía Exploradora del Istmo, S.A., the Mexican subsidiary of Texas Gulf.[17] The concessions granted Texas Gulf included the Nopalapa dome and portions of the Texistepec dome. The provisions of the contract were not at all in accord with the regulations applicable to the sulphur concessions outside the *Fomento* area. In 1949, both PASCO and Gulf Sulphur were subject to a 6 per cent royalty, a 15 per cent export tax, and a one per cent production tax; nothing was stipulated regarding a tax or royalty ceiling. The TGS contract, on the other hand, provided for a total tax and royalty load of 16 per cent during the first five years of operation, and a maximum of 21 per cent thereafter for the life of the contract (up to forty years). Faced with the prospect of such an inequitable tax, PASCO again drafted the services of Breceda and Urquidi. These two gentlemen succeeded in obtaining equal tax and royalty status for all sulphur producers by virtue of a Presidential Decree of 20 June 1950.[18]

Texas Gulf conducted a thorough exploration of their concession before deciding to construct a plant on the Nopalapa dome. The plant was not brought on stream until 8 February 1957. Production totaled 115,000 tons in 1957 and 1958 and 120,000 tons in 1959, all of which was stockpiled. In February 1960, production was suspended at the Nopalapa mine. Suspension of operations was attributed to the high costs of the operation, as compared with Texas Gulf's domestic mines, and the sharp reduction in sulphur prices throughout the world in the period from 1958 through 1962. During 1967, with sulphur in tight supply and prices rising, Texas Gulf announced plans to place the Nopalapa mine back into production.

In 1953, the Texas International Sulphur Company was formed to mine a surface deposit of sulphur in the State of Baja California. In 1956, the company purchased Central Minera, a Mexican firm which

17. Wionczek, *op. cit.*, describes the controversy that raged in Mexico over the opening of the Mexican Frasch sulphur industry to the "international sulphur trusts." Much of this opposition was led by the Breceda-Urquidi interests. Wionczek concludes that this resistance backfired. Not only did it not prevent the granting of the concession to Texas Gulf, but more importantly, it called attention to the presence of a foreign sulphur company in the country and strengthened the forces within the country that were pressing for the closer control of the mining sector.

18. Truett, *op. cit.*, pp. 87–90. In addition to the discrepancy in royalty tax arrangements between the TGS contract and the regulations applying to other concessionaires, other discrepancies existed between the two documents, particularly in terms of the investment required to maintain the concessions (or contract) and the required exploration program. Truett, *op. cit.*, pp. 92–94, and Acevedo, *op. cit.*, p. 118, contend that TGS appeared to have negotiated more with the view of blocking the sulphur mining efforts of potential competitors than of developing its own mining facilities.

had obtained a *Fomento* sulphur concession. Texas International installed a Frasch plant in the Texistepec concession in late 1959. No production was recorded for 1960, and production totaled only 50,000 tons in 1961. In 1962, shortage of capital forced the company to suspend operations, and no production has been recorded since then.[19]

Thus, of the five attempts to mine sulphur in Mexico, two were failures, and a third was discontinued. Of the two that remained, Pan American Sulphur Company was by far the more successful. Table 3 shows the rapid growth of Frasch sulphur output in Mexico, and PASCO's dominant position in the industry.

Table 3. Output of Frasch Sulphur in Mexico, 1954–65

Year	Total output	PASCO output	Other output	PASCO share of total output
	(............	*thousand long tons*	............)	*per cent*
1954	87.2	31.6	55.6	36.2
1955	475.5	391.8	83.7	82.4
1956	754.1	623.8	130.3	82.7
1957	993.4	723.1	270.3	72.8
1958	1,201.4	822.0	379.4	68.4
1959	1,266.8	886.9	379.9	70.0
1960	1,252.3	1,027.6	224.7	82.0
1961	1,171.8	882.7	289.1	75.3
1962	1,335.7	982.9	352.8*	73.6
1963	1,448.0	1,121.2	326.8*	77.4
1964	1,625.5	1,275.8	349.7*	78.5
1965	1,519.6	1,142.6	377.0*	75.2

SOURCE: Secretaría de Industria y Comercio, Dirección General de Estadística.

NOTE: All figures converted from metric tons to long tons. Conversion factor used = 0.98419.

* After 1962, Gulf Sulphur Company.

Relations between the Frasch producers and the Mexican government became increasingly strained after the passage of a new mining law in 1961 which required firms conducting mining operations in Mexico to be owned at least two-thirds by Mexican nationals. Pressures were exerted on both Pan American and Gulf Sulphur to mexicanize their operations. These pressures culminated in 1965, when the Mexican government abruptly imposed export controls on the Frasch sulphur industry. The stated objective of this action was to bring increases in exports into line with expansions in reserves. However, two equally important objectives which received little public attention were to encourage the development of a domestic chemical fertilizer complex,

19. *Sulphur* (June 1963), p. 17.

and to bring Frasch sulphur operations on the Isthmus into agreement with the provisions of the 1961 mining law.

As might have been expected, the initial reaction of the American financial press to the action taken by the Mexican government was quite hostile. One writer stated:

> For a quarter-century Mexico has sought, with considerable success of late, to live down its ill-advised expropriations of U.S. and British oil interests. Last month the government suddenly acted like a reformed bandit who can not give up his old tricks. Robbing the gringo, as everyone should have learned by now, is no way to get rich.[20]

The controls on sulphur exports proved much less restrictive than had been anticipated. Not only did the export authorizations in 1965 and 1966 not fall below previous levels, but they provided for a steady expansion of exports beginning in 1967 following the establishment of sizable new reserves. Without a doubt, the Mexican policy was highly successful in bringing about both an expansion in reserves and a program for the development of a chemical fertilizer complex in Mexico using Mexican sulphur.[21] At the same time, by demonstrating its power and will to influence the operations of the major Frasch producer, the Mexican government succeeded in bringing closer the mexicanization of the Isthmus sulphur industry. Late in 1966, negotiations proceeded to permit purchase by Mexican financial interests of a two-thirds ownership in Pan American Sulphur Company. Subsequently, PASCO was brought within the framework of the 1961 mining law.

The attitude of the Mexican government toward exploration and mining of sulphur by foreign firms was aptly summarized in April 1965 in a statement by the then-Secretary of National Properties, Alfonso Corona del Rosal:

> Concessions for sulphur exploration will be given to some companies that have sought them, within the framework of the present Mining Law; that is, to companies with at least 66 per cent Mexican capital, and preferably to those who promise to convert the sulphur into fertilizers for the demands of our agriculture and for export of the excess. Those companies will have the right, as an incentive to their explorations, to export 10 per cent of the sulphur reserves they discover.[22]

20. "Robbing the Gringo," *Barron's* (3 May 1965), p. 1.

21. Pan American, for example, spent $1 million in 1965 and 1966 in drilling 100 exploratory wells. They also entered into an agreement with two U.S. investment houses to establish a firm, 49 per cent owned by U.S. interests and 51 per cent owned by Mexican nationals, to build a $44 million fertilizer complex scheduled to commence production in late 1968. See "Pan American Sulphur Says '65 Profit, Sales Will Trail Last Year," *Wall Street Journal* (28 December 1965), p. 14.

22. Cited in "Scramble on for Mexican Sulphur," *The Engineering and Mining Journal* (May 1967), p. 105.

This policy, which appears to be still in effect, is a compromise that gives each of the interested parties significant advantages at minimum cost. The Mexican government gains control over the sulphur industry and the accompanying political advantages. Foreign-owned producers gain a fair return on their investment and the advantage of lower taxes on their operation. Finally, Mexican investors are given an opportunity to invest in the domestic sulphur industry.

Recovered Sulphur

When the practice of removing hydrogen sulphide from natural and manufactured gases was begun late in the nineteenth century, the hydrogen sulphide was treated as a waste and either vented to the atmosphere or burnt in a flare or under a boiler. Later, with the appearance of anti-pollution and conservation laws and the increasing use of gases with high concentrations of hydrogen sulphide, it became necessary to convert the hydrogen sulphide into either elemental sulphur or sulphuric acid. The shortage of sulphur in the early 1950s provided an economic incentive to accelerated recovery of sulphur from acid gas streams, and since 1954 sour natural and refinery gases have become a major source of sulphur.

Hydrogen sulphide can be separated from sour natural or refinery gases in several ways, but the processes most widely used today are ones such as the Girbotol process that recover hydrogen sulphide as a gas. However, as there is only a limited industrial demand for hydrogen sulphide, the gas is usually converted into a more marketable form of sulphur. Conversion into elemental sulphur is preferred to conversion into sulphuric acid because the process is simpler and the product is easier to store, handle, and transport. Today, most conversion plants use a method based on the Claus-Chance process to convert a concentrated gas stream containing hydrogen sulphide into sulphur dioxide and then into elemental sulphur.[23] The basic flow scheme of a Claus-Chance plant is shown in figure 3.

First, hydrogen sulphide-bearing gas is burned in a specially designed reaction furnace with a controlled amount of air, forming hydrogen sulphide. In some plants, as much as two-thirds of the hydrogen sulphide feed is bypassed around the furnace, in which case the stream passing through the furnace is burned all the way to sulphur dioxide. The gas passes from the reaction furnace, through a waste-heat boiler, and then

23. See James W. Estep, Guy T. McBride, Jr., and James R. West, "The Recovery of Sulphur from Sour Natural and Refinery Gases," in *Advances in Petroleum Chemistry and Refining*, vol. 6, ed. John J. McKetta, Jr. (New York: Interscience Publishers, 1962), p. 329.

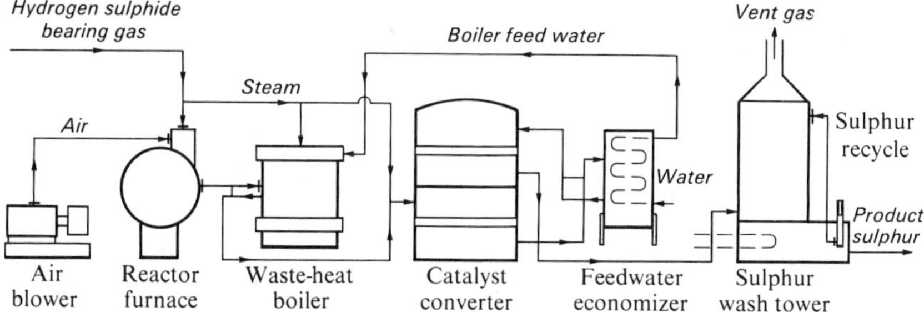

Figure 3. Flow scheme of sulphur recovery plant.

enters the catalyst converter. The hot gas from the first catalyst bed is cooled in a boiler feedwater economizer and then passes through a second catalyst bed which is operated at a lower temperature to give maximum conversion. Gas from the second catalyst chamber passes through a sulphur wash tower where condensation and removal of elemental sulphur occurs. The residual gas is vented to the atmosphere, while product sulphur is taken off to storage. With this process, up to 90 per cent of the sulphur may be recovered.

Domestic production of recovered sulphur

The discovery of several sour natural gas fields in southwest Arkansas in the early 1940s brought into existence the first commercial operation in the United States to recover elemental sulphur from sour gas streams. The Arkansas gas contained about 8 per cent hydrogen sulphide and an equal concentration of carbon dioxide. In 1941, the Southern Acid and Sulphur Company, now a part of Olin Mathieson Chemical Corporation, engaged the Ohio State University Research Foundation to develop in the laboratory a process for the recovery of sulphur from the acid gas separated from Arkansas sour natural gas, and in 1942 the company built a pilot sulphur recovery plant at Magnolia, Arkansas. About the same time, Susearch, an affiliate of the Texas Gulf Sulphur Company, built a pilot plant at McKamie, Arkansas, to conduct an independent study of the utilization of hydrogen sulphide derived from sour natural gas for the production of elemental sulphur. These pioneer efforts were instrumental in the commercial development of sulphur recovery from sour gas streams.

In 1944, Southern Acid constructed the first commercial sulphur recovery plant at McKamie, Arkansas. In 1949, sulphur recovery was begun from sour natural gas produced in the Worland-Manderson-Powell area of north-central Wyoming. The first company to recover sulphur from the natural gas of this region, which contained up to 30 per cent hydrogen sulphide, was the Stanolind Oil Company (later the Pan American Petroleum Corporation), which built a plant with a capacity of 75 tons per day at Elk Basin, Wyoming, in 1949.[24] In the 1950s, sulphur recovery operations were begun in the Permian Basin area of West Texas and southwestern New Mexico. The first sulphur recovery plant in this field was the 20-ton-per-day plant built by the Sid Richardson and Odessa Natural Gas companies at Odessa, Texas, in 1952.[25] The most recent discoveries of sour natural gas have been made in central Texas in the Smackover Trend, a geological formation extending from Mexico through central Texas to as far east as Alabama. Tide Water Oil Company built the first plant to recover sulphur from gas produced in this field in 1960 at Mt. Vernon, Texas.[26]

In each of the major sour natural gas fields, the first recovery plants were soon followed by additional plants having recovery capacities ranging from 10 tons to 300 tons per day. The only sulphur recovery plant in the United States having a capacity in excess of 300 tons per day is the Northeast Edgewood Field plant of Pan American Petroleum Corporation in Van Zandt County, Texas. The plant, built to process sour gas from the Smackover Trend, has a capacity of 900 tons of sulphur per day and was completed in 1964.[27]

Corresponding to the development of sulphur recovery from sour natural gas has been the recovery of sulphur at oil refineries processing sour crudes. The first large-scale sulphur recovery unit at an oil refinery in the United States was installed at Watson, California, by Hancock Chemical Company in 1949.[28] Since that time, additional recovery plants have come on stream at refineries in California and Texas and along the Eastern Seaboard, and sulphur is now being recovered at forty-nine refineries in the United States.

Factors that encourage sulphur recovery at oil refineries include: (1) laws controlling air pollution; (2) use of crudes with a high sulphur content; (3) demand for desulphurized products; (4) value of sulphur produced; and (5) use of sulphuric acid for oil refining purposes. Factors (1) and (3) have been particularly important in densely populated and highly developed areas. Thus, California, where stringent regula-

24. F. J. Kelly, "Sulphur Production and Consumption in Eight Western States," U.S. Department of the Interior, Bureau of Mines, *Information Circular 8094*, 1962, p. 72.

25. H. H. Jones and R. A. Graff, "West Texas' First Sulphur Recovery Unit," *The Oil and Gas Journal* (21 April 1952), pp. 122–23 and 153–54.

26. Leonard P. Larson and Victoria M. Roman, "Sulphur and Pyrites," U.S. Department of the Interior, Bureau of Mines, *Minerals Yearbook*, 1960, vol. 1.

27. See "New Sour Gas Plant Planned in Texas by Pan American," *The Oil Daily* (25 June 1963), and Robert B. Bizal, "Industry Adding 48 New Plants in '64," *The Oil and Gas Journal* (16 March 1964), p. 142.

28. See "U.S. Recovered Sulphur Capacity Shows New Growth Rate Peak in 1965," *Sulphur* (April/May 1966), pp. 13–16.

tions controlling air pollution exist and practically all hydrogen sulphide available from oil refineries is converted into either sulphur or sulphuric acid, accounts for over 24 per cent of total capacity for sulphur recovery from oil refineries in the United States.[29] Factor (2) is becoming increasingly important as larger amounts of sour crude are being refined. The importance of factor (4) will depend upon the distance of the oil refinery from sulphur markets and the state of the sulphur market. Undoubtedly, the shortage of sulphur in this country in the early fifties led to increased recovery of sulphur in the latter half of the decade. While factor (5) is not of major significance in the United States, it is important where refineries are located near the centers of oil production, such as Abadan or in the Caribbean.

At present, the forty-eight plants producing natural gas account for about 57 per cent of domestic recovered sulphur production. With the possible exception of the recently constructed plant in Van Zandt County, Texas, sulphur recovery facilities in the United States have been too small and too far removed from the major markets to have an appreciable impact on the total sulphur market. Only a few plants produce more than 50,000 tons per year, and only two firms, Pan American Petroleum Corporation and Getty Oil Company, are capable of producing as much as 100,000 tons of recovered sulphur per year.

Foreign production of recovered sulphur

While domestic production of recovered sulphur has had little impact on domestic Frasch sulphur markets, foreign production of recovered sulphur has made a major impact on world sulphur markets and, in particular, on U.S. exports of sulphur. Recovered sulphur is of major importance in Canada and France, and it is becoming increasingly important in the Middle East.

Canada. The existence of natural gas in Western Canada had been known since before the turn of the century; however, it was not until the late 1940s that oil discoveries in Alberta prompted extensive exploration for oil in the western provinces which brought to light extensive gas deposits.[30] The commercial development of natural gas in Western Canada was delayed until two conditions could be met: first, ample reserves to satisfy both domestic and export demands over a long period had to be proved; and second, the approval of both export agencies in Canada and import agencies in the United States had to be obtained and satisfactory long-term contracts negotiated. These conditions were not satisfied until the late fifties. Thus, the major growth in gas processing

29. See "Sulphur Recovery at Oil Refineries," *Sulphur* (February 1963), pp. 27–28.

30. See Eric J. Hansen, *Dynamic Decade* (Toronto: McClelland and Stewart, Ltd., 1958), pp. 223–25.

in Western Canada occurred after two major pipelines were brought on stream in August 1957—the Westcoast Transmission Company pipeline from the Peace River area of northern Alberta to Vancouver and the Pacific Northwest and the Trans-Canada Pipeline Company pipeline from central Alberta to eastern Canada and northeastern United States. In 1961, lines were extended to Montana and the midwestern section of the United States, and in 1962, a line built by Alberta Gas Trunk Line brought Canadian gas into California. The growth in demand for Canadian natural gas which attended the expansion of pipeline facilities is shown in table 4.

Table 4. Demand for Canadian Natural Gas, by Markets, 1960–63

million cubic feet per day

Markets	1960	1961	1962	1963
Domestic sales	886	1,000	1,100	1,300
United States sales:				
Pacific Northwest				
Via Westcoast Line	0	233	270	275
Via Alberta Natural Line	0	0	120	140
California	0	0	320	370
Montana	0	47	75	75
Midwest	0	166	179	170
Total U.S. sales	0	446	964	1,030
Total sales	886	1,446	2,064	2,330

SOURCE: *Oilweek* (27 January 1964), p. 23.

By the time pipelines were completed, demands for Canadian natural gas had risen to such an extent that it was necessary to tap sour gases to fulfill the contracts. The production of gas containing sizable amounts of hydrogen sulphide marked the birth of the Canadian recovered sulphur industry. The hydrogen sulphide content of natural gas being produced in the prairie provinces of Canada ranges from 1–2 per cent to as high as 30–40 per cent. If the hydrogen sulphide content of the raw gas stream is under 10 per cent, sulphur is generally looked upon as a by-product of natural gas processing. At hydrogen sulphide concentrations ranging from 10 to 20 per cent, sulphur and natural gas are considered coproducts. Where the hydrogen sulphide content of the crude gas stream is in excess of 20 per cent, the natural gas operation becomes a by-product of sulphur recovery operations. These classifications are arbitrary, and the divisions between by-product, coproduct, and main product status are affected by the relative prices of the two commodities.

A plant can vary the hydrogen sulphide content of its gas intake by drawing crude gas from more than one pool, or from several zones within a pool. By drawing on the sourer pools or zones, the plant operator can increase the output of sulphur without affecting the total gas throughput of the plant. In addition, where the hydrogen sulphide content of the raw gas stream is extremely high, it is possible to process the gas to recover the contained sulphur and recycle the gas back into the formation. At least one operation of this type is in operation in Canada today.

In 1953, only three natural gas processing plants were in operation in Western Canada. By 1956, the number of gas processing plants had grown to nine. The number of plants increased steadily after 1956, as did sulphur recovery from natural gas operations, and by the end of 1968, twenty-four sulphur recovery plants were in operation in Western Canada. The location of plants, the controlling companies, and recovery capacities are given in table 5. It should be noted that while these facilities have the capacity to produce over 3.4 million tons of sulphur per year, actual production of recovered sulphur in 1968 was only 2.6 million tons. Output will rarely if ever approach capacity because the plants are designed primarily to process gas, and gas sales contracts thus control sulphur production. Plants must be capable of meeting peak gas demands but will operate at such rates only briefly. Additional capacity under construction in 1968 and due for operation in 1969 will bring total annual capacity to nearly 5 million tons.[31]

France. Sulphur recovery from sour natural gas in France followed the discovery of a large gas field in the Lacq oilfield in southwestern France by the Société Nationale de Pétroles d'Aquitaine (SNPA) in December 1951. The hydrogen sulphide content of the gas was 15.3 per cent, and for nearly four years the French steel industry wrestled with the problem of engineering a metal alloy that could cope with the extensive corrosion that results from processing natural gas with such a high percentage of hydrogen sulphide. In 1955, the problem was finally solved with the development of a chrome-aluminum-molybdenum alloy.

Recoverable reserves in excess of 7 trillion cubic feet of sour gas having been proved, a Girbotol-type sulphur recovery plant was designed by the Ralph M. Parsons Company, and a multi-stage expansion program was adopted. The first unit, a 200-ton-per-day plant was completed in 1957. By the end of 1960, five units had been completed bringing total plant capacity to 4,100 tons per day, or about 1.5 million tons per year. Production of recovered sulphur at Lacq in 1968 was 1.575 million tons.

In 1965, SNPA discovered a sizable field of sour natural gas at

31. Letter dated 5 May 1969 from C. M. Bartley, Mineral Processing Division, Mines Branch, Department of Energy, Mines and Resources, Ottawa, Canada, to the author.

Table 5. Sulphur Recovery Plants in Western Canada, 1968

Operating company	Location (Alberta unless specified)	H_2S	Annual plant capacity	1968 production
		per cent	(..... *1,000 long tons* .....)	
Amerada Petroleum	1. Olds	11	63.0	55.5
Athabasca Oil	2. Mildred Lake	n.a.	105.0	23.5
Canadian Delhi Oil	3. Minnehik-Buck Lake	n.a.	6.3*	5.1
Canadian Fina Oil	4. Wildcat Hills	4	50.0	42.5
Canadian Superior	5. Harmattan-Elkton	53	300.0	240.3
Gulf Canadian	6. Nevis	3–7	45.0*	42.1
	7. Pincher Creek	10	114.0	87.0
	8. Rimbey	1–3	120.0	94.7
Home Oil	9. Carstairs	1	16.0	11.3
Hudson's Bay Oil and Gas	10. Edson	3	83.0	55.4
	11. Lone Pine Creek	8–17	38.3*	23.9
	12. Caroline	n.a.	6.3	—
	13. Kabob South	n.a.	365.4	—
	14. Fox Creek	n.a.	350.0	—
Imperial Oil	15. Redwater	3	4.5	2.0
Jefferson Lake Petrochemicals	16. Taylor Flats, B.C.	3	130.0	48.8
	17. Savannah Creek	13	140.0	26.6
Pan American Petroleum	18. E. Crossfield	38	518.0	—
	19. Bigstone	n.a.	110.0	—
Petrogas Processing	20. E. Calgary	31	700.0*	600.4
Royalite Oil Company	21. Turner Valley	4	10.5	5.7
Shell Canada	22. Jumping Pound	3–5	87.5*	55.2
	23. Innisfail	14	40.0	20.6
	24. Waterton	18–25	576.5	504.7
Standard Oil of California	25. Nevis	7	50.0*	44.3
Socony Mobil	26. Wimbourne	14	85.4	69.0
Steelman Gas	27. Steelman, Sask.	1	4.0	3.7
Texas Gulf Sulphur	28. Okotoks	33	150.0	130.4
	29. Windfall	16	495.0*	367.4
	30. Red Deer River	n.a.	175.0	—
Banff Oil	31. Rainbow Lake	n.a.	24.5	—
Total			3,414.0	2,560.1

SOURCE: Letter of 5 May 1969 to the author from C. M. Bartley, Mineral Processing Division, Mines Branch, Department of Energy, Mines and Resources, Ottawa, Canada.

* Indicates expansions planned for 1969. Total expansions estimated to equal 175,400 long tons.

n.a.—Not available.

Meillon, 15 miles southeast of Lacq, with a hydrogen sulphide content of 5–6 per cent. A 100,000–150,000 ton recovery unit was completed and placed in operation in 1967.

Middle East. The Middle East is also becoming an important source for sour gas and petroleum sulphur recovery. Within the past few years, several projects tied to fertilizer and petrochemical complexes have been announced. The largest of these is the $100 million sour gas plant being built in Iran by Allied Chemical Corporation and the National Petrochemical Company, a state-owned firm. The complex will have an initial daily capacity of 1,000 tons and an eventual one of 1,500 tons.[32]

32. *Chemical Week* (2 March 1968), p. 46.

Additional large plants being planned for Saudi Arabia, Kuwait, and Iraq show promise of expanding Middle East output of recovered sulphur in the next few decades.[33]

Growth since 1950

The increase in production of elemental sulphur from sour natural and refinery gases in the United States, Canada, and France for the period since 1950 is shown in table 6. While production of recovered sulphur has shown a continuous but moderate growth in the United States, its growth has been quite rapid in Canada and France. Taken together, recovered sulphur sources in the United States, Canada, and France now account for about 23 per cent of total world sulphur production (excluding Communist nations), and other recovered sulphur sources account for an additional 2 per cent. It appears likely that recovered sulphur will supply an increasing share of the world's sulphur requirements in the future. This possibility is discussed in chapter 8.

Table 6. Production of Recovered Sulphur in the United States, Canada, and France, 1950–67

1,000 long tons

Year	United States	Canada*	France	Total
1950	142	0	0	142
1951	184	0	0	184
1952	252	4	0	256
1953	342	16	0	358
1954	359	19	0	378
1955	399	26	0	425
1956	465	30	0	495
1957	511	96	28	635
1958	640	166	127	933
1959	686	263	419	1,368
1960	767	245	778	1,790
1961	858	352	1,080	2,290
1962	900	621	1,326	2,847
1963	947	1,116	1,386	3,449
1964	1,021	1,597	1,487	4,105
1965	1,215	1,847	1,497	4,559
1966	1,240	1,823	1,516	4,579
1967	1,268	2,073	1,719	5,060

SOURCE: U.S. Department of the Interior, Bureau of Mines, *Minerals Yearbook* for applicable years.

* Sales figures (1952–67).

33. See "New Sources of Sulphur Emerge," *Industrial Minerals* (December 1967), p. 29; and *The Engineering and Mining Journal* (February 1968), p. 97.

Chapter 3

Frasch Sulphur Costs of Production and Conditions of Entry

The supply function for an industry's product is influenced by the nature of costs and the conditions of entry, as well as by the size and distribution of sellers. This chapter contains an analysis of the costs of producing Frasch sulphur, followed by an examination of the conditions of entry into the industry and the general supply conditions for Frasch sulphur.

Costs of Producing Frasch Sulphur

In the short run, the number of plants and firms that can produce Frasch sulphur is relatively fixed. Costs per unit of output for existing plants and firms are dependent upon the rate of output; the prices of input factors; the production function, i.e., the physical productivity or efficiency of management, labor, and other factors which combine to produce output; and selling expenditures. In the long run, however, both the number of plants and firms in the industry and the scale of each plant and firm can be varied. The long-run supply curve for Frasch sulphur is thus related to the number of firms in the industry, the size or scale of each plant or firm, and the resulting marginal costs for these firms.

Technological considerations

When sulphur is mined by the Frasch process, the basic operations are: (1) drilling production wells into the deposit, and (2) supplying hot water for use in melting the sulphur contained in the deposit. The wells have a life of from a few days to two years, with about one year being average, and about 35,000 long tons can be extracted from an average sulphur well before the cavity becomes too large for effective production. The economics of a given deposit, however, depends primarily on the water ratio, i.e., the number of gallons of hot water required to mine one ton of sulphur, because the water ratio determines the maximum production rate that can be sustained from a given boiler plant.[1]

The water ratio itself is determined by the physical characteristics of the deposit. A typical formation of 25 per cent sulphur, 65 per cent rock, and 10 per cent water theoretically should require about 1,185 gallons of 330° F. water per ton of sulphur extracted. However, if the limestone formation containing the sulphur is too porous, much of the water pumped into the formation will be lost through leakage, and the amount of sulphur produced relative to the water input may be small. On the other hand, if the deposit is too tight, the water will be unable to circulate through the formation and the amount of sulphur obtained from each well will be small. Actual water ratios range from as little as 1,000 gallons to as much as 12,000 gallons per ton of sulphur recovered.[2] In general, it would appear that the water ratio varies inversely with the amount of recoverable sulphur in the deposit. Thus, water ratios are considerably lower for domes capable of producing 10 million tons over their life than for deposits with a yield of only one-half million tons.

In addition to varying between deposits, the water ratio varies over the life of the deposit and over the life of any single well. For any dome, the water ratio is an average of the ratios in each well. When a well is first drilled, the water ratio will be high because of the time required for the deposit to heat up. As production from a well continues, the water ratio usually falls until the minimum level of production is reached. Towards the end of the well's life the water ratio begins to increase as the outer limit of the area through which water from the well can circulate is reached. It is this increase in the water ratio which signals the end of a well's productive life. Over the life of a dome, the water ratio will also vary. As production wells approach the fringes of the deposit, the water ratio usually rises. If the deposit is highly faulted, the water ratio may vary greatly over the various sections of the deposit.

The size of Frasch plants (in terms of millions of gallons of water per day) varies directly with the size of the deposit. If the deposit is small—500,000 tons per year or less—the plant must be operated at full capacity in order to maintain production and prevent the dome from cooling. Since operating costs are fixed by the capacity of the

1. Because the amount of published technical information on sulphur production by the Frasch process is limited, this section is based largely on information obtained in interviews with officials of Frasch sulphur firms. These interviews are listed in the bibliography.

2. Texas Gulf Sulphur Company, *Modern Sulphur Mining* (rev. ed.; New York: Texas Gulf Sulphur Company, Inc., 1961), p. 7.

boiler plant, the tonnage over which these costs can be spread then depends upon the water ratio experienced. For larger deposits, a firm has an option of altering the rate of mining by varying the number of wells drilled. The larger plants can vary production in response to changes in demand, and generally operate within a range of 60–100 per cent of capacity.

Engineering cost estimates

There are no published cost estimates for Frasch sulphur mining that break down costs into variable and fixed components. Furthermore, the scarcity of Frasch sulphur deposits and the small number of plants and firms tend to make each Frasch operation unique, and it is difficult to make any generalizations regarding the size of plant and costs of production. The diversification of Frasch sulphur firms into production of other mineral products, which has occurred with increasing frequency in recent years, also limits the validity of conclusions regarding sulphur production costs based on statistical analysis of accounting records. On the other hand, the basic nature of all Frasch operations is the same, and the components of plant and equipment are similar to those found in other industries. Therefore, it is possible to derive generally valid engineering cost estimates which can be used to indicate both the range of unit costs over plants of differing size and domes of differing quality, and the behavior of unit costs over operations of a given plant at various levels of capacity.

In this section, investment costs for three Frasch plants of different capacities are first presented. Next, unit costs for these plants are computed, assuming operation at full capacity. Finally, unit costs for a given plant are evaluated over a range of capacity utilization. Where possible, estimates for both investment and operating costs have been compared with actual published figures, and appropriate adjustments have been made.

Estimates of investment costs for three Frasch plants within the normal daily water capacity range are as follows:

	Plant 1	*Plant 2*	*Plant 3*
Capacity (1,000 gal. water/day)	8,000	4,000	1,000
Estimated investment cost ($1,000)	7,200	4,720	1,500
Investment/1,000 gal. water capacity ($1,000)	900	1,180	1,500

These estimates were made by pricing the major items of equipment used in a Frasch sulphur plant. It was assumed that the largest plant could be scaled down to successively smaller capacities. The costs include only expenditures for physical plant and equipment for an onshore Frasch operation built in 1960 on the Texas-Louisiana Gulf Coast; they exclude all costs of exploration and development. The results are generally in agreement with costs that have been released by the sulphur companies. For example, the one-million-gallon-per-day plant of U.S. Sulphur Company at High Island was estimated to have cost $1.5 million new.[3] The 1.75-million-gallon-per-day Bay Ste. Elaine plant of Freeport Sulphur Company, built in 1952, cost $2 million. This amounts to $1,143 per 1,000 gallons of daily water capacity, which is below the estimated costs given above, but Freeport disclosed that the investment costs for this plant were below normal.[4]

These plant investment estimates indicate that costs for fixed plant and equipment rise sharply as the size of the plant increases, but that larger plants cost much less per unit of water capacity. Investment costs per thousand gallons of daily water capacity range downward from $1,500 for the one-million-gallon-per-day plant to $900 for the eight-million-gallon-per-day plant. Economies in construction costs tend to level off at the upper end of the range, but investment costs per unit of capacity continue to decline. Thus, the most economically sized Frasch plant to construct, in terms of investment cost per unit of capacity, would have a capacity in excess of eight million gallons per day.

The savings in investment costs per unit of capacity also generate savings in financial charges and depreciation expenses. These demonstrate the same trend as investment costs per unit of capacity. At an assumed 6 per cent, financial charges per thousand gallons of daily water capacity decline from $90 for the plant with a capacity of one million gallons per day to $71 for the plant with a capacity of four million gallons per day. Thereafter, the savings are less pronounced, declining $17 per thousand gallons between the four-million-gallon-per-day plant and the eight-million-gallon-per-day plant. The annual savings on financial charges caused by the $19 differential between the two smaller plants amounts to about $77,000 while the corresponding savings resulting from the $17 differential between the two larger plants totals $136,000. The significance of such savings varies directly with the rate level.

The decline in investment costs per unit of capacity realized in the construction of larger-scale plants also yields corresponding savings in depreciation charges. Assuming straight line depreciation on the basis of a fifteen-year life, the depreciation charges per thousand gallons of daily water capacity decrease from $100 for the one-million-gallon-per-

3. X. T. Stoddard, Scout Memo, "High Island Dome Sulphur Mine, Galveston County, Texas," for the Humble Oil and Refining Company, 22 July 1959, p. 14.

4. K. T. Price, "Freeport Mines Sulphur by Boat," *Engineering and Mining Journal* (December 1952), p. 102.

day plant to $79 and $60 respectively for the four-million and eight-million gallon-per-day plants. The unit depreciation charges thus reflect proportionately the reductions in investment costs per unit realized through the construction of larger scale plants.

A major portion of the total unit costs for full utilization of any single plant is accounted for by cost elements which are, for the most part, variable in nature. Production costs based on the average weighted figures for all three plant scales can be broken down approximately as follows:

	Per cent of total
Variable costs:	75.7
Natural gas	19.8
Treated water	1.8
Operating supplies	0.6
Production wells	22.0
Sulphur loading	11.2
Severance tax	20.3
Fixed costs:	24.3
Maintenance	2.7
Operating labor	5.7
Supervision	1.3
Labor and plant burden	7.0
Property taxes and insurance	1.6
Depreciation	6.0

In general, the larger plants have a somewhat higher percentage of fixed costs than shown above, and the smaller plants have a somewhat lower percentage. The breakdown of costs is an arbitrary one, and semivariable costs such as operating labor and supervision, which do not in fact vary over the normal range of operations, are listed as fixed costs. Production wells, however, are classified as variable costs, even though their average life is one year, because the only way a Frasch producer can vary production on a given deposit is to change the rate of drilling wells. The operators of the larger plants do consider wells as variable costs. For smaller plants operating with only a few wells, production wells are considered as fixed costs. The estimated unit costs given above do not include exploration and development costs, which are fixed, nor do they include royalty payments, which are variable in nature.[5]

In evaluating unit costs, consideration must be given not only to the

5. In general, exploration costs are capitalized and amounts equivalent to such exploration costs, together with the estimated related future federal income tax savings, are charged to income. There is no standard royalty agreement in the industry. Many royalty payments are based on a fixed percentage of net profits from the operation after all costs for development (including the cost of plant and equipment) are fully recovered.

size of the plant but also to the quality of the deposit, as reflected by the water ratio. Table 7 illustrates how each of these factors affects unit production costs. Of the variable costs in table 7, the estimates for natural gas and water costs were based largely on operating data published by the sulphur operators for the various domes. It should be noted that although gas consumption is the major heat requirement, it is not directly proportional to the water ratio experienced. Additional quantities of steam are used for driving the pumps, generating power, and heating sulphur transfer lines. Gas requirements decline slightly with increases in plant scale owing to the greater operating efficiency of larger boiler installations. The gas rate used ($0.23 per thousand cubic feet) is believed typical for the Gulf Coast during the period 1961–62. Production wells are short-lived, averaging about one year, and have been treated as an operating expense. Some companies, however, do capitalize them and recover the capital through depreciation. The wells are shallow (1,500 to 1,800 feet, in general), and on the basis of petroleum drilling costs in South Louisiana each well was estimated to cost $35,000, including the casing and pipe. Since pipe is often recovered and reused, actual well costs probably run under $35,000. Sulphur loading costs were computed on the basis of a flat charge of $0.57 per long ton of sulphur produced. The state severance tax on sulphur in both Texas and Louisiana is $1.03 per long ton, and this tax has been included as a variable cost.

Fixed costs were based largely on the amount of investment. Maintenance costs were estimated at 3 per cent of the investment per year, a rate that fits the nature of the plant—primarily a boiler installation. Since the number of employees engaged in production does not appear to vary with output over the range of likely plant operation, all labor requirements were considered as being fixed in nature. Operating labor was computed on the basis of an hourly wage of $3.00 with a shift requirement of fourteen men for plant 1 and ten men each for plant 2 and plant 3. Supervision was based on an estimate of eight shift foremen at $7,500 per year and a plant superintendent at $10,000 per year. Labor and plant burden were taken as being equal to operating labor and supervision costs. Local property and miscellaneous taxes and insurance costs were estimated to be 1.75 per cent of the investment per year, a rate generally applicable under normal circumstances. Depreciation was estimated on the basis of a fifteen-year life, which is common for some sulphur producers. Other producers have used a unit of production as the basis for depreciation, which leads to unit charges comparable to those shown for full capacity operation, assuming the plant's capacity in terms of units of output does not vary over its life.

The engineering cost estimates given in table 7 are in general agree-

Table 7. Estimated Unit Production Costs for Frasch Sulphur

Item	Case I. Plants of different capacity with the same water ratio			Case II. Plants of the same capacity with different water ratios		
	Plant 1	Plant 2	Plant 3	Plant 1	Plant 2	Plant 3
Plant investment	$7,200,000	$4,720,000	$1,500,000	$4,720,000	$4,720,000	$4,720,000
Capacity:						
Gallons of water per day	8,000,000	4,000,000	1,000,000	4,000,000	4,000,000	4,000,000
Tons of sulphur per day	5,000	2,500	625	2,500	1,000	444
Tons of sulphur per year	1,750,000	875,000	218,750	875,000	350,000	155,400
Water ratio	1,600	1,600	1,600	1,600	4,000	9,000
Investment per 1,000 gal.	$ 900	$ 1,180	$ 1,500	$ 1,180	$ 1,180	$ 1,180
Investment per ton of sulphur	$ 4.11	$ 5.39	$ 6.85	$ 5.39	$ 13.49	$ 30.37
Variable costs:	*$/ton*	*$/ton*	*$/ton*	*$/ton*	*$/ton*	*$/ton*
Natural gas	1.00	1.01	1.02	1.01	2.53	5.69
Treated water	.09	.09	.09	.09	.23	.51
Operating supplies	.03	.03	.03	.03	.08	.17
Production wells	1.12	1.12	1.12	1.12	2.80	6.31
Sulphur loading	.57	.57	.57	.57	.57	.57
State severance tax	1.03	1.03	1.03	1.03	1.03	1.03
Total	3.84	3.85	3.86	3.85	7.24	14.28
Fixed costs:						
Maintenance	0.12	0.16	0.21	0.16	0.40	0.91
Operating labor	.21	.30	1.20	.30	.75	1.60
Supervision	.04	.08	.32	.08	.20	.45
Labor and plant burden	.25	.38	1.52	.38	.95	2.14
Prop. taxes, insurance	.07	.09	.12	.09	.24	.53
Depreciation	.27	.36	.46	.36	.90	2.02
Total	0.97	1.38	3.83	1.38	3.44	7.74
Total unit costs	4.81	5.23	7.69	5.23	10.68	22.02

NOTE: The above are engineering cost estimates, made by the author; they are not intended to represent unit costs for any existing Frasch sulphur plant. It was assumed in making these estimates that each plant was operating at full capacity.

ment with published estimates of Frasch production costs. For example, Jefferson Lake Sulphur Company has reported the following costs for its Long Point Dome plant with a capacity of 3.5 million gallons per day:[6]

	Output	Operating costs	Water ratio
	long tons	*$/long ton*	*gal./long ton*
1961	230,042	13.63	4,905
1962	255,964	13.21	4,549
1963	234,362	12.74	4,909

There operating costs include royalties, severance taxes, and all other taxes except income. Estimated royalty payments on sulphur produced at Long Point during these years were equivalent to $3.81, $4.10, and $2.78 per ton.[7] When these payments are deducted, the resulting operating costs ($9.82, $9.11, and 9.96) appear consistent with the slightly higher estimate of $10.68 given in table 7 for a plant of similar size and a dome of comparable quality (case II—plant 2).

From table 7, case I, it can be seen that plants with identical water ratios experience decreasing average costs with increases in plant size. The reduction is due almost entirely to the decrease in average fixed costs that accompanies increases in plant scale. Only very minor savings in variable costs can be attributed to larger-scale plants. Case II demonstrates that average costs for plants of the same size operating at full capacity vary directly with the water ratio experienced in mining. The reason for this is that total costs, with the exception of sulphur loading charges and state severance taxes, are identical for each plant, while the amount of sulphur produced over which these costs can be spread varies inversely with the water ratio.

Thus far, the analysis of unit costs has been limited to full capacity operation. Figure 4 presents the average total unit costs for the three plants described above for operations ranging from 50 per cent to 100 per cent of capacity. The dashed line in figure 4 connects the empirical minimum average total unit cost points on the cost curves of the successively larger Frasch plants (which are based on 100 per cent capacity operations), and conveys some idea as to cost variation related to size.

6. This information was disclosed at the time of the acquisition of Jefferson Lake by Occidental Petroleum. See Occidental Petroleum Corporation, *Listing Application A-21482*, New York Stock Exchange, 23 January 1964, p. 38.

7. Jefferson Lake leases the Long Point Dome from Texas Gulf Sulphur under a contract which, as amended 1 October 1960, calls for royalty payments of the greater of: (a) 50 per cent of the annual net profits from the mine, or (b) $2 per long ton. The royalty estimates given above were obtained by dividing the payments to Texas Gulf by the annual output.

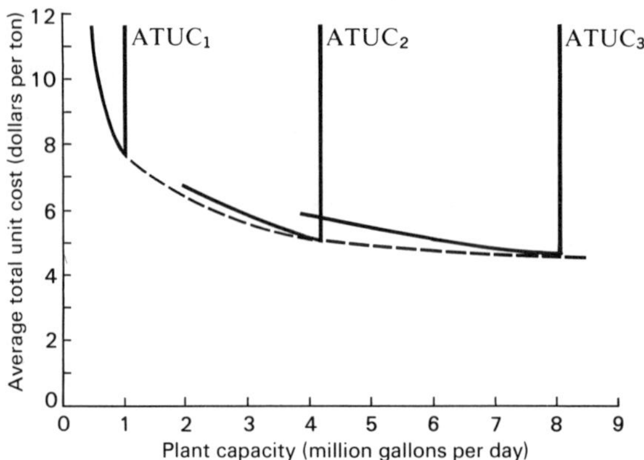

Figure 4. Effect of Frasch plant size and rate of operations on average total unit costs.

While unit costs continue to decline up to the maximum-size plant considered in this analysis, the flatness of the curve suggests that average total unit costs fall very slowly as plant size is increased beyond eight million gallons per day, and that the most significant economies are realized by the time the capacities in the range of four million gallons per day are reached.

In summary, this analysis of Frasch sulphur unit production costs has revealed the existence of substantial internal economies of scale. These economies result almost entirely from the savings realized in the use of fixed factors as plant size is increased and exhibit the common characteristic of increasing at a diminishing rate. They are, however, greatly overshadowed by the effect of ore deposit quality. The decline in unit costs accompanying declines in the water ratio (which reflect ore quality) over the actual range of water ratios experienced by firms in the industry is much more pronounced than the decline in unit costs accompanying increases in plant size, also taken over the range of existing plants. Finally, the high proportion of variable costs indicates that the penalty paid for operation at less than full capacity is not severe, at least not for plants of larger size.

Conditions of Entry into the Sulphur Industry

The sulphur industry has been characterized by extreme concentration throughout its history. In the United States, only five firms have achieved any significant production of Frasch sulphur, and two of these firms have produced over 85 per cent of the total Frasch sulphur output in this century. At the same time, several unsuccessful attempts have been made to enter the industry. The existence of only a few firms in an industry over a considerable time period leads one to inquire why other firms have not entered the industry. In a competitive situation, entry of new firms occurs in response to the long-run rate of profits; if the long-run rate of profit earned by existing firms is in excess of what can be earned in other industries in the economy, new firms should be attracted into the industry. If new firms have not entered an industry over time, analysis should then reveal that either (1) the long-run rate of profit earned by established firms in the industry has not been excessive; or (2) the established firms in the industry have significant advantages over potential entrant firms, these advantages being reflected in the degree to which the established firms can consistently maintain their prices above a competitive level without attracting new firms to enter the industry.

Profits earned by Frasch sulphur producers are analyzed in chapter 7. It is essential, however, before concluding the analysis of the market structure of the Frasch sulphur industry to determine if substantial advantages exist for established firms which would enable them to maintain a price level in the long run which would yield excess profits. These advantages, commonly called barriers to entry, have been classified into three groups: absolute cost barriers, product differentiation, and scale economies.[8] The existence of these barriers to entry is examined below.

Absolute cost barriers

If a potential entrant would have higher long-run costs than its established counterparts for any common scale of operations, the established firms can be said to possess an absolute cost advantage, and entry into the industry may be substantially restricted.

One source of such a cost advantage in the sulphur industry is the control by established firms of Frasch sulphur deposits. Since the sulphur industry is essentially a mining venture, holding a deposit is a necessary prerequisite to entry. However, Frasch sulphur deposits have been few in number and tightly controlled.[9]

The major Frasch sulphur producers acquired the sulphur rights to salt domes from the parties that had explored them for oil. Investigation of the relationship between the two largest sulphur producers and the major Gulf Coast oil companies reveals close ties between Freeport Sulphur and Texaco (formerly The Texas Company) and between Texas Gulf Sulphur and the Gulf Oil Corporation.

8. This classification follows Joe S. Bain, *Barriers to New Competition* (Cambridge: Harvard University Press, 1956), p. 12.

9. Strictly speaking, the nonavailability of Frasch sulphur deposits is an "absolute" barrier to entry only in the sense that the deposits which are not under the ownership of existing producers are of marginal quality, characterized by high water ratios, and having substantially higher unit costs than domes of better quality, even given the same scale of operation.

Freeport acquired at least four of the nine deposits it has mined from the Texas Company. In addition, the two companies have reciprocated directors. Since 1922 when Freeport leased the Hoskins deposit from the Texas Company with royalty payments of 70 per cent of the net profits from the mine, either the president or the chairman of the Texas Company has been a member of Freeport's board of directors. Since 1952, with the exception of 1956, two of Freeport's directors have also served on Texaco's board, and the chairman of Freeport has been a director of Texaco since 1955.

Texas Gulf Sulphur acquired at least three of the six deposits it has mined in the United States from the Gulf Producing Company, a subsidiary of Gulf Oil Corporation. From 1934 to 1948, Gulf Oil owned about 39 per cent of the outstanding Texas Gulf Sulphur stock. It continued to hold as much as 10 per cent until 1957. More recently, the two firms engaged in a joint venture to conduct offshore sulphur exploration.

Both Freeport and Texas Gulf, though closely associated with Texaco and Gulf Oil respectively, have also acquired deposits from Humble Oil and Refining and other Gulf Coast oil firms. As far as can be determined, no major petroleum company now owns as much as 10 per cent of the outstanding stock of either major sulphur producer.

Unlike their competitors, the two smaller Frasch sulphur producers were originally engaged in petroleum exploration. When their explorations turned up sulphur rather than oil, they entered the industry as sulphur producers. Both firms, however, were able to continue in the industry after their initial mines were exhausted by obtaining leases on marginal sulphur deposits from Texas Gulf Sulphur.

There are several reasons why more petroleum companies did not enter the industry. First, during the period when most of the salt domes were being discovered, petroleum exploration offered a high return on invested capital. The early wildcat drillers of the Gulf Coast were risk takers, and the promise of an above-average rate of return from sulphur production could not compete with the lure of the enormous potential return from a major oil strike.

Second, the Frasch sulphur companies were willing to pay a high price for the sulphur rights on salt domes with potential. Most contracts called for a royalty payment of 50 per cent of the net profits after the development expenses had been recovered. Thus, petroleum companies, without investing additional exploration and development funds, could reap 50 per cent of the benefits from sulphur production on their lands.

Third, after two firms were established in the industry with technical knowledge of the tricky Frasch process, access to markets, and, most importantly, tremendous aboveground inventories, successful entry became more difficult. This situation not only deterred entry by the oil companies but encouraged them to lease to the established firms rather than to potential entrants. Furthermore, the petroleum companies had no need to integrate backward into sulphur, as it was not until their acquisitions of agricultural chemical companies in the late fifties and early sixties that they became major consumers of sulphur.[10]

Product differentiation barriers

In some industries the preference of buyers for some or all of the products of established firms gives those firms a "product differentiation" advantage. However, as sulphur is a relatively homogeneous commodity purchased by professional buyers for large industrial firms, there is little opportunity for producers to differentiate their product. Thus, product differentiation has not acted as a barrier to entry in the sulphur industry.

Economies of scale barriers

The final barrier to entry, and the one that has perhaps received the greatest amount of attention in industry studies, is the barrier of economies of scale. If there are significant economies of scale throughout the range of possible industry output, the number of firms able to exist in the industry may be severely restricted. "Significant economies" means situations where the minimum optimal scale for a plant or firm in a particular industry, i.e., the smallest scale at which a plant or firm may achieve the lowest attainable unit cost, is a significant fraction of the total scale or capacity of the industry, and where unit costs at smaller than minimum optimal scales are significantly higher. In such cases, the entry of an additional firm may induce established firms to lower their price in order to preserve their market share. The entrant firm then faces the choice of entering the industry at a scale below its minimum optimal scale or entering the industry at its minimum optimal scale and facing a price after entry which is below the price prevailing prior to entry.[11] Any discussion of scale economies must be related to the plant

10. Thomas O'Hanlan, "The Great Sulphur Rush," *Fortune* (March 1968), p. 111, states: "Now, of course, with oil companies short of sulphur for their chemical and fertilizer divisions, the comfortable old camaraderie is over. From here on it's finders keepers."

11. There are actually two effects of scale economies on the conditions of entry. The one discussed here is known as the *percentage effect* and reflects the importance of the proportion of industry output supplied by an optimal sized plant or firm. A second effect, known as the *absolute-capital-requirements effect,* reflects the impact of large absolute amounts of capital investment required for optimum operation on the ease of entry into the industry. Since the absolute amount of capital required for construction of an optimal size Frasch sulphur plant is small, this effect has been omitted from the discussion of economies of scale.

and the firm, which are the functional units to which the economies are applicable.

The analysis of unit costs in the Frasch sulphur industry revealed economies of scale on the plant level, particularly up to the range of four million gallons of water per day. However, these economies do not appear to be large enough, relative to the demand for sulphur, to prevent the existence of a considerable number of plants in the industry. Annual domestic sales of Frasch sulphur in recent years have averaged over five million tons. If it is assumed that a plant with a water capacity of four million gallons per day can produce 500,000 tons of sulphur annually (reflecting an average water ratio of about 3,000 gallons per ton), then it would appear that a sizable number of "optimal size" plants could survive. Furthermore, the existence of several plants below this optimal size suggests that economies of scale at the plant level are not so large as to preclude profitable operation of suboptimal sized plants.

However, though about ten mines have generally been producing Frasch sulphur in the postwar period, these mines have been controlled by only four firms. Is it possible that larger economies of scale exist at the firm level? Certainly, multiplant firms have some significant advantages in the Frasch sulphur industry. The geographic centralization of Frasch mines makes it possible for a firm to construct a central terminal to serve several mines. Both Texas Gulf and Freeport conduct such an operation. It has been estimated that the installation of central handling and shipping facilities by Texas Gulf at its Beaumont terminal resulted in a 30–40 per cent reduction in its handling and shipping costs.[12] In addition, it is reasonable to assume that certain functions of the firm, such as research, financing, legal work, advertising, accounting, do not increase proportionally as the scale of the firm increases. It is therefore reasonable to assume that some economies of scale exist in these nonproduction functions of the firm. However, no evidence is available to suggest the magnitude of these firm economies. As has been the case in other industries, judgment as to the importance of economies of scale at the firm level must rest on indirect evidence. The existence of two small producers for over a twenty-five year period would seem to imply that economies of scale at the firm level are not of crucial importance in the Frasch sulphur industry, or that they are more than balanced by other factors, not necessarily connected with technology or economies, that elude analysis. However, survival is an imperfect test of efficiency because other elements, including antitrust legislation, can be respon-

12. See "Liquid Sulphur Terminal for TGS Cuts Costs, Eases Handling," *Sulphur* (February 1961), p. 27.

sible for the continuing existence of small firms in a concentrated industry.

General Supply Conditions for the Frasch Sulphur Industry

Sulphur production using the Frasch process is basically a mining operation. As such, its limits in time are set by the exhaustion of the ore deposit which is a nonreproducing form of capital. Nor (as Hotelling and Herfindahl have shown)[13] are these circumstances altered by long-run systematic exploration. However, the actual supply conditions of the Frasch sulphur industry must still be examined. In a perfectly competitive industry, the supply conditions could be shown by means of an industry supply curve depicting the lowest cost at which any given output could be produced. In the short run, the industry supply curve is simply the horizontal summation of the marginal cost curves of all firms in the industry. The long-run supply curve of the competitive industry will have a shape and position determined by the slopes of the marginal cost curves of the individual firms and the price at which each firm enters or leaves the industry.

However, Frasch sulphur is produced in an industry of few sellers. In such a situation, the industry supply curve is determined not only by the marginal cost curves of the individual firms, but also by the effect of a given shift in demand on the shape, slope, and position of the demand for individual producers. It is possible to isolate the supply response of the industry to a given change in price by constructing a schedule of what output would be forthcoming if the industry was given a set of alternative prices by an external source. For example, if the government agreed to purchase the entire output of the industry at various prices, the amount of output forthcoming at each price could be calculated by summing horizontally the marginal cost curves for all firms in the industry. In this manner, a supply price schedule could be derived. The curve reflecting such a schedule for the Frasch sulphur industry is given in figure 5. *ABC* is the short-run supply price schedule drawn to exclude the possibility of expanding the capacity of existing plants, but to include the possibilities of increasing production by substituting variable factors for the fixed capital, which is formed both by the ore deposit and by the plant associated with it.

The nearly flat portion of the curve, *AB,* represents production from the large, low-cost onshore deposits such as Boling and Grande Ecaille.

13. See Harold Hotelling, "The Economics of Exhaustible Resources," *Journal of Political Economy,* vol. 39 (April 1931), pp. 137–75; and Orris C. Herfindahl, "The Long-Run Cost of Minerals," *Three Studies in Minerals Economics* (Washington, D.C.: Resources for the Future, Inc., 1961).

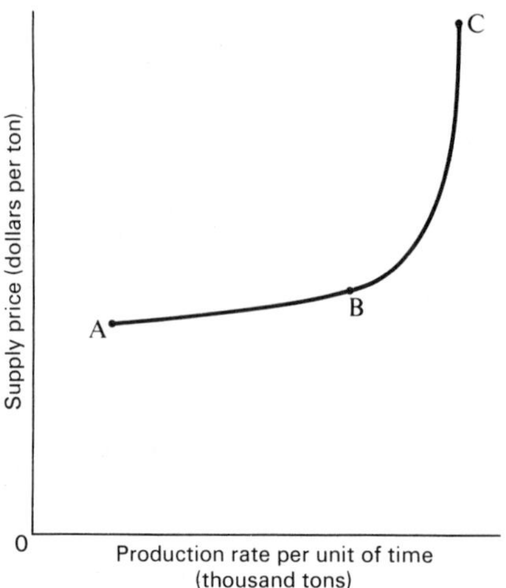

Figure 5. Supply price schedule for Frasch sulphur.

The rising portion, *BC,* depicts the production of increasingly higher-cost sulphur from poorer quality mines. Between 1963 and 1965, in the face of rising demand and increased prices, the four major Frasch producers were able to expand output by about 25 per cent. However, without opening new mines or increasing the capacity of existing plants, it is unlikely that the four firms could increase their total output by more than 10 per cent. Thus, the supply of Frasch sulphur in the short run appears relatively inelastic. Additional output of Frasch sulphur in the short run will be accompanied by significant increases in cost.

Of course, it does not follow that, because the Frasch sulphur industry is one of increasing cost in the short run, the supply price for Frasch sulphur must rise over time. It is reasonable, however, to expect that Frasch sulphur production is subject to diminishing returns in the long run as well. Increasing costs in the long run would result from resource depletion, which causes upward shifts in the industry's aggregate marginal cost curve. In the case of Frasch sulphur, the easily accessible sources of supply have already been explored. Barring the discovery of new onshore salt dome formations, it would appear that increments to sulphur reserves must come from development of offshore salt dome deposits or from working the known onshore deposits that heretofore have been regarded as submarginal. In either instance, additional reserves could be developed only at an increasing cost. Of course, technological advances in exploration or mining could offset the effects of depletion as has happened in other minerals, such as copper, for example. It must be stressed that the above discussion pertains only to the long-run supply of *Frasch* sulphur. The case is much less certain for the long-run supply for all forms of sulphur. While domestic Frasch sulphur reserves appear to be diminishing, recent discoveries of sour natural gas in Canada, France, and the Middle East, and Frasch sulphur deposits in Mexico, coupled with continuing advancement in sulphur recovery techniques promise adequate sulphur supplies in the foreseeable future. The effect of these developments on the long-run supply price is discussed in chapter 8.

Chapter 4

Market Structure of the Sulphur Industry: Demand Aspects

This chapter is concerned with an analysis of the structural elements of the demand for sulphur that significantly affect the conduct of Frasch sulphur firms. These elements include (1) the number and type of consumers; (2) the distribution system and marketing procedures of Frasch producers; and (3) the cyclical and secular nature of the demand for sulphur. Together these factors define the demand environment within which firms in the industry must operate.

The Number and Type of Consumers

With the exception of its direct application as a plant nutrient, sulphur enters into various processing and manufacturing industries as a raw material or factor of production. Over 85 per cent of the brimstone consumed in the United States is burned to form sulphur dioxide for conversion to sulphuric acid. Thus, the demand for sulphur is largely dependent upon, or derived from, the demand for the end products of industries that consume sulphur either directly or in the form of sulphuric acid. A partial listing of industries and products in which sulphur is employed is given in table 8.

The sulphuric acid industry

The percentage of sulphur going into the manufacture of sulphuric acid has increased in recent years, rising from 79 per cent in 1950 to 87 per cent in 1966. Sulphuric acid may be manufactured from elemental sulphur, pyrites, and smelter gases, or from hydrogen sulphide derived from the purification of coke-oven and refinery gases; it may also be refortified or obtained by burning spent acid in sludge conversion plants to form new acid (see table 9).

When by-product sulphur is unavailable, the acid producer must choose between using elemental sulphur or pyrites as his raw material input. His choice is not determined completely by the relative prices of

Table 8. Industries and Products in Which Sulphur Is Used

Acids	Inorganic or organic acids
Alcohols	Insecticides
Alum	Leather
Ammonium sulphate	Livestock food
Aniline	Lubricants
Bleaching agent	Magnesium
Bromine	Matches
Carbon dioxide	Medicine
Carbon disulphide	Metallurgy
Carbon tetrachloride	Paints and pigments
Casein	Paper pulp
Cellophane	Petroleum products
Celluloid	Pharmaceuticals
Cellulose esters	Phenol
Cements	Photography
Chlorine	Plastics
Coke	Plate glass
Copper	Rayon
Dehydrating agent	Refrigerants
Detergents	Resins
Dyes	Road-surfacing materials
Ebonite	Rubber goods
Electroplating	Soap
Explosives	Soda
Fertilizers	Solvents
Fire extinguishers	Steel pickling and galvanizing
Fireproofing agents	Storage batteries
Fireworks	Sugar
Food preservatives	Sulphonated oils
Fumigants	Synthetic fibers
Fungicides	Synthetic rubber
Glue	Textiles
Glycerin	Tires, rubber
Impregnant	Water purification

SOURCE: U.S. Bureau of Mines, *Mineral Facts and Problems, 1965 Edition*, Bulletin 630, p. 908.

Table 9. Domestic Sulphuric Acid Production by Raw Material Source

per cent of total acid

Year	Elemental sulphur	Pyrites	Smelter gases	Hydrogen sulphide	Reforti-fied	Acid sludge
1920	51.76	22.92	25.32			
1930	58.48	22.05	19.47			
1940	62.12	25.57	11.44	0.87		
1950	73.75	11.51	5.69	1.00	6.81	1.24
1960	69.84	10.46	6.62	1.84	4.46	6.78
1966	75.58	4.92	5.73	3.42	3.41	6.94

SOURCE: *Chemical Economics Handbook* (Menlo Park, California: Stanford Research Institute, 1961 and 1967), No. 792.5031 and No. 792.2010A–8030G.

these two raw materials at their source. Transportation costs are also important because only about 45 per cent of the weight of pyrites usually becomes available for acid production, while all of the weight of elemental sulphur is available. Another consideration is that acid production from pyrites results in a by-product sinter, having iron and other metal values. But freight costs are a factor here too, as the sinter must be moved to an appropriate smelter.

Because of its purity, elemental sulphur can be converted to sulphuric acid in a relatively simple and inexpensive acid plant. However, an acid plant designed to use pyrites is more complex and requires 30 to 60 per cent more investment than a comparable plant built to consume elemental sulphur,[1] and total factory costs are also greater.[2]

Sulphuric acid plants are widely scattered throughout the United States, chiefly because of the low bulk value of the acid, the difficulties of handling the acid in bulk, and the subsequent high costs of shipment. These factors have also contributed to the conspicuous absence historically of vertical integration in the sulphur industry. Few significant economies can be obtained from centralizing the production of sulphuric acid at or near Frasch sulphur mines.

Most acid produced is not sold on the open market. Large users, such as fertilizer, chemical, and explosives manufacturers, usually own and operate their own acid plants in locations determined by proximity to major markets or to other raw materials. In 1965, it is reported that 94 companies were producing sulphuric acid at 230 plants located in 42 states and Puerto Rico.[3] Although many of these companies are industrial giants, no single acid producer uses enough sulphur to exercise significant control over the sulphur market.

End-use analysis of sulphur consumption

The relative importance of the various end uses for sulphur in acid and non-acid forms is indicated in table 10 where domestic sulphur consumption is broken down by major industry. Four comments are in order regarding the nature of this breakdown of sulphur consumption by industry.

First, only a small proportion of sulphur is consumed directly in ground and refined form as a secondary plant nutrient, a fungicide, and

1. W. L. Faith, Donald B. Keyes, and Donald L. Clark, *Industrial Chemicals* (3d. ed.; New York: John Wiley and Sons, Inc., 1965), p. 753.

2. See "Rethinking Rejected Routes," *Chemical Week* (14 October 1967), p. 122.

3. Faith, Keyes, and Clark, *op. cit.*, pp. 754–56. Because a number of companies produce acid for use within their own plants, it is difficult to obtain accurate figures on the exact number of acid producers. Thus, these figures are only an approximation.

an insecticide; the rest is consumed indirectly in the production of other commodities. The demand curve of a firm for sulphur, as an intermediate product, depends upon four factors: (1) the technology, i.e., both the marginal rate of substitution between sulphur and alternative factors, and the relationship between marginal physical product and changes in sulphur input; (2) the nature of demand for the firm's products; (3) the prices of other factors; and (4) the elasticity of supply of other factors employed. While it is difficult to analyze each of these factors for the many firms using sulphur in one form or another, it is possible to make some broad judgments on the basis of the industries shown in table 10.

Table 10. Distribution of Domestic Sulphur Consumption, 1966

Consuming sector	Per cent of total sulphur consumption
Acid uses:	
Fertilizers	48
Chemicals	18
TiO_2 and other inorganic pigments	6
Iron and steel	3
Rayon and film	3
Petroleum	2
Others	7
Total acid uses	87
Nonacid uses:	
Pulp and paper	5
Carbon bisulphide	3
Ground and refined	2
Other	3
Total nonacid uses	13

SOURCE: Freeport Sulphur Company, *Sulphur—Ally of Agriculture and Industry* (1967).

The marginal rate of substitution between sulphur and other factors is relatively high in such industries as chemical fertilizers, paint and pigments, petroleum, iron and steel, and pulp and paper, where technically and economically feasible substitutes exist. On the other hand, the marginal rate of substitution is relatively low in the nonferrous metals, rayon, and rubber industries, where substitutes are technically inferior to sulphur or sulphuric acid. Thus, it would be expected that the elasticity of demand for sulphur would be higher for firms in the first group of industries than for firms in the second group, given the time required for substitution to occur.

In most cases, sulphur as sulphuric acid is combined in almost fixed proportions with other inputs; thus, the marginal physical product declines rapidly as additional units of sulphur input are added. For this reason, small price declines for sulphur will in general fail to increase sulphur consumption, particularly in the short run where only the input of sulphur can be altered with other factor inputs remaining fixed. This would establish a presumption in favor of an inelastic demand for sulphur in the short run.

The second comment regarding the breakdown of sulphur consumption given in table 10 is that in most of its uses sulphur represents only a small fraction of the total cost of the products in which it is used. For example, 100 pounds of sulphur (costing about $1.80 in 1967) are used in the production of 800–1,000 pounds of black powder, 2–2.5 tons of nitroglycerine, 100–125 pounds of viscose rayon, 5,000 pounds of soft rubber, and 885–1,060 pounds of superphosphate fertilizer.[4] As Stigler has pointed out, it cannot be said in general that the elasticity of demand for a factor of production is smaller the smaller the proportion of total cost the outlay on the factor is, without adding the qualification, "given the possibility of substituting other inputs."[5] For the sulphur industry, the statement with qualification added appears valid, particularly in the short run. A small or even moderate change in the price of sulphur is unlikely to induce short-term adjustments in the amount of sulphur used because a shift to a different input would involve changes in plants, processes, products, input proportions, and expenditures that would generally be more costly than any savings likely to result from substitution. Thus, the fact that sulphur in general accounts for only a small portion of the total cost of most of the products in which it is used, coupled with the unlikelihood of substitution in the short run, supports the presumption of an inelastic demand for sulphur in the short run.

In the long run, however, the demand for sulphur is probably elastic at least over some range of prices. The continued use of sulphur as an industrial raw material is dependent to a large extent on how the price of sulphur and the costs of sulphur-consuming processes compare with the price of technical substitutes and the costs of processes employing these substitutes. Unique uses for sulphur are few. In most instances, technical substitutes are available. In addition, since there are several

4. Texas Gulf Sulphur Company, *Facts About Sulphur* (New York, 1958) p. 24.

5. George J. Stigler, *The Theory of Price* (rev. ed.; New York: The Macmillan Company, 1952), pp. 190–91. Stigler asserts that "the smaller the fraction of total cost that a productive service constitutes, the more finely the productive service is classified as a rule, and the more finely the productive services are classified, the easier it is to substitute other productive services." Thus, he feels that the qualification is important, and "robs the statement of much of its importance."

sources of sulphur, the demand for any single source of sulphur (for example, Frasch sulphur) is more elastic than the demand for sulphur in general. Thus, the possibility of substitution tends to make the long-run demand for sulphur relatively price elastic.

However, it must be remembered that a decision to use sulphur generally coincides with a decision to use a particular process. Thus, the purchase decision has investment overtones. Changing from elemental sulphur to a technical substitute, or to another form of sulphur, generally will involve a change of processes, requiring both changes in input proportions of other raw materials and changes in plant and equipment. As price rigidity reduces the element of risk in a purchase decision with investment implications, purchasers of sulphur are felt to prefer a reliable source of sulphur at a reasonably stable price to widely fluctuating prices.[6]

The final comment regarding the end uses of sulphur by consuming industries is prompted by the observation that sulphur is used in a wide range of industries covering most segments of American industry. Liebig's axiom that the economic welfare of a nation can be most accurately measured by its consumption of sulphuric acid appears to be as valid today as it was when he advanced it in the middle of the nineteenth century, though we tend to use the term "welfare" more cautiously today. The diversity of uses for sulphur as an intermediate product subjects the demand for sulphur to the cyclical fluctuations that characterize the manufacturing segment of the economy. At the same time, it makes the long-run demand for sulphur dependent upon growth in industrial production. While sulphur is sold in relatively small lots to a great many firms, ranging in size from small independent acid manufacturers to large integrated concerns, one major Frasch producer estimates that its largest ten to fifteen customers account for 90 per cent of its domestic sales. Nevertheless, it is unlikely that any single purchaser constitutes enough of the sulphur market to be able to wield significant power over that market.

Export markets for sulphur

Sulphur consumption provides a reasonably good index of a country's stage of industrialization. For example, per capita consumption of sulphur in 1965 amounted to 95 pounds in the United States, as compared with 7 pounds in Latin America and only 2 pounds in India.[7] The dis-

6. See *Sulphur* (September 1957), p. 16. Peck and Phillips in their respective studies of the aluminum and synthetic rubber industries observe that price rigidity is often desired by consumers of intermediate products.

7. Estimates made by Freeport Sulphur Company.

tribution of free world consumption of sulphur in 1968 by geographic area and sulphur source is shown in table 11. As in the United States, the demand for sulphur worldwide is closely related to the production of sulphuric acid.

Table 11. Free World Consumption of Sulphur, 1968, by Geographic Area and Sulphur Source

thousand long tons, sulphur equivalent

Area	Elemental	Nonelemental	Total
North America			
United States	8,275	1,025	9,300
Canada	725	550	1,225
Subtotal	9,000	1,575	10,525
Latin America	725	75	800
Europe	3,700	5,550	9,250
Africa and Middle East	550	450	1,000
Far East	850	2,400	3,250
Oceania	650	275	925
Total, free world	15,475	10,275	25,750

SOURCE: *Engineering and Mining Journal* (March 1969), p. 160c.

The major export markets for Frasch sulphur traditionally were Canada, the United Kingdom, France, Brazil, India, and Australia. The advent of the recovered sulphur production in Canada and France and Frasch sulphur production in Mexico brought changes in the pattern of world trade in sulphur (see table 12). The U.S. share of total world sulphur trade fell from about 47 per cent in 1960 to less than 30 per cent in 1964. During the same period, Mexican Frasch producers managed to maintain a nearly constant share of about 30 per cent, while French and Canadian recovered sulphur producers significantly increased their share of world sulphur markets. In 1965, governmental export restrictions and production problems caused a sharp reduction in exports of Frasch sulphur from Mexico, and U.S. Frasch producers were able to reverse the downward trend in their export share.

From 1922 to 1952, most export sales of Frasch sulphur were made through the Sulphur Export Corporation (Sulexco), a Webb-Pomerene export association. Sulexco was disbanded in 1952, largely because a worldwide shortage of sulphur made such a sales organization superfluous. In 1958, in the face of growing competition in many of their traditional export markets, the four domestic Frasch producers reestablished Sulexco.

International trade in sulphur has for a long time been subject to

Table 12. World Sulphur Trade, 1960–65

thousand metric tons

Source and destination	1960	1961	1962	1963	1964	1965
U.S. Frasch (% of export market)	46.7%	41.4%	36.9%	30.9%	29.5%	35.5%
North America	301	307	180	144	138	153
Western Europe	733	632	626	626	712	1,214
Australia	238	216	199	229	228	276
S. and Cent. America and Caribbean	204	210	198	195	313	232
Asia	199	170	262	312	367	393
Africa	93	52	47	33	11	99
Communist countries	34	22	45	53	50	35
Total	1,802	1,609	1,557	1,592	1,819	2,402
Mexican Frasch (% of export market)	30.8%	29.6%	31.4%	28.4%	30.5%	23.9%
North America	599	650	735	870	917	789
Western Europe	293	249	308	353	667	527
Australia	122	105	95	135	71	143
S. and Cent. America and Caribbean	15	4	22	21	19	18
Asia	68	56	61	13	28	22
Africa	88	89	103	76	131	120
Communist countries	4	—	—	—	51	—
Total	1,190	1,153	1,324	1,468	1,884	1,619
France (Lacq) (% of export market)	10.8%	15.0%	12.5%	19.6%	15.7%	14.0%
North America	—	—	—	12	—	—
Western Europe	349	441	433	700	835	796
Australia	—	5	5	12	—	—
S. and Cent. America and Caribbean	8	6	6	49	9	—
Asia	10	45	13	21	8	8
Africa	44	59	48	129	92	125
Communist countries	6	25	24	87	23	17
Total	418	582	529	1,010	967	947
Western Canada (% of export market)	3.4%	5.0%	8.6%	14.4%	19.0%	20.0%
North America	130	188	297	485	574	681
Western Europe	—	—	15	17	103	66
Australia	—	—	22	51	174	214
S. and Cent. America and Caribbean	—	—	—	3	33	38
Asia	—	6	29	106	136	162
Africa	—	—	—	29	48	91
Communist countries	—	—	—	54	106	105
Total	130	194	363	745	1,174	1,357
Other exporters—free world	114	80	66	37	91	34
Communist bloc	208	275	388	312	240	422
World total	3,862	3,893	4,222	5,170	6,177	6,781

SOURCE: *Sulphur*, various issues.

NOTE: Totals may not add due to rounding.

controls and restrictions. For example, imports into the United Kingdom, Australia, and New Zealand are handled by purchasing cartels. In addition, some nations such as Japan and Italy traditionally have placed import quotas or high tariffs on sulphur in order to protect their domestic high-cost native sulphur ore and pyrites industry. While these restrictions have been relaxed somewhat in recent years, they still reduce sulphur sales in some export markets. Mexico, however, has raised tariff barriers in recent years, following the development of its domestic Frasch industry in the 1950s.

Distribution and Marketing of Frasch Sulphur

Markets, like people, appear to be creatures of habit. Forms of distribution and marketing practices, once established, usually persist for considerable periods of time. They play important roles in defining the nature of the price-making process and in determining the character of the responses by firms to changes in supply and demand. The absence of an organized commodity exchange for sulphur makes even more necessary a consideration of the distribution system and marketing practices of Frasch firms. In particular, it raises questions concerning the availability and validity of pricing data, the dimensions of price, and the degree of information concerning market conditions possessed by both sellers and buyers.

Institutional aspects of the Frasch sulphur market

The most striking feature of the manner in which Frasch sulphur is sold to domestic consumers is the directness and simplicity of the system. While small amounts of sulphur bypass the market through transfers to other parts of integrated companies, most Frasch sulphur is sold by the producer directly to the consumer, and not through agents, brokers, or other middlemen. Within the United States, Frasch sulphur is marketed through district sales offices located in the major market areas (Tampa, Florida, the Atlantic Seaboard, the Great Lakes, the Gulf Coast, and the inland water routes of the Mississippi, Ohio, and Illinois rivers). As mentioned previously, all export sales of Frasch sulphur were made through the Sulphur Export Corporation until 1952, and again since 1955. Until Duval withdrew in 1963, the ownership of Sulexco was divided as follows: Texas Gulf Sulphur Company—37 per cent, Freeport Sulphur Company—37 per cent, Jefferson Lake Sulphur Company—18 per cent, and the Duval Corporation—8 per cent. Sulexco, in turn, maintains a worldwide sales organization and has agents in every major foreign sulphur market.

Sulphur is generally sold under contracts on both domestic and export markets.[8] The contracts usually run for one year or more, but are

8. Historically, contract periods have varied in response to expectations concerning future supply and demand conditions. When a short supply of sulphur has been anticipated, consumers have pressed for long-term contracts to insure availability of future deliveries. In the early sixties, when sulphur was abundant and prices weak, buyers attempted to shorten the contract period. Usually, sulphuric acid manufacturers desire a contract period of at least one year to insure themselves twelve months' supply. A factor causing longer contract periods in recent years has been the inclusion in sulphur contracts of provisions calling for conversion of the buyer's plant to the storage, handling, and use of molten sulphur, sometimes at the seller's expense. In these instances, contracts were written for a longer period, generally either five or ten years. Even in these cases, how-

not full requirement contracts. As a rule, they contain provisions granting the seller the right to increase the price by notification to the purchaser. The buyer then has a specified period, usually thirty days, in which to accept or reject the price increase. If the price increase is rejected, the seller has the right to cancel the contract. On the other hand, if the purchaser receives a bona fide offer from another seller at a lower price, he may cancel his contract after giving the original seller the option of meeting the lower offer. In addition, the seller has an obligation to extend to the buyer any lower price agreed upon by the seller for a comparable sale to another buyer in the vicinity of the initial buyer's plant.[9] Consumers usually call for bids and then negotiate a contract with the most favorable supplier. Contracts generally call for minimum quantities to be purchased and specify delivery dates. There is some evidence that most purchasers of sulphur refrain from obtaining all their sulphur requirements from one seller in order to enhance their bargaining position and to ensure a continuing source of supply.

Distribution of Frasch sulphur

The geographical concentration of Frasch sulphur production and the widely dispersed locations of its primary consumers make the distribution of sulphur from the mines to the major consuming areas an important feature of the industry's market structure. Until recently, sulphur was marketed primarily from the mines. Union Sulphur Company shipped its output by rail directly to consumers or to Sabine, Texas, where it was loaded on freighters for transshipment either to the Atlantic Seaboard or abroad. Later, Texas Gulf Sulphur, Freeport Sulphur, Jefferson Lake Sulphur, and Duval Sulphur and Potash also shipped much of their product directly to the consumer by rail, and their ocean shipments were loaded on freighters at Texas City, Galveston, and Freeport, Texas. In time, major distribution points for sulphur developed on the Atlantic Seaboard in the port cities of New York, Baltimore, Portland, Searsport (Maine), and Quebec. Similarly, on the Pacific Coast, Portland, Oregon, and Vancouver, B.C., became major sulphur distribution points. Abroad, sulphur was distributed from Marseilles, Manchester, Hamburg, and Gothenburg.[10]

---

ever, the buyer has the option of cancelling the contract under certain provisions, provided he pays the seller the unamortized balance of any conversion cost incurred by the seller.

9. This obligation is not usually contained in the written contract. However, in conversations with both buyers and sellers, the author has ascertained that such an obligation is felt to exist by both parties.

10. See Albert G. Wolf, "Marketing of Sulphur," *The Engineering and Mining Journal* (1 July 1922), pp. 19–20.

Traditionally, sulphur has been marketed to three major groups of consumers: the pulp and paper manufacturers of New England and Eastern Canada; the chemical manufacturers of the eastern states; and the acid phosphate manufacturers of the southeastern states. Other consumer groups have been the various industries of the Great Lakes region, and the explosives, pulp and paper, insecticide, and fungicide manufacturers of the Pacific Coast. This grouping of major consuming areas has not changed greatly since the early days of the Frasch sulphur industry. The only important change has been the growth in sulphur consumption in the central and southwestern states. This occurred when the chemical industry spread into these areas as petroleum and natural gas became increasingly important as a raw material source.

For many years, sulphur was shipped in dry bulk form to the consumer. From the mine, the sulphur was moved through steamheated pipes to central points called relay stations, where it was discharged into steam-heated tanks and relieved of its contained air. From the relay stations, sulphur was pumped to the storage area where it was sprayed into vats to cool and solidify. When ready for shipment, the solid sulphur was broken up by power shovels, loaded onto conveyor belts, and moved to barges, freight cars, or ocean freighters for delivery to the consumer. At the consumer's plant, sulphur was again stored in dry bulk form until required for plant operations. In most instances, the sulphur had to be melted to liquid form before it could be used.

Beginning about 1955, some liquid shipments of sulphur were made by barge to consumers in Alabama, Arkansas, Mississippi, and Missouri via inland waterways. However, liquid shipments did not assume significance until after 1960, when major alterations were made in the distribution system for Frasch sulphur.

In 1958, Texas Gulf Sulphur Company constructed the first liquid storage terminal for sulphur at Cincinnati to serve customers in the Ohio Valley. In 1959, Texas Gulf began construction of a mammoth new $3 million storage and shipping terminal at Beaumont, Texas, on the Neches River. This terminal, completed in 1960, was designed to handle the bulk of the company's sulphur production from its four Frasch mines, both in the solid and liquid states. Rail, truck, barge, and ocean shipments could all be accommodated at this terminal. The centralization of shipping and storage facilities reduced Texas Gulf's handling and shipping costs by an estimated 30–40 per cent.[11] In addition, between 1958 and 1963, Texas Gulf constructed ten additional liquid storage terminals in major consuming areas. To carry liquid sulphur to the ter-

11. "Liquid Sulphur Terminal for Texas Gulf Sulphur Cuts Costs, Eases Handling," *Sulphur* (February 1961), p. 27.

minals in Tampa, Florida, and the Atlantic Seaboard, Texas Gulf chartered a converted T-2 15,000-ton tanker, the S.S. *Marine Sulphur Queen,* which went into service in January 1961. This was the first ocean-going vessel to be used exclusively for the transport of liquid sulphur.[12]

In mid-1959, the Freeport Sulphur Company launched a $23 million program to move sulphur in liquid form into major market areas for storage and transshipment to its customers. Freeport entered into long-term contracts with independent marine transportation companies to provide and operate new terminal facilities and marine equipment, estimated to cost about $20 million.[13] Additional facilities, costing between $3 million and $4 million were provided by Freeport. Freeport also leased two tankers, the S.S. *Louisiana Sulphur* and S.S. *Louisiana Brimstone,* to serve its domestic coastal markets.

In 1961, Pan American Sulphur Company constructed a liquid sulphur terminal at Tampa to handle part of its exports to the United States. PASCO later increased the size of the Tampa terminal and added a second terminal at Newark. In 1962, the other Mexican Frasch company, Gulf Sulphur Corporation, opened liquid sulphur terminals in Tampa and Baltimore.

In 1963, U.S. and Mexican Frasch producers shipped liquid sulphur to twenty-seven producer-controlled regional storage and transshipment terminals. (The location and the capacity of these terminals are listed in table 13.) The two small domestic Frasch firms, Jefferson Lake Sulphur and the Duval Corporation, ship liquid sulphur to customers in either tank trucks or railroad cars. Neither firm has built regional liquid sulphur terminals to handle water shipments. Duval ships only a small percentage of its sulphur in liquid form, and Jefferson Lake ships much of its liquid sulphur into areas where other producers also ship by rail or truck.

The movement of liquid sulphur to overseas markets began in 1964. Sulexco chartered two 25,000-ton tankers, the *Naess Texas* and the *Naess Louisiana,* and constructed an $18 million liquid terminal at Rotterdam, Netherlands, capable of handling approximately 500,000 tons of liquid shipments annually and storing more than 100,000 tons of solid sulphur. In 1965, Sulexco increased the capacity of its Rotter-

12. On February 2, 1963, the *Marine Sulphur Queen,* carrying a cargo of liquid sulphur, left Beaumont, Texas, for Norfolk, Virginia. Without distress signal, the ship disappeared with the tragic loss of its crew of thirty-nine. The disappearance remains a mystery to this day. In 1964, Texas Gulf chartered the 23,760-ton tanker, S.S. *Marine Texas* to replace the *Marine Sulphur Queen.*

13. See "Freeport Sulphur Company's Activities," *Sulphur* (February 1961), pp. 25–26; and "Trend to Molten Sulphur Grows Fast," *Chemical and Engineering News* (April 10, 1961), pp. 23–24.

Table 13. Liquid Sulphur Regional Storage and Transshipment Terminals in Operation in 1963

Producer-controlled terminals	Storage tanks	Total storage capacity
	number	*thousand long tons*
Freeport Sulphur Company:		
Baton Rouge, La.	1	6.5
Bucksport, Maine	2	20.0
Charleston, S.C.	1	10.0
Everett, Mass.	1	10.0
Joliet, Illinois	3	30.0
Nitro, W. Va.	2	18.0
Tampa, Florida	6	60.0
Warners, N.J.	2	12.5
Wellsville, Ohio	2	20.0
Total	20	187.0
Texas Gulf Sulphur Company:		
Baltimore, Md.	2	24.0
Carteret, N.J.	2	26.0
Cincinnati, Ohio	3	16.8
Jacksonville, Florida	1	11.0
Marseilles, Ill.	1	10.0
Newell, Pa.	1	10.0
Norfolk, Va.	2	20.8
Paulsboro, N.J.	2	24.0
Savannah, Ga.	1	11.0
Tampa, Florida	1	7.5
Wilmington, N.C.	1	8.0
Total	17	169.1
Pan American Sulphur Company:		
Newark, N.J.	1	10.0
Tampa, Florida	4	40.0
Total	5	50.0
Gulf Sulphur Corporation:		
Baltimore, Md.	1	10.0
Tampa, Florida	1	10.0
Total	2	20.0

SOURCE: U.S. Department of the Interior, Bureau of Mines, *Minerals Yearbook, 1965*, vol. 1 (Metals and Minerals—Except Fuels).

dam terminal by one-third and built a second liquid terminal at Dublin, Ireland. Customers are serviced from these terminals by self-propelled tanker barges and other carriers.

In 1965, PASCO also began liquid shipments abroad, placing in operation a 60,000-ton liquid sulphur terminal at Immingham, England. The company expects to ship about 225,000 tons of liquid sulphur annually through this terminal, which is serviced by three chartered tankers.

The change from solid to liquid shipment of sulphur occurred rapidly, with liquid shipments increasing from only 15 per cent of domestic shipments in 1959 to an estimated 90 per cent by 1963.[14] Producers had two major reasons for their sudden shift to liquid delivery. First, conversion to liquid sulphur made it possible to sell under longer-term contracts, which producers found desirable in a period of lagging sales and price competition. Conversion to liquid sulphur substantially reduced inventories held by both consumers and producers because of the added expense of maintaining the inventory in a liquid state. The reduction in producers' inventories made spot sales much more difficult. Distribution of sulphur from producer to consumer became subject to a greater degree of scheduling. As a result, producers were able to demand longer-term contracts. This trend to longer-term contracts was also encouraged by the willingness of sulphur producers to finance conversion of customers' plants to liquid sulphur in return for a longer-term purchase agreement. A second reason for the rapid switch to liquid delivery was that it required the use of special ships which reduce the freight advantage held by Mexican Frasch producers who were free to ship sulphur into the United States in foreign-registered tramp steamers.

Once the decision was made to move to liquid delivery of sulphur, it then became to the producers' advantage to convert as much of their shipments as possible to the new form of distribution. They were aided in this effort by the fact that liquid delivery benefited consumers also. Most sulphur, whether for acid or nonacid consumption, is used in liquid form, and liquid delivery eliminates fuel costs for sulphur melting and reduces handling costs. Liquid delivery also eliminates losses in handling, which average 0.5 per cent for dry sulphur. Furthermore, liquid sulphur is not subject to contamination from moisture, scale, and other foreign matter, and there is no dust to cause corrosion of adjacent equipment and create an explosion hazard.[15] It is estimated that

14. L. B. Gittinger, Jr., "Sulphur," *The Engineering and Mining Journal* (February 1964), p. 151.

15. John Doak, "Liquid-Sulphur Distribution," *The Oil and Gas Journal* (June 24, 1963), p. 101.

conversion of a plant to use of liquid sulphur lowers plant costs by as much as $2 per ton. In addition, conversion to liquid sulphur, combined with the establishment by producers of regional terminals, lowers the inventory requirements of sulphur consumers.

Nature of the price structure

As sulphur is normally sold under long-term contract with no formal market, both buyers and sellers must rely on their own initiative to collect price data. U.S. domestic list prices for Frasch sulphur are generally quoted per long ton, f.o.b., bulk, cars, mines; f.o.b., vessels, Gulf port (producer's port); and f.o.b., regional terminal. Prices are $1.50 lower at the mines than at the Gulf ports. The regional terminal prices vary with location. The current changes in freight prices do not affect the list prices at the mines and Gulf ports. U.S. export list prices, which are quoted per long ton, f.o.b., vessels, Gulf port, and c & f for certain destinations, are not based on domestic list prices, but are determined separately.

Two grades of Frasch sulphur are sold: bright (clear yellow sulphur not discolored by hydrocarbon impurities) and dark. Bright Frasch commands a $1.00 premium per long ton. Generally, the quoted list prices for spot and contract sales are the same. However, in the past, list price changes have been made effective on spot transactions and new contracts three to six months before they have been made effective for current contracts.

Fluctuations in the Demand for Sulphur

Seasonal fluctuations in the demand for sulphur do not exercise much influence on the behavior of firms within the industry. The demand for sulphur is, however, responsive to cyclical fluctuations in industrial production. This is illustrated in figure 6. The reason for this close relationship between sulphur demand and industrial production is the diversity of uses to which sulphur is put. Since sulphur is consumed in almost every sector of modern industry, the demand for sulphur tends to fluctuate with industrial activity in general, and "historical statistics show the remarkable harmony between the movement of sulphur consumption and that of industrial production."[16] It might be thought that the shifts in sulphur consumption that have occurred in recent years and, in particular, the increasing importance of the chemical fertilizer industry as the primary consumer of sulphur, would have weakened the

16. See Hans H. Landsberg, Leonard L. Fischman, and Joseph L. Fisher, *Resources in America's Future* (Baltimore: The Johns Hopkins Press for Resources for the Future, Inc., 1963), pp. 326–27.

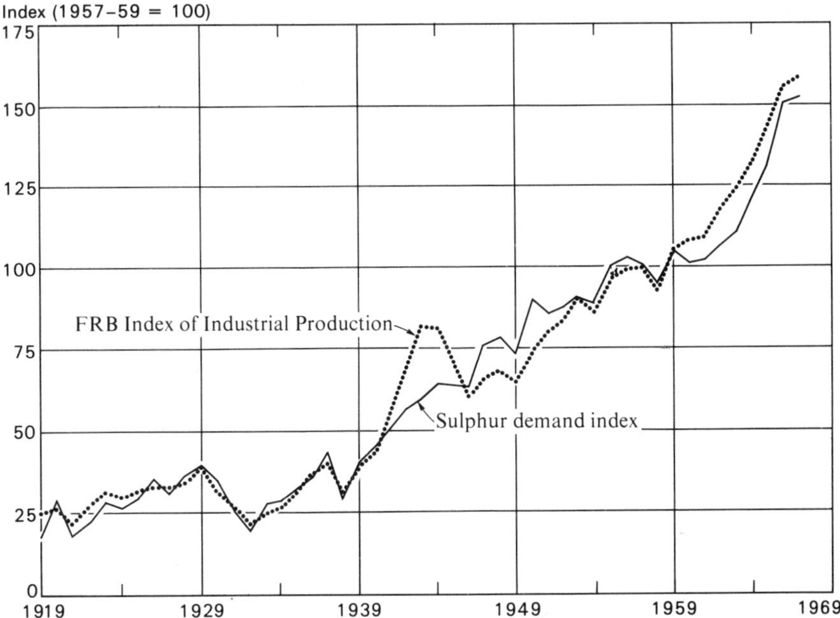

Figure 6. U.S. sulphur demand compared with industrial production, 1919–67.

historical relationship between sulphur consumption and industrial production. To test this hypothesis, two correlations of sulphur consumption with industrial production were made, the first for the period 1919–67 and the second for the period 1919–59. The resulting coefficients of determination were 0.9397 and 0.9675 respectively, indicating only a slight weakening in recent years of the relationship linking sulphur consumption and industrial production. Of course, it might be that the increased use of chemical fertilizers in the sixties has merely coincided with an increase in industrial production and that there is no permanent relationship between the two.

The demand for sulphur in the United States has increased significantly over time (see figure 7). The growth in consumption since 1952 shown in figure 7 is actually understated because it does not include (1) the sulphur values in suphuric acid reconstituted from acid sludges, or (2) reductions in consumers' inventories which accompanied the switch to liquid distribution of sulphur.[17] Exports, also shown in figure 7, have followed the general pattern of domestic consumption with the exception of the periods during World War II and Korea when exports

17. See William L. Swagger, *The Paley Report in Review: Sulphur* (Battelle Memorial Institute, 1961), pp. 5–6.

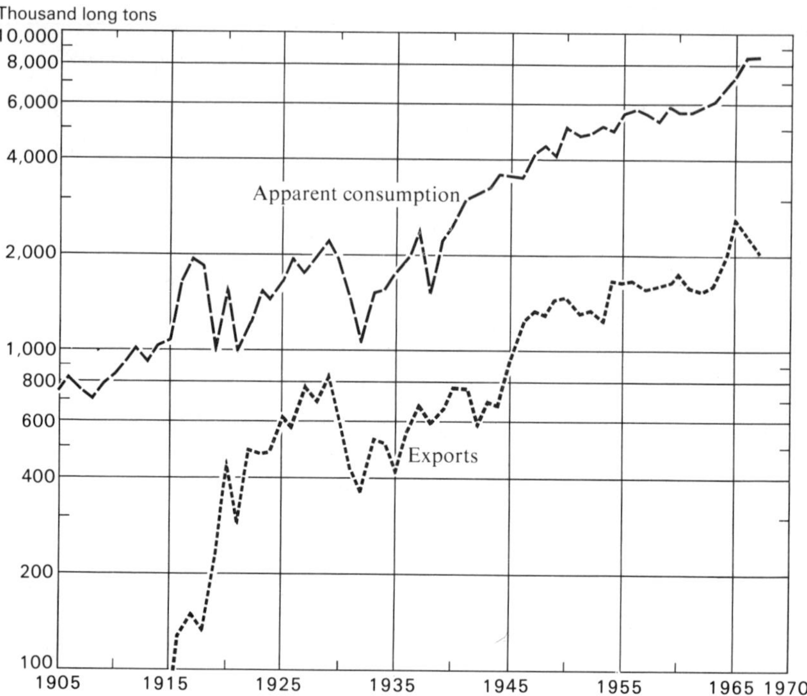

Figure 7. U.S. apparent consumption and exports of sulphur, 1905–67. (*Based on data in table A-2.*)

fell and domestic consumption increased. The extent of the increase in exports in recent years may have been somewhat overstated by including shipments that were intended to build up producers' stocks at newly opened terminals in Europe.

Part II

Market Behavior in the Sulphur Industry

Chapter 5

Output and Prices

In the introductory chapter to this study, the thesis was presented that an industry's price and output behavior could be related to the underlying factors of the industry's market structure. If the market structure of the industry undergoes significant change, it should be possible to observe resulting changes in market behavior within the industry. Earlier chapters of this study showed that the market structure of the Frasch sulphur industry underwent significant alterations during the fifties. In particular, new sources of supply, both domestic and foreign, entered into competition with Frasch sulphur for domestic and export markets. Thus, the Frasch sulphur industry affords an opportunity to test the hypothesis linking market behavior to market structure. As the structural characteristics of the Frasch industry have changed, similar changes should have occurred in market behavior within the industry.

It should be stressed, however, that while the market structure of the Frasch sulphur industry has changed over time, conditions in the industry have always closely approximated those of pure oligopoly. There have never been more than six domestic firms producing Frasch sulphur at any given time, and four firms have virtually dominated the industry. Entry of new firms has been restricted by the availability of workable deposits. Frasch sulphur has remained an essentially homogeneous commodity. Thus, the structural conditions in the industry have resulted in a maximum degree of interdependence among firms in the industry. The major changes in market structure have related to the degree to which the actions of Frasch producers have been independent of external restraint.

Frasch sulphur must compete in the market with other sources of elemental sulphur (recovered sulphur and native sulphur) and with various forms of nonelemental sulphur. Over the life of the industry, the market actions of domestic Frasch producers have been influenced to varying degrees by actual and potential competition from these other sources of sulphur, both domestic and foreign.

This chapter seeks to explain the observed market behavior of Frasch producers by relating price and output decisions to the changing structural characteristics of the industry. Output behavior in the Frasch sulphur industry is considered in section one of this chapter and price behavior is examined in section two. The following chapter contains a chronological explanation of market behavior in the industry by linking changes in the form of oligopolistic market behavior to changes in the industry's market structure.

Output Behavior in the Frasch Sulphur Industry

Short-run aspects of Frasch sulphur production

While quarterly production figures for Frasch sulphur are available back to 1924, a monthly production series extends back only to 1943. In the following analysis, three series have been used for the period 1951 to 1968. The first series is the monthly production of Frasch sulphur. The second is the month-end producers' inventories of Frasch sulphur. The third, computed from the first two, shows monthly shipments.

The first step taken in analyzing these three time series was to determine the extent of seasonal variation. To test for seasonal fluctuations, a 12-month moving total of the monthly observations was computed. To obtain a monthly moving average, the preceding and succeeding moving totals were averaged. Specific seasonals for each month were then computed by taking the ratio of the monthly observation to the monthly moving average. These specific seasonals for each month were then averaged for the period 1951–68, and the resulting means were then "leveled" to insure that they summed to 1200. The resulting monthly index of seasonal variation is given in table 14.

Analysis of the monthly seasonal indexes reveals that inventories are subject to only very minor seasonal variation, while both production and shipments exhibit a somewhat greater degree of seasonal sensitivity. Since Frasch plants operate on a continuous 24-hour-day basis, some monthly variation results from the varying number of days in the month. Frasch plants operate 672 hours in February, but 744 hours in 31-day months. Additional random variation results from the opening and closing of mines, holidays, and breakdowns.

Some of the seasonal variation in sulphur shipments stems from the highly seasonal nature of fertilizer consumption. As farmers make most of their purchases in the late spring and early summer, fertilizer manufacturers, who currently account for about half of Frasch sulphur sales, usually operate at full capacity during March, April, and May. Sulphur shipments are therefore higher during these months.

Table 14. Monthly Indexes of Seasonal Variation in Frasch Sulphur Inventories, Production, and Shipments, 1951–68

Month	Inventories	Production	Shipments
January	1.010	1.001	0.922
February	1.011	0.915	0.903
March	1.005	1.012	1.052
April	0.996	1.001	1.059
May	0.986	1.024	1.098
June	0.983	0.991	0.998
July	0.998	1.019	0.950
August	1.003	1.027	0.992
September	1.004	0.965	0.948
October	1.002	1.016	1.039
November	1.002	0.992	0.988
December	1.000	1.037	1.051

SOURCE: Computed from data in U.S. Department of Commerce, Office of Business Statistics, *Survey of Current Business* (1952–69).

Seasonally adjusted monthly Frasch sulphur production, end-of-month inventories, and shipments appear in figure 8. The striking feature of this chart is the stability of inventories and their size relative to output and shipments. Over the period from 1951 to 1968, the ratio of end-of-month inventories to monthly shipments has averaged 8.6 ranging from 15.7 in July 1958 to 2.5 in December 1967. While inventories never fell below 1.9 million tons, shipments never exceeded 866,000 tons.

Prior to the introduction of liquid storage of sulphur in 1959, the size of Frasch inventories could be explained by the ease with which sulphur could be stored in dry bulk form. Between 65 and 70 per cent of the inventory maintained by Frasch producers was being held by Texas Gulf Sulphur Company, even though this firm was accounting for only 40 to 45 per cent of total domestic Frasch production. Texas Gulf's management contended that large inventories had been maintained for two purposes: to achieve mining efficiency by maintaining sulphur production at a reasonably level rate; and to serve as a form of risk reduction for both producers and consumers.[1]

1. See Texas Gulf Sulphur Company, *Annual Report,* for 1956 and 1957. In testimony before the Federal Trade Commission, industry representatives stressed "that in the mining of sulphur, the process of 'steaming' wells is a continuous operation that normally is not interrupted because interruption increases production cost and may mean lessened potential recovery from a given operation. For this reason, wells are normally operated continuously until exhausted and their production accumulates above ground as unsold inventory." Federal Trade Commission, *Report on the Sulphur Industry and International Cartels* (Washington, D.C.: U.S. Government Printing Office, 1947), p. 93.

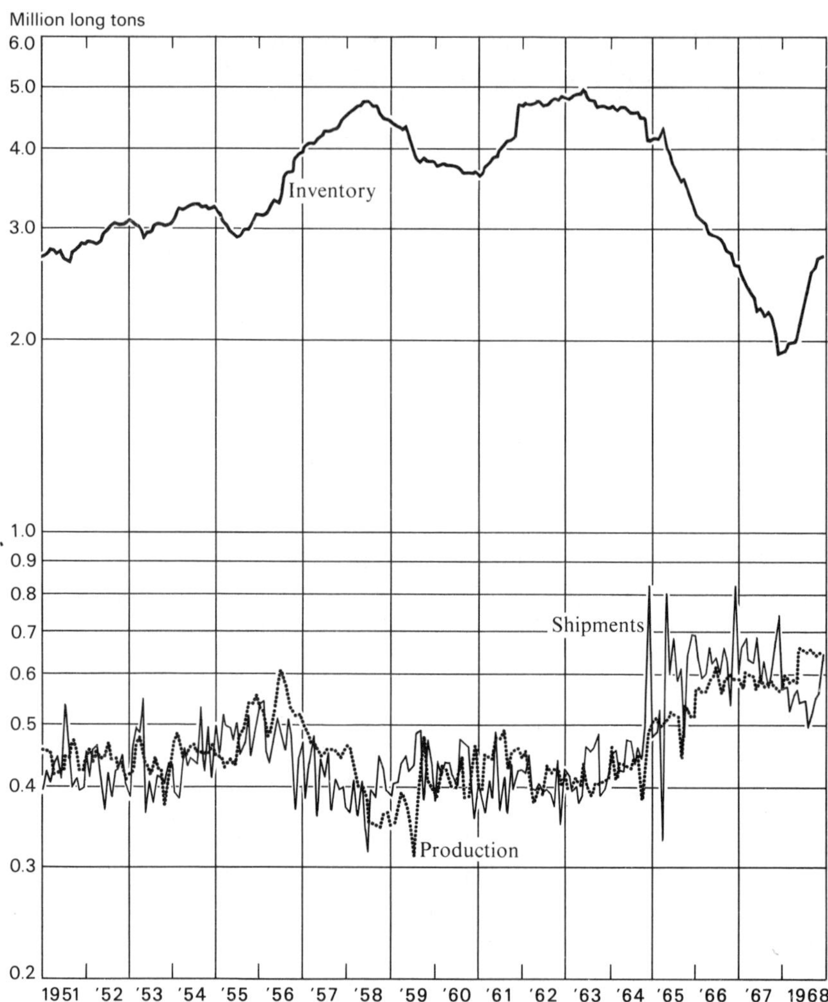

Figure 8. Monthly U.S. Frasch sulphur production, shipments, and inventories, 1951–68, seasonally adjusted. (Computed from data in U.S. Department of Commerce, Office of Business Statistics, Survey of Current Business, *1952 to 1969.)*

Since 1959, two forces have worked to reduce the size of inventories held by producers. The first was the switch to liquid distribution of sulphur which made storage of sulphur more costly and led to cutbacks in the inventories of consumers as well as producers. The second and more important force was the expansion of demand in recent years, which outstripped production and resulted in a steady decline in the industry's stocks from 1963 through 1967. At the end of 1967, producers' inventories amounted to 1.9 million tons, an all-time low for the industry.

The relationship between production and shipments shown in figure 8 is fairly close, particularly for the period prior to 1956. As might be expected, production appears to have fluctuated less than shipments, and the monthly changes in production have been consistently less than the monthly changes in shipments. As Frasch sulphur is generally sold on long-term contracts, producers have a fairly good idea of how much sulphur they will supply over the year, but they cannot be certain of the monthly distribution of shipments. It is not surprising that production tends to suggest the trend about which the shipments series fluctuates.

Trend in annual U.S. Frasch sulphur production

Annual domestic Frasch sulphur production from 1905 to 1967 is shown in figure 9. In order to depict the long-run movement of Frasch sulphur production, the method of least squares was used to derive a

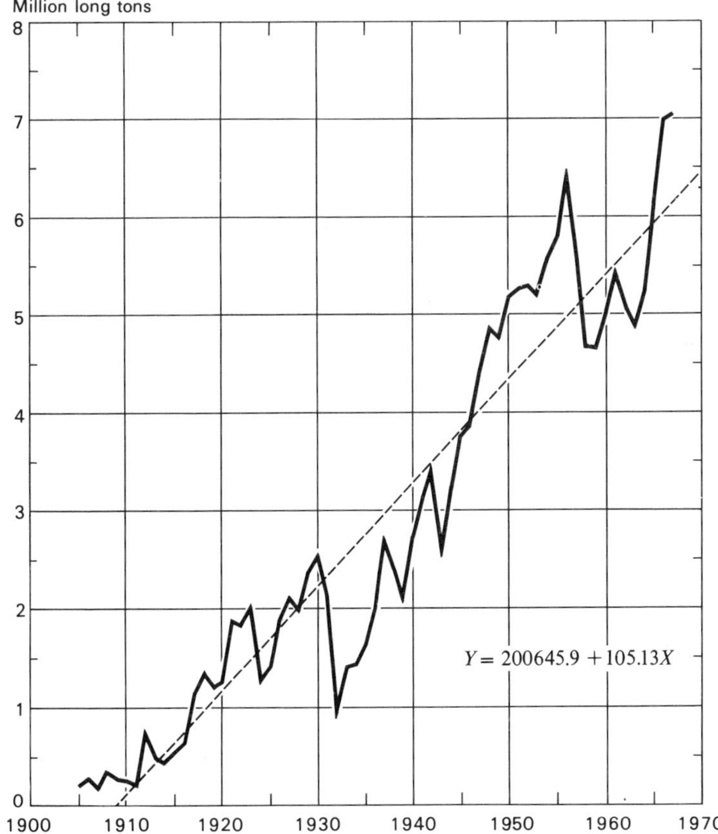

Figure 9. Annual U.S. Frasch sulphur production, 1905–67. (*Based on data in table A-1.*)

linear trend function for this period, depicted as the dotted line in the chart. The coefficient of determination for this trend was 0.8953.

Figure 9 indicates a nearly continuous upward trend in Frasch sulphur production from 1905 to 1967. Output was generally above the trend values until 1930 and below them from 1930 to 1945. In the post-World War II period, output again exceeded the trend values until 1957. The downturn in production from 1958 to 1964 is of interest because, unlike departures from the long-run trend in earlier years, it cannot be attributed to cyclical fluctuations in industrial activity. The slump during these years was the direct result of increased competition from other sources of sulphur.

Cyclical behavior of Frasch sulphur production

One method of evaluating the sensitivity of Frasch sulphur production to cyclical fluctuations in economic activity is to compute the percentage deviation of output from the trend values given in figure 9. Of course, deviations from the trend represent the influence of random or irregular factors as well as cyclical factors. However, if the deviations from the trend are compared with reference cycles in business activity, as in figure 10, some indication of the correspondence of fluctuations in output to fluctuations in economic activity can be gained.[2]

Analysis of figure 10 discloses a rough, but far from exact, correspondence between movements in the trend-adjusted Frasch sulphur production series and the timing of fluctuations in general economic activity. Frasch output closely followed movements in business activity during the early years, expanding during World War I and peaking in 1918. The 1920 reference cycle peak was not experienced in the sulphur industry. Sulphur production did not expand until 1921 and fell off slightly in 1922 before reaching a second peak in 1923. The relationship between the timing of output movements and of movements in economic activity was fairly close from 1924 to 1938. Between 1938 and 1945, the National Bureau recorded no turning points in general economic activity, but Frasch sulphur output was less consistent. Figure 10 reveals a clear peak in Frasch sulphur production in 1942 and a trough in 1943. From 1943 to 1948, sulphur output moved consistently upward with little response to the brief reference cycle contraction in 1945. From 1948 to 1956, there was little cyclical movement in Frasch sulphur output and little relationship with the timing of reference cycles. During this period, Frasch producers operated at full capacity and experienced difficulty in supplying domestic and export demands. During 1951 and 1952, shipments of Frasch sulphur were

2. Reference cycles taken from *Business Cycle Developments* (September 1966), p. 65.

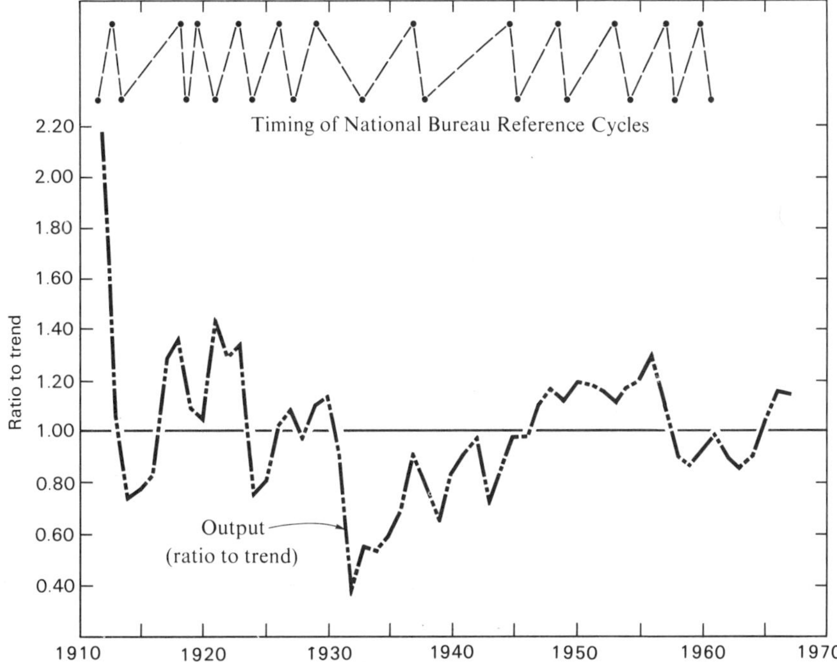

Figure 10. Annual U.S. Frasch sulphur output—ratios to trend. (Reference cycles from Business Cycle Developments, *September 1966, p. 65.)*

under the control of the Defense Production Agency. The slump in Frasch sulphur production from 1958 to 1963 and the steady increase in Frasch sulphur production since 1964 both appear to have been more closely related to changes in market structure, particularly the entry of new sources of sulphur, than to cyclical movements in economic activity.

Price Behavior in the Frasch Sulphur Industry

Short-run movements in posted Frasch sulphur prices

Frasch sulphur is a perfect textbook example of an industry in which prices are administered in the sense given it first by Gardiner C. Means as "prices . . . made by administrative decisions influenced to a greater or lesser extent by market conditions."[3] In his study of the fertilizer

3. See National Resources Committee, *The Structure of the American Economy*, Pt. I (Washington, D.C.: U.S. Government Printing Office, 1939), p. 109. Means contended that inflexible prices were the result of industrial concentration, and Frasch sulphur was one of the examples given. For a critical review of the arguments for and against the theory of administered prices see John M. Blair, "Means, Thorp, and Neal on Price Inflexibility," *Review of Economics and Statistics* (November 1956) pp. 427–35.

industry, Jesse Markham noted: "It is unlikely that American business annals contain a price less given to change than that of natural sulphur."[4]

The movement of posted prices for Frasch sulphur over the industry's history is summarized in table 15. The prices given pertain to the posted price for bright sulphur f.o.b. cars, mines. (Posted prices for dark sulphur are $1 per ton less than those for bright sulphur, and posted prices, f.o.b., Gulf port are $1.50 per ton more than the mines price.) Between 1926 and 1964, there were only seven changes in the posted price—an average of one price change every 5.6 years! Taken over most of this period, Frasch prices appear to have been established in response to long-run criteria and to have been relatively insensitive

Table 15. Summary of Frasch Sulphur Posted Prices, 1900–1968

Period	Posted price, bright sulphur ($/long ton, f.o.b. cars, mines)
1900–25[a]	$14.00–$22.00
1926–38	$18.00
1939–47	$16.00
1948–50	$18.00
1951–53[b]	$21.00–$24.00
1954–57[c]	$26.50
1958–64[d]	$23.50
1965–66[e]	$25.50
1967–68[f]	$28.00–$42.00

SOURCES: *Oil, Paint, and Drug Reporter;* U.S. Bureau of Mines, *Minerals Yearbook* for the applicable years.

[a] Initial price established by Union Sulphur Company was $17.00. Beginning in 1904, price increased to $18.00 where it remained until 1916. From 1917 to 1919, sulphur sold at $22.00 per ton to munitions and fertilizer manufacturers, although spot prices went much higher. From 1920 to 1926, posted price varied from $14.00 to as high as $22.00 per ton.

[b] In the fourth quarter of 1950, one producer increased his price to $22.00 and the other producer to $21.00 per ton. In 1951, the Office of Price Stabilization froze Frasch sulphur prices at $21.00 to $24.00 per ton.

[c] Price controls were removed in March 1953. Price immediately increased to $25.50 per ton. In 1954, price raised to $26.50 per ton.

[d] In September 1957, price reduced to $23.50 per ton. Between 1958 and 1964, posted price remained unchanged, but producer's realizations on sulphur sales fell to as low as $18.00 per ton due to freight absorption, discounts, etc.

[e] In July 1964, the posted price was increased to $25.50 per ton.

[f] In December 1966, the posted price increased to $28.00 per ton. Posted price increased to $32.00 in April 1967 and to $37.50 in September 1967. In 1968, trade journals were reporting a posted price of $39.00 per ton through March and $42.00 per ton for the remainder of the year.

4. Jesse W. Markham, *The Fertilizer Industry* (Nashville: The Vanderbilt University Press, 1958), p. 79.

to short-run changes in supply and demand. Short-run price stability was maintained by permitting inventories to fluctuate and by adjusting production schedules, when possible, to conditions of demand at the prevailing price.

In the period from 1965 through 1968, the price of Frasch sulphur was increased five times in the face of a severe worldwide shortage of the element. The increased responsiveness of posted prices to short-run conditions in the market represents a relatively recent phenomenon in the industry, but one that is likely to remain. It reflects the increased competitiveness of world sulphur markets since the introduction of new sources of supply in the past decade. The new pattern of pricing means that in periods when sulphur is plentiful, the posted price is likely to become less meaningful as sellers substitute freight absorption, discounts, and other hidden incentives for changes in the posted price. This type of behavior existed in the period from 1958 to 1964 when sulphur markets were glutted. In periods when the market is in short supply, the posted price is likely to increase quite rapidly as it did in the period 1965 through 1968, when price was used as a means of rationing existing supplies among consumers.

Trends and cycles in posted Frasch sulphur prices

Examination of the posted prices for Frasch sulphur given in table 15 reveals no clearly definable trend for the entire period from 1900 to 1968. Several short-run trend elements are identifiable, however, and each is related to a particular phase of the industry's development. A chronological description of industry price and output behavior is given in the next chapter.

Cyclical movements in Frasch sulphur prices are difficult to identify. The price decline in the period following World War I, the abrupt rise in 1926, and the decline in price in 1938 were generally consistent with movements in industrial activity in those years. However, the stable posted price from 1926 to 1937 gives little indication of the severe depression of the early thirties. In the post-World War II period, there appears to have been little relationship between cyclical movements in business activity and Frasch sulphur prices. Frasch prices remained constant during the recessions of 1949 and 1954. The price decline in 1957 preceded the general decline in business activity in 1958, and the posted price of Frasch sulphur remained constant during the 1961 recession. While Frasch prices rose dramatically from 1964 to 1968, the increases were in response to a fundamental imbalance between production and demand, rather than to the cyclical expansion in the economy. Over the entire period, it would appear that cyclical fluctuations in business activity have not affected Frasch sulphur prices. They perhaps have served to reinforce the pressure for revision of the posted price, but with the possible exception of the decline in 1938, they do not appear to have been responsible for the few changes in the posted price.

Price discrimination on the export market

Export prices in the Frasch sulphur industry have always been quoted separately from the domestic price, f.o.b. mines. In the early years of the industry, the export price was quoted on a c.i.f. basis at New York City; in recent years, it has been quoted f.o.b. vessels, Gulf port. Examination of the average values per ton of Frasch exports and Frasch domestic shipments reveals that both have differed significantly from the average annual posted price for Frasch sulphur. Over most of its life, the industry price for export has been higher than the domestic price. Does this constitute discriminatory pricing? Price discrimination may be defined as the "act of selling the same article produced under a single control, at different prices to different buyers."[5] This definition, however, would encompass both the sporadic short-lived discrimination found in many competitive markets and the systematic and persistent discrimination characteristic of monopoly.[6] Only the latter type of discrimination is of interest at this point because it represents the exploitation of market power.

Stigler has established three conditions which are required for price discrimination to exist. First, it must be possible to separate the market into two or more components. Second, demands in the various separable parts of the market must be considerably different. Third, the cost of separating the markets must not be too large.[7] To these conditions, a fourth requirement should be added: uniform pricing policies in the high-price market must be followed by all firms in the industry. The latter condition is essential if prices in the high-price market are not to be pulled down to those in the lower-price market by the actions of the independent marketers.[8]

5. Joan Robinson, *The Economics of Imperfect Competition* (London: Macmillan and Company, Ltd., 1961), p. 179.

6. See M. A. Adelman, "Effective Competition and the Antitrust Laws," *Harvard Law Review* (1948), pp. 1331–32.

7. Stigler, *op. cit.*, pp. 215–16.

8. Joe S. Bain, *The Economics of the Pacific Coast Petroleum Industry* (Berkeley: University of California Press, 1945), vol. II, pp. 195–204, found evidence of persistent and systematic discrimination in the West Coast Petroleum industry between "export" and "domestic" sales of prime fuels because of the existence of the "precise minimum conditions of concentration or of concurrent action which are necessary . . . to make some discrimination possible." On the other hand, Daniel C. Hamilton, *Competition in Oil* (Cambridge: Harvard University Press, 1958), pp. 129–34, found no such evidence of discrimination in the Gulf Coast refinery market and attributed his findings to the lack of concurrent action among sellers.

There are, of course, varying degrees of discrimination. The most common type of price discrimination consists in classifying buyers on the basis of the elasticity of their demand for the product and charging different prices for each class of purchaser. When this type of price discrimination is possible, profits will be maximized by adjusting total output to the level at which marginal cost of the entire output equals the sum of the marginal revenues in the various markets and marginal revenue in each separable market is equal. The analysis assumes that the conditions mentioned above for the existence of price discrimination are met. Over several periods in its history, these conditions have been fulfilled in the Frasch sulphur industry.

With the formation of the Sulphur Export Corporation in 1922, Frasch producers were able to separate their foreign and domestic markets at little or no cost to themselves, and by making all export sales through Sulexco they were able to achieve a uniform pricing policy in the export market.[9] Thus, by establishing a Webb-Pomerene export association, Frasch producers were able to sell at a higher price in export markets.

For discrimination to be profitable, however, the elasticity of demand had to be significantly different in the two markets. There is little reason to believe that at the time Sulexco was formed there was any marked difference between the elasticity of demand for sulphur in the domestic and export markets. Consumers of sulphur, both in the United States and abroad, however, could have been divided into two groups: (1) consumers requiring sulphur in its elemental form (rubber, sulphite wood pulp, insecticide, and pesticide manufacturers, for example), who represented about 20 per cent of the total market for sulphur, and producers of sulphuric acid for medicinal and other purposes requiring pure sulphuric acid which can only be made from elemental sulphur; and (2) manufacturers of sulphuric acid (other than those in the first group) who require sulphur in either elemental or nonelemental form, and who accounted for approximately 75 per cent of total sulphur consumption.

As might be expected, the demand for Frasch sulphur by the first group of consumers was much more inelastic than the demand by the second group of consumers because they could choose only between Frasch sulphur and native Sicilian sulphur. At that time, there was no economical process for recovery of elemental sulphur from gases containing hydrogen sulphide, and the small deposits of native sulphur

9. Canada, Cuba, Newfoundland, and the insular possessions of the United States were not covered by the Sulexco agreement nor by the later agreement with the Sicilian Consorzio. Therefore, there was no formal control over these markets which represented about 15 per cent of the total export market for Frasch sulphur.

that are scattered about the earth could not compete with Frasch sulphur or Sicilian brimstone at anything like the then prevailing price. Acid producers in the second group could have used either of the two forms of elemental sulphur or pyrites or smelter gases as the raw material for their process. Thus, they were much less dependent upon Frasch sulphur than the first group of consumers.

Frasch producers were able to discriminate in the European market by selling their product mainly to consumers in the first group. They further decreased the elasticity of demand in this market by formally agreeing with the Sicilians to divide the world elemental sulphur market (excepting the United States, Italy, Cuba, Canada, Newfoundland, and the insular possessions of the United States) on the basis of 75 per cent to Sulexco and 25 per cent to the Sicilian Consorzio. They cemented their complete control of the world market for elemental sulphur by fixing prices and establishing quotas.

In the United States, however, there was no way for Frasch sulphur producers to separate the domestic market into its component parts. Thus, they had to charge the same price to all domestic consumers, regardless of whether they were restricted to the use of elemental sulphur or not. Since the total demand for Frasch sulphur was more elastic than that for the elemental segment being supplied abroad, the price charged in the United States was lower than that charged for exports.

The above analysis raises two interesting questions, the answers to which shed considerable light on the behavior of Frasch producers. The first question relates to why domestic Frasch producers were willing to concentrate their selling efforts abroad in that portion of the market requiring elemental sulphur and to neglect the much larger acid market. The second question relates to the decision of Frasch producers to compete for the entire market for sulphur in the United States.

Why did Sulexco choose not to actively compete for the 75 per cent of the foreign sulphur market and restrict its main efforts to supplying the portion of the market requiring elemental sulphur? One obvious reason was the existence in Europe of a major combine of pyrites producers who controlled the European acid market. This combine, the European Pyrites Corporation, was owned jointly by the Rio Tinto marketing combine and the Metallgesellschaft, and controlled the marketing of Spanish, Norwegian, Cypriot, and Portuguese pyrites.[10] Much of the European acid market was directly controlled by pyrites producers who owned the principal acid plants. The competitive position of European pyrites was enhanced by the fact that much of the pyrites output was a by-product of copper, lead, and zinc operations. Supported

10. Theodore J. Kreps, *The Economics of the Sulfuric Acid Industry* (Stanford: Stanford University Press, 1938), pp. 100–01.

by such joint products, pyrites were in a virtually impregnable competitive position.

A second reason was the commanding position Sulexco held relative to the only other source of elemental sulphur, Sicily. In 1906, a Sicilian agent reported that the cost of Frasch sulphur landed at a European port was about 20 per cent below the cost of extracting and purifying Sicilian sulphur at the mine. The strong competitive position of Frasch sulphur at the time of the agreement between Sulexco and the Sicilian Consorzio is evidenced by reports which appeared in a leading trade journal in 1921, pointing out that Frasch sulphur could be landed in Europe at 520 lire/ton, while Sicilian sulphur sold for 650 lire/ton at Sicilian ports.[11] The situation in the Sicilian industry was so bad in 1921, that Italy passed legislation forbidding the importation of sulphur.[12] Thus, while Herman Frasch had been content to settle for only one-third of the world elemental sulphur market in his 1907 agreement with the Sicilians, Sulexco was able to demand and receive 75 per cent of the market. In fact, Sulexco was in a position to have eliminated altogether the Sicilian native sulphur industry through price competition, and might have done so had it not felt that the Italian Government would have come to the industry's defense with massive subsidies.

A third reason behind Sulexco's decision not to resort to price competition to gain a major share of the European acid market was the ability of Sulexco to supply some foreign acid markets at the same price that it charged to consumers restricted to using elemental sulphur. The cost of transporting a ton of sulphur in pyrites was over twice that of transporting a ton of sulphur in its elemental form. Therefore, in isolated markets such as Oceania, Asia, and South America, Frasch producers were able to compete with pyrites even at the higher export price. This was also true of some major inland markets in Europe.

Why did Frasch producers decide to compete for the entire sulphur market in the United States? Prior to World War I, Union Sulphur Company had not actively competed for the domestic acid market which was then being supplied by European pyrites. A 1919 study of the United States Tariff Commission concluded that prior to the war, domestic Frasch producers "were able to realize larger profits by maintaining the price of sulphur at $22 per ton f.o.b. New York and supplying the paper and chemical trade rather than by reducing the price of sul-

11. Henry L. Geissel, "Italian Sulphur Production Declining," *The Engineering and Mining Journal* (23 July 1921), p. 138, reported that between 1914 and 1920, the cost of producing Sicilian sulphur had risen from 80–85 lire/ton to 420–430 lire/ton. Also, see "Sulphur Crisis in Sicily," *The Engineering and Mining Journal* (17 December 1921), p. 977.

12. Kreps, *op. cit.*, pp. 103–04.

phur to a point where they could obtain the sulphuric acid business."[13]

The disruption of the pyrites markets during the war enabled domestic Frasch producers to gain a dominant position in supplying the domestic acid market. By 1919, nearly 50 per cent of domestic acid was being produced from Frasch sulphur.[14] However, the war had also aided the development of two additional Frasch producers. By 1920, the capacity of the industry was twice the level of prewar demand, stocks were sufficient to last for five years, and the industry was faced with the problem of expanding its sulphur sales. Expansion via Sulexco sales was limited by the need to maintain the high export price, and domestic Frasch producers were able to dispose of only 30 per cent of their production abroad. If they had chosen to restrict themselves to the elemental market at home as well, they would have been able to market only about half of their newly increased productive capacity. It is not surprising then that they adjusted the domestic price to enable them to secure about 60 per cent of the domestic acid market. The reasoning behind the price adjustment made between 1919 and 1926 is discussed in detail in the following chapter.

In the period from 1922 to 1940, price discrimination in the Frasch sulphur industry thus hinged on complete control of the world elemental sulphur market and close cooperation between the domestic producers of Frasch sulphur regarding export pricing. The extent of actual discrimination varied over the life of the industry depending upon the degree to which these two requirements were fulfilled.[15]

13. U.S. Tariff Commission, *Information Concerning the Pyrites and Sulphur Industry* (Washington, D.C.: U.S. Government Printing Office, 1919), p. 8.

14. Kreps, *op. cit.*, p. 105.

15. Truett, *op. cit.*, pp. 141–47, offers an alternative explanation of the persistent discrimination against the export market. Citing a case first mentioned by Jacob Viner in *Dumping: A Problem in International Trade* (Chicago: University of Chicago Press, 1923), p. 7, Truett contends that the lower domestic price of Frasch sulphur resulted from a "fear of utilizing monopoly power." This explanation would perhaps account for continued discrimination in the export market following the dissolution of Sulexco in 1952.

Chapter 6

Analysis of Behavior in the Frasch Sulphur Industry

In this chapter an attempt is made to relate the observed market behavior of Frasch sulphur producers to changes in the industry's market structure. For this purpose, the development of the industry is divided into three periods. The first period, 1900 to 1926, covers the birth of the Frasch sulphur industry and its growth to dominance of the world sulphur market. In the second period, 1927 to 1946, the industry is characterized by a stable market structure centered about an international cartel. The final period, 1947 to 1968, follows the dissolution of the international sulphur cartel and features the introduction of new sources of supply of both Frasch and other forms of elemental sulphur and their impact on world sulphur markets.

1900 to 1926: Formative Years

Entry of Union Sulphur Company

When the Frasch sulphur industry emerged in the first decade of this century, the world elemental sulphur market was being completely supplied by the native sulphur mines of Sicily, two-thirds of which were under contract to a single firm, the Anglo-Sicilian Company. The United States was one of the best customers for Sicilian sulphur, taking about one-third of the industry's annual output. Competition from Frasch sulphur reduced U.S. imports of Sicilian sulphur from 189,000 tons in 1906 to 20,000 tons in 1907. Falling prices and mounting stocks led to changes in the Sicilian sulphur industry, and in 1906, the Anglo-Sicilian Company was replaced by a cartel, the "Consorzio Obbligatorio per l'Industria Solfifera Siciliana," which was established under Italian law and given total control of all Sicilian sulphur production.

In 1907, after a brief round of price cutting, Union Sulphur Company and the Consorzio reached an agreement regarding the division of the world elemental sulphur market. At that time Union was the only U.S.

Frasch producer; Freeport began production in 1912 and Texas Gulf in 1919. The agreement specified that the world market, excluding the United States and Italy, was to be divided between the two companies on the basis of one-third to Union, and two-thirds to the Consorzio. The agreement established a minimum price for Louisiana sulphur of $22 per ton c.i.f. New York. It also specified that the price differential between Union and the Consorzio was never to exceed 2.5 per cent.[1]

Although the agreement with the Consorzio remained in effect for only four years, the price stability achieved through this accord lasted until after the outbreak of World War I. From January 1909 until February 1916 the posted price of Frasch sulphur remained constant at $22 per ton f.o.b. New York and $18 per ton f.o.b. the mine.

The impact of World War I

Between 1907 and 1915, the Union Sulphur Company had a virtual monopoly of the domestic market for elemental sulphur. During this period, Union concentrated on selling to the paper-pulp and other chemical industries which represented growing markets for elemental sulphur. No serious attempt was made to compete for the domestic sulphuric acid market which had been committed to pyrites since before the turn of the century.

During the First World War the domestic acid market opened up for Frasch sulphur when American sulphuric acid manufacturers were cut off from their supply of Spanish pyrites. While only 2.6 per cent of the acid produced in the United States in 1914 was made from Frasch sulphur, by 1918, approximately 48 per cent of the domestically produced acid was made from Frasch sulphur.[2] In 1916, the contract price of Frasch sulphur increased from $18 to $22 per ton f.o.b. mines. The price of sulphur to munitions and fertilizer manufacturers was voluntarily maintained at that level until 1 January 1919, although the spot price of sulphur in the New York market rose to $45 in the second quarter of 1917.[3]

The opening of the sulphuric acid market to Frasch sulphur and the increased price of sulphur during the war hastened the development of production by Freeport Sulphur Company and Texas Gulf Sulphur

1. *Investigations of Concentration of Economic Power,* Hearings before the Temporary National Economic Committee of the 76th Congress (1939), Part U, pp. 2219–26. (Hereinafter cited as TNEC Hearings.)

2. A. E. Wells and D. E. Fogg, *The Manufacture of Sulphuric Acid in the United States*, U.S. Department of the Interior, Bureau of Mines, Bulletin 184 (1920), p. 27.

3. United States Tariff Commission, "Industrial Readjustments of Certain Mineral Industries Affected by the War," *Tariff Information Series,* No. 21 (1920), pp. 238–39.

Company. With the end of the war, the use of Frasch sulphur to supplement pyrites in the manufacture of sulphuric acid ceased almost immediately. "During the spring of 1919, brimstone stocks at acid plants were gradually used up, and acid manufacturers were inclined not to replenish their stocks until it was apparent that brimstone could be purchased on a parity basis with pyrites ore, the importation of which was gradually resumed."[4] To make matters worse, 1920 ushered in a severe business recession, both in the United States and abroad, and the demand for sulphur declined.

The three domestic Frasch producers, faced with surface inventories nearly five times annual prewar consumption and current production nearly twice annual prewar demand, were primarily concerned with maintaining or increasing their wartime share of the domestic sulphur market. To do so, they had to adjust their prices to meet competition from both domestic and imported pyrites. The price adjustment between brimstone and pyrites which occurred in the seven years following 1919 is of much significance for it established the pattern of the industry price behavior for the next twenty years.[5]

Postwar price adjustments

From 1900 to 1916, with the price of sulphur at $22 per ton (22 cents per unit) f.o.b. New York and the price of pyrites at 13 cents per unit c.i.f. New York, 98 per cent of the sulphuric acid produced in the United States was made from pyrites.[6] A 1920 study by the U.S. Bureau of Mines concluded that if the consumer of pyrites received nothing for the by-product sinter, Frasch sulphur was worth to him only 3 to 4 cents per unit more for acid manufacturing purposes than sulphur in pure pyrites containing 40 to 43 per cent sulphur.[7]

Under these conditions, and with three firms producing a homogeneous product, it would be expected that the price of Frasch sulphur would have to fall if U.S. producers were to maintain their share of the domestic sulphuric acid market in the postwar period. The price of sulphur did fall from $45 per ton in 1917 to $14 per ton in 1922, the lowest point it had reached since 1906. For the next three and one-half years, the price remained at this level. Though pyrites prices fell during

4. Wells and Fogg, *op. cit.*, p. 24.

5. Much of what follows in the way of analyzing the behavior of Frasch prices from 1917 to 1926 is based on a study by Thurmond L. Morrison, "The Economics of the Sulphur Industry" (Ph.D. dissertation, Economics Department, University of Texas, 1939), pp. 100–20

6. A unit is one per cent of a ton (22.4 pounds in the case of a long ton). Thus a long ton of pyrites containing 45 per cent sulphur would contain 45 units (1,008 pounds) of sulphur.

7. Wells and Fogg, *op. cit.*, p. 24.

the same period, the percentage of sulphuric acid produced from Frasch sulphur increased to 75 per cent, as elemental sulphur almost entirely displaced imported Spanish pyrites in the manufacture of sulphuric acid. Much of the remaining 25 per cent of sulphuric acid production not being produced from elemental sulphur was supplied by domestic pyrites producers as a by-product of copper, lead, or zinc operations. In addition, some of the acid plants in the United States were owned by either domestic or foreign pyrites producers. Thus, decreases in the price of elemental sulphur below $14 per ton could not be expected to increase the share of the sulphuric acid market held by domestic Frasch producers because the remaining portion of the market was tied directly to pyrites consumption and insulated from competitive pressures.

It does not follow that $14 per ton was necessarily the price that maximized the industry's profit. Above $14 per ton, increases in the price of sulphur would cause a loss in sales because domestic acid producers would switch from elemental sulphur to pyrites. At a price elasticity less than unity, the loss in tonnage could have been more than compensated for by an increase in total revenue resulting from the higher price. Indeed, if the elasticity of the industry demand curve above $14 per ton were known, the most profitable output and price combination of the industry could be determined. However, there was no way for the firms in the industry, acting independently, to determine the elasticity of the industry's demand at such prices. Under the conditions described, any firm that increased its price above $14 per ton stood to lose all its sales.

In view of the homogeneous nature of the product, rival firms might be forced to follow a price decrease, but they would be reluctant to follow a price increase. Thus, once decreases in the price of sulphur were halted at the level of $14 per ton by the realization that further declines in the price would not increase sales, uncertainty as to a rival's response probably reinforced this price and led to its being maintained at this level.

In October 1922, the three American companies set up the Sulphur Export Corporation under the provisions of the Webb-Pomerene Act, which Congress had passed in 1918. One of the first acts of the corporation, which was formed to handle all export sales of Frasch sulphur, was to negotiate an agreement with the Sicilian producers through the Consorzio. The agreement, which was subject to renewal every four years, provided for the division and allocation of the world sulphur markets, with the exception of Italy and North America, on the basis of 75 per cent to the Sulphur Export Corporation and 25 per cent to the Consorzio. Prices, terms, and conditions of sale of all sulphur sold under the agreement were to be fixed from time to time by the parties in a manner that would best serve their mutual interest. To facilitate control over the world sulphur markets, each party was to furnish to the other party and to a central bureau a monthly statement showing the total tonnage shipped, total tonnage sold, the total tonnage delivered, destinations, prices realized, freight rates, and other such information as was from time to time deemed necessary for "proper forecast and allocation." A penalty of two tons was stipulated for each ton shipped in violation of the agreement. Finally, the two parties agreed that "the situation of the sulphur manufacturing industry in the countries covered by the agreement should be maintained throughout the life of the agreement." The agreement stated that "each party agrees not to do or encourage anything which would result in altering such present situation and any action of a nature to alter such present situation shall be jointly considered and both parties shall use their best endeavors to prevent any such alteration."[8]

The formation of the Sulphur Export Corporation and its subsequent agreement with the Sicilian Consorzio put an end to independent decisions by the three domestic Frasch producers on prices and output for the export market. It has been contended that the domestic Frasch producers used this newly created opportunity for formal cooperation to study the nature of the domestic demand for sulphur at prices above $14 per ton in order to determine the price that would be most profitable.[9] The subsequent behavior of pricing in the industry supports this judgment.

Within eight months of the date on which Sulexco reached an agreement with the Sicilians, the domestic price for Frasch sulphur began to rise. By 1925, the price of Frasch sulphur had risen to $18.50 per ton f.o.b. the mines, $22.00 per ton delivered in New York, Baltimore, and Philadelphia, and $22.50 per ton in Portland, Maine. At this time, imported Spanish pyrites were selling for 13 cents per unit (one per cent of a ton) in these markets.[10] As previously mentioned, the parity

8. The agreement is contained in its entirety in the TNEC Hearings, pp. 2214–17.

9. This view is expressed by Morrison, *op. cit.*, p. 109, *et passim*, pp. 110–15. Similar conclusions were reached by Markham, *The Fertilizer Industry*, pp. 80–83, and p. 178; and by George W. Stocking and Myron W. Watkins, *Cartels or Competition?* (New York: Twentieth Century Fund, 1948), pp. 260–61. The U.S. Federal Trade Commission, *loc. cit.*, pp. 14–16, concluded: "The domestic and export segments of the American sulphur industry are inseparable in interest. From an economic standpoint, the distribution and pricing activities of Sulphur Export Corporation had a natural relationship to the production, distribution, and pricing activities of its individual producing members."

10. Kreps, *op. cit.*, p. 103. The TNEC Hearings (p. 2203) give the price of imported pyrites at 11.5 cents per unit of sulphur in 1925. However, this includes the lower-valued Canadian imports as well as the Spanish imports.

prices for Frasch sulphur and pyrites, as established by the relative cost of manufacturing sulphuric acid from either material, were estimated in about 1920 to be three to four cents higher per unit of elemental sulphur than per unit of pyrites. Given the price of 13 cents per unit for imported Spanish pyrites and about 22 cents per unit for Frasch sulphur, both delivered to the major East Coast markets, it was to the advantage of acid producers in these markets to substitute imported pyrites for Frasch sulphur. Consequently, 85 per cent of the acid producers on the East Coast used pyrites.[11]

In inland markets, however, the relative costs of transporting Frasch sulphur and pyrites were the determining factor in the selection of a raw material for the manufacture of sulphuric acid. The cost of transporting a ton of sulphur in pyrites was over twice that of transporting a ton of sulphur in elemental form.[12] Thus, on shipments from the Atlantic Seaboard to inland markets any differential in price in favor of pyrites was quickly overcome by the freight differential.

It has been estimated that domestic consumption of sulphur fell from 1.6 million tons when the price of Frasch sulphur was $14 per ton f.o.b. the mines to 1.4 million tons when the price was raised to $18 per ton f.o.b. the mines; however, gross revenue rose from $22.4 million to $25.2 million. Even if it had cost nothing to produce the additional 200,000 tons of sulphur, it would still have been unprofitable for domestic Frasch producers to have lowered their price sufficiently to have secured the Atlantic Coast acid trade.

Increasing the price of Frasch sulphur above $18 per ton f.o.b. the mines, however, would have jeopardized the interior acid markets of Western New York, Indiana, Pennsylvania, Ohio, and Illinois, which represented about 30 per cent of the total domestic acid market. For example, it has been estimated that had the price of Frasch sulphur increased to $20 per ton f.o.b. the mines, at least 300,000 tons of sulphur sales would have been lost, causing gross sales revenue to decline from $25.2 million to $22 million.[13]

It was the possibility that acid makers might substitute pyrites for Frasch sulphur which exerted the greatest influence in determining domestic Frasch sulphur prices. As it was unprofitable for acid producers to substitute pyrites for sulphur as long as the price of sulphur was less than $14 per ton f.o.b. the mines and the price of pyrites was 12 to 13

11. Andrew M. Fairlie, *Sulfuric Acid Manufacture* (New York: Reinhold Publishing Corporation, 1936), p. 83. Actually, a larger proportion probably would have switched to pyrites had it not been for the fact that sulphuric acid for medicinal and other special purposes must be made from elemental sulphur.

12. About 45 per cent of the weight of pyrites, as opposed to over 98 per cent of the weight of elemental sulphur, becomes available for acid manufacture.

13. Morrison, *op. cit.*, pp. 112–14.

cents per unit, the demand for sulphur up to this point was quite inelastic. As the price of Frasch sulphur was increased above $14 per ton f.o.b. the mines, demand became increasingly more elastic. Apparently $18 per ton f.o.b. the mines was the price at which Frasch producers felt that their profits were at a maximum, i.e., the price at which the marginal cost of producing sulphur was equal to marginal revenue.[14]

1927 to 1946: Years of Stability

Early in this period the Union Sulphur Company was forced to retire from the industry owing to depletion of its Louisiana mine and its failure to secure additional production.[15] Texas Gulf and Freeport agreed to continue Sulexco and to share equally in its operation.[16] Two new domestic Frasch producers entered the industry—Duval Texas Sulphur Company in 1928, and Jefferson Lake Oil Company in 1932. In 1930, Orkla Grube Aktiebolag, a Norwegian pyrites producer, built a pilot plant in Norway to produce elemental sulphur from pyrites, and licensed the leading Spanish pyrites producer, Rio Tinto, and the leading Portuguese pyrites producer, Mason and Berry, to use its process in their respective countries. About the same time, the Montecatini interests in Italy developed sulphur production from pyrites outside the control of the Consorzio and began selling competitively in France and other markets covered by the Sulexco-Consorzio agreement. The net effect of these developments was to introduce new and, at the time of their development, unpredictable competition both in the domestic market and abroad.

The agreement between Sulexco and the Sicilian Consorzio became inoperative in 1932 because of the dissolution of the Consorzio by the Italian Government. The Sicilian sulphur industry, with the aid and encouragement of the Italian Government, was subsequently reorganized

14. It has been pointed out that there are many obstacles which prevent joint profit maximization even in an oligopoly producing a completely homogeneous product under conditions of identical and horizontal average total cost functions for each firm in the industry. If these latter conditions are relaxed, the problem becomes even more difficult, with joint profit maximization requiring interfirm transfers for the simultaneous maximization of the profits of each firm. See William Fellner, *Competition Among the Few* (New York: Alfred A. Knopf, 1949), pp. 120–36. Given the homogeneous nature of sulphur, and the existence of only two firms in the industry, $18.00 per ton f.o.b. the mines may be interpreted as the price which tended to maximize profits for both producers.

15. The following account of behavior in the Frasch sulphur industry during this period is based on information in the TNEC Hearings, and the Federal Trade Commission, *Report on the Sulphur Industry and International Cartels,* 1947 (hereinafter cited as the Federal Trade Commission Report).

16. A copy of this agreement between Texas Gulf and Freeport is contained in the TNEC Hearings, pp. 2235–36.

as Ufficio per la Vendita dello Zolfo Italiano. On 1 August 1934, an agreement containing provisions similar to the original Sulexco-Consorzio agreement was reached between Sulexco and Ufficio.[17]

Even with these major changes in the composition of the Frasch sulphur industry and its relationship with the Sicilians, which coincided with the severe worldwide depression of the thirties, the period from 1927 to 1946 was marked by an extremely rigid posted price for Frasch sulphur which changed only once during these two decades, and by consistently higher realizations on exports than on domestic sales. The practice of price discrimination, as emphasized earlier, depended upon the ability of Sulexco, through its agreement with the Consorzio, to control the supply of elemental sulphur. By exploiting this control, however, Sulexco encouraged both research aimed at lessening the dependence of foreign consumers upon the cartel and development of new sources of supply. The Federal Trade Commission aptly noted:

> The problem faced by the cartel participants (Sulexco and the Consorzio) was how to obtain the cartel objectives of price protection for the benefit of both Italian and American natural sulphur producers, without disturbing the existing status of the industry by fixing foreign market prices so high as to further stimulate increased production by independent producers of both natural and by-product sulphur.[18]

During the late 1920s, as Europe began to experience the severe depression which was to sweep the world during the next decade, Frasch sulphur export prices advanced, realizations on Frasch sulphur exports rising from $18.92 in 1926 to $21.68 in 1931. By the early thirties, developments on several fronts began to threaten the cartel's control of world markets for sulphur.

Entry of two independent U.S. producers

The entry of Duval in 1928 and Jefferson Lake in 1932 expanded the capacity of the domestic Frasch industry in the thirties when both domestic and export markets were shrinking. Since neither firm became a member of Sulexco, the entry of these two new firms posed a potential threat to Sulexco's cartel agreements covering export markets and to the domestic price stability that had existed in the industry since 1926. The pattern of domestic production and exports from 1932 to 1940 clearly reveals that Texas Gulf and Freeport met these threats by (1) cutting back on their production, permitting Duval and Jefferson Lake to gain a significant share of total production, and (2) through Sulexco aiding Jefferson Lake and Duval to find export markets, even though this meant relinquishing part of their own export sales.

17. A copy of this agreement is contained in the TNEC Hearings, pp. 2208–13.
18. Federal Trade Commission Report, p. 68.

Table 16. Production of Frasch Sulphur, 1930–40

		Production of Sulexco members			Production of nonmembers	
Year	Output	Texas Gulf	Free-port	Total	Duval	Jefferson Lake
	thousand long tons	(................		*per cent of total*	....	................)
1930	2,559	67.88	30.58	98.46	1.51	—
1931	2,129	60.95	37.42	98.44	1.63	—
1932	890	63.79	32.04	95.83	2.54	1.50
1933	1,406	46.13	29.45	75.58	2.70	21.61
1934	1,421	59.48	31.72	91.20	3.14	5.33
1935	1,633	56.55	37.54	94.09	3.94	1.50
1936	2,016	63.80	29.70	93.50	5.89	0.42
1937	2,742	63.60	25.95	93.55	4.82	3.44
1938	2,393	51.08	28.59	79.67	8.87	11.20
1939	2,019	39.14	37.83	76.97	12.97	9.95
1940	2,732	52.28	31.49	83.77	7.96	8.04

SOURCE: Jesse W. Markham, *The Fertilizer Industry* (Nashville, Tennessee: The Vanderbilt University Press, 1958), p. 77.

NOTE: Percentages may not add to 100 because of rounding and the inclusion of some non-Frasch sulphur in the output figure.

The adjustments in production made by Texas Gulf and Freeport in response to the entry of Duval and Jefferson Lake can be seen in table 16. From 1930 to 1934, the market share of the two major producers fell from 98 per cent to 76 per cent. The temporary increase in their market shares from 1935 to 1937 reflected the reduction in output of the two independent producers due to exhaustion of their initial mines. After 1937, the market share held by the two major producers again fell, as Jefferson Lake and Duval began exploitation of new deposits. Throughout the period from 1932 to 1935, shipments exceeded industry production as Texas Gulf and Freeport drew on large inventories accumulated prior to and during the early depression years. Thus, Texas Gulf and Freeport were able to maintain price stability in the domestic market during the 1930s by reducing their production, thereby permitting the two new entrants to dispose of their production at the existing price of $18.00 per ton.

The bulk of the production from the initial deposits exploited by Duval and Jefferson Lake came onto the market in 1933 and 1934, at a time when the agreement between Sulexco and the Consorzio was inoperative. Nevertheless, the price structure in European markets remained essentially the same as it had been under the cartel agreement. During these two years it became imperative that Sulexco obtain some control over the exports of the two independents or else face a disruption of the foreign price structure. The matter of exports by independent U.S. Frasch producers also became a factor in negotiations with the newly created Ufficio.

In 1933, Sulexco entered into direct agreements with Duval and Jefferson Lake to allocate export markets to these firms in return for their pledge to keep export prices intact, to limit their exports, and to confer with Sulexco as to destinations and prices before accepting any orders.[19] Similar agreements were made in 1934. As a result of these agreements, Sulexco marketed 86,519 tons for Jefferson Lake and 10,000 tons for Duval in European markets in 1933. In 1934, the two independents exported 117,216 tons, 110,700 tons of which were sold under agreement with Sulexco. Thus, nearly 94 per cent of the 125,128 tons produced by the two independents in 1934 was marketed abroad, leaving only 7,912 tons to be sold competitively either in the domestic market or elsewhere. In its 1934 agreement with Ufficio, Sulexco agreed to deduct from its quota any export shipments by independent American producers to the joint territory.

The record of cooperation between Sulexco and the two independent American Frasch producers in marketing sulphur abroad provides a good insight into the behavior of Frasch output and prices in the thirties. When exports of the American independent producers threatened to disrupt the foreign price structure and the negotiations with the Italians for a new cartel contract, Sulexco reacted by aiding Duval and Jefferson Lake in finding foreign markets, even though this meant relinquishing possible sales for its own members. Sulexco's actions during this period in which there was no international agreement in effect with the Sicilians enabled it to protect its foreign price structure, while at the same time removing from possible competition in the domestic market a corresponding quantity of independent tonnage. Thus, an attitude of cooperation based on mutual advantage was established in 1933 and 1934 between Sulexco members and nonmembers with respect to export trade.

Such cooperation was clearly to the advantage of Duval and Jefferson Lake. With export prices higher than domestic prices, and with Sulexco assisting Duval and Jefferson Lake to place export sales, neither of the two independents could have hoped to have reaped additional advantage from competing sharply in price with Sulexco members in the domestic market. To have done so would not only have reduced their realizations on sales in the domestic market, but would also have endangered their allocations in foreign markets.

19. Copies of these agreements are contained in the TNEC Hearings, pp. 2236–37.

After the renewal of the international agreement between Sulexco and the Italians, it appears that somewhat similar policies, again based on mutual advantage, were followed both at home and abroad. The large companies appear to have avoided using their superior economic strength and position in the market to compete with nonmembers in price either at home or abroad, because they appear to have realized that price competition with Duval and Jefferson Lake might have destroyed their cartel arrangements in Europe. With realizations on exports running $3 to $4 a ton above realizations on domestic sales, both Freeport and Texas Gulf had a vital interest in maintaining a stable price structure. With two larger firms in the industry taking this attitude, it would not have been wise for either Duval or Jefferson Lake to have initiated a price conflict.

Even though no arrangements existed between Sulexco and the two independent producers in regards to export markets after 1934, the two smaller firms were closely related to Texas Gulf Sulphur, the largest American producer. During the late thirties, after its initial mine had been depleted, Jefferson Lake obtained options from Texas Gulf on the Clemens Dome which it operated from 1937 to 1960. It paid sulphur royalties to Texas Gulf from 1937 to 1949. Duval operated a portion of Boling Dome by royalty agreement with Texas Gulf and obtained its options on Orchard Dome from Texas Gulf.

Diversion from domestic to export markets

Other developments both at home and abroad challenged Sulexco's position. The differential between domestic and export prices for Frasch sulphur encouraged American purchasers for domestic consumption to divert sulphur to the export market. Such diversions outside the control of the cartel became a disturbing factor to the cartel participants. American sulphur producers had always handled their own export sales and avoided setting up independent American exporters of crude sulphur either in the capacity of independent export merchants or as local agents for foreign buyers. Under the Sulexco agreement, Texas Gulf and Freeport agreed to turn over to the Corporation all orders or inquiries for sulphur to be shipped to the marketing territory covered by the agreement. In general, requests by nonconsumers for purchases for foreign producers were declined by Sulexco.

In the late 1920s, Sulexco found that its control of exports from the United States was being undermined by exports of domestic firms who were purchasing their sulphur from Sulexco members and diverting it to foreign markets. On 27 May 1929, Freeport and Texas Gulf sought to remedy this situation by making a supplemental agreement to their Sulexco contract. The proposed change read:

> No exporter shall sell to a domestic purchaser more crude sulphur than is necessary for the domestic sales requirements of such purchaser, if such sales would in any way interfere with or adversely affect the business of the exporters as carried on by the Sulphur Export Association or tend to deprive them of the benefits of the Webb Act.[20]

Upon submission of the proposed supplemental agreement to the Federal Trade Commission, Freeport and Texas Gulf were informed by the Commission that the clause represented an obvious attempt at restraint of trade. On 16 October 1929, the parties filed with the Commission a formal abrogation of the agreement, stating that no action had ever been taken under it.

The Norwegian episode

Still another challenge to Sulexco's dominance of the world elemental sulphur market came from the development of a process in Norway to produce elemental sulphur from pyrites. Prior to 1931, Texas Gulf Sulphur, realizing the potential of processes designed to extract elemental sulphur from pyrites, had conducted experiments with various processes, accumulating twenty-five to thirty patents. In 1930, Texas Gulf obtained an exclusive license for North and South America to use a process developed by a Norwegian firm, Orkla Grube Aktiebolag, for producing sulphur from pyrites.

Orkla itself began production on a commercial scale in 1931, and sold 7,600 tons in 1931 and 53,800 tons in 1932 to consumers in Scandinavia at prices less than the prevailing c.i.f. prices of the cartel. In January 1933, Sulexco made an agreement with Orkla, whereby Orkla would restrict its output to a maximum of 70,000 tons per year to be sold in Scandinavia at a minimum price agreed upon by both Sulexco and Orkla; in return, Orkla would receive a payment of $1 per ton by Sulexco for each ton of Orkla production up to 70,000 tons annually.[21] Thus, Sulexco was able to protect its European markets from competition with Orkla. Sulexco renewed its 1933 agreement with Orkla annually through 1936. Sulexco negotiated a new five-year agreement with Orkla beginning 1 January 1937. The new agreement provided that Orkla could increase its capacity beyond 70,000 tons per year, extended Orkla's market privileges to Europe, Asia, Africa, and adjacent islands, eliminated the tonnage payment by Sulexco, and divided sales in the joint territory on the basis of one-third to Orkla and two-thirds to Sulexco. The agreement provided that "in no case would an attempt be made to secure customers who would be in direct competition with pres-

20. Federal Trade Commission Report, pp. 53–54.
21. *Ibid.*, pp. 68–69.

ent users of brimstone without the mutual consent of both parties."[22] Bolstered by the new agreement, Orkla's production increased to 105,000 tons in 1937 and 108,000 tons in 1938 and 1939.

Sulexco's 1936 agreement with Orkla also stated that it might be desirable to obtain certain patents relating to sulphur production in the joint territory. The cost of acquiring any such patents was to be shared jointly, Orkla paying one-third and Sulexco two-thirds of the cost. The title to patents so acquired was to be held in trust by Orkla's subsidiary, A.B. Industrimetoder, Stockholm. No license for the use of such jointly owned patents would be issued without the consent of both parties. Later testimony before the Federal Trade Commission revealed that the patent purchasing clause was inserted in the 1936 Orkla agreement because one Orkla official knew of certain experiments underway in Norway and feared that the Norwegian Government would finance the development of the patents. Under this agreement, Sulexco contributed $35,000 as its share of the purchase cost of patents purchased by Orkla. Testimony revealed: "The development stopped on them."[23]

Behavior within the Frasch sulphur industry between 1927 and 1940 was aptly summarized by the Federal Trade Commission:

> The international picture, in its entirety, then is that low-cost, privately-owned American producers, organized as a Webb Act Association, combined, on the one hand, with a government sponsored Italian producing and marketing cartel and, on the other, with a privately owned Norwegian patent owner, to fix and maintain prices, divide markets, restrain competition and control sulphur developments in foreign countries. Controls broke down, or threatened to break down, from time to time due to the rise, or threatened rise, of new competition such as that of Orkla interests in the Baltic and other markets, Montecatini interests on the Italian mainland and in France, and that of Spanish, Portuguese, and independent American interests selling, or threatening to sell, into France and other countries. The fact that such failures and threats of failure were promptly met by efforts to rebuild and strengthen the cartel's structure and controls only serve to emphasize the real purposes and effects of the various cartel agreements on industrial developments and commerce in and with countries other than those of the participants.[24]

During the Second World War, all of the agreements between Sulexco and foreign sulphur producers became inoperative. On 13 September 1939, Sulexco gave notice to the Italians of complete suspension of the Ufficio contract effective as of 1 September 1939, because of war. On 15 March 1940 the Italians gave notice to Sulexco of the suspension of all agreements under which they were operating. Finally, pursuant to

22. A copy of this agreement is contained in the TNEC Hearings, pp. 2240–41.
23. Federal Trade Commission Report, p. 71.
24. *Ibid.*, p. 84.

action by its Board of Directors, on 15 February 1945, Sulexco notified Ufficio under date of 21 February 1945 of the cancellation of the agreement of 1 August 1934 as amended and supplemented. On 19 September 1939, Sulexco caused the complete suspension of the Orkla contract because of war conditions in Europe, and the contract was formally cancelled by Sulexco on 22 February 1945.

1947 to 1968: Years of Change

The period from 1947 through 1968 in the Frasch sulphur industry was dominated by successive phases of shortage and surplus in sulphur markets at home and abroad. The first shortage developed in the period following World War II, and culminated in controls being placed on the industry during the Korean crisis. This was followed by the development, beginning in 1953, of alternative sources of supply for elemental sulphur both within the United States and abroad. The introduction of new sources of supply created a surplus in sulphur markets from 1959 to 1963. During this period, the traditional pricing structure of the industry was destroyed, and a complete reorganization of Frasch sulphur marketing took place with the introduction of liquid shipment and regional terminals. The final years, 1964 to 1968, witnessed the reappearance of a shortage in sulphur markets as supply failed to keep pace with surging demand.

The patterns of production and consumption, exports and imports, and domestic and export prices in the sulphur industry over the period from 1947 to 1968 are shown in figures 11, 12, and 13. At the top of each chart the major factors affecting sulphur markets are indicated as well as the state of the U.S. sulphur market. U.S. production and consumption trends show the following pattern over the period: 1947 to mid-1956, shortage (drawing down of inventories); mid-1956 to mid-1959, balance; mid-1959 to mid-1963, oversupply (accumulation of inventories); mid-1963 to mid-1964, balance; mid-1964 to 1967, shortage; and 1968, balance.

Postwar adjustments

The 1947 Federal Trade Commission study of the sulphur industry and the operation of the Sulphur Export Corporation recommended that Sulexco refrain from entering into agreements with foreign producers to establish quotas which included domestic nonmember firms, to establish guarantees of tonnages to foreign producers, or to maintain the status quo in the manufactured sulphur industry; from acquisitions of patents "useful for or capable of being used in connection with the production of sulphur for commercial purposes"; from entering into any

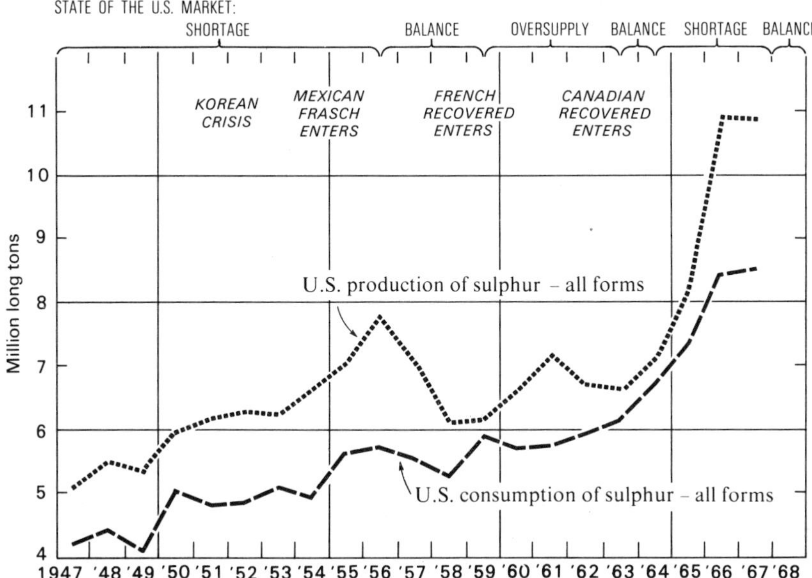

Figure 11. U.S. sulphur supply and demand cycle, 1947–67. (Based on data in tables A-1 and A-2.)

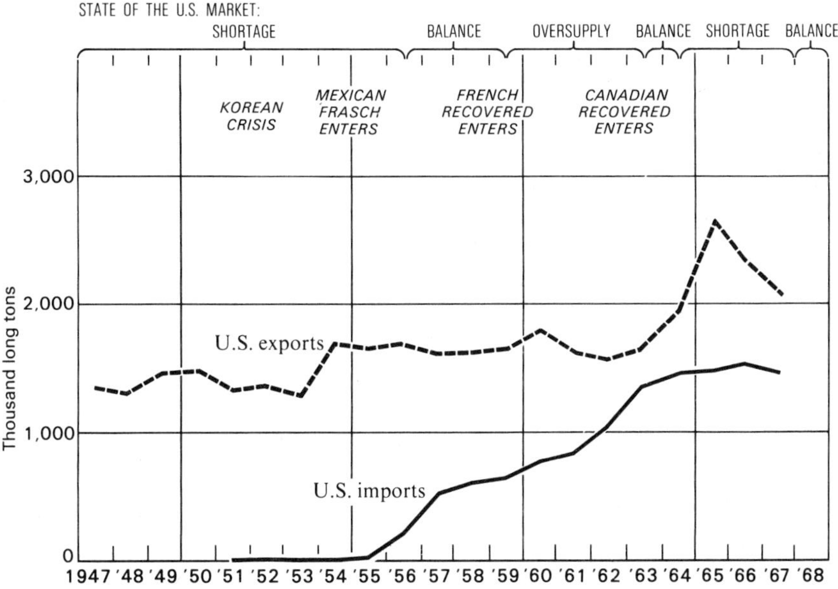

Figure 12. U.S. exports and imports of all forms of sulphur, 1947–67. (Based on data in table A-2.)

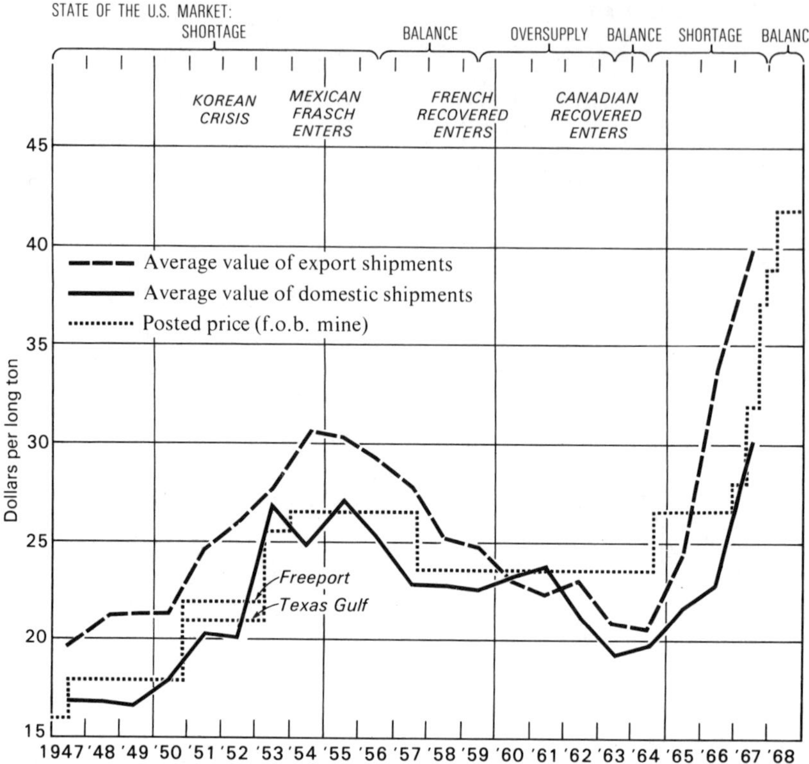

Figure 13. Average value of export and domestic shipments of U.S. Frasch sulphur and posted price, f.o.b. mine, 1947–68. (*Based on data in tables 15 and A-3.*)

agreement or understanding with nonmember domestic producers; and from selling or assisting in the sale of output from nonmember domestic producers.[25] However, by 1947 these were more or less academic issues because the Frasch sulphur industry had divorced itself from its international agreements during the war, and the Sulexco members had made no further attempt to obtain agreements with either domestic or foreign producers.

As shown in figure 11, the demand for Frasch sulphur increased rapidly in the years following the end of World War II. The largest domestic consumer of sulphur, the sulphuric acid industry, increased its output from 766,800 short tons in 1946 to 1,085,000 short tons in 1950. Exports of crude sulphur, depicted in figure 12, which had averaged 566,361 tons between 1935 and 1939, increased to an average of

25. *Ibid.*, pp. 102–3.

1,366,361 tons between 1947 and 1950. Responding to the expansion in demand, Freeport raised its price from $16 to $18 per ton f.o.b. the mine in June 1947, and two months later Texas Gulf met the price increase (see figure13).

Glenn Lehmann, in his study of the industry, has emphasized the effective role played by the Justice Department in the immediate post-war period in preventing additional price increases on Frasch sulphur.[26] Industry officials had experienced public scrutiny of their operations by the Temporary National Economic Committee of Congress in 1939 and by the Federal Trade Commission in 1947, and they were anxious to avoid any action that might draw public attention to the concentrated nature of the industry. Representatives of the major producers met frequently during the latter forties with the Head of the Economic Section in the Antitrust Division of the Justice Department to discuss developments in the industry and to sound out the government reaction to a price increase. As Lehmann puts it:

> In general the companies were given the impression that a price increase not justified by a cost increase might appear (to the public or to the Division) as a monopolistic exploitation of consumers and thus lead to an investigation of the industry.[27]

Within a few months after the outbreak of war in Korea in June 1950, an impending shortage of sulphur became apparent. By the beginning of 1951, Frasch producers had to curtail shipments to both domestic and export customers. In September 1950 Freeport increased its price by $4 per ton. Texas Gulf delayed until 30 November 1950, and then announced a price hike of $3 per ton. This represented the first difference in pricing between the two major producers since the establishment of Sulexco in 1922. Lehmann, basing his judgment on what he learned in personal contacts with company officers, suggests the action was motivated by a fear of antitrust prosecution:

> The lagged differential pricing by Texas Gulf particularly in the midst of a rapidly developing world shortage, can be viewed as entirely government oriented. From conversations with Texas Gulf officials, this writer can state: (1) that the increase to $21 was made as an added precaution against government investigation and prosecution (either at that time or some future time); (2) that the decision went counter to the advice of legal counsel, who advised that $22 was a perfectly safe price; and (3) that the plan was to later raise the price to $22.[28]

26. Glenn Albert Lehmann, "The Market for Sulphur: A Study in Duopoly" (Ph.D. dissertation, Economics Department, Harvard University, 1953), pp. 310–11.

27. *Ibid.*

28. *Ibid.*, pp. 312–13.

Be that as it may, the decision proved to be an extremely costly one to Texas Gulf. In 1951, the Office of Price Stabilization, under the provisions of the General Ceiling Price Regulation, froze sulphur prices at levels prevailing during the base period, 19 December 1950 to 25 January 1951. As it was not until 17 March 1953 that controls were removed on Frasch prices, Texas Gulf's price decision may have cost the company in the neighborhood of $3 million in forgone revenue.

During the Korean crisis controls were placed on domestic usage and exports, as well as on prices. Thus, there was little opportunity for the sulphur shortage to affect the behavior of Frasch producers at this time. The sulphur shortage is given credit, however, for the dissolution of Sulexco in 1952. Freeport requested the dissolution of Sulexco. In an interview, one industry official stated that, with sulphur being rationed by the government, there was little point in domestic producers continuing the expense of maintaining a sales organization for export shipments. At the time, there was certainly no need to encourage sulphur sales abroad; the problem was to limit export demands so that domestic demands could be met.

New sources of sulphur emerge

In June 1952, the President's Materials Policy Commission, established by President Truman, published *Resources for Freedom,* commonly called the "Paley Report," which presented a comprehensive review of the supply and demand for raw materials in the United States and the free world, including projections to the decade 1970–80.[29] The commission projected a 110 per cent increase in the demand for sulphur by 1975, and concluded that the country could not depend on major increases in the supply of Frasch sulphur to meet this expansion in demand. The Commission urged increased effort to recover more sulphur from pyrites and sour gases.

A decade later, in his review of the portion of the Paley Report pertaining to sulphur, William L. Swagger concluded: "Technology has been successful in providing increasing supplies of sulphur at no increase in real costs as the Paley Commission warned it would be required to do."[30] Between 1953 and 1960, aided by discoveries of additional deposits and technological improvements in recovery techniques, new sources of supply of elemental sulphur were developed both within the United States and abroad.

The development of new sources of supply in the years immediately following the sulphur shortage of the early fifties represented, at least

29. The President's Materials Policy Commission, *Resources for Freedom* (Washington, D.C.: U.S. Government Printing Office, 1952).

30. William L. Swagger, "The Paley Report in Review: Sulphur," Battelle Memorial Institute, 1961, p. 13.

in part, a response by the Frasch sulphur industry and others to market conditions during the shortage. While it is tempting to attribute all the change in the sulphur industry in the fifties to the sulphur shortage, it must be recognized that other developments, in particular the growth in production of sour natural gas, complemented the search for new sources of supply. Nevertheless, the influx of new capital into the sulphur industry in response to higher rates of return served to widen the base of the industry and brought changes in the pattern of market behavior which had remained unchanged for thirty years.

As mentioned above, the initial response to the sulphur shortage was the imposition of governmental controls over sulphur shipments and prices. At the same time, the government provided incentives, such as rapid tax amortization and exploration loans, to stimulate the development of new sulphur capacity. While domestic prices were controlled, the price on the open market, particularly in Europe, rose to very high levels with some sales at over $200 per ton being reported. In addition, some customers in Europe experienced long delays in obtaining their sulphur requirements. After the removal of price controls in March 1953, the price of Frasch sulphur rose in two successive increments to $26.50 per ton for domestic shipments f.o.b. the mine; $31.00–$33.00 per ton for export shipments f.o.b. vessels, Gulf port; and $28.00–$33.00 per ton for domestic and Canadian shipments f.o.b. vessels, Gulf port in January, and $28.00–$29.50 per ton from February to December.[31]

Entry of Mexican Frasch production

Production of elemental sulphur by the Frasch process in Mexico began in 1954, and reached nearly a half million tons in 1955. The Frasch producers in Mexico, led by the Pan American Sulphur Company, had initially intended to market their output mainly in Western Europe to take advantage of the $3.00 per ton differential between the export and domestic prices of U.S. Frasch producers.[32] Mexican Frasch sulphur was initially priced at $29.00 per ton f.o.b. the Mexican port, or $2.00 per ton below the comparable U.S. posted price. The policy proved to be so successful that, in February 1956, Freeport Sulphur cut its export price by $3.00 per ton in an attempt to maintain its share of foreign markets. In April, Texas Gulf reduced its export prices by $3.00 per ton, charging $28.00 per ton for bright sulphur to all destinations. Jefferson Lake and Duval made similar price reductions.

However, with the price umbrella removed from the European mar-

31. U.S. Department of the Interior, Bureau of Mines, *Minerals Yearbook*, 1954, vol. 1, p. 1127.

32. This information was confirmed in an interview with Mr. Henry Webb, President of Pan American Sulphur Company.

ket, Mexican Frasch sulphur producers decided that Mexican sulphur at $28.00 per ton f.o.b. the Mexican port was competitive in the United States as well as in other export markets. In addition, the Mexican firms had the advantage of being able to transport sulphur to the U.S. coastal markets at $1.50 per ton less than the U.S. Frasch producers who were required by law to use U.S. vessels to serve domestic ports.[33] Freeport, which had initiated the abolishment of the export differential and which sold most of its domestic sulphur in the inland markets of the Mississippi Valley, was not as much affected by the freight differential as was Texas Gulf, which supplied most of the East Coast markets.

By 1957, Mexican production of Frasch sulphur had reached nearly one million tons and had made marked inroads into both the domestic and export markets for U.S. Frasch sulphur as shown in figure 12. On 18 September 1957 Texas Gulf Sulphur Company announced a price reduction of $3 per ton on domestic and Canadian shipments of Frasch sulphur, thus reestablishing the export differential and bringing the domestic price to $23.50 per ton f.o.b. the mine, $25.00 per ton f.o.b. vessels, Gulf ports. Within hours, Freeport Sulphur Company announced a straight-across-the-board cut of $3 per ton on all shipments, both domestic and export.[34] Texas Gulf then amended its initial action, going along with Freeport's broader reductions in the export market. The other domestic producers followed with similar reductions.

Thus, Texas Gulf was unsuccessful in its attempt to reestablish the export differential and encourage Mexican tonnage to move to European markets. Two additional factors prompting the price reductions were the advancements made by Mexican producers in improving the grade of Mexican sulphur through filtering and a decision by Pan American Sulphur to build a stockpile at Tampa, Florida, thus increasing its competitive potential in the large Florida fertilizer market in which Texas Gulf was the largest seller.[35]

The 10 per cent reduction in Frasch sulphur prices made in 1957 was designed to enable domestic producers to regain the share of domestic and foreign markets which had been lost to Mexican Frasch sulphur. However, one Mexican producer, Gulf Sulphur Corporation, immediately reacted by reducing its posted price by $2.00 per ton to $23.00 f.o.b. the Mexican port for filtered (bright) Frasch sulphur,

33. W. G. Brese, *An Analysis of the Sulphur Industry in Alberta* (Calgary, Alberta: Research Council of Alberta, Information Series, No. 38, 1962), p. 44. The Mexican port of Coatzacoalcos was about equidistant with the major sulphur exporters of the Gulf Coast to the important sulphur markets on the Eastern Seaboard of the United States.

34. See *Chemical Week*, 28 September 1957, p. 85.

35. *Sulphur* (September 1957), p. 16.

while the other Mexican Frasch producer, Pan American Sulphur, reestablished its competitive position in the United States and overseas markets by adjusting discounts and freight allowances without resorting to changes in its posted prices. The price cutting did not succeed in stopping the entry of Mexican Frasch sulphur into the United States, though it may have been responsible for leveling off Mexican imports. As shown in figure 12, from 1957 through 1959, imports of Frasch sulphur from Mexico averaged about 600,000 tons per year. Over this period, the reduction in price, however, is estimated to have cost domestic Frasch producers $35 million in forgone revenue.[36]

1958 to 1963: years of surplus

Following the major price reduction in 1957, the posted price for Frasch sulphur became increasingly less meaningful. By 1958, all Frasch producers, both U.S. and Mexican, had begun quoting prices on a delivered basis, thus breaking the pattern of f.o.b. pricing adopted by Herman Frasch in the industry's infancy and maintained for over five decades. Freight contributions and discounts began to be used to obtain contracts in the more competitive markets, particularly along the East Coast of the United States.[37] In December 1960, Pan American Sulphur reacted to a brief upturn in sulphur markets by raising its posted price by $2.00 per ton. Domestic Frasch producers responded by withdrawing part of the transportation allowances which represented the gap between their posted price and actual realizations (see figure 13).[38]

The development of recovered sulphur production in Western Canada and at Lacq, France, brought additional supplies of elemental sulphur into world markets during the late fifties and early sixties and further reduced the market shares held by U.S. Frasch producers. The substitution of delivered pricing for f.o.b. pricing and the development of several sources of supply for elemental sulphur resulted in a trend toward regional pricing with relative freight rates becoming the decisive factor in securing markets.

The competitive position of the Canadian recovered sulphur industry in U.S. markets was greatly enhanced during 1961 by the reduction in

36. Brese, *op. cit.*, p. 54.

37. See *Sulphur* (September 1960), p. 4, where it was pointed out that posted prices "apply only in an ever decreasing and now very small number of protected markets and the bulk of domestic and export sales are based on 'delivered' prices which include freight contributions and discounts generally of up to $3.50 per ton although the recent intensification of the price war has augmented this concealed factor to over $5. In effect, therefore, the bulk of U.S. Frasch sulphur sells today at an f.o.b. equivalent of $21.50 for bright and $20.50 for off-colour materials, while some bright sulphur is sold at prices equivalent to as little as $18.50."

38. *Oil, Paint, and Drug Reporter* (26 December 1960), pp. 3 and 8.

rail freight rates from Alberta to Chicago from $19.94 per ton to $12.88 per ton. The new rate, which became effective in August 1961 and which was unsuccessfully challenged in federal court by Freeport Sulphur Company,[39] enabled Canadian recovered sulphur to be sold in midwestern markets at about $26.00 per ton, a price that included $12.00 to $13.00 in freight costs. Domestic Frasch producers responded by reducing their delivered prices in markets facing competitive pressures from the Canadians. In 1963, both Texas Gulf and Freeport challenged the rail rates from Alberta to midwestern markets in Interstate Commerce Commission hearings. The rail rate of $12.88 per ton paid on shipments from Alberta to Chicago was substantially the same as that paid by U.S. producers on shorter shipments from the Gulf Coast to Chicago. Nevertheless, the challenge was denied on appeal in January 1966.[40]

Domestic Frasch producers, after their futile attempts to maintain their share of domestic and foreign markets by price competition with the Mexican Frasch producers, adopted nonprice competition as a secondary line of defense during the early sixties. The switch from solid to liquid delivery of Frasch sulphur was particularly helpful in maintaining domestic market shares. By agreeing to finance the conversion of customers' plants to the storage, handling, and use of liquid sulphur, domestic producers were able to secure long-term contracts and develop a closer tie between the customer and the supplier.[41] By placing greater emphasis on customer service, the domestic Frasch producers were able to retard the erosion of prices in domestic markets.

In export markets, the four domestic Frasch producers responded to competition from Mexican, Canadian, and French sulphur by moving in 1958 to reestablish the Sulphur Export Corporation, with the following distribution of ownership: Texas Gulf, 38 per cent; Freeport, 38 per cent; Jefferson Lake, 18 per cent; and Duval, 8 per cent. Sulexco was reformed to bring unity to the efforts of domestic Frasch producers in competing for foreign markets. In addition, Sulexco could offer its

39. U.S. Department of the Interior, Bureau of Mines, *Minerals Yearbook,* 1961, vol. 1, p. 17. Also see *Chemical Week* (6 January 1962), p. 21.

40. U.S. Department of the Interior, Bureau of Mines, *Mineral Industry Surveys* (Sulphur), September 1963, p. 2. Also see Arthur D. Little, Inc., *The Free World Sulphur Outlook* (April 1966), p. 17.

41. The leading trade journal made the following observation regarding the effect of transition to liquid sulphur delivery: ". . . to date the liquid sulphur programme has contributed significantly to the prevailing relatively stable marketing conditions in the U.S.A. . . ." "Sulphur Price War—World Brimstone Prices Drop Over $3," *Sulphur* (December 1962), p. 1. As with most customer-oriented innovations, for example, the showing of in-flight movies on domestic airlines, the switch to liquid sulphur delivery was soon implemented by competitors, in this case, Pan American Sulphur Company, Gulf Sulphur Corporation, and SNPA.

customers technical aid and ocean freight assistance—matters of increasing importance with the growth of liquid sulphur deliveries.[42]

Some foreign consumers showed a marked aversion to purchasing from a marketing cartel. Differences in scale and nature of operations between the four members of Sulexco also hindered the development of a unified marketing policy. In particular, the willingness of Texas Gulf and Freeport to reduce prices in order to maintain tonnage appears to have worked to the detriment of Duval and Jefferson Lake, which were operating on marginal deposits with higher operating costs. As a result, they were not in a position to benefit from a sacrifice of incremental revenue for additional tonnage. Thus, Duval and Jefferson Lake were in the uncomfortable position of having only a minority interest in determining the policy under which 60 per cent of their output was being sold.[43]

Even with the formation of Sulexco, however, domestic Frasch producers continued to lose their share of world export markets. Between 1960 and 1963, as shown in figure 12, their share of world markets fell by 35 per cent. Not all of Sulexco's competition in world sulphur markets came from Mexican and Canadian sulphur. In 1963, SNPA, the state-controlled firm producing recovered sulphur at Lacq, France, undertook an aggressive, price-slicing policy to obtain a larger share of the world market and unload sizable inventories. It managed to increase its share of the Western European export market, particularly in the United Kingdom, by from 25 to 36 per cent. As a result, the proportion of U.S. sulphur exports to imports fell, and realizations on both domestic and foreign shipments hit a twenty-year low (see figure 13).

1964 to 1967: years of shortage

The sulphur market abruptly reversed itself in mid-1963, and suppliers and consumers found themselves faced with a shortage for which they were unprepared. The underlying forces causing this switch were the restricted growth in sulphur capacity during the early sixties when prices were depressed, and a rapid surge in demand, both at home and abroad, particularly in the chemical fertilizer industry. From 1963 through 1967, sulphur consumption continued to rise, increasing 38 per cent in the United States and 32 per cent in the noncommunist countries. While production of sulphur in all forms increased 29 per cent, it could not keep pace with demand. The result was a drawdown in sulphur stocks of about 1 million tons in 1964, 1.1 million tons in

42. Brese (*op. cit.*, p. 48) estimated that Sulexco was able to reduce handling and shipping charges by as much as $3.00 per ton through pooling its shipments and transporting sulphur in large quantities.

43. *Chemical Week* (11 June 1960), p. 101.

1965, 0.6 million tons in 1966, and 0.3 million tons in 1967 (see figure 11).

Reacting to the pressure for increased supply, Texas Gulf initiated a $2.00 per ton increase in the posted price of sulphur, effective 1 July 1964. Other U.S. producers and Mexican producers quickly followed Texas Gulf's lead. However, discounts by domestic Frasch producers remained at $1.50 per ton where Mexican sulphur was sold and $3.00 per ton where the competition was Canadian.[44] Throughout 1965, published prices for domestic sales remained unchanged at $27.00 per ton f.o.b. Gulf ports and $25.50 per ton f.o.b. mines, with $1.00 per ton less for dark or acid grade sulphur. However, as shown in figure 13, producers gradually terminated competitive discounts and began a program of charging realistic delivered prices that fully covered transportation and terminal costs.

Undoubtedly, the domestic posted price for sulphur would have been raised during 1965 had not the President's Council of Economic Advisors and other administrative agencies made it clear that such action would bring about a quick response from a highly price-conscious administration.[45] During 1965, the export price for bright Frasch sulphur climbed from $27.50 per ton in January to $31.00 per ton on 15 February and to $36.00 per ton in mid-June. The widening differential between domestic and foreign prices during 1965 made exports extremely attractive to domestic Frasch producers (see figure 13), and they responded, as shown in figure 12, by increasing their exports to 2.67 million tons, an all-time high representing 32.4 per cent of total U.S. production in 1965.

During 1965, it became apparent that further expansion of exports would lead to shortages in the domestic market and increase pressures on the domestic price. Thus, for Frasch producers, it became a question of selling abroad at higher prices thereby creating a domestic shortage and threatening the posted price, or of curtailing exports in order to satisfy domestic demands at the existing posted price. Government pressures eventually forced Frasch producers to restrict their exports. During 1966, Sulexco worked with the State Department in an informal arrangement to ration sulphur exports. Sulexco sent to the State Department an estimate of exports for 1966 broken down by country. The Department in turn informed Sulexco of its "views" regarding total

44. *Oil, Paint, and Drug Reporter* (6 July 1964), p. 27.

45. While not generally publicized, Administration efforts to persuade domestic producers to hold the line on sulphur prices were quite effective. During 1965, the Administration, acting through the Council of Economic Advisors, turned down requests by the major domestic Frasch producers to increase their domestic prices. Had sulphur prices risen without approval by the Administration, it is likely that the industry would have faced either export controls or antitrust action.

export tonnage and its allocation among countries.[46] The rationing of exports produced difficulties in some markets that were hard hit by a reduction in exports from Mexico due to a production failure on a portion of Pan American's mine.

Early in 1966, the two Mexican Frasch producers increased their price for sulphur to U.S. consumers by $5.00 per ton. The major U.S. Frasch producers did not respond by increasing their domestic prices, but continued the program begun in 1965 of eliminating allowances and adjusting transportation and handling charges in order to recover the costs of transportation and terminals. Realizations on domestic sales, as shown in figure 13, climbed throughout 1965 and 1966. Sulphur markets continued to tighten during 1966, bringing additional pressures on the domestic posted price. Finally, effective 1 December 1966, Freeport Sulphur increased its domestic price by $2.50 per ton for dark sulphur f.o.b. Port Sulphur, the company's main shipping point. Transportation and handling charges for sulphur shipped by Freeport beyond Port Sulphur remained unchanged from the levels established earlier in 1966. Texas Gulf increased its price for domestic sales by $2.50 per ton to $28.00 per ton for bright sulphur f.o.b. mines, effective 15 December 1966.[47]

In the middle of December, Pan American announced an increase of $10.00 per ton on all sulphur sold in the United States effective 1 January 1967. Gulf Sulphur reported that upward price adjustments had been made in its contracts as they came up for renewal. Prices in other parts of the world continued to run substantially above those in the domestic market. Toward the end of 1966, export prices for U.S. Frasch sulphur were $39.00 per ton and upwards for bright sulphur f.o.b. U.S. Gulf ports (see figure 13). Export prices for Mexican Frasch sulphur and recovered sulphur were reported to be at even higher levels.

The continuing sulphur shortage led to two price increases for domestic sulphur in 1967. Published prices increased $4.00 per ton f.o.b. Gulf ports in April and were increased an additional $5.50 per ton in October. Year-end prices for bright sulphur were $39.00 per ton f.o.b. Gulf ports. Like the 1966 increase, the 1967 price hikes were initiated by Freeport, indicating its position as the leading Frasch producer. The increases in posted prices during 1966 and 1967 were insufficient to ration existing supplies of sulphur among consumers. It became necessary for sulphur deliveries to be allocated by the major producers. In

46. This arrangement was described by Edward Getzin, Chief, Industrial and Strategic Minerals Division, United States Department of State, in an interview with the author in Washington, D.C., on 11 August 1966.

47. L. B. Gittinger, Jr., "Sulphur," *The Engineering and Mining Journal* (February 1967), p. 170.

September 1966, Texas Gulf cut deliveries to domestic consumers to 75 per cent of their 1965 level, and in December 1967, customers were notified that they would be limited in 1968 to 65 per cent of their 1965 purchases.[48] Freeport, early in 1967, told customers it could deliver only 90 per cent of their base tonnage.

Export prices continued to rise during 1967. In August, Pan American Sulphur increased its run-of-the-mill sulphur price to $50.00 per ton for sales to regular contract customers and to $55.00 per ton for spot sales, f.o.b. Coatzacoalcos, Mexico. Bright sulphur prices were increased to $52.00 and $57.00 per ton respectively, maintaining the $2.00 per ton difference.[49] Canadian recovered sulphur, early in 1968, was reported to be selling as high as $56.50 per ton f.o.b. Vancouver.[50]

1968: balance achieved

World sulphur markets returned to balance in 1968 when, for the first time since 1962, production exceeded shipments in the noncommunist countries. The return to balance between supply and demand was attributed to two factors: (1) an increase in sulphur production, primarily brimstone production in Western Canada augmented by increased output of Frasch sulphur in the United States and Mexico; and (2) a reduction in the rate of growth of sulphur consumption, primarily due to the fact that there was no increase in U.S. consumption.[51] Late in 1968, prices in Western Europe and some other overseas markets were reduced by $2.00 per ton. In January 1969, similar price reductions were made in the domestic and Canadian markets. With the sulphur shortage at an end, both suppliers and consumers were left pondering whether the feast or famine pattern of sulphur markets during the past two decades would be repeated in the coming years. This question is considered in chapter 8.

48. "Texas Gulf Again Cuts Sulphur Allocations to 65% of '65 Deliveries, as Shortage Grows," *The Wall Street Journal* (5 December 1967), p. 34.

49. "Mexican Concern Increases Prices On Its Sulphur," *The Wall Street Journal* (29 August 1967), p. 28.

50. Thomas O'Hanlan, "The Great Sulphur Rush," *Fortune* (March 1968), p. 109.

51. L. B. Gittinger, "Sulphur," *The Engineering and Mining Journal* (March 1969), pp. 160C–160F.

Part III

Performance in the Sulphur Industry

Chapter 7

Evaluation of Competitive Performance

Analysis of the market structure and behavior of an industry provides observations upon which an evaluation of the industry's performance can be made. However, in contrast to the analysis of market structure and behavior, performance evaluation is largely qualitative in nature. It is simply a judgment of an industry's effectiveness vis-à-vis some norm or standard. The commonly accepted norm is that of pure competition. However, the use of the competitive standard is based upon an implicit value judgment. Given different value judgments, other norms might replace the competitive standard. For example, if progressiveness is an accepted criterion of performance, the competitive standard may not offer any basis for comparison.[1] If the problem of resource utilization is a matter of sole concern, monopoly may be preferred to competition.[2] Even if one accepts the value judgments behind the use of the competitive standard, its application to any given industry is very difficult. In the final analysis, evaluation of the performance of an industry must rest upon an appraisal of the overall impact of industry behavior upon what is thought to represent the public welfare.

Earlier chapters in this study pointed up the oligopolistic nature of the Frasch sulphur industry's market structure. Analysis of the industry's market behavior revealed a rigid pricing policy and the existence of price discrimination between domestic and export markets over much of the industry's history. However, it was also revealed that the indus-

1. Phillips, *Competition in the Synthetic Rubber Industry,* p. 202, states ". . . there are no analytical standards to measure progressiveness since innovation has not been dealt with by competitive models." The same point is made by Hamilton, *Competition in Oil*, p. 153.

2. Anthony Scott, *Natural Resources: The Economics of Conservation* (Toronto: The University of Toronto Press, 1955), p. 84, contends that monopoly, through the restriction of output, serves the cause of resource conservation more effectively than competition. "It may even follow that when conservation policy has the higher priority, the state should actively encourage monopoly as an ally in this programme."

try's market behavior has undergone a significant change during the past decade in response to fundamental alterations in its market structure. Evaluation of the industry's performance, therefore, must be made not only in light of the industry's history, but also in light of the recent changes in market structure and behavior and their implications for future performance.

The most important indicators of industry performance are the level of profits and the relationship between costs and prices. These factors are examined in detail in this chapter. Another indicator—and one that is important in a resource-based industry—is the utilization of the sulphur resource and the outlook for sulphur as a mineral resource. This aspect of performance is examined in the following chapter.

The Level of Profits

Profit levels as a competitive standard

The clearest indication of how well an industry meets competitive standards is the long-run record of its profits. A basic premise of competition is that the rate of return to capital invested in various sectors of the economy, for a given degree of risk, will be approximately equal, given the time required for adjustment. Thus, while an industry may experience an above-normal rate of return during periods of rapidly growing demand or dynamic innovation, these profits will in time be bid down to competitive levels through the attraction of new capital into the industry, the expansion of output, and the reduction of prices. While the process of equalization may be retarded by factors limiting the mobility of capital, particularly at the international level, evidence indicates that the economy in general performs this task fairly well.[3] Of course, it should be emphasized that while persistent above-average profits are almost *prima facie* evidence of noncompetitive performance, the existence of an average rate of return in an industry does not prove that the industry is competitive.[4] However, as a first approximation of competitiveness, the level of profits over the long run is a very useful tool for evaluating the performance of an industry.

Profits in the Frasch sulphur industry

The Frasch sulphur industry developed from an ingenious and unique innovation, the Frasch hot-water mining process. It would be expected

3. George J. Stigler, *Capital and Rates of Return in Manufacturing Industries* (Princeton: Princeton University Press for the National Bureau of Economic Research, 1963).

4. *Ibid.*, p. 55.

that after perfecting the process, the innovator would have received a rate of return during the industry's early phase that would have been significantly above the normal rate of return for capital invested in other parts of the economy. The existence of above-normal rates of return, however, should have induced entry into the industry and lowered the rate of return. Unfortunately, data on profits earned by the Union Sulphur Company are not available. In any event, new producers were soon attracted into the industry.

In its 1947 study of the sulphur industry, the Federal Trade Commission computed average invested capital, profits before and after taxes, and the rate of return before and after taxes for the four principal Frasch sulphur producers over the period from 1919 to 1946. During this period, Texas Gulf, Jefferson Lake, and Duval were engaged only in the production of Frasch sulphur. Freeport was also engaged in mining manganese and nickeliferous iron ore in Cuba during this period, but the Commission excluded these operations so that the reported rate of return on investment represented only profits on the production and sale of sulphur. To compensate for the high income and excess profits taxes during the period from 1941 to 1946, the Commission calculated the before-tax rate of return by relating the profit before federal taxes to the average invested capital adjusted for such tax provisions.

Since 1947, data on profits earned on Frasch mining operations are less reliable because all Frasch producers have diversified their operations into related fields of mining and chemicals. Accounting data published in the annual reports of these firms incorporate all their activities, and separate information regarding investment in Frasch mining and profits earned on Frasch sales is not available. Nevertheless, since sulphur mining remained the principal activity of both Texas Gulf and Freeport through 1966 and Jefferson Lake through 1962 (in 1964, Jefferson Lake was acquired by Occidental Petroleum), accounting data for these firms provide a reasonably good basis for computation of the rate of return on Frasch mining activities. However, over the past two decades, sulphur mining has become an increasingly smaller element of Duval's operations and has not been a dominant activity of the firm since 1953. Thus, table 17, which lists average invested capital, after-tax profits, and the after-tax rate of return on invested capital both for the entire Frasch industry and for each of the individual producers, includes no data for Duval after 1953 and no data for Jefferson Lake after 1962.

Table 17 shows that the average rate of return on invested capital for all firms in the Frasch sulphur industry was 23.60 per cent for 1919–53 and 21.23 per cent for 1919–66. Most economists would agree that

Table 17. Average Investment and After-Tax Profits and Rate of Return for the Frasch Sulphur Industry, 1919–66

	Rate of return after taxes on invested capital				Frasch Sulphur Industry		
Year	Texas Gulf	Freeport	Jefferson Lake	Duval	Invested capital*	Income after taxes	Rate of return
	per cent	*per cent*	*per cent*	*per cent*	*thousand dollars*	*thousand dollars*	*per cent*
1919	18.76	11.48	—	—	14,791	2,073	14.02
1920	37.04	6.94	—	—	17,387	3,911	22.49
1921	16.58	(5.82)	—	—	19,727	1,374	6.97
1922	31.24	(2.53)	—	—	22,198	3,555	16.02
1923	36.39	6.33	—	—	25,042	5,453	21.77
1924	36.01	(2.65)	—	—	25,502	4,437	17.40
1925	42.44	6.37	—	—	25,032	6,378	25.48
1926	62.85	14.40	—	—	27,356	11,105	40.59
1927	67.86	27.01	—	—	31,516	15,738	49.94
1928	66.49	24.59	—	—	34,991	17,871	51.07
1929	58.66	33.07	—	—	39,210	20,028	51.08
1930	41.99	23.94	—	20.66	44,826	16,706	37.27
1931	24.99	18.51	—	14.76	47,496	11,059	23.28
1932	16.34	21.35	—	9.98	47,089	8,067	17.13
1933	19.85	22.94	35.77	(6.54)	51,971	10,687	20.55
1934	13.69	11.70	33.85	3.61	65,501	9,124	13.93
1935	12.50	12.07	5.51	6.54	75,686	9,170	12.12
1936	16.66	16.73	n.a.	24.03	73,565†	12,140†	16.50†
1937	19.60	17.30	(0.51)	14.07	77,011	14,242	18.49
1938	11.75	10.87	33.27	19.69	77,658	9,672	12.45
1939	13.22	10.87	47.01	26.92	79,516	11,447	14.40
1940	15.40	12.36	28.70	20.62	82,556	12,701	15.38
1941	15.34	13.63	10.46	25.13	83,198	12,585	15.13
1942	14.97	10.60	(13.81)	28.99	83,413	11,329	13.58
1943	13.55	12.54	6.46	30.91	82,887	11,338	13.68
1944	16.38	11.57	16.20	31.12	82,582	12,984	15.72
1945	16.91	14.40	13.40	30.00	84,546	13,667	16.17
1946	24.79	15.52	11.52	35.73	89,204	19,987	22.30
1947	32.86	9.10	11.41	25.65	103,396	25,843	24.99
1948	42.11	12.77	11.55	19.45	97,135	29,503	30.37
1949	47.47	17.01	13.61	21.64	92,323	31,051	33.63
1950	45.13	19.32	28.65	18.28	104,340	35,311	33.84
1951	39.44	16.26	26.13	14.05	117,459	34,365	29.26
1952	36.48	17.82	21.67	25.60	126,658	36,451	28.78
1953	33.37	19.43	23.58	24.78	124,638	37,772	30.31
1954	36.56	20.95	30.22	—	139,515	42,946	30.78
1955	33.75	21.82	21.03	—	161,751	46,666	28.85
1956	26.51	19.94	18.52	—	182,442	43,237	23.70
1957	15.92	17.88	13.24	—	193,037	31,924	16.54
1958	11.95	12.99	(6.05)	—	235,420	27,341	11.61
1959	11.58	10.11	(11.74)	—	278,199	27,341	9.83
1960	10.63	9.47	1.68	—	277,610	25,464	9.17
1961	10.09	9.19	10.15	—	277,505	26,724	9.63
1962	9.17	8.75	10.76	—	288,879	26,031	9.01
1963	6.58	8.43	—	—	295,111	22,248	7.54
1964	7.63	9.55	—	—	312,872	26,967	8.62
1965	11.02	12.71	—	—	337,325	40,084	11.88
1966	14.11	17.17	—	—	389,869	60,844	15.61
1919–53 Avg.	—	—	—	—	—	—	23.60
1919–66 Avg.	26.35	13.68	15.59	20.28	—	—	21.23

SOURCE: Appendix B.

NOTE: Jefferson Lake was acquired by Occidental Petroleum in 1964; data not available after 1962. Data for Duval not available after 1953; owing to diversification, accounting data no longer reflect results from sulphur mining.

( ) Loss.

n.a.—Not available.

* Beginning and end of year.

† Excludes Jefferson Lake.

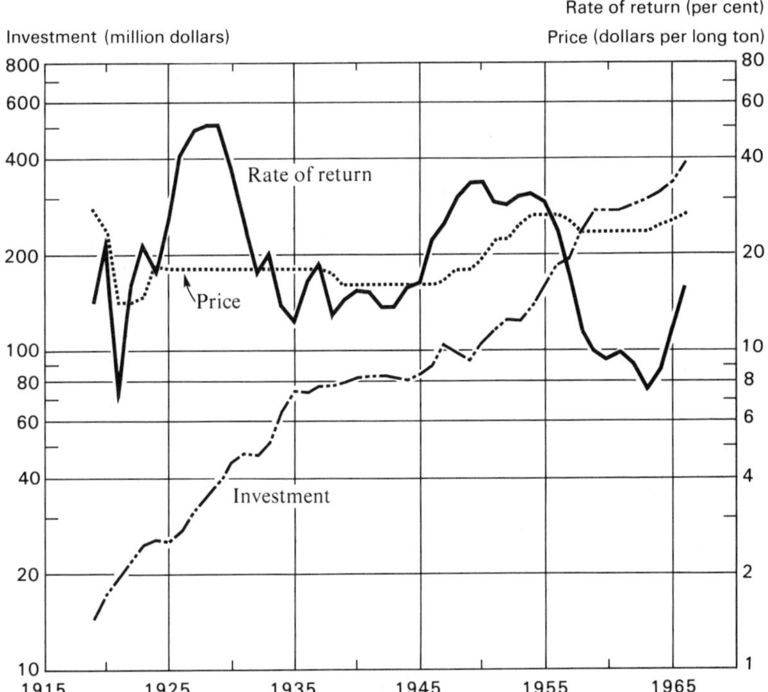

Figure 14. Annual average investment, price, and rate of return for the U.S. Frasch sulphur industry, 1919–66. (Based on data in tables 17 and *A-3.)*

these are abnormally high rates of return for any industry over such a long period.[5] In figure 14, the rate of return for the industry, the average annual investment, and the posted price for Frasch sulphur are plotted for the period 1919 through 1966. Under competitive conditions, it would be expected that as investment grew both the rate of return and the price would decline. However, as figure 14 shows, while investment increased steadily in the Frasch sulphur industry, the additional capital came not from new entrants but from expansion by existing producers, and the price of sulphur has shown no tendency to decline. The rate of return for the industry, except for the period from 1958 through 1965, remained above 12 per cent.

An exceptionally high level of profits was earned during the period

5. For example, John G. McLean and Robert W. Haigh, *The Growth of Integrated Oil Companies* (Boston: Division of Research, Graduate School of Business Administration, Harvard University, 1954), pp. 680–81, report that the average rate of return on invested capital for 120 oil companies between 1920 and 1952 ranged from 6.6 per cent to 10.9 per cent. Phillips, *op. cit.*, p. 210, found synthetic rubber firms earned from 6 per cent to 9 per cent on their investment.

from the formation of the Sulphur Export Corporation in 1922 to the commencement of the depression in 1930. The average return for all firms during this period was 38.82 per cent. While the depression reduced industry profits, the average rate of return for all firms in the industry between 1930 and 1939 was still a very healthy 17.54 per cent. Profits in the industry remained at a high level until about 1953 when they began to fall. The decline in profits continued unabated through 1963. Thus, the pattern of profits, like those for prices and output, changed significantly in the mid-fifties, responding to the development of alternative sources of supply for elemental sulphur, particularly in Mexico, Canada, and France, which produced major changes in the market structure and behavior of the domestic Frasch industry.

Table 17 shows considerable divergence between the rates of return earned by the individual firms producing Frasch sulphur. Texas Gulf, largely on account of its ownership of the industry's lowest cost and largest deposit, Boling Dome, led in profits, earning an average of 26.35 per cent on invested capital over the period from 1919 through 1966. The two smaller firms, Duval and Jefferson Lake, averaged 20.28 per cent and 15.59 per cent respectively over the periods shown in table 17. Freeport Sulphur averaged only 13.68 per cent for 1919–66. Comparison of the profits earned by Texas Gulf and Freeport reveals that Freeport earned considerably lower profits in the twenties and in the period from 1940 to 1957. This can be attributed to Freeport's having higher costs because it was operating on domes of lower quality than Texas Gulf during these periods. In particular, Freeport's Grande Ecaille mine was located in the Louisiana swamps where the costs of producing sulphur were higher than in the salt plains of the Texas coast. Since 1957, profits of both Freeport and Texas Gulf have followed a similar pattern, although Freeport has had a slightly higher rate of return. Freeport has also become the leading producer of Frasch sulphur during this period.

Table 18 compares the rates of return on invested capital after taxes for the domestic Frasch sulphur producers with the rates of return earned by the two Mexican producers. (Duval is omitted from the comparison because sulphur constituted a minor part of its operations over much of this period.) It can be seen that Pan American consistently exceeded the rate of return of the major domestic producers throughout this period. The return earned by Gulf Sulphur, after its initial period of losses, also exceeded the comparative rates of return earned by the domestic Frasch producers.[6]

6. PASCO's mine is on a dome of high quality and its costs are undoubtedly similar to those of the major U.S. Frasch mines (Boling Dome and Grande Ecaille). However, Gulf Sulphur's mine is of average quality and its costs are

Table 18. Frasch Sulphur Producers: Comparative Rates of Return on Invested Capital After Deduction of Income Taxes, 1955–66

Year	Pan American	Gulf Sulphur*	Texas Gulf	Freeport	Jefferson Lake†
1955	6.60		33.75	21.82	21.03
1956	29.33		26.51	19.94	18.52
1957	34.09		15.92	17.88	13.24
1958	27.11		11.95	12.99	(6.05)
1959	20.97		11.58	10.11	(11.74)
1960	16.28		10.63	9.47	1.68
1961	12.30	4.94	10.09	9.19	10.15
1962	15.36	22.75	9.17	8.75	10.76
1963	16.48	15.06	6.58	8.43	
1964	22.02	10.99	7.63	9.55	
1965	17.03	20.66	11.02	12.71	
1966	28.85	22.66	14.11	17.17	
Average	20.54	16.18	14.08	13.17	7.20

SOURCE: Appendix B.
( ) Loss.
* No operating profit prior to 1961.
† Data not available after 1962; acquired by Occidental Petroleum, 1964.

Several limitations on the use of accounting data to obtain rates of return should be mentioned at this point. The accounting concepts used in calculating corporate profits differ in many respects from the corresponding economic concepts appropriate to the measurement of income.[7] Similarly, the use of invested capital probably does not reflect the actual value of the firm's investment in plant and equipment. While these limitations are important and must be recognized, the use of accounting data for calculating rates of return on investment must rest on the practical grounds of data availability.

Depletion and royalties

Two additional aspects of using accounting data for computation of rates of return on invested capital for the Frasch sulphur industry should

more nearly in line with the smaller domestic mines. The $1.50 per ton freight differential on shipments to U.S. buyers probably helps to explain the higher profits earned by the Mexican firms. See Dale B. Truett, "Sulphur and the Development of a Chemical Fertilizer Industry in Mexico" (Ph.D. dissertation, The University of Texas, 1967).

7. For a comprehensive discussion of this problem, see Edgar O. Edwards and Philip W. Bell, *The Theory and Measurement of Business Income* (Berkeley: University of California Press, 1961). The major problems are accounting for capital gains and losses as they arise; distinguishing between gains from normal operations and gains from merely holding assets as prices rise; and promptly recognizing changes in the general price level which affect both the level of reported profit and the statement of net worth.

be noted. Percentage depletion increases the after-tax earnings of Frasch sulphur firms, while royalties, which are taken as a cost of doing business, reduce the income of Frasch sulphur firms.

In 1932, sulphur was placed under the depletion provisions, which allow depletion of up to 23 per cent of gross income from the sulphur-producing property but not to exceed 50 per cent of net income. The extent to which the net income limitation restricts the percentage depletion claimed is a function of the relationship between net and gross income and the statutory rate of depletion. In the case of sulphur, Frasch producers are affected by the net income limitation if their ratio of net to gross income is less than 46 per cent.[8] However, data indicate that the net income limit does not severely restrict the amount of depletion claimed by Frasch producers. Depletion claimed by these producers was equal to 20.3 per cent in 1958, 20.6 per cent in 1959, and 24.2 per cent in 1960 of gross income from mineral extraction.[9]

The available evidence suggests that the main result of depletion in the Frasch sulphur industry has been to increase profits, rather than to stimulate exploration and development of new sulphur deposits. This is understandable since sulphur is one mineral which is seldom found intentionally. Indeed, most of the existing Frasch sulphur deposits were discovered in the process of petroleum exploration. It is not surprising, then, that exploration expenditures in the sulphur industry have been extremely low related to the average net income of firms in the industry or to the amount of percentage depletion which the industry receives.[10] In recent years, exploration expenditures have increased, but exploration efforts have been largely unsuccessful. In one of the few major

8. U.S. Congress, House Committee on Ways and Means, *President's 1963 Tax Message*, Hearings on the tax recommendations of the President contained in his message to the Congress, 24 January 1963, pt. 1, 88th Cong., 1st Sess., 1963, p. 297.

9. *Ibid.*, p. 309. Total depletion claimed can exceed both the gross rate of percentage depletion and the 50 per cent unconsolidated net income from the taxpayer's mineral activities, because: (1) percentage depletion must be computed on a property-by-property basis, and cost depletion must be used where higher than percentage depletion; (2) in deriving total net income, losses from producing properties and deductions on nonproducing properties are subtracted from positive net income.

10. For example, see James R. Nelson, "Percentage Depletion and National Security," in *Federal Tax Policy for Economic Growth and Stability*, Joint Committee Print, of the 84th Cong., 1st Sess. (Washington, D.C.: United States Government Printing Office, 1955), p. 473. In describing depletion in the sulphur industry, Nelson states: "During the 19 years 1930 through 1948, average net income was $13 million per year; average dividend payments, $11 million; and average annual exploration expense, $369,603. In 1946, allowable depletion was $11.2 million, and in 1947, $13.8 million. Total exploration expense was $7 million during the entire period, 1930–1948." Due to the diversification of sulphur firms into other mining activities during the fifties, these figures are the latest available on sulphur exploration expenditures.

explicit efforts to find Frasch sulphur, the off-shore exploration program of the major Frasch companies in the mid-fifties, and again in the mid-sixties, the expenditure of sizable funds failed to turn up any new commercial deposits of Frasch sulphur.[11]

In addition to percentage depletion, royalties also play an important role in determining the rate of return on investment in the Frasch sulphur industry. The rates of return shown in tables 17 and 18 were calculated after deductions for royalty payments had been made. In general, two types of royalty payments are made on sulphur deposits (see table 19). The first type—a fixed fee per ton of sulphur produced—is paid to the owner of the mineral rights to the property. A second

Table 19. Summary of Royalties Paid by Frasch Producers

Company and mine	Description of royalties
Freeport:	
Hoskins	Subleased from The Texas Co. A fixed royalty of $1.06 per ton is payable to the fee owner, and 70 per cent of the net profits after deducting the fixed royalty is payable to the Texas Co.
Grande Ecaille	Subleased from Gulf Oil Corp., Humble Oil and Refining Co., and Shell Canadian Exploration Co. Fixed royalties to owners are $1.05 per ton. An additional fixed royalty of $1.00 per ton is payable to the three oil companies. The three oil companies also receive an additional royalty based on the sales price for sulphur. Freeport's share of the net profits from this property amounts to between 60 and 65 per cent of the total.
Lake Pelto, Bay Ste. Elaine, and Garden Island Bay	Subleased from The Texas Co. Net profits are shared equally with The Texas Co.
Grand Isle	Leased from Humble Oil and Refining Co. Net profits after recovery of all construction and development costs are shared equally with Humble.
Chacahoula, Nash, and Bryan Mound	Data unavailable.
Duval:	
Orchard	Leased from individuals. Fixed payment of $1.00 per ton for the first 6,000 tons produced each month and $2.00 per ton on all output beyond 6,000 tons per month. In addition, a fixed fee of $0.84 per ton is paid to the fee owners.

11. See "Sulphur Prices Hit New High," *Chemical Week* (7 October 1967), p. 32. Freeport Sulphur Company spent $14.8 million between 1965 and 1967 in searching for offshore Frasch deposits without success. Other firms reportedly spent $21 million on offshore exploration for Frasch sulphur during this period without finding a commercial deposit.

Table 19. (Continued)

Company and mine	Description of royalties
Palangana and Boling Dome	Data unavailable.
Jefferson Lake:	
Lake Peigneur	Leased from the State of Louisiana. Royalty of $0.75 per ton paid to the state.
Clemens	Leased from individuals and subleased from Texas Gulf Sulphur. Amount of royalty unknown. Until 1949, payment to Texas Gulf was made in the form of sulphur. In 1949, royalty payments were substituted.
Long Point	Leased from Texas Gulf Sulphur. Texas Gulf receives 50 per cent of the output.
Starks	Leased from Texas Gulf Sulphur and Carter Oil Co. No data available on royalties.
Texas Gulf:	
Boling	Subleased from Gulf Production Co. (85.065 per cent), The Texas Co. (9.113 per cent), Sun Oil Co. (0.825 per cent), Vacuum Oil (1.972 per cent), and others (2.909 per cent). Royalty payments to Gulf are $1.00 per ton including payment of the underlying royalty; $3.00 per ton paid to The Texas Co. including the underlying royalty; and $1.00 per ton paid to the remaining interests plus the underlying royalty. Further, Texas Gulf agreed to share equally with the oil companies in the net profits after all development expenses were recouped. In 1934, Gulf Oil exchanged its interest in this property for 1.3 million shares of Texas Gulf stock or 38.83 per cent of the stock thereafter outstanding. On 3 November 1948, Texas Gulf repurchased 500,000 shares from Gulf Oil at $55 per share. Gulf Oil sold its remaining shares in 1956.
Long Point	Leased from Gulf Production Co. under the Boling Dome lease agreement.
Moss Bluff	Leased from Gulf Production Co. and Humble Oil and Refining Co. No data available on royalty payments.
Fannett, Gulf, and Spindletop	Data unavailable.

SOURCE: All data taken from Moody's *Manual of Industrial Investments.* Additional information taken from William Haynes, *Brimstone: The Stone That Burns* (Princeton, New Jersey: D. Van Nostrand Company, Inc., 1959).

NOTE: All sulphur mines developed prior to 1967 are included in the above listing except the original Sulphur Mine of Union, the Big Creek mine of Union, Standard Sulphur Company's Damon mine, and U.S. Sulphur Company's High Island mine. Data on these mines are unavailable.

royalty is paid when the Frasch producers sublease the sulphur rights from petroleum companies. This second royalty is sometimes paid to the petroleum company or companies in the form of a fixed payment per ton of sulphur mined, but more often is combined with a payment of a percentage of net profits from the operation.

Royalty payments are considered a cost of production, but when these payments amount to 50 per cent or more of the net profits from the operation, as shown in table 19 for several of the major deposits, the relationship between the lessor and lessee resembles that of a limited partnership. In such cases, royalties ought to be included in net income, and looked upon as part of the return on investment of capital in the firm. In the case of Boling Dome, Texas Gulf and Gulf Oil decided that an exchange of stock for sulphur rights would be preferable to a profit-sharing royalty agreement. In this case, royalties do not show up as a cost of operation (except for the royalty payments to the initial owners of the lease) but are included in net income and distributed to shareholders in the form of dividends. Of course, the stock given to the oil company in return for its deposit would represent an expansion of investment in the firm and the rate of return would reflect this expansion.

Royalty payments are not listed separately from other costs in the financial statements of Duval and Jefferson Lake. However, both Texas Gulf and Freeport list royalty payments as supplementary information to their profit and loss statements. Examination of royalty payments from 1934 through 1962, given in table 20, reveals two interesting facts. First, even though Texas Gulf was the larger producer during this period, Freeport paid two and one-half to three times more royalties. This is due to the fact that Texas Gulf's largest mine, Boling Dome, had been largely freed of royalty payments by the exchange of stock with Gulf Oil. A second point of interest is that royalty payments by both firms declined in the period 1957–62, reflecting the downward trend in output.

Cost-Price Relationships

Competitive performance would require that firms in an industry pass forward reductions in costs to buyers in the form of reductions in price; thus, prices would be closely related to the level of marginal costs. It is apparent from previous chapters that the Frasch sulphur industry does not have a competitive market structure. In the period prior to 1955, the Frasch sulphur industry was an oligopoly, selling a completely homogeneous product, and protected from entry by absolute cost barriers (stemming from possession of the lower-cost sulphur deposits). Thus, its prices at home and abroad reflected its market power and

Table 20. Royalty Payments by Texas Gulf Sulphur and Freeport Sulphur, 1934–62

thousand dollars

Year	Texas Gulf Sulphur*	Freeport Sulphur
1934	984	2,278
1935	963	2,751
1936	1,088	3,788
1937	1,149	4,435
1938	1,017	3,325
1939	656	3,083
1940	1,793	3,788
1941	2,173	4,469
1942	2,113	4,915
1943	2,094	5,332
1944	1,850	5,488
1945	1,850	6,116
1946	1,836	5,515
1947	2,216	5,001
1948	2,319	6,781
1949	2,211	8,266
1950	2,800	9,047
1951	3,385	10,493
1952	3,841	11,316
1953	4,013	13,858
1954	4,341	16,421
1955	4,945	17,329
1956	4,902	18,167
1957	4,501	15,296
1958	3,533	11,552
1959	3,798	11,468
1960	3,595	11,486
1961	3,403	11,134
1962	3,860	10,470

SOURCE: Moody's *Manual of Industrial Investments* for the applicable years.

* Includes both royalty payments on output and "advanced royalties" paid for renewal or extensions of rights.

yielded, as seen in this chapter, above normal profits for the industry. Prices were clearly not related to the level of marginal cost. Since 1955, the entry of new firms in response to expanding demand has significantly altered both the market structure and market behavior of Frasch sulphur firms. As might have been expected, the initial impact of entry was to reduce industry profits and cause major alterations in market behavior. Despite the changes in market structure and behavior that have occurred since 1955, the Frasch sulphur industry has remained an industry of few sellers producing a completely homogeneous commodity, but it has become increasingly difficult for Frasch sulphur firms to supply the entire market for elemental sulphur. As a result, higher-cost sources of supply have been brought into production. Sulphur prices now tend to reflect the higher costs of mining marginal deposits. The lower-cost sources of supply are thus earning pure economic rent. Therefore, in analyzing the relationship between costs and prices, it is necessary to examine the relationship as it existed prior to 1955, and as it exists today.

Cost-price relationships prior to 1955

Given the purely oligopolistic structure of the Frasch sulphur industry prior to 1955, the best explanation of industry pricing is that of tacit collusion on the domestic market and cartel pricing on the export market. Tacit collusion on the domestic market refers to the behavior of Texas Gulf and Freeport, acting as duopolists, in setting the domestic price that maximized industry profits. Tacit collusion, it should be stressed, means only that the dominant sellers in the market reached an implicit understanding regarding pricing and output behavior, not that they formally met or agreed to a common pricing policy. As the economic literature on oligopolistic pricing clearly reveals, this type of pricing behavior is the only way in which rational oligopolists can act if they are to avoid constant turmoil in their market.[12]

Chamberlin has shown that with only two firms in the market selling a homogeneous commodity and pricing independently, if both sellers recognize their mutual dependence and act accordingly, the industry price will stabilize where marginal cost is equal to marginal revenue, thus maximizing industry profits.[13] The stabilization of the domestic price of Frasch sulphur at $18.00 per ton f.o.b. the mine during 1925 and 1926 appears to correspond closely to the theoretical model of duopoly behavior.

Once established, such an oligopolistic price would be unlikely to change frequently. Where the degree of mutual dependence among the oligopolists is extreme, as is the case in an industry of very few sellers producing an undifferentiated product, prices are likely to be very sticky because each firm is uncertain of the reaction of its rivals to a change in price. This tendency toward price inflexibility would be reinforced in the case of Frasch sulphur by the extreme inelasticity of demand at prices below the profit maximizing level. (For example, it was shown in chapter 6 that, at a price of $14.00 per ton, Frasch sulphur would be used by all domestic acid manufacturers except those tied to

12. See Stigler, *The Theory of Price*, chap. 13; Martin Shubik, *Strategy and Market Structure* (New York: John Wiley and Sons, Inc., 1959); and H. H. Liebhafsky, *The Nature of Price Theory* (Rev. ed., Homewood, Illinois: The Dorsey Press, 1968), chap. 13.

13. Edward H. Chamberlin, *The Theory of Monopolistic Competition* (6th ed., Cambridge: Harvard University Press, 1950), pp. 46–51.

the use of another form of sulphur or those consuming by-product sulphur.) Small shifts in marginal costs would not cause the profit-maximizing price to depart significantly from the existing level. Finally, where entry is restricted by a high barrier—in this case, an absolute cost advantage—the initial determination of price is made with the purpose of limiting entry; upward adjustments in price would be resisted because they might induce unwanted entry into the industry. Thus, once the equilibrium price was established, strong forces would operate to prevent its change. Again, the behavior of domestic Frasch prices, which changed only once between 1926 and 1947, conforms closely to the behavior expected from firms in a purely oligopolistic industry.

Shifts in demand, however, if of significant magnitude, would cause the profit-maximizing price to change. However, the oligopolists would be likely to respond only if they became convinced that the shift in demand was to be permanent, and no firm would initiate a change in price until it was reasonably certain that its actions would be followed by its rivals. Thus, while prices would eventually respond to shifts in demand, the response would be slower than under a more competitive market structure. This analysis helps to explain the failure of the posted price of Frasch sulphur to fall in the face of the severe drop in demand caused by the depression of the thirties. Not until 1938 did Frasch producers reduce their posted price. It also helps to explain the rather sluggish response of Frasch sulphur prices to the rapid expansion in demand which occurred following World War II.

On the export market, the Webb-Pomerene Act made it legally possible for the two major Frasch producers to act jointly through the Sulphur Export Corporation in determining export prices. They responded by entering into a formal market-sharing agreement with the Sicilians. As discussed in chapter 5, the practice of price discrimination in export markets rested on the complete control over the supply of elemental sulphur. The cartel participants established export prices that reflected the costs of Sicilian sulphur, which were higher than those of Frasch sulphur. Thus, export prices were consistently higher than domestic prices, and sales in export markets were restricted to consumers requiring elemental sulphur. Even though the cartel agreements were abandoned by 1940, export prices continued to run above domestic prices throughout the existence of Sulexco.

Cost-price relationships after 1955

Higher-cost marginal Frasch mines, such as Bay Ste. Elaine, Damon, Starks, Chacahoula, and Nash, were brought into production after World War II when additional supplies were needed to meet the rapidly expanding demand. Prices for Frasch sulphur moved steadily upward from 1947 to 1956, interrupted only by the two-year period of governmental controls during the Korean crisis, and the low-cost mines of Texas Gulf and Freeport earned significantly higher economic rents. Beginning in 1955, U.S. Frasch sulphur met increasing competition both at home and abroad, first from Mexican Frasch sulphur and then from Canadian and French recovered sulphur. This increase in the supply of elemental sulphur brought about a reduction in sulphur prices, and resulted in the closing of many of the marginal mines.[14]

The period from 1955 to 1958 witnessed an apparent conflict in pricing objectives between Texas Gulf and Freeport. As described in chapter 6, the leadership efforts of Freeport in 1956 led to the abolishment of the export differential. This occurred during the six-year period 1952–58, in which the Sulphur Export Corporation did not exist. Freeport's actions, however, were followed by all other producers. An attempt by Texas Gulf in 1957 to reestablish the export differential met with opposition from Freeport and ended in a decrease in both domestic and export prices. Freeport emerged in a stronger position during this period because of its control of the interior, more protected domestic markets.

After 1958, the pricing structure of Frasch sulphur underwent a complete change as producers reestablished Sulexco, moved to liquid delivery, established regional storage terminals, and switched to a system of delivered pricing characterized by substantial concessions being made in terms of absorption of freight and handling charges in order to combat competition from other sources of sulphur. The experience of the Frasch sulphur industry during this period confirms the presence of competitive forces in the economy. The discovery of new sources of supply and the entry of new firms into the market were sufficient to upset the pattern of market conduct that had persisted for several decades. The developments in the Frasch sulphur industry bear out Fellner's conclusion that "The broadening of oligopolistic groups is likely to loosen the coordination of business policies, particularly with respect to market variables other than price."[15] While price reductions did occur following the entry of new sources of supply, the more important changes from the point of view of the long-run impact on the Frasch sulphur industry have been the significant alterations in both the price structure and distribution channels for Frasch sulphur.

14. The major reason given by Texas Gulf for abandoning its efforts to produce Frasch sulphur in Mexico in 1960 was the higher costs of the Mexican operation. Other mines abandoned prematurely during the period of declining sales realizations included Nash and Chacahoula. All of these mines were later reopened during the sulphur shortage of 1964–68, when increased prices made possible further production from these marginal deposits.

15. William Fellner, "Collusion and Its Limits Under Oligopoly," *American Economic Review* (May 1950), p. 60.

When rapid expansion in demand both in the United States and abroad beginning in the early sixties once more created a need for additional supplies of elemental sulphur, Frasch producers responded by first eliminating their special discounts and concessions, and then by instituting sizable increases in the posted price on both the domestic and export markets. However, prices continued to be established on the basis of delivered costs to regional markets. The pattern of the early fifties was repeated as higher prices once again brought forth additional elemental sulphur onto the market by the tapping of marginal sources of supply. The rents earned by the lower-cost Frasch producers again increased to sizable proportions.

It now appears that sulphur prices will be established at the level required to bring in the additional amounts of elemental sulphur needed to fill the gap between the demand for elemental sulphur in world markets and the available supply from low-cost sources such as Frasch deposits. The price level will be related not to the marginal costs of the Frasch producers, but to the marginal costs of mining lower quality sulphur deposits and utilizing non-Frasch sources of supply to the extent required to bring the market into balance. It is likely that Frasch producers will continue to earn a significant amount of economic rent. However, the regionalization of sulphur markets and the continued practice of delivered pricing provide more room for flexibility in sulphur pricing today than at any time in the past. The greater number of suppliers of elemental sulphur should help to ensure this flexibility.

Other Standards of Competitive Performance

In addition to the level of profits and the relationship between costs and prices, industry studies have employed a number of other indicators of competitive performance. These include: plant-output relations (the existence of plants of optimum scale and the absence of chronic excess capacity); selling expenditures (as a measure of the degree of product differentiation); and progressiveness (the existence over time of innovation and technological change). None of these standards is particularly suitable for analyzing the performance of the Frasch sulphur industry. The industry appears to have achieved reasonable long-run efficiency in scale and capacity utilization. Selling expenditures are not significant, as might be expected for an industry producing a homogeneous commodity that is purchased by industrial buyers. The industry appears to have been progressive, although it is difficult to determine a standard for comparison. Consideration of these factors would not appear to add much to our understanding of the Frasch sulphur industry's performance.

Chapter 8

The Industry and the Resource

The Frasch segment of the sulphur industry is engaged in exploitation of an exhaustible resource. In evaluating the industry's performance the question arises, how effective has the industry been in utilizing this resource? Has the mining been efficient? Has there been an adequate investment in the discovery and development of new resources? Have consumers been assured of an adequate supply? These are questions closely related to the market structure of the industry and the market behavior of Frasch sulphur producers.[1]

An equally important consideration is the outlook for sulphur as a resource, and, in particular, the supply-demand balance that may be expected to prevail in coming years. Can expected future demands on the sulphur resource be met without substantial increases in cost? What extensions of the resource base are likely to occur?

Effective Utilization of the Sulphur Resource

The Frasch sulphur firms seem to have been very efficient in exploiting the sulphur resource. In particular, the practice of exploiting each deposit as a unit under single management has avoided the waste so often associated with multiple ownership of a specific block of resources. On the other hand, until the past decade, exploration for new Frasch sulphur deposits was undertaken almost entirely by petroleum firms. Indeed, most of the Frasch deposits were discovered in the process of petroleum exploration. As discussed in chapter 7, exploration expenditures in the Frasch sulphur industry have been extremely low in relation to the average net income of the firms in the industry or to the amount of percentage depletion which the industry receives.

As the analysis of the industry's development has demonstrated, resource development takes place in response to needs that are transmitted through the market mechanism, either through changes in the

1. See Edward S. Mason, "The Political Economy of Resource Use," in *Perspectives on Conservation,* ed. Henry Jarrett (Baltimore: The Johns Hopkins Press for Resources for the Future, Inc., 1958), pp. 157–86.

supply conditions for a given resource or through changes in the demand for that resource. In general, increases in supply occur in response to prices that yield above-normal profits and lead to entry and the development of sources of supply that have not previously been competitive. Decreases in supply occur through the closing of marginal mines in response to prices which yield below-normal profits and lead to the exit of firms from the industry. Changes on the demand side occur in response to a change in relative factor costs, i.e., a change in the cost of a given resource input as compared with the cost of alternative resource inputs will encourage consumers to attempt to alter their consumption of the resource.

For resource development to be responsive to the market, it is essential that the market mechanism be free of artificial impediments. During the period from 1922 to 1955, sulphur prices remained high enough to yield an above-normal rate of return to Frasch sulphur producers. Changes in supply did not occur, however, primarily because ownership by the existing producers of the high-quality deposits made the cost of entry into the Frasch segment of the industry too high. The existence of an international cartel controlling the entire supply of elemental sulphur over much of this period also acted to restrict the market and to permit Frasch producers to engage in entry-preventing pricing. The price of Frasch sulphur was maintained below the price at which other forms of sulphur could profitably be produced, but above the level that would lead to normal profits for Frasch producers. At the same time, the output of Frasch sulphur during this period was generally in excess of the quantity demanded, with the major producers maintaining large stocks. Since Frasch sulphur was easy to obtain and its price was below that of alternative inputs, industrial consumers were not encouraged to develop sulphur-saving innovations or switch to substitute inputs.

The shortage of sulphur in the late forties and early fifties was the result of several factors. First, development of at least one new deposit was held up during World War II by a shortage of plant and equipment.[2] Second, the postwar expansion in demand could not have been foreseen. Finally, attempts by the government to maintain sulphur prices in the face of expanding demand discouraged resource development and led to a situation where available supplies of sulphur had to be rationed among consumers. Consumers then turned to other sources of sulphur (for example, gypsum in England) and developed sulphur-conserving processes. After Frasch sulphur prices were freed from artificial control, the market reacted quickly and prices increased. At this point, entry did occur with the development of other sources of supply, including

2. See Haynes, *Brimstone: The Stone That Burns*, pp. 162–64.

Frasch sulphur in Mexico, and recovered sulphur in Canada, France, and the United States.

A second shortage of sulphur occurred in the period from 1964 to 1967. Since the turn in the market began in mid-1963, it would appear that the industry had ample time to increase capacity. However, several factors must be considered before a judgment can be made. First, a part of the shortage was caused by the failure of Mexican Frasch exports to increase as anticipated. Second, Freeport was the only domestic Frasch producer that could increase output significantly in the short run. Third, the supply of recovered sulphur is inelastic in the short run owing to its by-product nature, and Canadian and French producers could not increase output immediately. Finally, because elemental sulphur had been in ample supply at low prices for several years, many consumers had switched from pyrites, and the surge in demand fell primarily on elemental sulphur. There was also government intervention in this period to prevent the domestic Frasch price from increasing. Without a price increase, there was less incentive to search for other sources of supply or to reduce sulphur consumption.

The lesson that emerges is that when an industry is based upon a depletable resource, public policy should have a broader focus than influencing the number of firms in the industry or the price level. At the same time, the oligopolistic structure of the industry, and its vulnerability to antitrust investigation, should not be used by the government to achieve price stability during periods in which the market is out of adjustment. Rather, emphasis should be placed on potential new sources of supply, new technologies, and new applications of existing techniques, and efforts should be made to ensure that resource development is not impeded by artificial barriers, such as selective price controls and export cartels.

The Outlook for Sulphur as a Resource

The sulphur market's performance in the next decade will depend upon the growth in demand, the extent to which the resource base can be expanded to meet this growth, and the resulting cost of sulphur to consumers. In the following sections, factors affecting each of these elements are discussed.

Growth in demand

The simplest method of projecting aggregate sulphur demand is to assume that the demand for sulphur will continue to grow at about the same rate as industrial production. A long-run annual growth rate of 4.4 per cent in industrial production, the rate actually experienced over the period from 1947 to 1957, would imply a rise in annual sulphur consumption in the United States from 8 million long tons in 1965 to 12.3 million long tons in 1975. However, such projections assume that the pattern of sulphur consumption will not change. To test the validity of that assumption, potential changes in the industrial consumption of sulphur are examined below, first for industries other than the fertilizer industry, and then for the fertilizer industry.

The pattern of industrial consumption of sulphur remained very stable for many years, the major components being chemicals, inorganic pigments, iron and steel pickling, production of man-made fibers, petroleum refining, and pulp and paper manufacture. In recent years, however, the use of substitutes for sulphur (or sulphuric acid) has reduced sulphur's share of some of these major industrial markets. One of the primary reasons for substitution has been the difficulty of disposing of spent sulphuric acid and the high cost of regeneration. As public tolerance of pollution has diminished, the search for less offensive alternatives to sulphuric acid has proceeded in many industries.

In iron and steel pickling, a component representing about 4 per cent of total domestic sulphur demand, the consumption of sulphuric acid increased 23 per cent between 1963 and 1965, while consumption of hydrochloric acid during the same period rose fivefold.[3] Of the 75 large picklers in the United States, 57 have decided to switch to hydrochloric acid.[4] The primary reason is that hydrochloric acid presents much less of a disposal problem. In addition, spent sulphuric acid is 8 to 10 per cent acid and too costly to regenerate, while hydrochloric liquor is less than 0.1 per cent acid, and with one of the newer processes about 80 per cent of the acid can be recovered from the pickling bath. Also, hydrochloric processes are said to give a better looking sheet than sulphuric acid processes and overpickling is less of a problem.

The rate at which hydrochloric acid will replace sulphuric acid in iron and steel pickling is difficult to estimate. The average life of a pickling line is fifteen years, which offers opportunities for replacement. However, even though pickling is much faster with hydrochloric acid than with sulphuric acid, some of the existing pickling plants are too slow to take full advantage of the speed of the hydrochloric process. Thus, while new plants will probably use hydrochloric processes, many of the existing plants will not be converted from sulphuric acid. The best estimate is that use of hydrochloric acid will increase to 700,000 tons by 1970, while the use of sulphuric acid will fall to about 400,000 tons. This would represent a decline of over 60 per cent in consumption by the iron and steel industry.[5]

3. *Chemical and Engineering News* (6 September 1965), p. 107.

4. "Hydrochloric Acid Dominates Steel Pickling," *Chemical and Engineering News* (3 March 1969), p. 38.

5. *Ibid.*

Another application in which sulphuric acid is facing stiff competition is in the manufacture of inorganic pigments. Traditionally, titanium dioxide pigments have been made by digesting ilmenite ore with sulphuric acid. Because of the varying content of iron and other impurities in ilmenite ores, the quantity of sulphuric acid used in digestion varies between 3 to 4 tons per ton of titanium dioxide pigment. Titanium slag may also be used to manufacture pigment and thereby acid requirements are reduced to 1.0 to 1.5 tons per ton of pigment. In 1965, about 560,000 tons of sulphur were used in the United States in the manufacture of titanium dioxide pigments, representing 7 per cent of the total domestic sulphur demand.

In the late fifties, DuPont introduced a process for manufacturing titanium dioxide pigments from rutile ore using chlorine. This process has gained wide acceptance in recent years because of several factors. Construction costs are about 60 to 70 per cent less than those for the sulphuric acid leaching process. Waste from the chlorine process is about one-eighth of that from sulphuric acid, and chlorine disposal problems are reduced because the chlorine process is continuous and the chlorine recycled. The chlorine process also has a small cost advantage, despite the fact that it can only be used with rutile ore which costs over twice as much as ilmenite or titanium slag.

Two additional components of sulphur demand which appear to be diminishing are petroleum refining and pulp and paper manufacture. Use of sulphuric acid in petroleum refining is decreasing due to the increasing application of solvent-extraction and hydrogenation. Alkylation, a major user in the oil refining industry, is not expanding, mainly due to the changeover in aviation fuel from high octane to kerosene type fuels and the growing application of hydrofluoric in place of sulphuric acid. In pulp and paper manufacture, the newer sulphate process, which uses sodium sulphate, is steadily replacing the sulphite process which uses sulphuric acid. The principal advantage offered by the sulphate process is the possibility of recovery and regeneration, and the smaller pollution problem.

Only in its application in the manufacture of chemicals and man-made fibers does sulphur appear to have a favorable outlook among major consumers. The use of sulphuric acid in the chemical industry is so widespread that curtailment in its use in the manufacture of any single product would probably have little effect on total consumption by the industry, and there is no indication that its use in many or most product lines will decline. In the synthetic fiber industry, however, a great deal will depend on the product mix in the industry. (Table 21 depicts the 1965 product mix in the industry and the resulting sulphur requirements.) In the next few years, it is likely that rayon's share of the total man-made fiber market will diminish in favor of such newer

Table 21. The Use of Sulphur in Man-Made Fibers, 1965

Fiber	Fiber putput, 1965	Sulphur requirements
	million lbs.	*1,000 long tons*
Rayon	1,082	350
Acetate	445	22
Nylon 6 (Allied Chemical process)	712	132
Nylon 6/6 (DuPont process)	225	—
Polyester	361	3
Olefin	68	10
Acrylic	311	—
Spandex	8	—
Total		517

SOURCE: Interview with Delbert L. Rucker, Director of Information, The Sulphur Institute, Washington, D.C., 9 August 1966.

fibers as polyester and olefin which have much smaller sulphur requirements. In addition, at least two processes have been developed for the manufacture of rayon which use little or no sulphur. Nonetheless, barring a dramatic shift in product mix, the overall growth expected in the man-made fiber industry should mean that sulphur requirements will continue to expand.

In summary, the major characteristic of industrial consumption of sulphur other than by the fertilizer industry is that sulphur requirements will not increase as rapidly as demand for the products in which sulphur is used. Thus the share that sulphur holds in most of these industrial markets will continue to decline.

In recent years, the decline in certain industrial uses of sulphur has been more than offset by the increase in consumption of sulphur in the manufacture of fertilizers. For example, in 1963 fertilizer manufacture accounted for an estimated 40 per cent of total domestic sulphur consumption. It is estimated that about 77 per cent of the growth in demand for sulphur in the United States in the two ensuing years was for the fertilizer industry, with the result that by 1965, the fertilizer industry accounted for 45 per cent of total domestic sulphur consumption. It is likely, therefore, that the future growth in demand for sulphur will depend primarily upon the rate at which sulphur consumption expands in the manufacture of fertilizer.

The production of sulphur-containing fertilizers should continue to give strong impetus to growth of sulphur consumption over the next decade. Much of this growth will result from continued worldwide pressure on food production. Most of the world's agricultural lands including those in the United States can profitably utilize additional fertilization, and steep increases in fertilizer demand seem likely.

Sulphuric acid is used in the manufacture of both phosphatic and nitrogen fertilizers. (The amount of sulphur consumed in the manufacture of various types of fertilizer and the substantial growth in sulphur consumption by the fertilizer industry over the period from 1955 to 1965 are shown in table 22.) One of the most important factors behind the increased demand for sulphur for use in the manufacture of fertilizers has been the trend away from low-analysis fertilizers such as ammonium sulphate and normal superphosphate toward highly concentrated fertilizers such as triple superphosphate and ammonium phosphate. Since high-analysis fertilizers require up to 40 per cent more sulphur per unit of P_2O_5 in their manufacture, this trend has led to steadily increasing sulphur consumption by the fertilizer industry.

Table 22. Sulphur Used in Domestic Fertilizer Manufacture

Product	Analysis	Sulphur per ton	Sulphur consumption 1955	1962	1965
		lb.	(....	*million tons*	....)
Ammonium sulphate	21% N	521	0.5	0.4	0.6
Normal superphosphate	20% P_2O_5	268	0.9	0.7	0.7
Triple superphosphate	45% P_2O_5	597	0.4	0.5	0.9
Ammonium phosphate	18% N 46% P_2O_5	880	0.1	0.5	1.0
Other	—	—	—	0.3	0.5
Total			1.9	2.4	3.7

SOURCE: L. B. Gittinger, Jr., Assistant Vice President, Freeport Sulphur Company, in a talk to the Chemical Marketing Research Association, 3 May 1966.

The sulphur used in the manufacture of the low-analysis products, ammonium sulphate and normal superphosphate, is an end component of these materials. In fact, there is more sulphur than nitrogen in a bag of ammonium sulphate and more sulphur than phosphorus in a bag of normal superphosphate. On the other hand, phosphoric acid, triple superphosphate, and ammonium phosphates contain little or no sulphur and the movement toward high-analysis fertilizers may soon create a need for direct addition of sulphur as a secondary plant nutrient. Soil sulphur deficiencies, which limit crop yields, have been noted in various parts of the world, including Australia, New Zealand, and Brazil, and at least sixteen states in the United States.[6]

6. See *Sulphur, The Essential Plant Food Element* (Washington, D.C.: The Sulphur Institute, 1962). Also see David W. Bixby, Samuel L. Tisdale, and Delbert R. Rucker, *Adding Plant Nutrient Sulphur to Fertilizer*, Technical

While sulphur consumption by the fertilizer industry increased substantially from 1955 to 1965, substitution of either fertilizers or processes not requiring sulphur inputs may dampen future increases in the demand for sulphur by this industry. An example of the first type of substitution is the use of non-sulphur nitrogen fertilizers such as urea, anhydrous ammonia, and ammonium nitrates in place of ammonium sulphate. Since each of these substitutes is of higher analysis than ammonium sulphate, this movement, which has been occurring on a large scale, is taking place regardless of the need or desire to lessen sulphur requirements.

Substitution of the second type is likely to come by the introduction of different methods of making phosphoric acid. Today, over one-third of the sulphur consumed in the United States enters into the production of wet-process phosphoric acid. The substitute most commonly suggested for sulphuric acid in the manufacture of fertilizers is nitric acid. "The nitric phosphates processes are the most attractive sulphur-saving methods . . . any further increase in the cost of sulphur, or a shortage of sulphur, could initiate a phenomenal swing toward nitric phosphates."[7] Annual production of nitric phosphates in European countries totals several million tons. In the United States, however, nitrophosphates are presently being manufactured in only six plants.[8] These plants use either a process that employs a mixture of nitric and sulphuric acids, the extract being ammoniated to produce diammonium phosphate, ammonium nitrate, and calcium sulphate, or a process using a mixture of nitric acid and phosphoric acid. Thus, in both types of plants, sulphur requirements are reduced, but not eliminated. The Norwegian Odda process, which is widely used in Europe, removes the calcium nitrate by refrigeration and crystallization and requires neither sulphuric nor phosphoric acid.

It is estimated that nitric phosphates currently have a small but significant cost advantage over ammonium phosphates and ammonium

---

Bulletin Number 10, October 1964, The Sulphur Institute. One of the primary sources of sulphur today is the gas released into the atmosphere by the burning of fuels such as coal. The sulphurous gases are captured by moisture in the air and are deposited in the soil by rainfall, fog, smog, and dew. It has been estimated that in the United States plants receive about 11 million tons of sulphur each year from the atmosphere. If strong pollution abatement measures were enacted nationally, about half of this sulphur could be recovered. However, soils would be deprived of sulphur required for plant growth, thus creating an enlarged market for direct application of sulphur as a plant nutrient.

7. Travis P. Hignett, Director of Chemical Development, Tennessee Valley Authority, in a paper presented at the National Plant Food Institute Annual Convention, White Sulphur Springs, West Virginia, 7–9 June 1965.

8. "Fertilizer Process Bypasses Sulphuric Acid Entirely," *Chemical and Engineering News* (20 November 1967), p. 19.

nitrate in large plants.[9] However, incomplete water solubility and inflexibility in N-P ratios continue to present a severe marketing problem. Further, the need for a large-scale plant limits the adaptability of most phosphoric acid operations to the use of nitric acid.[10]

The furnace method of producing phosphoric acid contains none of the product difficulties associated with the nitric acid substitution. However, costs appear to be prohibitive at present. It has been estimated that, even if electric power were free, the furnace method could not compete so long as sulphur costs less than $39.50 per long ton.[11] Of course, where a producer has surplus phosphorus from making other products, such as detergents, he can afford to use the excess to produce phosphoric acid.

At present, no producer is likely to build a plant to produce hydrochloric acid for use in fertilizer manufacture. However, if he is producing hydrochloric acid for some other type of manufacturing operation that requires it, he might well invest his surplus production in the manufacture of phosphatic fertilizers.

In summary, demand for fertilizers should continue to expand over the next decade, both within the United States and abroad. The most dynamic growth area for sulphur consumption by the fertilizer industry appears to be phosphate fertilizers, which already account for about 36 per cent of U.S. sulphur consumption and more than 30 per cent of the free world sulphur consumption. The trend toward use of high-analysis phosphate fertilizers should continue, while consumption of low-analysis products will have limited growth. Since high-analysis products require 40 to 50 per cent more sulphur in their manufacture than low-analysis products, the average annual growth of sulphur consumption by the fertilizer industry will be higher than the rate of increase in fertilizer output. Substitution possibilities, both product and process, appear unlikely to affect this outcome significantly over the next decade.

Supply outlook

The world will require new sources of supply to meet the continuing growth in demand. Fortunately, relatively abundant reserves of sulphur are available, though at higher production costs, and technology already

9. Hignett, *loc. cit.* This view was also supported by David Bixby, Chemical Engineer with The Sulphur Institute, in an interview in Washington, D.C., 3–4 August 1966.

10. A 600-ton-per-day nitrophosphate plant would require about 90 tons per day of nitrogen. An economically sized ammonia plant, however, would produce 820 tons per day of nitrogen.

11. Information obtained from David W. Bixby, Chemical Engineer with The Sulphur Institute. This assumes a plant making 54 per cent phosacid, and producing 200 short tons of P_2O_5 per day.

exists to tap these additional supplies. Further, as these new sources of supply become more important, competitive pressures should act to improve technology and lower the cost of recovery. Table 23 summarizes the world resource situation of sulphur. While it includes all sources of supply which have been identified, table 23 should not be taken to imply that all sources will be tapped. The outlook for each major source of sulphur is described below, and the figures given in the table are qualified as to origin and meaning.

The lowest-cost form of sulphur is Frasch sulphur obtained from the salt domes of the U.S. Gulf Coast and the anticlines of the Isthmus of Tehuantepec in Mexico. The U.S. Bureau of Mines estimates the reserves of known offshore and onshore U.S. salt dome deposits at 200 million long tons.[12] Intensive past exploration by the oil and gas industry suggests that additional sulphur-impregnated domes will not be discovered on the mainland at depths favorable for the recovery of sulphur. However, there are abandoned onshore Frasch mines that can be reworked, and plans to reopen five such mines were announced during the most recent shortage.

The offshore area of the Gulf Coast has not been thoroughly explored for sulphur, and the extent of potential offshore reserves may not be known for several years. It is likely that additional deposits of sulphur will be discovered in the offshore area, but they may prove too costly to mine to be classified with other salt dome mines as law-cost sources. Offshore exploration is estimated to be five times as costly as onshore exploration, and operating costs offshore probably run at least 1.5 to 2.5 times higher than those for an onshore mine of similar size and quality.

Estimated reserves in known Mexican anticline deposits on the Isthmus of Tehuantepec range from 50 million to 60 million tons.[13] However, Mexican sources indicate that the bulk of the Tehuantepec area has not been carefully surveyed by geologists. Further exploration on the Isthmus will probably result in the discovery of additional deposits of sulphur, but the irregular structure of the Isthmus formations makes it difficult to estimate the commercially recoverable quantities that might be added.

Sulphur ore also occurs in volcanic, hot spring, sedimentary, and replacement deposits. The sulphur content of these native ore deposits is

12. Paul M. Ambrose, "Sulphur and Pyrites," in *Mineral Facts and Problems, 1965 Edition* (U.S. Department of the Interior, Bureau of Mines, Bulletin 630), p. 909.

13. Marlin E. Sandlin, Chairman of the Board of Pan American Sulphur Company, has indicated the company estimates its reserves at 50 million tons. See *Chemical Week* (8 May 1965), p. 27. Gulf Sulphur is thought to have 7 to 10 million tons of reserves.

Table 23. Estimated World Sulphur Resources

million long tons

Type and leading sources	Estimated resources
Elemental	
Frasch (salt dome)	250*
United States	200
Mexico	50*
Native	410*
United States	50*
Poland	100
Iraq	150*
Andes	75
Japan	35
Recovered	850*
United States:	
Gas	10*
Petroleum	45
Canada: Gas	350
France: Gas	35
Middle East:	
Gas	75
Petroleum	200
Rest of World:	
Gas	35
Petroleum	100
Oil shale, tar sands, and similar material	830*
United States	50
Canada	780
Nonelemental	
Metal sulphides	1,250*
United States	125
Spain: Pyrites	375
Other	750*
Anhydrite and gypsum	Enormous
Coal	15,000
United States	5,000
Sea water	Enormous

SOURCES: The information given represents a summary of available estimates of sulphur resources. It combines estimates of proven reserves with those of potential reserves. Where a range of estimates have been made, a representative figure has been arbitrarily selected. Those estimates thought to be conservative are noted. See Paul H. Ambrose, "Sulphur and Pyrites," *Mineral Facts and Problems, 1965 Edition* (U.S. Department of the Interior, Bureau of Mines, Bulletin 630), p. 909; "Sulphur Market Tight; Reserves Adequate," *The Oil and Gas Journal* (27 November 1967), pp. 71–74; and Arthur D. Little, Inc., *The Free World Sulphur Outlook* (April 1966).

NOTE: See the text section, "Supply outlook," for comments on the origin and meaning of the estimates in this table.

* Published estimates thought to be conservative.

similar to that of the Gulf Coast salt dome deposits—20 to 40 per cent—though occasional deposits contain up to 95 per cent sulphur. Most of these native ore deposits are located in remote areas, many of them are quite small, and production and transportation costs are higher than for either Frasch or recovered sulphur. In general, these sources are used to supply local markets. However, a large native sulphur deposit in the Mishraq area of northern Iraq is thought to be commercially feasible. Early in 1968, twelve companies were reported to be bidding for this deposit. The Iraq government was said to be demanding royalties of 80 per cent of net profits and requiring construction by 1972 of a million-ton-per-year plant and distribution facilities, estimated to cost about $40 million. The cost of sulphur from this deposit, delivered to the nearest port, Basra on the Persian Gulf, was estimated to be about $25 per ton.[14]

In the United States, small hot spring, volcanic, and sedimentary native sulphur deposits have been found in the Rocky Mountain and western states. Perhaps the most important domestic sulphur-bearing formations, outside the salt domes of the Gulf Coast, occur in Pecos County and Culbertson County, Texas. Two firms are attempting to mine the Pecos County deposit which is estimated to contain between 10 and 30 million tons of sulphur.[15] The Culbertson County deposit, being mined by the Duval Corporation, is estimated to have reserves of 50 million tons.[16]

The largest known deposits of volcanic ores occur in the 3,000 mile Andes Mountain chain in South America, where reserves have been estimated to contain as much as 100 million tons of sulphur.[17] The most important of the 100-odd deposits are found in Chile, where occurrences of high-grade (45 to 95 per cent) sulphur are estimated at 40 million tons. Similar deposits, generally having lower sulphur content, are known to exist in Peru, Argentina, Bolivia, Colombia, Ecuador, Mexico, Venezuela, Costa Rica, and the Galapagos Islands.

Japan has at least forty known deposits of volcanic sulphur with sulphur content estimated as ranging from 25 to 50 million tons.[18] Other Asiatic countries and many European countries also have volcanic

14. Thomas O'Hanlan, "The Great Sulphur Rush," *Fortune* (March 1968), p. 211.

15. F. F. Netzeband, Thomas R. Early, J. P. Ryan, and W. C. Miller, *Sulphur Resources and Production in Texas, Louisiana, Missouri, Oklahoma, Arkansas, Kansas, and Mississippi, and Markets for the Sulphur* (U.S. Department of the Interior, Bureau of Mines, Information Circular 8222, 1964), p. 11.

16. James C. Tanner, "Brimstone Supplies in 1968 Seen Equaling Consumption: Prices Start to Level Off," *The Wall Street Journal* (26 August 1968), p. 28.

17. Ambrose, *Mineral Facts and Problems, 1965 Edition,* p. 910.

18. W. T. Lundy, "Known and Potential Sulphur Resources of the World," *Industrial and Engineering Chemistry* (November 1950), p. 2200.

sulphur deposits, but most of them are too small and too remote to be considered as recoverable reserves under almost any conditions.

The most important sedimentary deposits are found in the southeastern portion of Poland in the Tarnobrzeg basin. Reserves are estimated at 108 million long tons.[19] Open-pit mining is employed with flotation and filtration processing. Experiments are also underway with hot water and chemical solvent processes in an effort to reduce costs. The Solec-Grzybow deposit, a smaller but significant source located in the same area, is also being developed. Other areas having large sedimentary deposits include the U.S.S.R., Sicily, and mainland China.

The most important addition to the world's elemental sulphur reserves since the Korean War sulphur shortage has been the increased recovery of elemental sulphur from sour natural and refinery gases. Since the factors governing the availability of elemental sulphur from natural gas are quite different from those governing availability from petroleum, the two sources of recovered sulphur are considered separately below.

The sulphur content of U.S. natural gas averages about 0.05 per cent by weight. The sulphur content occurs as hydrogen sulphide in concentrations ranging from none to 70 per cent. In Canada, the concentration of hydrogen sulphide in gas presently being processed ranges from 1.0 to 38.1 per cent. Several of the planned recovery operations in the Middle East will be processing gas having a hydrogen sulphide content of 10 to 15 per cent. French plants at Lacq and nearby Mellion process gas which has a 5 to 15 per cent hydrogen sulphide concentration. Current technology enables the extraction of up to 95 per cent of the sulphur contained in the gas stream.

When it comes to estimating the reserves of sulphur that might be recovered from the gas fields, it is difficult to set a standard criterion for inclusion. Gas transported to fuel markets must be "sweetened" (the sulphur removed) if the hydrogen sulphide content is too high. If the gas contains more than 0.25 grain of sulphur per 100 cubic feet it is generally disqualified for sale to domestic consumers (0.25 grain is approximately 0.078 per cent sulphur by weight or 0.83 per cent hydrogen sulphide by weight). This suggests that natural gas fields with a sulphur content of over 0.078 per cent by weight should properly be considered as sulphur reserves *provided* a market exists for the gas, for if the gas is to be marketed the hydrogen sulphide must be removed. Natural gas fields having sulphur concentrations lower than 0.078 per cent by weight should not be included in reserve estimates unless sulphur prices increase substantially. Sour gas fields having concentrations

19. See "Poland Pushes Ambitious Chemical Plans," *Chemical and Engineering News* (5 October 1964), p. 65.

of sulphur above the maximum allowable but without access to markets must be treated individually.[20]

Reasonably accurate reserve estimates have been developed for sour gas fields in Canada, France, and the United States where sulphur is presently being recovered. For other areas of the world, only very rough approximations can be made. The U.S. Bureau of Mines estimates domestic sour gas sulphur reserves at 7 million tons from proven gas fields.[21] They might be five to ten times as high if they included gas not yet proven. The potential reserves of sulphur in the sour gas fields of Alberta have recently been estimated by the Canadian Petroleum Association at 350 million tons.[22] In making this estimate, the ratio of present proved sulphur reserves to proved reserves of natural gas with which they are associated was applied to the estimates of potential reserves of natural gas. Estimates of reserves at the two sour gas fields in France range from 25 to 50 million tons. Based on proven reserves in excess of 10 trillion cubic feet of gas, having an average concentration of hydrogen sulphide of 15 per cent, and allowing for 80 per cent recovery, an estimate of 35 million tons appears reasonable.

Middle East sour gas reserves are difficult to estimate. In 1965, Iran announced the discovery of a major sour gas field at Masjed Soleymān. Other sour gas fields exist in Iraq, Kuwait, and Saudi Arabia. Estimates of sulphur reserves in the Middle East range from 50 to 250 million tons, but a range of 50 to 100 million tons seems more realistic.[23] The distance of these fields from markets for natural gas means that only the development of fields with the highest hydrogen sulphide concentrations would be feasible. A recent study indicated that it might be more economical to import ammonia into the United States than to bring in LNG feedstock to make it here.[24] Such a development would have important implications for the development of sour gas fields in the Middle East. Gas from these fields might be processed to remove the natural gas liquids and sulphur for use in a local fertilizer complex. The gas could then be recycled into the formation, and the fertilizers exported. Thus, future development of sour gas fields in this area might not have to rely on a nearby market developing for the gas.

20. Arthur D. Little, Inc., *The Free World Sulphur Outlook* (April 1966), pp. 39–40.

21. Ambrose, *Mineral Facts and Problems, 1965 Edition*, p. 909.

22. U.S. Department of the Interior, Bureau of Mines, *Mineral Trade Notes* (July 1969), pp. 29–30.

23. Estimate made by H. W. Manley, president and managing director of Jefferson Lake Petrochemicals of Canada, Ltd., and cited in "Sulphur Market Tight; Reserves Adequate," *The Oil and Gas Journal* (27 November 1967), p. 73.

24. See "Ammonia Going One Way, Sulphur Another," *The Oil and Gas Journal* (16 October 1967), pp. 70–71.

Crude oils have widely varying sulphur content, ranging from 0.04 per cent (Pennsylvania) to 4.5 per cent (Mexico). In the United States the average sulphur content of crude petroleum is 0.6 per cent. Crudes containing higher amounts are usually blended with low-sulphur crude oils. In the past, because of the added difficulty of processing high-sulphur crude, many sources of high-sulphur crude were bypassed in favor of low-sulphur content crude. However, in recent years, it has become necessary to process crudes with an increasingly higher average sulphur content.

Refinery gases, but not heavy oil fractions, are generally desulphurized, and altogether only a small fraction of the contained sulphur is recovered from the crude. This leads to widely varying methods of estimating sulphur availability in crude oil. Thus, as with natural gas, estimates of recoverable sulphur contained in proven world petroleum reserves must be vague. It has been estimated conservatively that recoverable sulphur content in world proven oil reserves amounts to 330 million long tons.[25] Since proven oil reserves are a conservative measure, sulphur resources measured more broadly (including undiscovered pools, unproved portions of known fields, and secondary recovery) could be as much as 10 to 20 times the above estimate.

Large potential reserves of sulphur exist in the known deposits of other hydrocarbons such as bituminous rock, tar sands, and shale oil, but the range of estimates is very wide, depending on the estimator's judgment of the timing and feasibility of developing the hydrocarbon resource itself.

Operations began in 1967 to recover synthetic crude oil from the Athabasca tar sands in Alberta, which have an average sulphur content of 5 per cent by weight. Through February 1969, 13,165,761 barrels of raw bitumen had been processed, yielding 34,675 tons of sulphur. If future production is in the same ratio, the potential reserves of sulphur can be calculated at 780 million tons.[26] This estimate does not include the sulphur reserves of the Cold Lake oil sands in Northern Alberta, reported to contain 4 to 5 per cent sulphur, or those associated with certain structures in the Arctic Islands.[27] Based on estimated oil content in tar sands deposits of 2.6 billion barrels for the United States and 490 billion barrels for the world, and assuming a recovery factor

25. Arthur D. Little, Inc., *loc. cit.*, p. 41. Manley (cf. footnote 23) estimates proved reserves of sulphur in sour petroleum crude oil at 40 million tons and probable reserves at an additional 800 million tons.

26. U.S. Department of the Interior, Bureau of Mines, *Mineral Trade Notes* (July 1969), pp. 29–30. This is the estimate made by the Canadian Petroleum Association.

27. *Ibid.* Also, see "Where Are the Largest Native Sulphur Reserves?" *Oilweek* (7 April 1969), p. 23.

of 60 per cent, the sulphur content of bituminous rock and tar sands would be 10 million tons for the United States and 2 billion tons for the world.[28]

Shale oil, which to date has not been exploited in the United States, has an estimated sulphur content of 0.75 per cent. Assuming that estimated deposits could eventually yield 850 billion barrels for the United States and 1,297 billion barrels for the world, the sulphur contained in shale oil would be 846 million tons for the United States and 1,290 million tons for the world.[29] However, using a conservative approach toward the exploitability of shale, the Bureau of Mines places domestic sulphur reserves from this source at only 50 million tons.[30]

Metal sulphides, such as iron-bearing pyrites and various nonferrous ores that are smelted or refined for their copper, lead, and zinc content, are important sources of sulphur. These are widely distributed and can be found in all types of rocks. Practically all of the sulphur in nonferrous sulphides is released as sulphur dioxide in waste gas, and is normally recovered only when plants are located near sulphuric acid markets. Potential world reserves of sulphur in metal sulphides are estimated to be 1 to 1.5 billion tons.[31] The U.S. Bureau of Mines estimates that 100 to 150 million tons of sulphur content are available in domestic sulphides alone.[32] The principal producing countries for nonferrous sulphides are Japan, the United States, Canada, and the U.S.S.R. Spain has the largest reserves of pyrites, about 1 billion tons of ore. Other important sources are the U.S.S.R., China, Canada, Cyprus, France, West Germany, India, Italy, Japan, the Philippines, Norway, Portugal, Sweden, Turkey, Brazil, and North Korea. But given the very wide dispersal and the variety of conditions under which sulphur may or may not be recovered, these estimates actually list only rough orders of magnitude of eventually recoverable resources.

Sulphur may also be obtained from anhydrite and gypsum (calcium sulphate). Reserves of these sources are enormous and widely dispersed throughout the world. Gypsum is decomposed in the presence of silica, alumina, and carbon to produce sulphur dioxide and portland cement. The Elcor Chemical Company of Midland, Texas, is reported to have developed a process that permits the recovery of one ton of sulphur from about ten tons of gypsum, and the company has constructed a

28. Arthur D. Little, Inc., *loc. cit.*, p. 44.

29. *Ibid.*

30. Ambrose, in *Mineral Facts and Problems, 1965 Edition,* p. 909.

31. Lundy, *loc. cit.*, p. 2201, cites an estimate of world reserves of pyrites of 908 million tons, made in 1926 by the 14th International Geological Congress at Madrid, with the warning that subsequent discoveries may have caused reserves to increase by 50 per cent or more.

32. Ambrose, in *Mineral Facts and Problems, 1965 Edition,* p. 909.

350,000-ton-per-year recovery plant in Texas.[33] Gypsum and anhydrite are also reacted with ammonia and carbon to produce ammonium sulphate. In recent years, the United Kingdom has met its need for additional sulphur by using more anhydrite. For example, 700,000 tons of anhydrite can be substituted for 140,000 tons of sulphur for the manufacture of 400,000 short tons of sulphuric acid, with the residue from the decomposition of the anhydrite being used to manufacture cement.[34]

Coal is another substantial source of sulphur. At the present time, the sulphur content is generally discharged to the atmosphere as sulphur dioxide in stack gases, although some is recovered in Europe. According to the U.S. Bureau of Mines, the average sulphur content of U.S. coal is about 2.6 per cent. The sulphur content of recoverable U.S. coal reserves alone, taken at a conservative 220 billion tons, would come to 5 billion tons or more.[35] How much of the sulphur content will be recovered is another matter, depending not only on the amount of coal that will be burned, but on the fraction that will be considered as innocuous if left in the stack gas and on the economy of the recovery process.

The final source of sulphur is the sea. Sulphur is the fourth most abundant element in sea water following chlorine, sodium, and magnesium, but unless sulphur is obtained as a by-product in the production of rarer minerals from sea salts, there is no foreseeable economic justification for investment in the advanced technology required to extract sulphur from the sea.

About 4 billion tons of sulphur are potentially available from sources considered either to be economic or to approach economic exploitation levels, and some of these sources (Frasch, native, recovered, and pyrites) may prove to have substantially higher reserves. Coal, gypsum, anhydrite, and sea water provide an enormous backup potential which brings the sulphur content of known sources to over 20 billion tons. The question, then, is not whether or not the resource base can expand to meet increases in demand, but, rather, at what price additional supplies of sulphur will be forthcoming, and in what order.

Outlook implications

This brief survey of the demand and supply outlook for sulphur, coupled with the earlier analysis of the industry's development, makes

33. O'Hanlan, *loc. cit.*, p. 212. Also, see "Trouble Ahead for Non-Frasch Sulphur?" *Chemical Week* (28 December 1968), p. 8, where Elcor officials are quoted as saying that there is enough gypsum on the company's 28,000 acre tract to last 100 years at the present rate of mining.

34. See "Acid from Indigenous Anhydrite," *Chemical Trade Journal and Chemical Engineer* (London: 20 May 1965), p. 618.

35. Ambrose, in *Mineral Facts and Problems, 1965 Edition,* p. 909.

possible some general conclusions regarding the future course of the industry. Demand for sulphur should continue to expand over the next decade at a rate equal to, or perhaps slightly above, the rate of growth in industrial production, depending on the degree to which losses in some of its industrial markets are offset by increases in the demand for sulphur for use in fertilizers. On the supply side, there are ample reserves of low-cost sulphur (including both domestic and foreign Frasch and recovered sulphur) to ensure that forthcoming demands will be met notwithstanding temporary dislocations. However, *with present recovery techniques,* supplies may become available at slightly higher prices than those that prevailed from 1926 to 1964. Moreover, the geographical dispersion of the primary sources of supply will tend to create regional markets for sulphur, differentiated by differences in freight costs.

At the same time, prices for sulphur should become increasingly the result of competition. The domestic Frasch industry can no longer supply the world's elemental sulphur needs. The new sources of supply have created a competitive environment for this industry. Domestic and foreign Frasch producers will continue to earn an economic rent as a reward for possession of the lowest-cost sources of supply, but the amount of that rent should diminish over time as these low-cost sources are depleted.

To anticipate both a more competitive price structure for sulphur and higher prices for sulphur consumers as well may appear paradoxical. However, if changes in technology lead to lower recovery costs, the more competitive environment will help to ensure that prices to consumers will also be lower.

Chapter 9

Summary and Conclusions

Analysis of the market structure, behavior, and performance of the Frasch sulphur industry was undertaken with the view in mind of investigating the use of market power and evaluating the implications of such use for the public welfare. The purpose of this chapter is to summarize the important aspects of the domestic sulphur industry's market structure, behavior, and performance and to set forth the author's conclusions regarding the workability of competition in the industry.

Characteristics of the Industry—Summary

Market structure

1. The U.S. Frasch sulphur industry came into existence at the turn of the century when a unique technological innovation gave producers using the Frasch process a significant cost advantage over the Sicilian native sulphur industry, which had been supplying most of the world's elemental sulphur. (Chapter 2, pp. 11–14.)

2. The U.S. Frasch sulphur industry has been one of few sellers. From 1896 to 1912, Union Sulphur Company enjoyed a complete monopoly on Frasch sulphur production by virtue of the patent granted to its founder, Dr. Herman Frasch. In 1912, Freeport Sulphur Company entered the industry, followed in 1919 by Texas Gulf Sulphur Company. In 1925, depletion of its mine forced Union to cease production. In 1928, Duval Texas Sulphur Company entered the industry, followed four years later by Jefferson Lake Sulphur Company. From 1932 to 1968, these four companies controlled the entire Frasch sulphur output of the United States, with Texas Gulf and Freeport accounting for nearly 90 per cent. The industry is not only concentrated, but production is centralized in a few mines located within a small region of the Texas and Louisana Gulf Coast. (Chapter 2, pp. 14–20.)

3. Frasch sulphur currently accounts for about 75 per cent of the

total output of sulphur in the United States, and about 85 per cent of domestic production of elemental sulphur. Most of the other U.S. elemental sulphur is recovered from sour natural or refinery gases. The primary form of nonelemental sulphur is pyrites. While all forms of elemental sulphur are perfect substitutes for one another, the degree of substitutability between elemental and nonelemental sulphur is limited. (Chapter 1, pp. 1–2.)

4. Foreign sources currently account for about 47 per cent of the total output of elemental sulphur in non-Communist countries, Mexico, Canada, and France having become important suppliers in the 1950s. (Chapter 2, pp. 20–33.)

5. Sulphur is used in an extremely large number of chemical and manufacturing processes, predominantly in the form of sulphuric acid, the production of which currently absorbs 86 per cent of sulphur output. There is no formal commodity exchange for sulphur. In general, it is sold on a contract basis directly to industrial consumers. Two important changes in sulphur marketing took place in 1959: a switch from solid to liquid delivery of Frasch sulphur, accompanied by an expansion in the number of services provided for customers; and a change from prices quoted f.o.b. mines or Gulf port to pricing on a delivered basis at regional terminals. Over most of its history, the Frasch sulphur industry has handled the bulk of its exports through a Webb-Pomerene Export Association, the Sulphur Export Corporation (Sulexco). (Chapter 4, pp. 50–52 and 55–64.)

6. The demand for Frasch sulphur is derived from the demand for the products in which it is used. Demand is inelastic in the short run, but becomes more elastic in the long run since there are few unique uses for sulphur. Demand for Frasch sulphur is subject to only moderate seasonal fluctuations. In the past there has been a strong correlation between demand for sulphur and the index of industrial production, reflecting the pervasive use of sulphur throughout the industrial sector of the economy. Thus, demand is responsive to cyclical fluctuations in business conditions, and expands when industrial production rises. (Chapter 4, pp. 52–55 and 64–66.)

7. Investment costs per unit of capacity decline significantly with increases in the scale of plant. Engineering cost analysis reveals that about 75 per cent of total production costs are variable in nature. The crucial determinant of cost is the water ratio, i.e., the number of gallons of hot water required to produce a ton of sulphur. Water ratios vary with the quality of the deposit being worked and range from as low as 1,000 gallons to as high as 12,000 gallons of hot water per ton of sulphur recovered. Plants having identical water ratios experience decreasing average unit costs with increases in plant scale over the range of plant sizes currently found in the industry. By the same token, the

average unit costs of plants of identical size were found to vary directly with the water ratio. However, the water ratio is more important than plant size in determining the level of average unit costs. Thus, Frasch sulphur unit production costs reflect the existence of substantial internal economies of scale, resulting from savings realized in the use of fixed factors as plant size increases. When the industry is operating at full capacity, it is not possible to increase output in the short run without increasing average costs per ton. (Chapter 3, pp. 34–42 and 47–49.)

8. Entry into the Frasch sulphur industry is very difficult, the principal barrier being one of absolute cost resulting from control by the established producers of the better deposits. Neither product differentiation nor economies of scale seemed to constitute a major barrier to entry. (Chapter 3, pp. 42–47.)

Market behavior

9. Shipments of Frasch sulphur are subject to some seasonal variation. However, seasonal and irregular fluctuations in monthly consumption were found to be unimportant in earlier years because producers maintained extraordinarily large inventories. Production schedules were found to lag behind demand changes by as much as six months to a year. Inventories began to decline after producers had shifted in 1959 to liquid delivery of sulphur, and from 1962 to 1968 shipments exceeded production. (Chapter 5, pp. 69–74.)

10. Frasch sulphur production has grown steadily. While movements in production roughly coincide with cyclical movements in industrial activity, the correspondence is far from exact, particularly in the past decade. (Chapter 5, pp. 74–75.)

11. Frasch sulphur prices were found to belong to the class of prices commonly termed "administered"—they did not move to equate short-run demand and supply. Posted prices changed only once between 1926 and 1947, and only seven times between 1926 and 1964. In recent years, sulphur prices have risen to the highest levels in the industry's history in the face of a worldwide shortage of sulphur. There is no general trend in Frasch sulphur prices over the history of the industry, though definable shorter-term elements can be isolated. Net realized prices for exports were consistently higher than those for domestic shipments. In general, however, the direction and timing of movements in net realized prices for both export and domestic shipments coincided with movements in the posted price. The only period in which major departures were noted was between 1957 and 1963 when posted prices remained stable, but net realizations on both export and domestic shipments continued to decline. (Chapter 5, pp. 75–78, Chapter 6, fig. 13, p. 98.)

12. Price discrimination between the domestic and export markets was found to have existed over the industry's history with the exception of the period from 1960 to 1964. Higher prices on the export market prior to 1940 were found to have been closely related to the cartel agreements reached by the Sulphur Export Corporation and major foreign producers of elemental sulphur. (Chapter 5, pp. 78–82.)

Performance

13. Analysis of the rate of return earned by the industry on average invested capital revealed an abnormally high rate of return averaging 23.60 per cent from 1919 to 1953. While data on profits and invested capital pertaining to Frasch operations alone are only partially complete for the period since 1953, evidence indicates that rates of return remained above normal until about 1955 and then fell consistently until 1963. Investigation also disclosed that the average rates of return for the four firms in the industry had ranged from a high of 26.35 per cent for Texas Gulf to a low of 13.68 per cent for Freeport. (Chapter 7, pp. 111–17.)

14. The high rates of return in the sulphur industry were shown to have prevailed despite the fact that large royalty payments were made to the owners of the mineral rights to salt dome properties, mainly large oil companies. The 23 per cent depletion allowance on sulphur contributed to the high earnings of firms in the industry. But because sulphur deposits are almost always found in the search for oil, the effectiveness of the depletion allowance as an incentive to search for additional sulphur reserves has been modest, as evidenced by the fact that exploration expenditures in the past have been low in relation to the net income of firms in the industry and the amount of depletion which the industry receives. (Chapter 7, pp. 117–21.)

15. Frasch sulphur prices have not in general been closely related to the level of marginal cost. Prior to 1955, the Frasch sulphur industry was a pure open oligopoly (few firms, homogeneous product, high barriers to entry), and domestic prices were established to maximize industry profits. Export prices were determined by the Sulphur Export Corporation and, from 1926 to 1940, Sulexco set export prices through a cartel agreement with the Sicilian producers. Export prices exceeded domestic prices in part reflecting the higher marginal costs of the Sicilians. After 1955, the entry into the industry of two Mexican Frasch producers and the development of competition from recovered sulphur production in Canada and France significantly altered the market structure and behavior of Frasch firms. The expansion in demand in recent years resulted in marginal costs becoming more important in the determination of Frasch prices. However, it is the marginal costs of pro-

ducing sulphur from lower quality deposits and non-Frasch sources that determine Frasch prices. The major Frasch producers are able to earn significant amounts of economic rent. (Chapter 7, pp. 121–26.)

16. The industry was found to have utilized the sulphur resource effectively. In particular, the practice of unit management of deposits has fostered efficient mining practices. (Chapter 8, pp. 127–29.)

17. The outlook for sulphur as a resource is for continuing growth in demand, with increased consumption of sulphur in fertilizers more than offsetting a loss of market share in some industrial markets. The supply of sulphur should be adequate to meet foreseeable demands, but increased supplies will become available at prices slightly above those prevailing over the period from 1926 to 1964 unless there are improvements over current recovery techniques. At the same time, increased competition among sources should exert downward pressure on sulphur prices. (Chapter 8, pp. 129–44.)

Is the Frasch Sulphur Industry Workably Competitive?

As pointed out in the introductory chapter, the key elements in any evaluation of the workability of competition in an industry are the degree to which actual performance has departed from desired performance and the possibility of remedial public action. Over most of its life the Frasch sulphur industry has not performed in a competitive manner. The record of stable prices and soaring profits in the face of a constant expansion in investment in the industry clearly indicates the dominance of monopolistic elements. These elements have been dormant in recent years and are unlikely to reappear now that there is competition from other sources of sulphur.

The scarcity of low-cost Frasch sulphur deposits has limited the industry to a few firms, and the differential quality of the workable deposits gives power over the market to at best one or two firms. The strongest factor working to make the Frasch industry perform competitively is the existence of other sources of sulphur. Much of the competitive pressure from other sources of supply has come from foreign producers.

In recent years, the development of the Frasch deposits of Mexico and the growth in recovery of sulphur from sour natural gas in Western Canada and France, have challenged the market power held by domestic Frasch producers. Because sulphur could be produced from these sources at a cost competitive with U.S. Frasch sulphur produced on the Gulf Coast, the foreign suppliers were able to bring pressure to bear on both the domestic and export markets. As shown in this study, this pressure resulted in lower prices, increased customer services, and reduced profits for domestic Frasch producers. Although prices and profits recovered before long and have recently climbed to historic highs, it is unlikely that the Frasch industry can ever return to its pre-1957 structure. Other sources of supply, both domestic and foreign, should become increasingly important over the next decade.

It is perhaps unlikely that the Frasch sulphur industry can be made truly competitive. In the long run, the fate of competition in the sulphur industry will rest on the expansion of the resource base. The discovery of new sources of supply, innovations reducing the cost of existing sources of supply, and the development of substitutes for use in some of the processes that currently require sulphur offer the best possibilities for protecting the interests of the public. The task of public policy should be to make certain that the market is sufficiently free of artificial restraints to enable these forces to exert their full influence.

Appendixes

APPENDIX A

Statistics on Production, Trade, Consumption, and Prices

Table A-1. U.S. Sulphur Output from All Sources, 1880 to 1967

thousand long tons

		By-product sulphur				Pyrites		
Year	Native sulphur	Gas & coal	Cu, Zn mining	Hydrogen sulphide	By-product total	Ore	Sulphur content	Total
	(1)	(2)	(3)	(4)	(5)	(6)	(7)	(8)
1880	0.54					2.0	0.9	1.8
1881	.54					10.0	4.5	6.4
1882	.54					12.0	5.4	7.6
1883	.89					25.0	11.0	15.0
1884	.45					35.0	16.0	20.0
1885	.64					49.0	22.0	30.0
1886	2.23					55.0	25.0	35.0
1887	2.68					52.0	23.0	34.0
1888	0					54.3	24.0	31.0
1889	.40					93.7	42.0	54.0
1890	0					99.9	45.0	58.0
1891	1.07					106.0	48.0	63.0
1892	2.40					110.0	50.0	67.0
1893	1.07					75.9	34.0	45.0
1894	.45					106.0	48.0	62.0
1895	1.61					99.5	45.0	61.0
1896	4.70					116.0	52.0	74.0
1897	2.03					143.0	64.0	85.0
1898	1.07					193.0	87.0	114.0
1899	4.31					175.0	79.0	107.0
1900	3.15					205.0	92.0	122.0
1901	6.87					235.0	106.0	145.0
1902	7.44					200.0	90.0	125.0
1903	7.38					226.0	102.0	140.0
1904	85.00					207.0	93.0	232.0
1905	220.00					253.0	114.0	425.0
1906	295.00					261.0	117.0	530.0
1907	189.00					247.0	111.0	390.0
1908	364.00					223.0	100.0	590.0
1909	274.00					247.0	111.0	490.0
1910	247					242	109	460
1911	205		99		100	302	140	440
1912	788		139		140	351	160	1,090
1913	491		143		140	341	150	780
1914	418		173		170	337	150	740
1915	521		205		200	394	180	900
1916	650		264		260	439	200	1,110
1917	1,134		330		330	483	220	1,680
1918	1,354		n.a.		255	464	210	1,820
1919	1,191		184		180	421	170	1,540

Table A-1. (Continued)

Year	Native sulphur	By-product sulphur: Gas & coal	By-product sulphur: Cu, Zn mining	By-product sulphur: Hydrogen sulphide	By-product sulphur: By-product total	Pyrites: Ore	Pyrites: Sulphur content	Total
	(1)	(2)	(3)	(4)	(5)	(6)	(7)	(8)
1920	1,255		279		280	311	120	1,660
1921	1,880		140		140	157	70	2,090
1922	1,831		n.a.		160	173	80	2,070
1923	2,036		178		180	191	80	2,300
1924	1,221		198		200	168	70	1,490
1925	1,409		228		230	194	80	1,720
1926	1,890		236		240	227	70	2,220
1927	2,112	2.5	236		240	303	120	2,470
1928	1,982	2.5	264		270	313	113	2,365
1929	2,362	2.5	286		290	334	121	2,773
1930	2,559	2.5	269		272	343	124	2,955
1931	2,129	2.5	196		198	331	121	2,448
1932	890	2.5	136		138	190	66	1,094
1933	1,406	2.5	139		142	284	108	1,656
1934	1,422	1.5	131		132	432	168	1,722
1935	1,633	1.5	137		139	514	203	1,975
1936	2,016	1.5	166		167	547	217	2,400
1937	2,742	1.5	189		191	584	232	3,165
1938	2,393	4.0	156		160	556	219	2,772
1939	2,091	4.0	177	13	194	519	220	2,505
1940	2,732	4	191	16	211	627	262	3,205
1941	3,139	5	208	21	234	645	270	3,643
1942	3,461	5	218	19	242	720	307	4,010
1943	2,540	5	279	18	302	802	337	3,179
1944	3,219	19	263	22	304	789	333	3,856
1945	3,754	25	246	19	290	723	296	4,340
1946	3,862	35	209	18	262	813	337	4,461
1947	4,443	43	212	21	276	941	392	5,111
1948	4,870	44	187	26	257	929	388	5,515
1949	4,747	57	167	38	262	888	378	5,387
1950	5,193	142	216	42	400	931	393	5,986
1951	5,280	184	241	60	485	1,018	433	6,198
1952	5,295	252	253	67	572	994	418	6,285
1953	5,194	342	253	80	675	923	380	6,249
1954	5,579	359	259	73	691	909	405	6,675
1955	5,800	399	325	94	818	1,007	410	7,028
1956	6,484	465	348	89	902	1,070	432	7,818
1957	5,579	511	391	88	990	1,067	436	7,005
1958	4,646	640	360	92	1,092	974	403	6,141
1959	4,640	686	317	88	1,091	1,057	437	6,168
1960	5,037	767	345	95	1,207	1,016	416	6,660
1961	5,477	858	332	106	1,296	987	399	7,172
1962	5,025	900	355	98	1,353	916	379	6,757
1963	4,882	947	356	116	1,419	825	344	6,645
1964	5,228	1,021	366	123	1,510	847	354	7,092
1965	6,116	1,215	388	139	1,742	875	354	8,212
1966	7,001	1,240	424	134	1,798	872	356	10,953
1967	7,014	1,268	364	134	1,766	861	355	10,901

SOURCES: 1880–1957 data from Neal Potter and Francis T. Christy, Jr., *Trends in Natural Resource Commodities* (Baltimore: The Johns Hopkins Press for Resources for the Future, Inc., 1962), pp. 417–18. 1958–67 data from U.S. Department of the Interior, Bureau of Mines, *Minerals Yearbook*, vol. 1.

n.a.—Not available.

Table A-2. U.S. Imports, Exports, and Consumption of Sulphur, 1880 to 1967

thousand long tons

Year	Native sulphur imports	Native sulphur exports	Native sulphur shipments	Apparent consumption of native sulphur	Sulphur content of pyrites output	Sulphur content of pyrites imports	By-product sulphur output	Apparent consumption of all forms of sulphur
	(1)	(2)	(3)	(4)	(5)	(6)	(7)	(8)
1880	88		1	89	1		10	110
1881	105		1	106	5		10	130
1882	98		1	99	5		10	130
1883	95		1	96	11		20	140
1884	105		*	105	16	8	20	150
1885	97		1	98	22	3	20	140
1886	118		2	120	25	1	20	170
1887	97		3	100	23	8	20	150
1888	98		0	98	24	n.a.	30	150
1889	136		*	136	42	n.a.	30	210
1890	163		0	163	45	n.a.	30	240
1891	117		1	118	48	45	40	250
1892	101		2	103	50	69	40	260
1893	106		1	107	34	88	40	270
1894	125		*	125	48	75	40	290
1895	122		2	124	45	86	40	290
1896	139		5	144	52	90	50	340
1897	137		2	139	64	117	50	370
1898	151		1	152	87	114	60	410
1899	140		4	144	79	121	60	400
1900	167		3	170	92	145	70	480
1901	175		7	182	106	182	70	540
1902	171		7	178	90	198	80	550
1903	191		7	198	102	189	80	570
1904	130	3	85	212	93	190	90	580
1905	84	12	220	292	114	230	100	740
1906	74	14	295	355	117	270	100	840
1907	23	36	272	259	111	280	100	750
1908	21	28	206	199	100	300	100	700
1909	31	37	258	252	111	310	120	790
1910	31	31	251	251	109	360	120	840
1911	29	28	254	253	140	450	100	940
1912	30	58	305	277	160	440	140	1,020
1913	23	89	319	253	150	380	140	920
1914	26	98	342	270	150	460	170	1,050
1915	25	37	294	282	180	430	200	1,090
1916	21	129	767	659	200	560	260	1,680
1917	1	153	1,120	968	220	435	330	1,950
1918	*	131	1,267	1,136	210	220	255	1,820
1919	*	225	678	453	170	175	180	980
1920	*	477	1,518	1,041	120	150	280	1,590
1921	*	286	954	668	70	98	140	980
1922	*	486	1,344	858	80	125	160	1,220
1923	*	473	1,619	1,146	80	120	180	1,530
1924	1	482	1,537	1,056	70	110	200	1,440
1925	*	629	1,858	1,226	80	120	230	1,660
1926	*	577	2,073	1,490	70	160	240	1,960
1927	3	789	2,072	1,272	120	110	240	1,740
1928	5	685	2,083	1,383	113	210	270	1,980
1929	1	855	2,437	1,566	121	230	290	2,210
1930	*	609		1,381	124	160	272	1,940
1931	0	420		957	121	160	198	1,440
1932	0	360		749	66	110	138	1,060
1933	5	531		1,111	108	170	142	1,530
1934	6	517		1,102	168	160	132	1,560
1935	2	413		1,223	203	180	139	1,740
1936	1	567		1,403	217	190	167	1,980
1937	1	689		1,778	232	235	191	2,440
1938	3	592		1,040	219	150	160	1,570
1939	14	653		1,595	220	215	194	2,220

Table A-2. (Continued)

Year	Native sulphur imports	Native sulphur exports	Native sulphur shipments	Apparent consumption of native sulphur	Sulphur content of pyrites output	Sulphur content of pyrites imports	By-product sulphur output	Apparent consumption of all forms of sulphur
	(1)	(2)	(3)	(4)	(5)	(6)	(7)	(8)
1940	28	766		1,820	262	180	211	2,470
1941	29	761		2,344	270	165	234	3,010
1942	26	586		2,472	307	135	242	3,160
1943	17	682		2,528	337	115	302	3,280
1944	*	675		2,905	333	80	304	3,620
1945	*	943		2,907	296	85	290	3,580
1946	*	1,246		2,848	337	88	262	3,530
1947	*	1,350		3,490	392	61	276	4,220
1948	*	1,296		3,720	388	52	257	4,420
1949	*	1,461		3,410	378	58	262	4,110
1950	*	1,479		4,158	393	100	400	5,050
1951	2	1,312		3,786	433	106	485	4,810
1952	5	1,338		3,728	418	142	572	4,860
1953	1	1,271		3,932	380	91	675	5,080
1954	1	1,675		3,700	405	134	691	4,930
1955	35	1,636		4,246	410	171	818	5,640
1956	212	1,675		4,268	432	175	902	5,780
1957	499	1,593		3,997	436	169	990	5,590
1958	591	1,602		3,652	403	164	1,092	5,311
1959	642	1,636		4,232	437	134	1,091	5,894
1960	741	1,787		3,950	416	146	1,207	5,719
1961	832	1,596		3,908	399	135	1,296	5,738
1962	1,040	1,554		4,065	379	145	1,353	5,942
1963	1,351	1,612		4,302	344	93	1,419	6,158
1964	1,462	1,928		4,738	354	120	1,510	6,722
1965	1,486	2,624		5,134	354	160	1,742	7,390
1966	1,514	2,326		6,113	356	160	1,798	8,427
1967	1,474	2,043		6,260	355	165	1,766	8,546

SOURCES: 1880–1957 data from Neal Potter and Francis T. Christy, Jr., *Trends in Natural Resource Commodities* (Baltimore: The Johns Hopkins Press for Resources for the Future, Inc., 1962), pp. 490–91. 1958–67 data from U.S. Department of the Interior, Bureau of Mines, *Minerals Yearbook*, vol. 1.

NOTE: Column 4 is derived from columns 1, 2, and 3 through 1924, but represents a Bureau of Mines independently calculated series beginning in 1925. Column 8 represents a rounded addition of columns 5, 6, and 7, adjusted in 1880–83 to allow for lack of data.

* Less than 500 long tons.

n.a. Not available.

Table A-3. Average Revenue and Posted Price per Ton, U.S. Shipments of Sulphur, Domestic and Export, 1900 to 1967

Year	Total value			Average value			
	All shipments (1)	Export shipments (2)	Domestic shipments (3)	All shipments (4)	Export shipments (5)	Domestic shipments (6)	Average posted price (7)
	(....... *thousand dollars* ....)			(.............. *dollars/long ton* ....)			
1900							
1901							21.15
1902							22.00
1903							23.45
1904	1,256						22.34
1905	3,305			20.90			21.79
1906	3,702	298	3,404	20.40			21.28
1907	4,771	735	4,036	17.30	20.67	19.95	22.16
1908	3,727	562	3,165	17.50	20.45	17.11	21.50
1909	4,782	737	4,045	18.10	20.13	17.72	21.81
				18.50	19.84	18.30	22.00
1910	4,522	533	3,969	18.00	17.99	18.03	22.00
1911	4,573	545	4,028	18.00	19.41	17.85	22.00
1912	5,289	1,076	4,213	17.30	18.64	17.01	22.00
1913	5,617	1,600	4,017	17.60	17.93	17.46	22.00
1914	6,214	1,807	4,407	18.20	18.41	18.07	22.00
1915	4,959	725	4,234	16.90	19.42	16.50	22.00
1916	12,246	2,506	9,740	16.00	19.46	15.26	31.36
1917	23,987	3,501	20,486	21.40	22.92	21.17	43.33
1918	27,868	3,627	24,241	22.00	27.66	21.35	28.62
1919	10,252	6,326	3,926	15.10	28.15	21.18	28.00
1920	30,000	8,994	21,006	20.00	18.84	20.19	23.85
1921	17,000	4,525	12,475	17.80	15.83	18.66	25.80
1922	22,000	7,096	14,904	16.40	14.61	17.37	14.08
1923	26,000	7,105	18,895	16.10	15.04	16.48	14.00
1924	25,000	7,793	17,207	16.30	16.16	16.31	14.02
1925	29,000	11,000	18,000	15.60	17.48	14.65	14.69
1926	37,300	10,918	26,382	18.00	18.92	17.64	18.22
1927	38,300	16,254	22,046	18.48	20.59	17.05	18.00
1928	37,500	14,345	23,155	18.00	20.94	16.56	18.00
1929	43,800	17,629	26,171	17.97	20.61	16.54	18.00
1930	35,800	12,416	23,384	17.99	20.93	16.74	18.00
1931	24,800	8,837	15,963	18.02	21.68	16.47	18.00
1932	20,000	7,179	12,821	18.04	20.36	16.95	18.00
1933	29,500	9,878	19,622	18.02	18.90	17.60	18.00
1934	28,900	9,365	19,535	17.91	18.47	17.65	18.00
1935	29,300	7,852	21,448	17.92	19.51	17.43	18.00
1936	35,400	10,147	25,253	17.98	18.54	17.19	18.00
1937	44,300	12,155	32,145	17.96	18.00	17.95	18.00
1938	27,300	10,379	16,921	16.76	17.92	16.12	17.51
1939	35,500	10,772	24,728	15.89	17.16	15.40	16.00
1940	40,900	13,042	27,858	15.98	17.47	15.37	16.00
1941	54,400	12,520	41,880	15.99	17.16	15.67	16.00
1942	50,100	10,943	39,157	16.01	19.26	15.29	16.00
1943	47,300	12,522	34,778	16.01	19.05	15.14	16.00
1944	56,300	12,236	44,064	16.00	18.72	15.38	16.00
1945	61,300	16,643	44,657	15.99	18.12	15.32	16.00
1946	66,100	21,590	44,510	16.01	18.16	15.14	16.00
1947	85,200	25,388	59,812	17.65	19.54	16.95	16.51
1948	89,600	26,779	62,821	18.00	21.20	16.91	18.00
1949	86,200	30,490	55,710	18.00	21.31	16.59	18.00
1950	104,000	30,951	73,049	18.99	21.48	17.98	19.02
1951	107,300	31,760	75,540	21.51	24.66	20.41	22.01
1952	110,925	33,515	77,410	21.57	25.70	20.17	22.01
1953	141,054	34,554	106,500	27.00	27.83	26.74	24.74
1954	142,014	50,362	91,652	26.65	30.62	24.88	26.50
1955	163,156	48,708	114,448	27.94	30.42	27.00	26.50
1956	150,356	48,305	102,051	26.49	29.25	25.36	26.50
1957	122,915	43,940	78,975	24.41	27.84	22.85	25.51
1958	109,272	39,975	69,765	23.53	25.04	22.75	23.50
1959	121,777	39,975	81,802	23.32	24.80	22.66	23.50

Table A-3. (Continued)

Year	Total value: All shipments (1)	Total value: Export shipments (2)	Total value: Domestic shipments (3)	Average value: All shipments (4)	Average value: Export shipments (5)	Average value: Domestic shipments (6)	Average posted price (7)
	(....... *thousand dollars* ....)			(............... *dollars/long ton* ....)			
1960	115,494	40,880	74,614	23.09	23.02	23.12	23.50
1961	117,884	35,370	82,514	23.19	22.31	23.60	23.50
1962	107,069	35,496	71,573	21.77	23.09	21.18	23.50
1963	99,014	39,651	81,126	19.82	20.91	19.31	23.50
1964	120,777	39,651	81,126	20.01	20.64	19.71	24.50
1965	164,654	64,278	100,376	22.71	24.49	21.69	25.50
1966	201,292	78,759	122,533	26.07	33.86	22.71	26.75
1967	251,670	81,492	170,175	32.76	39.91	30.18	33.50

SOURCES: 1900 to 1932 data taken from U.S. Department of the Interior, Bureau of Mines (Geological Survey before 1924), *Mineral Resources of the United States* (Washington, D.C.: 1900–1932). Data after 1932 taken from U.S. Department of the Interior, Bureau of Mines, *Minerals Yearbook* (Washington, D.C.: 1932–33 to the present). Data on posted price taken from U.S. Department of Labor, Bureau of Labor Statistics, *Wholesale Prices*, Bulletin No. 320 for 1890–1912, Bulletin No. 493 for 1913–1928, annual bulletins for 1929–1948, summaries for 1947–1950 and 1951–1953, and annual bulletins for 1954–1967.

NOTES: Column (2) subtracted from Column (1) to obtain Column (3). Columns (4), (5), and (6) obtained by dividing total tons shipped, total tons exported, and total tons shipped minus total tons exported into Columns (1), (2), and (3) respectively. (Data on shipments taken from sources listed above, but not given in the table.)

APPENDIX B

Financial Data for Frasch Sulphur Producers

The investment and rate of return series for the period from 1919 to 1946 were taken from the United States Federal Trade Commission, *Report on the Sulphur Industry and International Cartels* (Washington, D.C., 1947). The Commission computed investment in the sulphur industry for each of the four producers. Annual balance sheet investment for each company at the end of the year was adjusted to more nearly reflect actual investment in the sulphur industry by eliminating items such as investment in governmental and other securities and surpluses arising from reappraisal of assets. The balance sheet information of Freeport Sulphur Company was adjusted to exclude its manganese and nickeliferous iron ore mining activities in Cuba. Similarly, net profits before taxes were adjusted for other income, other expenses, and like revenue items to obtain only the net revenue arising from sulphur operations. Average investment, computed from investment at the beginning and end of each year, was divided into net profits to obtain the rate of return for each company. Both before-tax and after-tax rates of return are shown for Texas Gulf Sulphur Company, Freeport Sulphur Company, and Jefferson Lake Sulphur Company. Since Duval did not publish before-tax profits, only after-tax rates of return are shown.

The investment and rate of return series for the period since 1946 were computed from information reported to the Securities and Exchange Commission and published in *Moody's Manual of Industrial Investments.* The average invested capital data represent the sum of the par value of capital stock, paid-in capital, retained earnings, and any surplus or reserve appropriated from retained earnings. No attempt was made to adjust for investment in activities other than sulphur mining or for income and expense arising from other than sulphur mining.

The compilation of an investment and profit series for the Frasch segment of the domestic sulphur industry is made easier by the fact that prior to 1950 only Freeport was engaged to any extent in activities other than the production of sulphur. During the 1950s, however, the four domestic Frasch producers diversified into other lines of activity. Nevertheless, sulphur mining remained the dominant activity of both Texas Gulf and Freeport through 1966 and of Jefferson Lake through 1962. (In 1964, Jefferson Lake was acquired by Occidental Petroleum Corporation.) However, over the past two decades sulphur mining has become an increasingly smaller element of Duval's operations. Presently, sulphur accounts for about 9 per cent of Duval's net income.

Both of the Mexican Frasch producers were engaged solely in the production of sulphur in the period prior to 1967. For Pan American, investment and profits are shown over the life of the firm from 1955 to 1966. For Gulf Sulphur, the data cover only the period from 1961 to 1966. While this firm began sulphur operations in 1956, it was not until 1961 that the firm showed a profit.

Table B-1. Summary of Investment, Profits, and Rates of Return on Investment for Texas Gulf Sulphur Company, 1919 to 1966

		Profit		Rate of return	
Year	Average invested capital*	Before federal taxes	After federal taxes	Before federal taxes	After federal taxes
	(.........thousand dollars		.........)	(....per cent	.....)
1919	5,159	994	968	19.27	18.76
1920	8,981	3,519	3,327	39.18	37.04
1921	11,261	1,941	1,866	17.24	16.58
1922	12,193	3,999	3,809	32.80	31.24
1923	12,867	4,972	4,683	38.64	36.39
1924	13,224	5,089	4,762	38.48	36.01
1925	13,260	6,028	5,627	45.46	42.44
1926	14,790	10,036	9,296	67.86	62.85
1927	17,687	13,110	12,002	74.12	67.86
1928	21,673	15,661	14,411	72.26	66.49
1929	27,589	17,624	16,185	63.88	58.66
1930	33,272	15,101	13,972	45.39	41.99
1931	35,791	9,772	8,943	27.30	24.99
1932	36,179	6,374	5,910	17.62	16.34
1933	37,506	7,957	7,444	21.21	19.85
1934	49,238	7,337	6,743	14.90	13.69
1935	59,739	8,178	7,468	13.69	12.50
1936	59,133	10,843	9,633	18.34	16.66
1937	59,131	12,864	11,589	21.76	19.60
1938	59,353	7,634	6,964	12.86	11.75
1939	59,349	8,922	7,847	15.03	13.22
1940	59,375	10,851	9,141	18.28	15.40
1941	58,770	12,966	9,016	21.05†	15.34
1942	58,642	13,449	8,779	21.36†	14.97
1943	58,789	14,416	7,966	22.40†	13.55
1944	58,721	16,820	9,620	25.66†	16.38
1945	59,089	18,193	9,993	27.24†	16.91
1946	61,485	21,590	15,240	31.40†	24.79
1947	65,940	30,665	21,665	46.50	32.86
1948	57,545	34,081	24,231	59.22	42.11
1949	50,273	33,238	23,863	66.12	47.47

Table B-1. (Continued)

Year	Average invested capital*	Profit: Before federal taxes	Profit: After federal taxes	Rate of return: Before federal taxes	Rate of return: After federal taxes
	(........*thousand dollars*........)			(....*per cent*....)	
1950	57,367	38,889	25,889	67.79	45.13
1951	64,502	40,942	25,442	63.47	39.44
1952	68,830	38,612	25,112	56.10	36.48
1953	73,530	40,284	24,534	54.79	33.37
1954	83,576	46,245	30,555	55.33	36.56
1955	95,878	49,856	32,356	52.00	33.75
1956	106,139	42,386	28,136	39.93	26.51
1957	110,259	20,257	17,557	18.37	15.92
1958	111,987	16,883	13,383	15.08	11.95
1959	115,211	17,438	13,338	15.14	11.58
1960	119,304	17,434	12,684	14.61	10.63
1961	124,680	17,333	12,583	13.90	10.09
1962	132,352	15,887	12,137	12.00	9.17
1963	142,245	10,904	9,354	7.67	6.58
1964	151,448	15,060	11,556	9.94	7.63
1965	164,813	24,158	18,161	14.66	11.02
1966	199,164	39,928	28,096	20.05	14.11

SOURCES: U.S. Federal Trade Commission, *Report on the Sulphur Industry and International Cartels* (Washington: U.S. Government Printing Office, 1947) for years through 1946; and *Moody's Manual of Industrial Investments* (New York: Moody's Investors' Service, various issues) for 1947 to 1966.

* Beginning and end of year.

† Because of the high income and excess profits taxes during the war years, rates of return were computed by relating profit before federal taxes to the average invested capital adjusted for such tax provisions.

Table B-2. Summary of Investment, Profits, and Rates of Return on Investment for Freeport Sulphur Company, 1919 to 1966

Year	Average invested capital*	Profit: Before federal taxes	Profit: After federal taxes	Rate of return: Before federal taxes	Rate of return: After federal taxes
	(.........*thousand dollars*		.........)	(....*per cent*	.....)
1919	9,632	1,185	1,105	12.30	11.48
1920	8,406	584	584	6.94	6.94
1921	8,446	(492)	(492)	(5.82)	(5.82)
1922	10,005	(253)	(253)	(2.53)	(2.53)
1923	12,175	770	770	6.33	6.33
1924	12,228	(326)	(326)	(2.65)	(2.65)
1925	11,772	750	750	6.37	6.37
1926	12,566	1,809	1,809	14.40	14.40
1927	13,830	3,925	3,736	28.38	27.01
1928	13,318	3,460	3,276	25.98	24.59
1929	11,621	4,216†	3,843†	36.28†	33.07†
1930	10,434	2,834	2,502	27.12	23.94
1931	10,364	2,177	1,918	21.00	18.51
1932	9,392	2,253	2,005	23.99	21.35
1933	10,807	2,714	2,479	25.11	22.94
1934	12,628	1,625	1,477	12.87	11.70
1935	12,363	1,642	1,492	13.28	12.07
1936	13,158	2,488	2,201	18.91	16.73
1937	14,122	2,713	2,443	19.21	17.30
1938	13,913	1,678	1,513	12.06	10.87
1939	14,927	1,828	1,622	12.25	10.87
1940	17,534	2,547	2,167	14.52	12.36
1941	18,933	3,281	2,581	16.85‡	13.63
1942	19,655	2,808	2,083	13.79‡	10.60
1943	19,340	3,310	2,425	16.43‡	12.54
1944	19,087	3,658	2,208	18.06‡	11.57
1945	20,156	4,902	2,902	22.40‡	14.40
1946	21,697	4,453	3,368	19.16‡	15.52
1947	29,924	3,446	2,723	11.52	9.10
1948	32,025	4,895	4,088	15.28	12.77
1949	34,583	7,190	5,882	20.79	17.01
1950	37,114	9,363	7,169	25.23	19.32
1951	39,453	8,728	6,415	22.12	16.26
1952	41,670	9,162	7,426	21.99	17.82
1953	44,801	10,786	8,706	24.08	19.43
1954	48,711	13,406	10,207	27.52	20.95

Table B-2. (Continued)

Year	Average invested capital*	Profit: Before federal taxes	Profit: After federal taxes	Rate of return: Before federal taxes	Rate of return: After federal taxes
	(........*thousand dollars*		........)	(....*per cent*....)	
1955	57,737	15,163	12,599	26.26	21.82
1956	67,665	15,908	13,493	23.51	19.94
1957	73,387	16,928	13,124	23.07	17.88
1958	112,541	16,398	14,617	14.57	12.99
1959	151,672	16,097	15,332	10.61	10.11
1960	147,517	14,349	13,965	9.73	9.47
1961	142,902	13,374	13,135	9.36	9.19
1962	146,989	12,997	12,868	8.84	8.75
1963	152,866	13,596	12,894	8.89	8.43
1964	161,424	17,011	15,411	10.54	9.55
1965	172,512	26,047	21,923	15.10	12.71
1966	190,705	39,163	32,748	20.54	17.17

SOURCES: See table **B-1**.

* Beginning and end of year.

† 13 months.

‡ Because of the high income and excess profits taxes during the war years, rates of return were computed by relating the profit before federal income taxes to the average invested capital adjusted for such tax provisions.

( ) Loss.

Table B-3. Summary of Investment, Profits, and Rates of Return on Investment for Duval Corporation, 1930 to 1966

Year	Average invested capital*	Profit after federal taxes	Rate of return after federal taxes
	(..... *thousand dollars*	.....)	*per cent*
1930	1,121	232	20.66
1931	1,341	198	14.76
1932	1,517	151	9.98
1933	1,307	(85)	(6.54)
1934	1,080	39	3.61
1935	1,196	78	6.54
1936	1,275	306	24.03
1937	1,571	221	14.07
1938	1,923	379	19.69
1939	2,421	652	26.92
1940	2,817	581	20.62
1941	2,820	709	25.13
1942	2,743	795	28.99
1943	2,616	809	30.91
1944	2,566	799	31.12
1945	2,619	786	30.00
1946	2,832	1,012	35.73
1947	4,183	1,073	25.65
1948	3,928	764	19.45
1949	3,609	781	21.64
1950	5,510	1,007	18.28
1951	8,448	1,187	14.05
1952	10,474	2,681	25.60
1953	12,289	3,045	24.78
1954	14,182	3,072	21.66
1955	15,996	3,063	19.15
1956	17,531	2,507	14.30
1957	21,339	3,110	14.57
1958	26,501	2,645	9.98
1959	28,845	2,349	8.14
1960	30,691	4,595	14.97
1961	33,415	4,104	12.28
1962	35,863	4,463	12.44
1963	39,756	4,364	10.98
1964	45,240	5,442	12.03
1965	58,071	9,604	16.54
1966	73,919	11,036	14.93

SOURCES: See table B-1.

* Beginning and end of year.

( ) Loss.

Table B-4. Summary of Investment, Profits, and Rates of Return on Investment for Jefferson Lake Sulphur Company, 1933 to 1962

		Profit		Rate of return	
Year	Average invested capital*	Before federal taxes	After federal taxes	Before federal taxes	After federal taxes
	(........ *thousand dollars* ....)			(.... *per cent* .....)	
1933	2,351	1,019	841	43.33	35.77
1934	2,554	1,005	864	39.36	33.85
1935	2,389	.....	132	.....	5.51
1936	n.a.	n.a.	n.a.	n.a.	n.a.
1937	2,188	(11)	(11)	(.51)	(.51)
1938	2,469	977	821	39.56	33.27
1939	2,819	1,529	1,325	54.23	47.01
1940	2,830	1,075	812	37.98	28.70
1941	2,676	323	280	12.09	10.46
1942	2,374	(328)	(328)	(13.81)	(13.81)
1943	2,142	149	138	6.78	6.46
1944	2,207	431	358	19.54	16.20
1945	2,682	424	359	15.80	13.40
1946	3,191	395	368	12.22	11.52
1947	3,349	431	382	12.87	11.41
1948	3,637	622	420	17.10	11.55
1949	3,858	1,027	525	26.62	13.61
1950	4,349	1,898	1,246	43.64	28.65
1951	5,056	2,150	1,321	42.52	26.13
1952	5,684	2,086	1,232	36.70	21.67
1953	6,307	2,288	1,487	36.28	23.58
1954	7,228	3,841	2,184	53.14	30.22
1955	8,136	2,652	1,711	36.60	21.03
1956	8,683	2,569	1,608	29.59	18.52
1957	9,391	1,350	1,243	14.38	13.24
1958	10,892	(538)	(659)	(4.94)	(6.05)
1959	11,316	978	(1,329)	8.64	(11.74)
1960	10,789	867	181	8.04	1.68
1961	9,916	2,104	1,006	21.22	10.15
1962	9,538	2,060	1,026	21.60	10.76

SOURCES: See table B-1.
n.a.—Data not available.
* Beginning and end of year.
( ) Loss.

Table B-5. Summary of Investment, Profits, and Rates of Return on Investment for Pan American Sulphur Company, 1955 to 1966

Year	Average invested capital*	Profit: Before federal taxes	Profit: After federal taxes	Rate of return: Before federal taxes	Rate of return: After federal taxes
	(........*thousand dollars*........)			(....*per cent*.....)	
1955	5,725	623	378	10.88	6.60
1956	7,236	3,775	2,122	52.17	29.33
1957	10,135	6,319	3,455	62.35	34.09
1958	13,188	6,878	3,575	52.15	27.11
1959	16,512	6,547	3,462	39.65	20.97
1960	19,155	6,149	3,119	32.10	16.28
1961	19,628	5,465	2,415	27.84	12.30
1962	20,067	6,846	3,082	34.12	15.36
1963	21,037	8,029	3,467	38.17	16.48
1964	23,254	11,200	5,120	48.16	22.02
1965	25,432	8,230	4,330	32.36	17.03
1966	28,780	16,389	8,303	56.95	28.85

SOURCE: Pan American Sulphur Company, Annual Reports.
* Beginning and end of year.

Table B-6. Summary of Investment, Profits, and Rates of Return on Investment for Gulf Sulphur Corporation, 1961 to 1966

Year	Average invested capital*	Profit: Before federal taxes	Profit: After federal taxes	Rate of return: Before federal taxes	Rate of return: After federal taxes
	(....... *thousand dollars* ....)			(....*per cent*.....)	
1961	5,145	254	254†	4.94	4.94†
1962	5,006	1,614	1,139	32.24	22.75
1963	6,082	1,143	916	18.69	15.06
1964	6,978	1,014	767	14.53	10.99
1965	8,307	2,529	1,716	30.44	20.66
1966	10,476	3,200	2,374	30.55	22.66

SOURCE: Gulf Sulphur Corporation, Annual Reports.
* Beginning and end of year.
† No income tax paid in 1961.

Bibliography

I. Books, Monographs, and Theses

Acevedo Escobedo, Antonio. *El azufre en Mexico*. Mexico, D.F.: Editorial Cultura, 1956.

Adams, Walter, and Gray, Horace M. *Monopoly in America: The Government as Promoter*. New York: The Macmillan Company, 1955.

Arthur D. Little, Inc. *The Free World Sulphur Outlook*. 1966.

Bain, Joe S. *The Economics of the Pacific Coast Petroleum Industry*. Berkeley: University of California Press, 3 vols., 1944, 1945, 1947.

———. *Barriers to New Competition*. Cambridge: Harvard University Press, 1956.

Barger, Harold, and Schurr, Sam H. *The Mining Industries, 1899–1939*. New York: National Bureau of Economic Research, 1944.

Barnett, Harold J., and Morse, Chandler. *Scarcity and Growth*. Baltimore: The Johns Hopkins Press for Resources for the Future, Inc., 1965.

Baruch, Bernard M. *Baruch, My Own Story*. New York: Henry Holt and Company, 1957.

Bernstein, Marvin D. *The Mexican Mining Industry*. New York: State University of New York, 1965.

Bixby, David W.; Tisdale, Samuel L.; and Rucker, Delbert R. *Adding Plant Nutrient Sulphur to Fertilizer*. Washington, D.C.: The Sulphur Institute, Technical Bulletin no. 10, 1964.

Brese, W. G. *An Analysis of the Sulphur Industry in Alberta*. Calgary, Alberta: Research Council of Alberta, Information Series, no. 38, 1962.

Chamberlin, Edward H. *The Theory of Monopolistic Competition*. 8th ed. Cambridge: Harvard University Press, 1962.

Clow, Archibald, and Clow, Nan L. *The Chemical Revolution*. London: The Batchworth Press, 1952.

Duecker, Werner W., and West, James R. *The Manufacture of Sulfuric Acid*. New York: Reinhold Publishing Corporation, 1959.

Earp, M. H. "The Frasch Sulphur Industry of Mexico." Master's thesis, Southern Methodist University, 1960.

Edwards, Edgar O., and Bell, Philip W. *The Theory and Measurement of Business Income*. Berkeley: University of California Press, 1961.

Fairlie, Andrew M. *Sulfuric Acid Manufacture*. New York: Reinhold Publishing Corporation, 1936.

Faith, W. L.; Keyes, Donald B.; and Clark, Ronald L. *Industrial Chemicals*. 2nd ed. New York: John Wiley and Sons, Inc., 1957.

Fellner, William. *Competition Among the Few*. New York: Alfred A. Knopf, 1949.

Hamilton, Daniel C. *Competition in Oil*. Cambridge: Harvard University Press, 1958.

Hansen, Eric J. *Dynamic Decade*. Toronto, Canada: McClelland and Stewart, Ltd., 1958.

Haynes, Williams. *The Stone That Burns*. New York: D. Van Nostrand Company, Inc., 1942.

———. *Brimstone: The Stone That Burns*. Princeton: D. Van Nostrand Company, Inc., 1959.

Kaysen, Carl. *United States v. United Shoe Machinery Corporation*. Cambridge: Harvard University Press, 1956.

Kreps, Theodore J. *The Economics of the Sulfuric Acid Industry*. Stanford: Stanford University Press, 1938.

Landsberg, Hans H.; Fischman, Leonard L.; and Fisher, Joseph L. *Resources in America's Future*. Baltimore: The Johns Hopkins Press for Resources for the Future, Inc., 1963.

Lehmann, Glenn Albert. "The Market for Sulphur: A Study in Duopoly." Ph.D. dissertation, Harvard University, 1953.

Liebhafsky, H. H. *The Nature of Price Theory*. Homewood, Illinois: The Dorsey Press, Inc., 1963. Rev. ed., 1968.

Liebig, Justus. *Familiar Letters on Chemistry*. Edited by John Gardner. New York: J. Winchester, New World Press, 1843.

Markham, Jesse W. *Competition in the Rayon Industry*. Cambridge: Harvard University Press, 1952.

———. *The Fertilizer Industry*. Nashville: The Vanderbilt University Press, 1958.

Mason, Edward S. *Economic Concentration and the Monopoly Problem*. Cambridge: Harvard University Press, 1957.

McKie, James W. *Tin Cans and Tin Plate*. Cambridge: Harvard University Press, 1959.

McLean, John G., and Haigh, Robert William. *The Growth of Integrated Oil Companies*. Boston: Division of Research, Graduate School of Business Administration, Harvard University, 1954.

Montgomery, R. H. *The Brimstone Game*. Manchaca, Texas: The Chaparral Press, 1949. First published, 1940.

Morrison, Thurmond L. "The Economics of the Sulphur Industry." Ph.D. dissertation, University of Texas, 1939.

Peck, Merton J. *Competition in the Aluminum Industry, 1945–1958*. Cambridge: Harvard University Press, 1961.

Phillips, Charles F., Jr. *Competition in the Synthetic Rubber Industry*. Chapel Hill, North Carolina: The University of North Carolina Press, 1961.

Robinson, Joan. *The Economics of Imperfect Competition*. London: Macmillan and Company, Ltd., 1961.

Schumpeter, Joseph A. *Capitalism, Socialism, and Democracy*. 3rd ed. New York: Harper and Brothers Publishers, 1950.

Scott, Anthony. *Natural Resources: The Economics of Conservation*. Toronto, Canada: The University of Toronto Press, 1955.

Shubik, Martin. *Strategy and Market Structure*. New York: John Wiley and Sons, Inc., 1959.

Stigler, George J. *The Theory of Price*. New York: The Macmillan Company, 1946. Rev. ed., 1952.

———. *Capital and Rates of Return in Manufacturing Industries*. Princeton: Princeton University Press for the National Bureau of Economic Research, 1963.

Stocking, George W., and Watkins, Myron W. *Cartels or Competition?* New York: The Twentieth Century Fund, 1948.

Stoddard, X. T. "Scout Memo, High Island Dome Sulphur Mine, Galveston County, Texas." Memorandum, Humble Oil and Refining Company, 1959.

Swagger, William L. "The Paley Report in Review: Sulphur." Unpublished monograph, Battelle Memorial Institute, 1961.

Texas Gulf Sulphur Company. *Facts About Sulphur.* New York: Texas Gulf Sulphur Company, 1958.

———. *Modern Sulphur Mining.* New York: Texas Gulf Sulphur Company, 1961.

Truett, Dale B. "Sulphur and the Development of a Chemical Fertilizer Industry in Mexico." Ph.D. dissertation, University of Texas, 1967.

Tuller, William N., ed. *The Sulphur Data Book.* New York: McGraw-Hill Book Company, Inc., 1954.

Viner, Jacob. *Dumping: A Problem in International Trade.* Chicago: University of Chicago Press, 1923.

II. Public Documents

Federal Trade Commission. *Report on the Sulphur Industry and International Cartels.* 1947.

President's Materials Policy Commission. *Resources for Freedom.* 1952.

United States Congress. *Hearings before the Temporary National Economic Committee.* 76th Congress, 1st Session, Part V, 1939.

United States Department of the Interior, Bureau of Mines. *Minerals Yearbook.* Annual issues.

———. *Mineral Trade Notes.* Monthly issues.

United States House of Representatives. *President's 1963 Tax Message.* 88th Congress, 1st Session, Part I, 1963.

United States Tariff Commission. *Information Concerning the Pyrites and Sulphur Industry.* 1919.

———. "Industrial Readjustments of Certain Mineral Industries Affected By the War." *Tariff Information Series, Number 21.* 1920.

III. Articles and Periodicals

Ambrose, Paul M. "Sulphur and Pyrites." In *Mineral Facts and Problems, 1965 Edition.* United States Department of the Interior, Bureau of Mines, Bulletin 630, 1965.

Adelman, M. A. "Effective Competition and the Antitrust Laws." *Harvard Law Review* (1948), 1289–1350.

Bain, Joe S. "Workable Competition in Oligopoly: Theoretical Considerations and Some Empirical Evidence." *American Economic Review* (1950), 35–47.

Blair, John M. "Means, Thorp, and Neal on Price Inflexibility." *Review of Economics and Statistics* (1956), 427–35.

Brooks, David B. "The Supply of Individually Mined Minor Metals and Its Implications for Subsidy Programs." *Land Economics* (1964), 18–24.

Butterworth, C. D., and Schwab, J. W. "Sulfur Mining as a Processing Industry." *Industrial and Engineering Chemistry* (1938), 746–51.

Carsey, J. Ben. "Geology of Gulf Coastal Area and Continental Shelf." *Bulletin of the American Association of Petroleum Geologists* (March 1950), 361–85.

Clark, J. M. "Towards a Concept of Workable Competition." *American Economic Review* (1940), 241–56.

DeGolyer, E. "Origin of North American Salt Domes." *Bulletin of the American Association of Petroleum Geologists* (August 1925), 831–74.

Deschamps, Federico. "Los domas del sal del Istmo de Tehuantepec desde el punto de vista de su importancia económica." *Revista Mexicana de Ingenieria y Arquitectura* (November and December 1937), 711–23 and 777–99.

Doak, John. "Liquid-Sulphur Distribution." *The Oil and Gas Journal* (June 24, 1963), 101.

Estep, James W.; McBride, Guy T.; and West, James R. "The Recovery of Sulphur from Sour Natural and Refinery Gases." In *Advances in Petroleum Chemistry and Refining*, edited by John J. McKetta, Jr. New York: Interscience Publishers, 1962.

Fellner, William. "Collusion and Its Limits Under Oligopoly." *American Economic Review* (1950), 54–62.

Gittinger, L. B., Jr. "Sulphur." *The Engineering and Mining Journal* (February 1964), 151.

———. "Sulphur." *The Engineering and Mining Journal* (February 1967), 170.

———. "Sulphur." *The Engineering and Mining Journal* (March 1969), 160C–160F.

Graff, R. A. "Elemental Sulphur from Petroleum Gases." *The Oil and Gas Journal* (17 February 1949), 103–4.

Gray, L. C. "Rent Under the Assumptions of Exhaustibility." *Quarterly Journal of Economics* (May 1914), 446–89.

Hanna, Marcus A., and Wolf, Albert G. "Texas and Louisiana Salt Dome Cap Rock Minerals." In *Gulf Coast Oil Fields*, edited by Donald C. Barton and George Sawtelle. Tulsa, Oklahoma: The American Association of Petroleum Geologists, 1936.

Hartley, Burton. "The Petroleum Geology of the Isthmus of Tehuantepec." *Economic Geology* (October–November 1917), 581–88.

Hawkins, M. E., and Jink, C. F. "Salt Domes in Texas, Louisiana, Mississippi, Alabama, and Offshore Tidelands: A Survey." United States Department of the Interior, Bureau of Mines, *Information Circular 8313* (1966).

Herfindahl, Orris C. "Some Fundamentals of Mineral Economics." *Land Economics* (1955), 131–38.

Hotelling, Harold. "The Economics of Exhaustible Resources." *Journal of Political Economy* (1931), 137–75.

Hunt, Walter F. "The Origin of the Sulphur Deposits of Sicily." *Economic Geology* (1915), 543–79.

Huntley, Stirling. "Oil Development on the Isthmus of Tehuantepec." *Transactions of the American Institute of Mining and Metallurgical Engineers* (1923), 1150–66.

Jones, H. H., and Graff, R. A. "West Texas' First Recovery Unit." *The Oil and Gas Journal* (April 21, 1952), 122–23 and 153–54.

Kearney, John H. "A New Empire of Frasch Process Sulphur Is Rising from the Jungles of Mexico." *Engineering and Mining Journal* (January 1955), 72–77.

Kelly, F. J. "Sulphur Production and Consumption in Eight Western States."

United States Department of the Interior, Bureau of Mines, *Information Circular 8094* (1962).

Lee, C. O.; Bartlett, Z. W.; and Feierabend, R. H. "The Grand Isle Mine." *Mining Engineering* (June 1960), 578–90.

Lundy, W. T. "Sulphur and Pyrites." In *Industrial Minerals and Rocks*. 2nd ed. New York: American Institute of Mining and Metallurgical Engineers, 1949.

———. "Known and Potential Sulphur Resources of the World." *Industrial and Engineering Chemistry* (November 1950), 2200.

Mason, Donald B. "The Sulphur Industry." *Industrial and Engineering Chemistry* (1938), 740–46.

Mason, Edward S. "The Political Economy of Resource Use." In *Perspectives on Conservation*, edited by Henry Jarrett. Baltimore: The Johns Hopkins Press for Resources for the Future, Inc., 1958.

Means, Gardiner C. "Basic Characteristics of the American Economy." In National Resources Committee, *The Structure of the American Economy*. Part I (1939).

Nelson, James R. "Percentage Depletion and National Security." In *Federal Tax Policy for Economic Growth and Stability*. Joint Committee Print of the 84th Congress, 1st Session, 1955.

Netzeband, F. F.; Early, Thomas R.; Ryan, J. P.; and Miller, W. C. "Sulphur Resources and Production in Texas, Louisiana, Missouri, Oklahoma, Arkansas, Kansas, and Mississippi, and Markets for the Sulphur." United States Department of the Interior, Bureau of Mines, *Information Circular 8222* (1964).

O'Hanlan, Thomas. "The Great Sulphur Rush." *Fortune* (March 1968), 109.

Price, K. T. "Freeport Mines Sulphur by Boat and Barge at Bay Ste. Elaine." *Engineering and Mining Journal* (December 1952), 98–102.

Reed, Robert M., and Updegraff, Norman C. "Removal of Hydrogen Sulphide from Industrial Gases." *Industrial and Engineering Chemistry* (1950), 2269–77.

Rogers, Sherburne. "The Intrusive Origin of the Gulf Coast Salt Domes." *Economic Geology* (September 1918), 447–85.

Sawtelle, George. "Salt Dome Statistics." In *Gulf Coast Oil Fields,* edited by Donald C. Barton and George Sawtelle. Tulsa, Oklahoma: The American Association of Petroleum Geologists, 1936, 109–18.

Shearon, Will H., Jr., and Pollard, J. H. "Modern Sulphur Mining." In *Modern Chemical Processes,* edited by William J. Murphy. vol. 2. New York: Reinhold Publishing Corporation, 1952, 219–29.

Sheehan, Robert. "The 'Little Mothers' and Pan American Sulphur." *Fortune* (July 1960), 96–103.

Shibler, B. K., and Hovey, M. S. "Processes for Recovering Sulphur from Secondary Source Materials." United States Department of the Interior, Bureau of Mines, *Information Circular 8076* (1962).

Sosnick, Stephan H. "A Critique of Concepts of Workable Competition." *Quarterly Journal of Economics* (1958), 380–423.

Villard, H. H. "Competition, Oligopoly, and Research." *Journal of Political Economy* (1958), 483–97.

Villarillo, Juan D. "Algunas Regiones Petroliferas de Mexico." *Boletin del Instituto Geologico de Mexico* (1908), 69–92.

Viner, Jacob. "Cost Curves and Supply Curves." *Zeitschrift fur National-Okonomie* (1932), 23–46.

Wells, A. E., and Fogg, D. E. "The Manufacture of Sulphuric Acid in the United States." United States Department of the Interior, Bureau of Mines, *Bulletin 184* (1920).

Williamson, Oliver E. "Innovation and Market Structure." *Journal of Political Economy* (February 1965), 67–73.

Wionczek, Miguel. "Foreign-Owned Export-Oriented Enclave in a Rapidly Industrializing Economy: Sulphur Mining in Mexico." In *El nacionalismo mexicano y la inversión extranjera.* Mexico, D.F.: Siglo XXI Editores, 1967.

Wolf, Albert C. "Marketing of Sulphur." *Engineering and Mining Journal* (July 1, 1922), 19–22.

Zimmerman, J. B., and Thomas, Eugene. "Sulphur in West Texas: Its Geology and Economics." The University of Texas at Austin, Bureau of Economic Geology, *Geological Circular 69–2* (1969).

IV. Personal Interviews

———. Personal interview with William Amos, Chief, Division of Agricultural and Inorganic Chemicals, Business and Defense Services Administration, United States Department of Commerce, Washington, D.C., August 5, 1966.

———. Personal interview with Clarence O. Babcock, Commodity Specialist (Sulphur), Minerals Division, United States Department of the Interior, Bureau of Mines, Washington, D.C., August 1964.

———. Personal interview with David W. Bixby, Chemical Engineer, The Sulphur Institute, Washington, D.C., August 3–4, 1966.

———. Personal interview with Hal H. Bybee, Geologist, Continental Oil Company, Houston, Texas, February 1964.

———. Personal interview with J. C. Carrington, Vice President, Freeport Sulphur Company, New York City, August 15, 1966.

———. Personal interview with Shelby M. Darbishire, Executive Vice President, Gulf Sulphur Company, Houston, Texas, May 21, 1964.

———. Personal interviews with Raymond Devine, Vice President, Pan American Sulphur Company, Houston, Texas, July 24, 1963 and January 30, 1964.

———. Personal interview with Eugene Germain, Vice President, Duval Corporation, Houston, Texas, February 1964.

———. Personal interview with Edward Getzin, Chief, Industrial and Strategic Minerals Division, United States Department of State, Washington, D.C., August 11, 1966.

———. Personal interview with William C. Hawk, Geologist, Continental Oil Company, Houston, Texas, February 1964.

———. Personal interview with I. E. McKeever, Jr., General Manager of Mines, Texas Gulf Sulphur Company, Newgulf, Texas, March 1964.

———. Personal interview with Delbert L. Rucker, Director of Information, The Sulphur Institute, Washington, D.C., August 9, 1966.

———. Personal interview with H. W. Strickland, Senior Vice President, Texas Gulf Sulphur Company, Houston, Texas, February 14, 1964.

———. Personal interview with H. C. Webb, President, Pan American Sulphur Company, Houston, Texas, January 1964.

FORAGING NEW YORK

Finding, Identifying, and Preparing
Edible Wild Foods

"Wildman" Steve Brill

GUILFORD, CONNECTICUT

FALCONGUIDES®

An imprint of Globe Pequot
Falcon, FalconGuides, and Outfit Your Mind are registered trademarks of Rowman & Littlefield.

Distributed by NATIONAL BOOK NETWORK

British Library Cataloguing-in-Publication Information available

Library of Congress Cataloging-in-Publication Data

Names: Brill, Steve.
Title: Foraging New York: Finding, Identifying, and Preparing Edible Wild Foods / Steve Brill.
Description: Guilford, Connecticut : FalconGuides, [2017] | Includes index.
Identifiers: LCCN 2016046004 (print) | LCCN 2016046705 (ebook) | ISBN 9781493024285 (pbk.) | ISBN 9781493024292 (e-book)
Subjects: LCSH: Wild plants, Edible—New York (State) | Plants, Edible—New York (State)
Classification: LCC QK98.5.U6 B748 2017 (print) | LCC QK98.5.U6 (ebook) | DDC 581.6/32097471—dc23
LC record available at https://lccn.loc.gov/2016046004

∞™ The paper used in this publication meets the minimum requirements of American National Standard for Information Sciences—Permanence of Paper for Printed Library Materials, ANSI/NISO Z39.48-1992.

Printed in the United States of America

To all the wonderful people who attended my foraging tours over the decades, spread their love of nature, and helped make our planet a greener place.

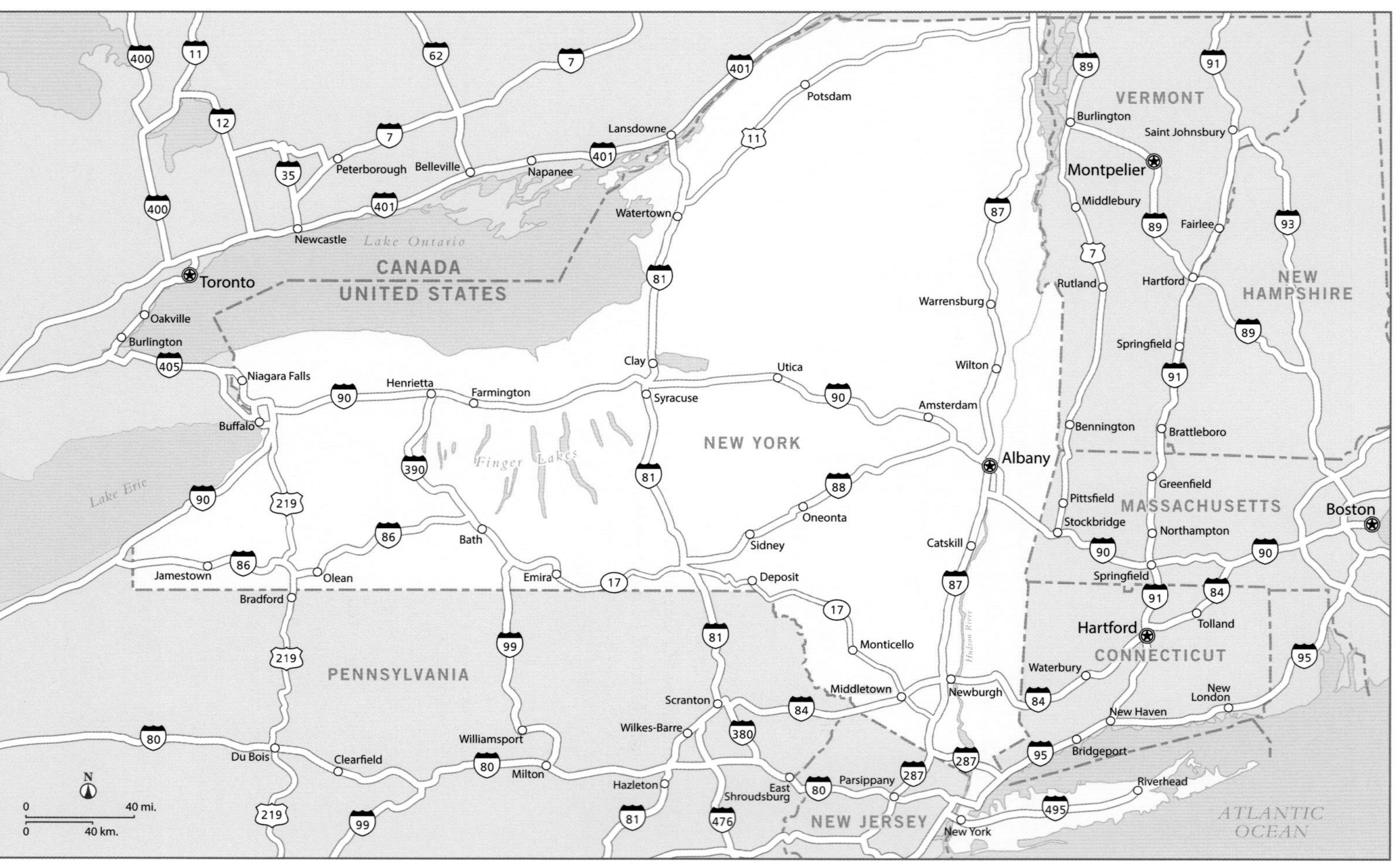

VERMONT
NEW HAMPSHIRE
MASSACHUSETTS
CONNECTICUT
NEW YORK
NEW JERSEY
PENNSYLVANIA
CANADA
UNITED STATES
Lake Ontario
Lake Erie
Finger Lakes
Hudson River
ATLANTIC OCEAN
Toronto
Oakville
Burlington
Newcastle
Peterborough
Belleville
Napanee
Lansdowne
Watertown
Potsdam
Niagara Falls
Buffalo
Henrietta
Farmington
Clay
Syracuse
Utica
Amsterdam
Albany
Warrensburg
Wilton
Catskill
Jamestown
Olean
Bradford
Bath
Emira
Sidney
Oneonta
Deposit
Monticello
Middletown
Newburgh
Scranton
Wilkes-Barre
Hazleton
East Shroudsburg
Parsippany
New York
Du Bois
Clearfield
Williamsport
Milton
Burlington
Montpelier
Middlebury
Rutland
Bennington
Pittsfield
Stockbridge
Saint Johnsbury
Fairlee
Hartford
Springfield
Brattleboro
Greenfield
Northampton
Springfield
Hartford
Tolland
Waterbury
New Haven
Bridgeport
New London
Riverhead
Boston
N
0 40 mi.
0 40 km.

CONTENTS

ACKNOWLEDGMENTS

I want to thank my daughter, foraging expert Violet Brill, for her curiosity and perceptiveness in the field, and in the kitchen. She discovered new ways to use several of the plants in this book that would never have occurred to me, and also contributed recipe ideas starting from when she was a very young child.

I also want to thank Wisteria, Violet's parakeet, for flying onto my shoulder, talking into my ear, and dictating everything I should write in this book!

INTRODUCTION

ABOUT FORAGING

Dozens of edible wild plants grow, unnoticed, in virtually every possible habitat throughout New York State. Many of these are so common, or even invasive, that people destroy them as "weeds," although, in fact, they're more tasty and nutritious than anything you can buy from a store.

Here's how you can discover and identify them, harvest them ecologically and safely, and use them to make delicious, healthful recipes, as well as home remedies. This is based on my experience as a naturalist and an environmental educator who has been leading thousands of foraging tours. I've worked with the public, and with schools, day camps, museums, nature centers, land trusts, farmer's markets, teaching farms, parks departments, and other organizations throughout the Greater New York Region since 1982. I' also draw on extensive research, and collaboration with other foragers.

You'll learn to enjoy our incredible bounty of wild herbs, shoots, greens, fruits, berries, roots, nuts, seeds, flowers, and even seaweeds in the field and in the kitchen. These species are really good to eat and practical to collect, not the ones that take forever to collect and process and result in tiny amounts of "food" that tastes so bad, you'd wish there was still less!

I chose these species not only because they're the ones I know best, but also because they're common, widespread, and easy to harvest ecologically. Also, they're fun and easy to use for making some great meals.

GROUND RULES

The first thing to know about foraging is that you need to identify anything you're going to eat with 100 percent certainty *before* you eat it. Each plant has key identifying characteristics that let you distinguish it from all other plants. When you think you've found a plant from this book, carefully go over every single characteristic the plant should have at the time of year you're collecting it, one by one. If the characteristics aren't there, don't eat the plant. You can keep following it throughout the seasons as different features appear and try it later on, when you're completely sure you have the right plant.

POISONOUS PLANTS

Some poisonous plants resemble edible plants. I warn about these in the text and describe the features that distinguish the two species. Seek out those attributes.

If you're a novice, learn the most common species that lack toxic look-alikes and follow them through their life cycles. If you're not sure, be patient.

No one was teaching foraging when I began in 1982, so I had to learn everything by myself. Using field guides full of inaccuracies and mistakes, written by botanists who didn't forage or cook, I was still able to identify Kentucky coffee tree and greenbrier (see p. 82) right away, but had to wait almost 2 years before I could eat daylily (see p. 23) shoots safely, and even longer before I found out that cornelian cherries—which no foraging book covered—were actually edible.

Be especially careful not to collect a different plant that's growing along with an edible species. It doesn't help if the characteristics are completely different if you don't notice that you've picked two different species. (See the story under lamb's quarters [p. 127] for an extreme example of this.)

POLLUTION

Plants can pick up pollution from the environment. Quickly growing leaves and stems are good at this, while fruits, nuts, and seeds pick up the least contamination.

Avoid obvious polluted places. Heavy metals tend to settle within 50 feet of heavy traffic and persist in the soil, even decades later. Arsenic was used before DDT, for spraying fruit in orchards, and that's still around in those places too. Railroads spray toxic herbicides around their tracks, so avoid foraging near those. Golf courses are just as bad. Disheveled-looking old buildings, which look like sites where people dumped all sorts of toxic substances, are obvious places to avoid. The same is true in the vicinity of farms that use toxic chemicals on their crops. Polluted waterways should also be avoided.

Rinse off everything you take home under running water, and use common sense to avoid foraging from sites that are likely to be contaminated. Most of the plants in this book are so common, once you've learned them, you should be able to find them in unspoiled natural habitats.

PLANT NAMES

Common names are ambiguous and vary regionally, so two different plants may have the same name. Scientific names are hard to memorize, but you can look them up in this book and use them as references, to make sure you don't get poisoned by nomenclature! Family names are included too, as members of plant families have some common characteristics, especially their reproductive parts (which is why they were put into one family in the first place), making it easier to get a handle on all the botanical diversity you're going to encounter. All members of the legume family, for example, have pods that look recognizably like a variant of peapods.

SEASONAL CHANGES

When you look at the info about plant seasons, keep in mind that these periods are relative. Spring starts later, and autumn and winter come sooner, in northernmost regions and sectors of higher elevation, for example, and—as everyone but politicians knows—long-range climate change is altering plants' seasons too, as we heat up the atmosphere with massive carbon dioxide emissions. When I began foraging on a colder planet in 1982, spring plants appeared close to a month later than they do now, and fruits ripened earlier or later too: For some species, an earlier spring gives the flowers that produce the fruit a head start. For other species, a longer autumn stretches out the time during which the fruit is available. Hopefully foragers and other conscientious people who are in touch with the earth will force politicians to change their destructive ways!

HABITATS

While I list all the habitats where plants grow, some places are better than others. A plant that can grow in partial shade may do even better in full sunlight, and one fruit tree may be genetically constituted to have better-tasting berries than the one next to it. Often, those with the largest, most abundant, and brightly colored fruits are the best. Again, look around and sample before you start collecting.

THE DANDELION POLICE, FORAGING, AND CONSERVATION

It's also good to collect where it's legal to do so, although this can sometimes be difficult. Check out my arrest for eating a dandelion in Central Park (see p. 45). As you'll see, in this case, my civil disobedience paid off, enabling me to teach foraging and appreciation of nature to many thousands of adults and kids in the ensuing decades. The bottom line is that no edible "weeds" have ever been damaged as a result of my activities. Hopefully readers will be able to avoid confrontations with self-serving public officials!

Foraging is good for the environment. Picking small proportions of very common plants where they're common has no detrimental environmental impact whatsoever, but it naturally motivates people to protect the habitats where these species grow, and, by extension, other ecosystems and the rest of our planet. Children who first became aware of the natural environment and the science that illuminates it while attending one my tours with their school class, or with parents, e-mailed me decades later, writing how this activity first sparked their interest in nature and conservation. Some of them have become ecotourist guides, science teachers, or dedicated conservationists.

NUTRITION

Wild foods are usually more nutritious than store-bought foods. Wild plants depend on nutrients and other helpful substances (phytochemicals) for survival, while store-bought plants are bred to be larger, heavier, less perishable, and more beautiful. Therefore, if you put the store-bought produce into a juicer, you get more juice. Juice is mostly water, so these plants have a greater proportion of water to nutrients, phytochemicals, and flavor compared to wild plants.

PLANTS FOR MEDICINE

Wild plants, of course, have been used for medicine ever since humans first walked the earth. Plants use such substances to take care of many of their needs, from making food to defense against herbivores, so they're replete with biologically active chemicals, which people use to their advantage.

These can be both helpful and dangerous. Using plants to treat mosquito bites and tummy aches is fine. (It also works!) Using them to treat symptoms of serious illnesses, where you don't even have a diagnosis of the cause of the symptoms, can be disastrous. Consult a qualified practitioner for anything that might be a major problem, and then use herbs if they're going to be helpful.

RECIPES AND FORAGING

Once you've identified and harvested your wild food, what can you do with it? Some plants are great to eat in the field. Eating fruit berries on the spot is as much fun for adults as it is for kids. But I've also provided you with what I think are very tasty and healthful recipes, from simple to complex, for most of the plants I've covered. Here's how my approach of combining gourmet cooking with nutrition came to be.

Decades ago, the scientific indications that a diet high in processed foods; refined, concentrated, simple carbohydrates (sugar and white flour); and animal fats—which is also necessarily a low-fiber diet—is unhealthful looked very compelling to me. The early deaths from heart disease and cancer, of family members in my parents' and grandparents' generations, only reinforced this. In consequence, I've been an organic whole-foods vegan since 1990. I also swim laps, bicycle, do rapid walking, practice yoga, use light weights, and meditate regularly. Chances are it's this lifestyle that's keeping me fit and healthy as I approach my late sixties.

The scientific evidence that eating what Big Food wants us to buy is fueling the current epidemics of obesity, diabetes, heart disease, strokes, and cancer is now greater than ever. The inhumane treatment of factory-farmed animals and the accompanying harm to the environment caused by inefficiently growing plants to feed animals are additional factors influencing my choice of lifestyle.

So the recipes in this book are all vegan, although they do include lamb's quarters, sheep sorrel, and cattails! I use healthful, whole ingredients, some of which you may have to buy in health food stores or online, just as you'd go to specialty stores or sites if you're going to make Japanese or Indian recipes. I've melded traditional concepts from cuisines from around the world, plus modern culinary ideas, with wild foods and vegan ingredients in new ways to make delicious, healthful recipes.

I'm not trying to force anyone to adopt my lifestyle, but I think the idea that you've to give up eating tasty food to be healthy is wrong. You can make healthful and tasty meals, significantly lowering your risk of contracting these diseases of civilization, and have fun in the process. In other words, you can have your cake and eat it too!

If you try these recipes, according to what people on my tours tell me when I share samples of dishes made with the plants I have found, they taste really good, no matter what kind of foods these people normally eat (or maybe they're just being polite, to ensure that they're still alive when the tour ends!). Whether my ideas of preventing illness are right or wrong, I hope you enjoy the results of my decades of experimenting with wild food recipes!

Wild foods make these dishes special, but the recipes still work very well with store-bought ingredients, so I offer such substitutions whenever possible, in case you haven't found the wild food that's called for, or it's out of season.

ORGANIZATION OF THIS BOOK

As much as possible, the plants in this book are grouped both by food groups and season, starting with the cold-weather shoots and greens that come up in early spring and often again in fall, progressing to flowers that mostly span from early to mid spring. Then, I move to warm-weather veggies, some of which may persist though fall. Fruits and berries, which start toward the end of spring and keep coming until late fall, appear next. They're followed by nuts and seeds, in season, mainly in autumn. Subsequently come root vegetables, which are at their peak both in autumn and early spring, but persist through the winter if it's warm enough. I arbitrarily end with seaweeds, which are mostly in season all year.

Of course, not all plants fit into neat categories. Frustratingly, some plants are good to go all year. Wintergreen (see p. 255), for example, provides leaves for making tea all year, plus berries that are ripe from autumn sometimes up to early spring. Since berries are more spectacular than tea, I arbitrarily include this species at the end of the fruit section. Sassafras (see p. 2) I simply place in the beginning of the book, since you can start foraging for them in the winter.

FINAL HINTS

Study the plants you may find in the habitats you're about to explore in advance. Look at the pictures carefully. You may spot some of the plants right away. Others may take time to recognize.

Teaching myself, I first recognized some plants when they were in flower and easiest to identify, although not necessarily in an edible stage. Every subsequent year, I was able to spot these plants earlier and earlier, until finally I'd notice their first traces as they emerged from the soil.

Of course, if there's a foraging teacher in your area, study with him or her. I've found that people who attend about ten of my tours in different parks through the course of nine months become so familiar with the vast majority of the wild foods in the region that I have a hard time showing them two new species in the course of a subsequent 4-hour tour. Under these circumstances, learning to become an expert forager takes about the same amount of time and effort as learning to drive a car, an order of magnitude easier than mastering a musical instrument or martial arts, for example. I hope these suggestions and the information in this book make learning to forage easier and more fun for you!

Early Spring Shoots and Greens

These are the first plants to appear when winter ends, and many of the cold-resistant greens are the last ones you'll be able to collect in late autumn, as they come up for a second time and they're cold-resistant by necessity. If winter is exceptionally warm, some of these will continue to grow even then. Some of these plants spread out their leaves close to the ground, radiating in a circle from the root system, in a configuration called a basal rosette. This maximizes sunlight and minimizes cold. Later on, when it's warmer, some of these develop stems, reaching upward toward the sun.

Other plants form shoots, stems with immature leaves wrapped around them, growing upwards toward the sunlight right away. These are less likely to reappear in autumn.

Sassafras
(*Sassafras albidum*)

Family: Lauraceae, the laurel family

Other names: White sassafras, gumbo filé, cinnamon wood, mitten tree, ague tree, saxifras, tea tree

This very common, medium-sized native tree, 30–40 (sometimes up to 80) feet tall, smells lemony or like root beer when broken. The irregularly furrowed brown bark, red-orange underneath, has vertical ridges and horizontal slits. The many green, minutely hairy, lemon-scented saplings, with upward-curved, candelabra-like tips, only reach maturity in full sunlight.

The smooth, stalked, alternate, toothless, medium-sized leaves may be oval, one-lobed, or two-lobed. Tiny, inconspicuous, five-petaled, long-stalked, radially symmetrical yellow flowers bloom on small racemes in the spring, while the leaves are forming. Female flowers become small, blue-black, ovate fruits, about half an inch long, set in long-stalked, red cups.

Look for sassafras in sunny and partially sunny habitats, on dry acidic soil, in old fields, along the borders of woods, in open woodlands, on bottomlands, in thickets, along fencerows and roadsides, on lower slopes, in urban parks, and sometimes along residential streets, anywhere in the eastern United States and Ontario.

Available whenever the ground isn't frozen, especially after it's rained, pull up the smaller, renewable saplings' roots (or use twig). Young, green leaves are good from late spring into mid-summer.

Simmer the scrubbed roots (which you can reuse), covered, for 20 minutes for tea. Chill this, and stir in chilled sparkling water and a sweetener to make root beer. The root's cambium, without any bark, fresh or dried, makes a superb sweet seasoning, like cinnamon, root beer, anise, and ginger. The young, light green leaves are edible raw, great in salads and sandwiches too. Dried and ground into *filé powder,* they thicken soups, creating gumbos. Stir 2 tbsp into a completed pot of soup to serve six. The soup thickens instantly. Puréeing the leaves with some of the broth in a blender before returning it to the the soup works too.

Sassafras contains oils, fats, resins, wax, camphor, albumen, starch, gum, lignin, tannin, salts, safrole, and sassafrid. Native Americans used the tea as a blood purifier (detoxifier) and spring tonic, and American herbalists used it as a diaphoretic for colds and fever, to treat chronic arthritis, gout, high blood pressure, kidney problems, stomachaches, eczema, and other skin diseases. Compresses have been applied to infections, burns, and poison ivy rash, and a distilled aromatic oil has been used for menstrual obstruction and childbirth, although it hasn't been tested scientifically.

Caution: The FDA (Food and Drug Administration) has removed sassafras from the market. It can increase your risk of liver cancer, if you take the equivalent of 200 cups of tea made from artificial concentrate every day for only 2 years, and you just happen to be a rat! Rodents metabolize safrole differently from humans. No human has ever gotten sick from drinking sassafras tea. Furthermore, beer, which due to its alcohol content is fourteen times as carcinogenic to humans as sassafras is to rodents, is still on the market. So the experiment proves two important points:

1. There are more beer lobbyists in Washington than sassafras lobbyists.
2. There are lots of rats in the FDA!

Also, a population study indicated that the tea lowers the risk of liver cancer!

RECIPE

Vegan Sour Cream

Here's an especially good vegan version of sour cream you can use the same way you use the dairy version.

2 cups silken tofu, well drained

¼ cup lime juice

1 tbsp brown rice vinegar or wine vinegar

¼ cup lecithin granules

2 tbsp sweetened miso coating (see below)

2 tbsp fresh dill weed

2 tbsp vegan butter substitute or flaxseed, corn, or olive oil

1. Puree all ingredients in a food processor, or with a whisk or fork.
   Makes 2⅓ cups
   Preparation time: 5 minutes

RECIPE

Sweetened Miso Coating

Here's a very tasty condiment you can use to coat vegetables before baking them, as a spread or to add flavor to potatoes, grains, soups, or stews.

2 cups white miso

½ cup sesame oil

½ cup pine nuts or lecithin granules

8 Medjool (soft) dates, pitted

2 tbsp liquid stevia or other sweetener

2 tsp freshly grated orange rind or orange extract

½ tsp dried sassafras cambium, ground; or 1 tsp powdered cinnamon

2 tsp slippery elm powder (available in herb stores and online), or 1 tsp maple extract

2 inches of the scrapings from the inside of a vanilla bean, or 2 tsp vanilla extract

1. Purée all ingredients in a food processor.
   Yields: 3 cups
   Preparation time: 5 minutes

Chickweed
(*Cerastium* spp.)

Family: Caryophyllaceae, the pink or carnation family
Other names: Chickenwort, craches, maruns, winterweed (*Stellaria* spp.), mouse-ear chickweed

This small, sprawling European herbaceous plant, which often forms dense mats along the ground, gets its name because chickens love it. A row of fine hairs, grows along the slender stem. The tiny, opposite, spade-shaped to oval leaves are smooth edged and hairless. Common chickweed (*Stellaria media*) has leafstalks, while star chickweed (*S. pubera*) lacks them. Tiny white flowers bloom in early spring and late fall. The "V"-shaped petals are split so deeply, you could count them as ten, although there are only five. Surrounding the petals are five tiny, green sepals. A tiny, ovate, stalked capsule, contains even smaller oval, yellow-brown seeds. Mouse-ear chickweed (*Cerastium* spp.) is quite similar to common and star chickweeds, except that it's fuzzy everywhere.

This annual tolerates the cold. Best in late fall and early spring, it also grows in warm, snow-free spots in the winter. Chickweed finishes its life cycle by mid-spring, sets seed, and dies; but the seeds can germinate in the summer and new growth can occur then; so you may find it any month of the year. However, when it produces seeds and starts to die, it becomes stringy and tastes grassy.

Chickweed grows in full sun and partial shade, on lawns, in parks, and along trail- and roadside, although I've found it under trees where some sunlight penetrates in the summer.

Several plants look enough like chickweed that you may collect them along with your chickweed if you're careless: Doorweed (*Polygonum aviculare*) grows in the same habitats as chickweed, but in a basal rosette; and with alternate, not opposite leaves; joints on the stem; and no row of hair on the stem. The flowers are different too. It's nonpoisonous, but tastes like wire. Cooked, it tastes like cooked wire!

Spotted spurge (*Euphorbia supina*) has opposite leaves and trails along the ground like chickweed, but a blackish line runs the length of each elliptical leaf, and the white flowers are nothing like chickweed's. A distinct, white sap pervades the plant, oozing out of the cut stem. This looks poisonous, and it is!

The scarlet pimpernel (*Anagallis arvensis*) looks the most like chickweed, creeping along the ground, with opposite or whorled, oval leaves, ¼–1¼ inches long. However, the leaves are shiny and, yet again, the row of hairs running along the stem is missing. The flowers are scarlet-orange. This plant is also poisonous, especially if you're French. (Download the hilarious movie of same name, and you'll see why!)

Look for the thickest, greenest mats of pure chickweed before collecting, to avoid having to sort out grass or the like. Grab bunches in one hand and cut it at the base, or hold down the bottom of the bunch with one hand and tear out the rest with the other hand.

You can eat everything but the roots, raw or cooked, and it tastes like corn or corn silk. Chop it into bite-sized pieces and add it to salads or sandwiches, or any recipe that calls for sprouts. Cook it in any recipe that calls for greens, adding it 5 minutes before a recipe is done. Don't overcook.

Waterless steaming works quite well too. Place the rinsed, drained, and chopped pieces in a heavy saucepan and cook, covered, over low heat until just wilted. Don't add water. Season with any seasoning you prefer: Garlic sautéed lightly in olive oil, plus tamari soy sauce, is great, as are Thai seasonings, such as lemongrass, basil, a hot pepper, ginger, and salt, plus some coconut oil.

Chickweed is loaded with nutrients, such as vitamins C, A, D, folic acid, riboflavin, niacin, and thiamin; and minerals including calcium, magnesium, potassium, manganese, zinc, iron, phosphorus, sodium, copper, and silica. Not bad for a garden "weed."

This is a very important plant in traditional herbal medicine and it's completely safe, so long as you're not suffering from an untreated serious disease. In the past, herbalists had people who'd survived serious illnesses drink a chickweed infusion, or a soup with chickweed, to rebuild their strength. With bodies greatly depleted of vitamins and minerals, due to the initial illness, they'd be immunocompromised, and chickweed would replace these essential nutrients, speeding up recovery.

An infusion of the whole aboveground plant is also a safe, gentle diuretic. You can also chop up the plant and apply it topically for skin sores and irritations.

RECIPE

Savory Chickweed Dip

Conceived by my then-eleven-year-old daughter, Violet Brill, this somewhat spicy dip features the spectacular flavor of chickweed, enhanced by the other seasonings. Use it with chips, celery, or anything else that's dipable! We first made this in January, during a mild winter, when this hardy but delicate plant was thriving. The onion is soaked to make it less spicy—important if you're going to serve the recipe to kids!

4 cloves of garlic

2 tbsp red onion, finely chopped and soaked in water for 30 minutes, then drained and patted dry with paper towels

2 cups chickweed or other greens

2 cups corn chips, coarsely ground

2 tbsp white (mellow) miso

1 tbsp vegan butter substitute or olive oil

1 tsp coarse salt, or to taste

½ tsp wild carrot seeds or celery seed, ground

½ tsp paprika

¼ tsp nutmeg, ground

1. Chop the garlic in a food processor.
2. Add the chickweed and chop.
3. Add the remaining ingredients and process until well mixed and finely chopped.
   Yields: 2¼ cups
   Preparation time: 40 minutes

Garlic Mustard
(*Alliaria petiolata*)

Family: Brassicaceae or Cruciferae, the mustard, crucifer, or cabbage family
Other names: Jack-by-the-hedge, garlic root, hedge garlic, sauce-alone, Jack-in-the-bush, penny hedge, hedge garlic, poor man's mustard

This European biennial is one of the most common and invasive of wild foods, with many different forms. It begins in very early spring as a nondescript, flag-shaped sprout, with a single slender, reddish stalk about 2 inches in height and one strap-shaped leaf about ½ inch long. The sprout, as well as the subsequent leaves, stem, flower buds, and flowers, all emit the distinct smell of garlic when crushed, a good defense against insects (unless Italian insects find it, when all bets are off!).

The sprout soon develops into a basal rosette, supported by a fleshy, white, horseradish-scented taproot that increases in size in proportion to the basal leaves. Dark green, kidney-shaped, scallop-edged, deeply veined, and long-stalked, the basal leaves sometimes grow up to 5 inches across.

The basal rosette persists throughout the first year, persevering through mild winters, or returns in early spring of the second year; but by mid-spring of the second year, a single, erect, slightly hairy stem grows 1–3½ feet tall. Its deeply veined, triangular, alternate leaves are more pointed and larger-toothed than the basal leaves.

A small, broccoli-like flower bud develops into clusters of four-petaled white flowers, each ⅓ inch across. The petals of the alternating flowers form a cross, like all mustards, and these become long, slender, cylindrical, alternating seedpods called siliques. They are 1–1½ inches long and curve upward from long stalks.

The plant dies in its second summer, leaving behind the short-stalked, needle-shaped siliques, which are now dry and whitish. The frequent large stands of this invasive plant you encounter produce so many of these needles, you'd think you were in the South Bronx! The seedpods split lengthwise to disclose two rows

of tiny, oblong, blackish, finely lined, spicy flavored seeds, guaranteeing further proliferation of this delicious nuisance.

Garlic mustard is a highly invasive species that takes over woodlands, disturbed habitats, parks, roadsides, trail sides, edge habitats, and wetlands. One reason it's so successful is that it excretes fungicides from its roots that inhibit the growth of fungi that support tree growth. Garlic mustard grows throughout northeastern North America, much of the middle of the country, and in the Pacific Northwest.

Each part of the plant has its own season. The sprouts come up in early spring. The basal leaves are available all year if winter isn't harsh. The leaves of the leafstalk, the top of the leafstalk, the flower buds, and the flowers are good to go in mid-spring. The roots are good to use in the fall, during winters mild enough for the leaves to survive and mark their location, and in early spring. The seeds are most abundant in mid-summer, but some remain into autumn.

Pinch off the sprouts and handfuls of basal leaves with your fingers. Strip leaves, tender upper stems, flower buds, and flowers from mature plants. You can sometimes uproot the taproot under the basal rosette with your fingers too; but if it doesn't come up readily, use a shovel or trowel. Break off the dead plants with their seedpods and stuff them into a large paper bag. Rub out the seeds over a tray at home, blow away the chaff, and store the seeds in a jar. They last indefinitely.

Add the young basal leaves and sprouts, which taste like garlic with an overtone of bitterness, to salads and sandwiches. They're excellent in pesto.

The bitterness concentrates when you cook them and they shrink, so use them sparingly in recipes that call for greens. They cook in about 5 minutes. The mature basal leaves are more bitter than the young ones, but roasting them with oil, salt, and spices; or in a coating of white (mellow) miso, olive oil, and lecithin granules or pine nuts, with sweet or savory spices, makes them delicious.

The immature leaves on the stem are spicy, less bitter than the basal leaves, garlicky, and a little sweet. They're even better in pesto, salads, sandwiches, and cooked veggie dishes than the basal leaves.

Use the taproots just like horseradish. Both roots contain the same glucosinalates, which turn into highly volatile oils called isothiocyanates when the plant is cut, making it spicy. The grated or chopped root is wonderful in dips, spreads, and dressings, and in bland dishes like beans, potatoes, or pasta. Heat destroys the flavor, so add them to cold dishes. Oxygen destroys the flavor too, so store the roots—chopped, grated, or whole—covered in vinegar. The root freezes well, since it's adapted to do this in nature during the winter.

The seeds are quite spicy, like crunchy horseradish with an overtone of sunflower seeds. You don't have to grind them, like store-bought mustard seeds, and they add texture to recipes, raw or cooked. Use them in the same kind of recipes as the roots, sprinkle them on salads, or bake them into breads, like fiery caraway seeds. You can also grind them in a blender, covered with vinegar, to make prepared mustard. Add salt or white miso, and the same kinds of additional spices used in traditional prepared mustard recipes.

Calling some products superfoods is mainly a marketing gimmick; but if there were such things, garlic mustard would qualify as one. It provides vitamins A, C, and E; omega-3 fatty acids; some B vitamins; plus the minerals potassium, calcium, magnesium, copper, iron, manganese, and selenium. The sprouts, like other microgreens, have four to six times the concentration of nutrients of the mature plant.

The leaves also contain plant estrogens adapted to interfere with insect reproduction, and also inhibit human and synthetic estrogens from signaling human cells to proliferate, thereby reducing the risk of cancer. Furthermore, the sulfur-containing amino acids that produce the garlic aroma dilate the blood vessels, just as garlic does, reducing the risk of cardiovascular disease; although because of this effect, people with low blood pressure should check their blood pressure after eating the leaves, to make sure it's not exacerbating the condition.

Garlic mustard isn't used much in traditional herbal medicine, but people have used an infusion of the leaves as a diaphoretic for fevers, to stimulate the immune system, and for bronchitis. They've heated the root in oil and applied this ointment to the chest for bronchitis. This hasn't been tested, although the juice from the leaves inhibits the growth of gram-negative bacteria, such as those that cause typhoid and gastroenteritis. Yet again, more study is called for. The crushed leaves have been applied to insect bites and stings, although jewelweed and common plantain are more effective.

RECIPE

Garlic Lover's White Bean Dip

Wild seasonings (for which you can substitute store-bought ones) make this dip so tasty, you may not be able to stop to open a bag of chips for scooping before devouring it.

1¼ cups white beans

4 cups vegetable stock

¼ cup olive oil

1 tsp tarragon, ground

2 bay leaves, enclosed in a tea bag or tea ball

8 large cloves of store-bought garlic, chopped

1 tsp Vege-Sal or seasoned salt, or ½ tsp salt, or to taste

2 tbsp whole garlic mustard seeds or 1 tsp commercial mustard seeds, ground, or to taste

1. Rinse the beans, transfer them to a pressure cooker or saucepan, cover them with water, bring the water to a boil, remove the pressure cooker or saucepan from the heat, and let the beans steep for 1 hour (or soak the rinsed beans in room temperature water to cover overnight).
2. Drain and rinse off the beans.
3. Return the beans to the pressure cooker with the vegetable stock, 2 tbsp of olive oil, epazote, and bayberry leaves, and pressure cook this under the highest pressure for 20 minutes (or simmer in a covered saucepan for 3 hours, or until the beans are tender, stirring occasionally).

4. Meanwhile, lightly sauté the wild garlic in the remaining olive oil in a small frying pan for 3–5 minutes, or until very lightly browned. Remove the wild garlic from the pan immediately, to prevent it from burning and becoming bitter. Reserve the olive oil.
5. Drain the beans, discard the bayberry leaves, and reserve the stock.
6. Purée the beans with the reserved olive oil from the sauté pan, plus the Vege-Sal, in a food processor. If you prefer a thinner dip, add some of the stock or additional olive oil to taste.
7. Add the garlic and garlic mustard seeds, and process until just mixed.
   Makes 3 cups
   Preparation time: 25 minutes
   Cooking time: 20 minutes

RECIPE

Garlic Mustard Salad Dressing

Garlic mustard roots add the zing to this dressing, which will make even the best salad even better.

2 cups vegan mayonnaise

½ cup brown rice vinegar

¼ cup garlic mustard taproot

2 tsp smoked paprika

2 tsp tarragon, ground

1 tsp sage, ground

½ tsp Celtic Sea Salt or other coarse salt

¼ tsp powdered or liquid stevia

1. Purée all ingredients together in a blender.
   Yields: 2½ cups
   Preparation time: 5 minutes

Field Garlic
(*Allium vineale*)

Family: Amaryllidaceae, the amaryllis family
Other names: Onion grass, meadow garlic, wild onion, Canada garlic, wild garlic, rose leek, meadow leek, tree onion

This delicious, common, widespread Eurasian/North African perennial, which smells like onions and garlic, was incredibly hard to find when I first taught myself foraging. I saw line drawings in the field guide I was using, but just couldn't spot the plant, so I went swimming (I like to stay fit) in the local YMCA. After my mile of laps in the pool, I held on to the edge of the pool and conversed with an acquaintance named Chuck:

"Chuck, you know I like to cook. Now I'm trying to learn foraging."
"I know one wild edible plant, Steve. It's called onion grass."
"Chuck, you have to tell me where it grows! I've been looking for it for a year! WHERE IS IT? WHERE IS IT!? YOU HAVE TO TELL ME!"

After making the CIA waterboard agents at Guantanamo look like wimps, a half-drowned Chuck spluttered out its location, near the baseball field close to the Grand Central Parkway in Alley Pond Park in Queens, New York. The next day was my bike riding exercise day. I sped off first thing in the morning, and there it was!

After collecting all I could use, I pedaled back home. To my surprise, I started seeing field garlic in other places in the park, in green areas on my route home, and finally, right in front of the service entrance to my apartment building, as I was dismounting my bike. Turns out I was confusing it with grass, unaware that grass has flat blades, while field garlic has basal leaves that are cylindrical.

Unlike what you'd expect, new leaves begin growing in early autumn. Long, slender, unbranched, hollow, round, and grooved, they often survive the winter, growing more during warm spells. If severe winter weather does them in, they resume growing very early in the spring, as soon as the snow and ice are gone, and it's above freezing during part of the day.

The leaves grow from 6 inches to 24 inches long, coming from small clusters of layered underground bulbs that look tiny onions in the fall, winter, and early spring. The bulbs grow to almost 1 inch across, and look more like garlic cloves in mid-spring, when the bulbs partially split.

By late spring, a spherical cluster or whitish, green-tinged, or reddish bulblets, ¾–2 inches across, grows above a single, smooth, erect, green, leafless scape, 1–3½ feet tall. The tiny bulblets are ovoid, with one flat side and one curved side. Sometimes a tiny, slender, green shoot grows out of the top of the bulblet.

Additional stalks of tiny, lilac-colored, six-petaled, short-stalked flowers, about ¾ inch long, sometimes also emerge from the tops of the bulblets.

A membrane surrounding the bulblets eventually bursts. The garlic-scented bulblets fall to the ground, and eventually grow into new plants (unless Italian herbivores find them first!).

Wild garlic resemble field garlic. They're both edible, but they have flat leaves, not cylindrical ones.

Some poisonous lilies have narrow leaves and bulbs, but they're odorless, and all the other characteristics are different too.

One poisonous plant, Star-of-Bethlehem (*Ornithogalum umbellatum*), greatly resembles field garlic in early spring (it doesn't reemerge in autumn), and they sometimes grow side by side.

However, Star-of-Bethlehem has flat leaves, not cylindrical ones. A white stripe runs down the length of each leaf and the plant has no odor, so you have to be careless to confuse the two. The flowers (which bloom in mid-spring) and seeds are completely different too.

Poisoning is so rare, I have had only one fatality since I first began teaching foraging in 1982: Soon after warning tour participants who were about to harvest field garlic to beware of Star-of-Bethlehem, I saw that one woman had been putting the toxic species into her bag. I stopped her before she could eat any, but the unfortunate lady still succumbed—she died of embarrassment!

Field garlic grows throughout most of the eastern United States and eastern Canada, plus the Pacific States and western Canada. You'll find it in partially shaded and sunny habitats. It grows along edges; in lawns, meadows, pastures, and fields; along roadsides, riversides and stream sides; in backyards; on disturbed soil; in parks; and in open woods. It's a very common plant. Dairy farmers hate it, because if cows eat it, their milk tastes like garlic!

The leaves are in season when they're young, in the fall and early spring, as well as during mild winters. By mid-spring, they become too tough to eat. The aboveground bulblets are in season from late spring through mid-summer, before they fall to the ground. The underground bulbs are edible all year, although you won't be able to locate them after mid-summer when the aboveground parts vanish or during very cold winters.

You can tear or cut off the young basal leaves, or dig up the whole plant with a shovel or trowel. I swing the mass of bulbs against a tree, and pull apart the bunch of leaves into smaller groups, to get rid of the soil quickly. You can pull off the bulblets with your fingers.

Cooking "authorities" put down this plant in print, because they don't know what they're doing and pick the mature leaves in mid or late spring, when they're awful. But the young leaves are great, with a flavor of their own, yet still similar to onions and garlic. Use them accordingly, in salads, sandwiches, soups, stews, sauces, grains, casseroles, or any savory dish, the way you'd use scallions or chives. They cook in about 15 minutes, and any cooking method works with them.

This plant hasn't been analyzed nutritionally; but if it's similar to its relative, garlic, it should be a good source of antioxidants, flavonoids, carotenoids and chlorophyll. Because of the garlic odor, it must contain sulfur compounds that may help reduce LDL (bad) cholesterol levels and aid digestion.

Herbalists consider it to be a blood purifier, carminative, diuretic, expectorant, stimulant, and vasodilator. The raw bulbs may lower blood pressure, good to try if your blood pressure is being monitored, to see whether it works. However, if you've low blood pressure, be careful with it, starting with very small amounts, lest it lower your blood pressure further.

A tincture of the bulbs has been used to prevent colic and croup, and the plant may have antiasthmatic properties, although this should be tested. It also reputedly stops kids from getting worms, but this hasn't worked with my young daughter, who collects field garlic with one hand, while unearthing and collecting earthworms with the other!

RECIPE

Indian Field Garlic Soup

With its spicy flavor, field garlic is ideal in Indian recipes. This recipe combines field garlic with store-bought garlic, and it's quick and easy to make.

¼ cup vegan butter substitute or olive oil

2 cups field garlic leaves or scallions, coarsely chopped

1 tsp fresh ginger, coarsely chopped

1 tsp cumin, ground

½ tsp coriander seed, ground

½ tsp thyme, ground

½ tsp black pepper, ground

2 heads of garlic, peeled but not chopped

2 cups chopped lettuce

4 cups vegetable stock

1 cup cooked yam or potato, coarsely chopped

1 medium tomato

1 tbsp white (mellow) miso

1. Sauté the field garlic in the vegan butter substitute, along with the ginger, cumin, coriander, thyme, black pepper, and garlic, for 5–10 minutes or until the garlic is lightly browned.
2. Meanwhile, simmer the lesser celandine in water to cover for 2 minutes, drain, and discard the water (not necessary if you're using lettuce).
3. Combine the field garlic mixture, lesser celandine, and all remaining ingredients in a saucepan, bring to a boil over high heat, stirring often, reduce the heat to low, cover, and simmer for 10 minutes.
4. Purée in batches in a blender, holding down the cover with a towel and beginning on low speed to prevent eruptions.
   Serves: 4
   Preparation time: 25 minutes
   Cooking time: 20 minutes

Daylily
(*Hemerocallis fulva*)

Family: Xanthorrhoeaceae, the aloe family
Other names: Orange daylily, tawny daylily, tiger daylily, ditch daylily

This extremely common invasive Asian perennial produces four crops: shoots, flower buds, flowers, and tubers. One of the first plants to appear in late winter, the first thing you see are shoots, composed of sword-shaped, light green basal leaves, with the parallel veins typical of the lilies. The leaves eventually reach 1–3 feet in length and flop over, but when they first appear, they're still upright and tightly wrapped together, united at the whitish, ellipsoid or cylindrical base. This base grows 1–2 inches tall, before the young leaves begin to curve away from both sides, in the same plane.

Fleshy, light brown rhizomes—with the thickness of shoelaces, about ¼ inch in diameter—spread into the ground from the base, each ending in a small, ellipsoid, light brown tuber, about ¾ inch long. Roots emanate from the ends of the tubers. In late spring, a smooth, leafless flower stalk grows ¼–½ inch in diameter and 3–4 feet tall. It's unbranched for most of its length, then produces short branches near the top, ending in six to fifteen cylindrical, lined, yellow-orange flower buds, 1½–3 inches long. These open into large, showy, short-stemmed, upward-facing, orange, funnel-shaped flowers. Nearly identical, the three-reflexed tepals and three sepals, about 4 inches long, with ruffled edges, curve backward at their tips. A pale yellow line runs along each tepal's length. In the center of each flower, six short stamens surround a single long pistil. The flower clusters often consist of the flowers, each of which lives for only one day; unopened flower buds of different lengths and levels of maturity; and wilted flowers from previous days. Wild daylilies produce no seeds. Squirrels dig up and eat some of the tubers, bury what they don't eat, and forget some of their stashes, thereby spreading clones of this plant.

Bred as show flowers, cultivated daylilies come in a variety of colors and are sometimes bred to have more than six tepals and sepals. These varieties are edible, but not as good as the common feral orange ones.

Tiger lilies (*Lilium tigrinum*), which also have edible flowers, resemble day-lilies, but they have leaves growing from the stem, whereas daylily scapes are

bare. I only see tiger lilies in gardens, but they're supposedly capable of escaping into the wild.

Caution: The daffodil (*Narcissus pseudonarcissus*) is a poisonous garden plant that escapes into the wild. It's long, sword-like leaves resemble the daylily's at first, but there's no cylindrical base, the white flowers are completely different, and there are no tubers. The poisonous iris (*Iris* spp.) has sword-like leaves as well, but, again, completely different flowers, no cylindrical base, and a single, thick rhizome, rather than tubers.

Daylilies grow in cultivated areas, parks, disturbed habitats, edges, lawns, parks, thickets, along trail- and roadsides, and in open woodlands. The shoots are in season in early spring; the flower buds, flowers, and wilted flowers from late spring to mid-summer; and the tubers are available all year, although they're at their best from fall through early spring.

The first time I found what I thought might be daylilies was right after they'd finished flowering, in mid-summer. When I returned early the following spring and saw the shoots, I still wasn't confident of my identification and didn't eat them. I waited another three months until they flowered, when it was easy to identify them. I enjoyed using the flowers, but had to wait still longer, until the following spring (twenty long months in total), to enjoy the shoots, and it was worth it. Not only were the shoots delicious, but I was still alive!

Growing in dense stands, daylily shoots are easy to harvest in quantity. Simply break off the shoots with your fingers or cut them off (the shoots, not your fingers!) with a sharp knife. Break off the flowers, flower buds, or wilted flowers with your fingers, and dig up the shallow tubers with a shovel or a trowel, easy if there are no rocks, and if rain has loosened the soil.

Like related onions, daylily shoots have a sharp, spicy flavor, plus an overtone of string beans. Excellent chopped into salads and sandwiches, any cooking method works wonderfully with them. They cook in about 10 minutes, and taste great in any savory dish, such as grains, beans, casseroles, soups, curries, stir-fries, and soups.

The flowers are both sweet and spicy. However, the bottom one-tenth of the flower, which is colored greenish, is acrid and should be discarded. The stamens and pistils, however, are edible. Chop the flowers into salads, but eat the salad the same day, before the flowers self-destruct. Italian and Chinese people dip the flowers in batter and deep-fry them. You can also put them in pancake batter and cook them into savory fritters. I've stuffed them with a vegan cottage cheese of my own devising, nuts, and dried apricots; sealed the flowers with toothpicks; and served them at parties. The flowers are also superb in soups, cooking in about 5 minutes. In fact, they're essential in Chinese hot and sour soup. The Chinese call them golden needles, and you can buy them dried in Chinese grocery stores and online, although there's no excuse for not getting them for free in the wild. This invasive plant grows in great abundance everywhere.

The larger flower buds that are just about to open taste like string beans. They're excellent sautéed, stir-fried, or cooked in soups or casseroles. The newly wilted flowers are great in soups too. The tubers taste like turnips. Scrub them, slice thinly, and sauté them or add them to soups. You can also mix them with oil and herbs and bake them. Use firm tubers only. The soft ones are awful.

Caution: Daylilies make about one out of fifty people sick, causing diarrhea or vomiting. Eat a couple of bites at first, then eat a little more each day to assure yourself that this plant is safe for you. If you feel queasy this plant is not for you. Also, on very rare occasions, a particular strain of daylilies can cause digestive distress in everyone. I've never encountered such a stand myself in over 35 years of foraging, and I know of only one foraging teacher who has. So, again, start slowly if you find daylilies somewhere new.

The shoots haven't been analyzed, but the flowers and flower buds are good sources of beta-carotene, vitamin C, and iron, and the tubers are high in protein and essential fatty acids.

The rhizomes and tubers show antimicrobial and anti parasitical effects, and could even inhibit the growth of cancer cells, but more research is needed to find out how to use them effectively.

Chinese herbalists (who also use it for pain, fever, childbirth, and as a sedative) call the daylily the flower of forgetfulness and use it for post-traumatic stress disorder (PTSD). I know one Chinese woman for who grew up under the rule of Chairman Mao, constantly in fear of the secret police, who could lock up anyone with impunity. She became a medical doctor, learned traditional Chinese herbal medicine, made friends with Westerners when that became possible, and emigrated to Boston. There she used daylily flower infusion to rid herself of the constant fear and anxiety that had become a way of life. I'd love to see this tested. Someone could give a large group of unprepared people a difficult math test, then give half the group daylily flower tea and the other half a placebo. Next they'd have everyone rate their symptoms. Sadly, such an inhumane experiment would never be approved by any ethics committee!

RECIPE

Sautéed Daylilies

Just a few seasonings turn daylilies into a perfect early spring cooked green. Serve over toast or with whole grains.

6 cups daylily shoots, chopped

6 tbsp olive oil

6 cloves of garlic, chopped

1 tsp Vege-Sal or seasoned salt, or ½ tsp salt, or to taste

1 tsp fennel seeds, ground

1 tsp paprika

1 tsp marjoram, ground

1 tbsp garlic mustard seeds **(see pp. 11)** or 1 tsp hot sauce, or to taste

1. Sauté all ingredients except the garlic mustard seeds together for 10–15 minutes, or until the daylilies are tender.
2. Serve sprinkled with the garlic mustard seeds or hot sauce.
   Serves: 6
   Preparation/cooking time: 15 minutes

RECIPE

Daylily Sherbet

Daylily flowers make any recipe luxuriant, and this sherbet is no exception.

3½ cups almond or soy milk

¼ cup silken tofu

¼ cup lecithin granules

¼ cup raw cashews

¼ cup grape seed oil

¼ cup vegetable glycerin

2 tsp clear liquid stevia

1 tsp cinnamon, ground

1 tsp dried mint leaves, ground

1 inch vanilla bean, scraped, or 1 tsp vanilla extract

¼ tsp salt

2 cups daylily flowers

1. Purée all ingredients in a blender except for 1 cup of the daylily flowers.
2. Chop the remaining daylily flowers in the blender, but don't purée them.
3. Transfer everything to an ice cream machine and freeze according to the manufacturer's directions.
   Yields: 5½ cups
   Preparation time: 10 minutes
   Freezing time: 120 minutes (varies)

Sheep Sorrel
(*Rumex acetosella*)

Family: Polygonaceae, the smartweed or buckwheat family
Other names: Red sorrel, sour weed, field sorrel

One of the best-tasting and most common wild foods, you don't want to be sheepish about trying this one! A European perennial, it spreads via rhizomes, but also has taproots.

The cold-hardy plant produces a basal rosette very early in the spring. The long-stalked leaves reach 1½–3 inches in length. The youngest leaves are briefly oval, but soon become arrow-shaped, like a sheep's face: the pointed tip is the nose and the two spreading lobes at the leaf base are the ears.

In mid-spring, a slender, branched, deeply ridged stem 1½–9 (sometimes up to 18) inches long arises. The stem is jointed and papery sheaths wrap around the stem adjacent to the leaf axils, just like its much larger relative, Japanese knotweed (see p. 54). The alternate leaves on sheep sorrel's stem look like the basal leaves, only smaller.

Tiny, yellow-green male flowers, and diminutive, reddish female flowers, bloom on long, lacy, loosely branched racemes on the upper stalks in late spring and early summer. Tiny, inconspicuous, reddish to yellow-brown fruits ripen in yellow-brown, papery wrappers in the summer as well.

Bindweed (*Convolvulus* spp.) is an inedible plant with arrow-shaped leaves, but it's a vine, not an upright plant, with funnel-shaped flowers and it never forms a basal rosette. Wood sorrel (see p. 99) sounds and tastes like sheep sorrel,

but looks completely different in all its forms. The word "sorrel" means sour in Old French.

The basal leaves grow in early spring and throughout the fall, and the aerial leaves are available in the summer. Sheep sorrel grows on sunny lawns, in fields and openings in the woods, along trail- and roadsides, in disturbed habitats, and on acidic soil throughout most of the United States and Canada.

The basal leaves are the largest and best ones to eat, although the stem leaves certainly aren't b…a…a…a…d either! Grasp a bunch of basal leaves with one hand, hold down the leafstalks with the other hand, and pull off the leaves, which are more tender than the leafstalks. You can also cut the entire rosette from the roots with a knife and trim off the leafstalks and roots. You can strip the aerial leaves off the stems with your fingers.

Sheep sorrel is strongly lemony and very delicious. Add the leaves raw to salads and sandwiches, or cook for around 10 minutes in soups, stews, grain and bean dishes, or any recipe that calls for greens. Nothing will drown out its strong flavor, and it adds zing to mild ingredients such as potatoes and squash.

This plant is replete with vitamins C, A, B-complex, D, E, K, P and U, plus the minerals calcium, phosphorus, magnesium, potassium, silicon, iron, sulfur, copper, iodine, manganese, and zinc. It also contains tartaric acid; the anthraquinones chrysophanol, emodin, and rhein; glycosides such as hyperoside; and quercetin 3-D-galactoside.

Because of its vitamin C content, it was used by herbalists to cure scurvy before vitamins were discovered. It's also been used as a diuretic, for inflammation, cancer, diarrhea, worms, intestinal parasites, and fever. With all its biologically active compounds, it should be tested to see if it can help any of these conditions.

RECIPE

Steve's Schav

Sheep sorrel gets its English name from the arrow-shaped leaf resembling a sheep's face, but it also looks like a calf's face and *schav* means calf in Yiddish. If you like tart flavors, you'll especially love sheep sorrel and the traditional Jewish cold sour soup it produces. It's particularly cooling on a hot day, but you can serve it hot as well.

8 cups vegetable stock

4 cups sheep sorrel, curly dock (see p. 94), wood sorrel (see p. 99), or garden sorrel

2 medium red onions, finely chopped

1 tbsp flaxseeds, ground

½ tbsp Vege-Sal or ¾ tsp salt, or to taste

¼ tsp black pepper, or to taste, ground

1 tbsp lemon juice

1 tbsp vegan butter substitute, or corn or olive oil

½ tbsp lecithin granules or pine nuts

1 cup silken tofu, diced

1. Bring ¾ of the stock, the sheep sorrel, onion, flaxseeds, Vege-Sal, and black pepper to a boil in a saucepan over medium heat; reduce the heat to low; and simmer, covered, for 5 minutes.
2. Meanwhile, puree the lemon juice, vegan butter substitute, and lecithin granules in a blender with the remaining stock.
3. Stir this into the soup with the tofu, adjust the seasonings to taste, and add additional lemon juice if desired.
4. Serve hot or chilled.
   Serves: 6
   Preparation/cooking time: 30 minutes

Common Mallow
(*Malva neglecta*)

Family: Malvaceae, the mallow family

Other names: Buttonweed, cheeseplant, cheeseweed, dwarf mallow, roundleaf mallow

This common, unobtrusive, mild-flavored European perennial is not to be neglected. Growing from a long, slender taproot, it can stand upright or creep along the ground.

The crinkled, toothed, slightly hairy, long-stalked basal leaves are round to heart-shaped, and the smaller leaves on the main stem are similar. The leaves grow from ¾ to 2½ inches across. They have five to seven shallow lobes and are notched where they connect with the leafstalk, which can get up to 7 inches long.

The flower is similar to the garden hibiscus flowers, only smaller. Less than ¾ inch across, it's five petals, plus a bushy column consists of many stamens, and one pistil in the center. White to pale pink or lavender, the petals are notched at the tips and pink lines run down their lengths. The stalked green fruit resembles a tiny wheel of cheese. It is ¼ inch across, flattened, rounded, and segmented.

Ground ivy (Glechoma hederacea) is a medicinal plant used as tea. It has-looking similar leaves, but they're opposite, not alternate, and quite hairy. Also, the whole plant smells minty.

Marsh mallow (*Althea officinalis*) has flowers similar to common mallow, but they're an order of magnitude larger and the leaves, which are heart-shaped to three-lobed, are velvety. This European relative of coastal marshes is edible, used much like common mallow, but very rare in the Mid-Atlantic states.

Common mallow grows in sunny and partially shaded places. You can find it in parks and gardens, along roadsides and paths, in empty lots, and on disturbed soil. It grows across North America.

To harvest, simply strip off the leaves, flowers, and "cheeses" with your fingers. You can eat the mild-flavored, mucilaginous leaves, flowers, and fruits raw or cooked. They're mild-tasting to bland, but have a wonderfully chewy texture, which will thicken soups, stews, and casseroles—the way okra, a relative, does. They cook in about 10 minutes. People have boiled the roots to create a thickener out of the water and tried eating the roots, like marsh mallow, but they're small and fibrous, so this isn't going to be very successful.

Common mallow provides vitamin C, iron, calcium, copper, and trace minerals. Tea made from boiling the roots of this plant and its relative, marsh mallow, has been used by herbalists, externally and internally, for skin sores, gastric and duodenal ulcers, digestive tract irritations, urinary tract irritations, cystitis, sore throats, irritated air passages, coughs, and bronchitis for centuries. The texture gives this demulcent a soothing effect, but it's never been tested scientifically to see where it has the most (and least) impact.

RECIPE

Unmellow Mallow

Common mallow loses its blandness completely with this wonderful combination of seasonings. Try one bite of these greens and you won't be able to stop eating them.

¼ cup peanut oil

¼ cup vegan butter substitute or olive oil

4 cups common mallow leaves, cheeses (the mallow fruits), or flowers

2 tsp whole cumin seeds

¼ tsp crushed red pepper

¼ cup fresh basil, chopped

1 tbsp wild or store-bought garlic, chopped

½ tsp coriander, ground

6 tbsp nutritional yeast

¼ tsp cloves

1 tsp tamari soy sauce

1. Sauté the mallow leaves for 10 minutes in 1 tbsp of the peanut oil and 1 tbsp of the vegan butter substitute.
2. Add the remaining vegan butter substitute and peanut oil, cumin seeds and crushed red pepper, and cook over low heat for 2–3 minutes, stirring constantly.
3. Add the basil and garlic and cook over low heat for another minute, stirring often.
4. Stir in the remaining ingredients, remove from heat, and allow to cook in the hot pan for another 2 minutes, stirring often.
   Serves: 4
   Preparation/cooking time: 10 minutes

Goutweed (*Aegopodium podagraria*)

Family: *Apiaceae or Umbelliferae*, the umbelliferous, celery, carrot, or parsley family
Other names: Bishopsweed, ground elder, herb gerard, snow-in-the-mountain

Goats love this plant, so it was first called "goatweed"; but after someone misheard it and it became changed to "goutweed," people began using it to treat gout! As a chess player, I prefer the name "bishop's weed," although it acquired that name after having been planted on the grounds of European monasteries centuries ago and had time to spread everywhere and take over.

An invasive European colonial perennial that smells and tastes like parsley, celery, and carrots, it spreads by means of long, white branching rhizomes, forming a ground cover. In late winter and early spring, it grows close to the ground, with hairless, long-stalked, three-parted palmate-compound basal leaves. The oval, pointed, sharp-toothed, irregularly lobed leaflets grow from 1 to 4 inches long, and the larger leaflets then divide into another two or three lobes.

In mid-spring, a hollow, furrowed stem grows from 1½ to over 3 feet tall, with alternate leaves similar to the basal ones. Flat-topped, umbrella-like flower clusters 2–4 inches across grow at the top of this stem. The clusters consist of many tiny, five-petaled, white flowers, growing at the tops of the branching stems in late spring and summer. Later in the summer, the flowers change into small, elongated, flattened, green seeds. New basal leaves appear in the fall and persist until multiple hard frosts do them in.

People have confused goutweed with water hemlock (*Cicuta maculata*), which is deadly, even though water hemlock grows in the water and goutweed doesn't. The flowers are different, water hemlock doesn't form dense stands, and its leaves are feather compound, not palmate compound. You'd really have to ignore all the features of both plants to confuse the two.

People have also confused wild carrot (see p. 295) with goutweed, because the related plants have similar flowers, but the leaves and roots are completely different. Other relatives have similar flowers too, but are also different in other ways.

Goutweed grows in partially shaded, fully shaded, or sunny habitats. You'll find it in parks, along trailsides, on moist soil, in old gardens, in forests where trees have been cut, and in old fields, pastures, and disturbed habitats. It grows throughout the Northeast, and in the Pacific Northwest.

Early spring and mid to late fall are the best times to harvest the basal leaves in quantity, although there are always plenty of new, tender, young leaves growing at ground level, under the larger leaves, in late spring and summer too.

Simply pick the young basal leaves with your fingers, tearing off as many leaves with as few stems as possible.

Use the young leaves the same way you'd use parsley in salads, sandwiches, spreads, soups, sauces, dips, casseroles, and grain or bean dishes fresh or dried. I find them too strong-flavored to use as a green by themselves and too small to roast. You could boil them to turn them into milder greens, but that destroys much of the nutritional content.

Goutweed leaves are a rich source of beta-carotene, bioflavonoids, minerals, and vitamins E and C. Research has shown that high doses of vitamin C help alleviate the symptoms of gout, so its use for this ailment is justified after all, even though the plant's current name arose by accident.

Herbalists use an infusion made from the leaves for joint pain and swelling, and boil the leaves and roots together and apply this externally to inflamed joints inflammation and sciatica.

The infusion of the leaves is also considered a diuretic, cleansing the urinary tract and promoting the flow of urine. It's also supposed to be a sedative. People have also inhaled the crushed seeds into the nose to relieve congestion caused by the common cold. None of this has been verified scientifically, and while this herb was used much more widely in medieval Europe than in the present.

RECIPE

Vegan Hollandaise Sauce

Vegan ingredients improve on the traditional eggs and butter, while goutweed adds a wild touch to this lemony sauce. Use it on everything from artichokes to potatoes. It also freezes well.

1 cup silken tofu, drained

½ cup lemon juice (made from 2 lemons)

½ cup olive oil

¼ cup goutweed, Virginia waterleaf, honewort, or parsley

3 tbsp lecithin granules or pine nuts

1 tsp lemon extract

½ tsp yellow mustard seeds, ground

½ tsp white pepper, ground

½ tsp nutmeg, ground

¼ tsp turmeric

½ tsp Vege-Sal or ¼ tsp salt, or to taste

¼ tsp liquid or powdered stevia

1 tsp konjac (a thickener available in health food stores)

1. Bring all ingredients except the konjac to a boil in a saucepan over medium heat, stirring often.
2. Reduce the heat to low, cover, and simmer for 5 minutes, stirring occasionally.
3. Transfer to a blender, hold down the cover with a towel, start blending on low speed, then increase the speed to high, and purée.
4. Pour in the konjak while the blender is running and blend until thickened, about 30 seconds.
   Yields: 4 cups
   Preparation time: 10 minutes

Trout Lily
(*Erythronium americanum*)

Family: Liliaceae, the lily family

Other names: Yellow trout-lily, American trout-lily, adder's tongue, fawn lily

This is a spring ephemeral that forms dense colonies, spreading by runners as well as seeds. A solid, light brown, tooth-shaped corm, ⅓–1 inch long and white inside, grows underground.

With mottled, purple brown spots on the green leaves, it does look like a speckled trout (*Cynoscion nebulosus*). This plant has basal leaves only: one for sterile plants and two for fertile plants. The leaves are smooth-edged, shiny, lance-shaped, ovate to elliptical, pointed, and fleshy. They grow 3–6 inches long and about 1 inch wide, with nearly no leafstalks.

From early to mid spring, a solitary, nodding, yellow, six-tepaled flower, 1–2 inches wide and streaked with reddish lines grows on top of a long, smooth, slender, leafless stalk, 4–10 inches tall. The tepals are bent backward, exposing six brown stamens and 1 thick pistil. In late spring, it becomes an ovate fruit. Then the plant dies to the ground.

This native perennial grows in partially shaded habitats, often near water, in rich moist woods, and on wooded slopes throughout most of eastern North America. You can eat the young leaves and corms in early spring, before the flowers appear. The plant becomes slightly toxic after the flower blooms.

Harvest by grasping a few plants at a time, then break off the young leaves. You can also dig up the corms with a shovel or a trowel while the leaves are still small and the corms' food reserves haven't been used up. This is labor intensive, so do this where the plants are the most dense.

The leaves taste like cucumbers. They're great chopped and added raw to salads or sandwiches, or cooked for 5–10 minutes using any cooking method in recipes that call for greens. You can also cook the corms like micro potatoes, although digging up and cleaning such small vegetables is labor intensive.

Caution: This plant doesn't agree with everyone, so start with small quantities.

Trout lilies provide vitamin C plus α-methylene-γ-butyrolactone, which shows antimutagenic activity and could help prevent cells from becoming cancerous.

Cherokees and other Native American tribes crushed the plant to make a soothing emollient for inflamed surfaces, such as rashes, bruises, and sores that don't heal. They also drank infusion of the corms for fever, although the plant hasn't been tested scientifically for antimicrobial activity.

RECIPE

Tofu in Peanut Sauce

Here's a great way to season tofu to create a satisfying entrée, with trout lilies giving it an exotic touch. This will even taste good to tofu-haters. Serve alongside brown rice.

2 cup apple juice

¼ cup Chinese preserved radish in chili (optional)

¼ cup peanut butter

¼ cup mellow (light-colored) miso

¼ cup fruit juice sweetened ketchup

½ tsp coriander, ground

¼ tsp cloves, ground

¼ cup peanut oil

2 tbsp powdered arrowroot

2 tbsp umeboshi plum vinegar

½ tsp allspice, ground

½ tsp clear liquid stevia

2 14-oz. packages extra firm tofu, drained and sliced

2 cups trout-lily leaves or lettuce, chopped

1. Purée all ingredients except the tofu and trout-lily leaves in a blender.
2. Place the tofu and trout-lily leaves in an oiled casserole dish, pour over the sauce, cover, and bake for 45 minutes or until bubbly.
   Serves: 4–6
   Preparation time: 10 minutes
   Cooking time: 45 minutes

Common Dandelion (*Taraxacum officinale*)

Family: Asteraceae or Compositae, the aster, daisy, composite, or sunflower family
Other names: Lion's tooth, priest's crown, swine's snout

This very tasty and prolific common garden weed proved to be quite dangerous to me. I ate one leaf of this perennial at 4 p.m. on March 29, 1986, and was promptly surrounded, handcuffed, and arrested by New York's finest, in response to a radioed emergency distress call by two undercover park rangers who had infiltrated my foraging tour. They had pretended to be a married couple, and since they never held hands or kissed in the course of the four-hour tour, I believed them.

I was taken to the police station in Central Park, where I was fingerprinted, photographed, and issued a desk appearance summons to appear in court. I was charged with criminal mischief for "removing vegetation from the park," because I'd eaten a dandelion leaf. I faced up to a year in jail if convicted.

Things looked very grim until the cops made a huge blunder: They let me go. I went home and called every newspaper, TV station, radio station, and wire service. The next morning, on the way to the newsstand to see if I'd had any success, five police officers accosted me. Turned out, they'd recognized me from the papers and all wanted my autograph.

I was in front pages of newspapers around the country, including page 1 of *The Chicago Times*. I was summoned back to Central Park, where I got on *CBS Evening News* for 5 minutes. Local TV crews were waiting on line behind them to cover the story on their own. I eventually got on everything from NBC's *Late Night with David Letterman* and *The Today Show* to MTV. Even the BBC covered the story.

When they took me to court, I served "Wildman's Five-Boro Salad" to reporters and passersby on the steps of the Manhattan Criminal Courthouse. Again, the press ate it up!

Embarrassed city officials negotiated with me, dropped the charges, and hired me to teach foraging as a NYC (New York City) Parks Department employee, which I did for the next four years, until a new, unfavorable administration came into power and reneged on the previous administration's negotiated agreement. I went back to leading freelance foraging tours and have been doing so ever since.

Years later, Parks Commissioner Adrian Benepe told me that the real reason I'd been arrested was because Parks Department officials were terrified of frivolous lawsuits, fantasizing that I might inspire someone to pretend to have poisoned themselves and sue the city. Arresting someone for hidden motives not stated on the charges is official wrongdoing. It's called false arrest. I hope they do that again!

This European perennial grows from a beige, perennial taproot. Up to 10 inches long, it's thick and brittle. All parts of the plant exude a white, milky sap where cut.

The dandelion has jagged leaves, 3–12 inches long, and ½–1½ inches wide. They always grow in a basal rosette. Unlike the similar and edible wild lettuce and chicory the teeth always point toward the base of the leaf and there are no hairs anywhere on the plant. Unlike sow thistle which is also edible, the leaves are never prickly. Poor man's pepper (see p. 90), also edible, starts as a basal rosette with narrow, toothed leaves, but the teeth don't point to the leaf base, and there's no white, milky sap.

New leaves of the Common Dandelion emerge in late fall and persist until destroyed by severe winter weather, only to reemerge in early spring. After the leaves have grown for a while, also in early spring, a cluster of short, stubby, green, flattened flower buds that look like a bunch of buttons form in the rosette's center. You've to look carefully to see them. Soon after, a smooth, slender, leafless flower stalk elevates each bud about 18 inches into the air—less if subjected to mowing.

The yellow composite flower heads reach 1–2 inches across. Unlike some other members of this family, there are no central disk flowers, only strap-like ray flowers. Reflexed (bent) green bracts curl under each flower.

Overnight, the flower transforms into a spherical, white seed head. Tiny brown seeds, shaped like sunflower seeds, grow in the center of the sphere and extend tiny, white parachutes outward.

Dandelion leaves are at their best when they first come up in very early spring, then again in late fall, and sometimes into the winter, if the ground isn't frozen and it's above freezing for part of the day. By the time the plant flowers, unless you prepare them with strong seasonings like kale chips, the leaves get super-bitter. They won't kill you, but they taste so bad, they'll make you wish you were dead. If that doesn't happen, they might make you hallucinate, but you'll have only one hallucination: that you're eating food in an English restaurant!

The flowers are best when the greatest number have just opened, still in early spring, when the leaves are large and the flowers are mostly bright yellow. Some new, bright yellow flowers appear throughout the rest of the growing season, but they're few and far between.

You can dig up the root any time, but it's probably at its best when there's the most food stored underground for rapid spring growth: in the fall and early spring, as well as in the winter, if you can locate it and the ground isn't frozen.

Dandelions aren't very particular about where they'll grow. In addition to lawns and gardens, you'll find them in disturbed habitats, edgy habitats, fields, marshes, parks, thickets, along trail- and roadsides, and in parks, marshes, and thickets.

Pick dandelion greens by inserting a pocket knife into the ground next to the center of the rosette at a 45° angle to the ground and cut in an arc to sever the root. Then you can pick up the whole rosette and shake off any extraneous leaves or debris. This is much faster than picking the leaves one at a time. You can collect the flower buds, which are best when they're still embedded in the center of the rosette, the same way.

Pick the flowers with your fingers and cut off the sepals, which are bitter. The best way to dig up the roots is with a shovel. Choose a rock-free location, and harvest after rain has softened the soil.

The young leaves taste like lettuce, but more intense, and with an overtone of bitterness. They're good in salads and sandwiches with other ingredients. Use the amount that won't make the dish too bitter for you.

They're also good sautéed; however, they shrink and concentrate their bitterness then, but that disappears if you stir in a sauce and cook them further. You can add dandelion leaves to any dish that calls for greens, again sparingly, depending on how much bitterness you can handle. They cook in 10–20 minutes. You can use the flower buds the same way you use the leaves.

The flowers taste a little like carrots. In the field, you can take a bite right out of the center of a very fresh flower, something my foraging expert daughter discovered at the age of 9, to get a burst of nectar. You can also cook the flowers in batter and make fritters with them. They're also a superb ingredient for making wine. Just make sure to get rid of all the very bitter green sepals that surround the flower's base.

The taproots are hard and bitter. Some people eat them anyway, but they're best sliced and simmered, covered, for 20 minutes to make a medicinal decoction. Although the English make a tea of dandelion mixed with burdock, the roots don't taste good to most people, so the decoction is mainly used as a medicine. You can also roast the roots until they're black, grind them to the size of coffee in a blender, and put them in a coffeemaker, like chicory to make a caffeine-free coffee substitute.

Dandelion flowers are a good source of beta-carotene, which your body turns into vitamin A, and the leaves are super nutritious, beating any store-bought vegetables hands-down. They provide vitamins B1, B2, B5, B6, B12, C, E, P, and D, as well as biotin and inositol. Minerals include calcium, potassium, phosphorus, magnesium, and zinc.

Dandelion root decoction (made from 1 tbsp chopped roots simmered in 1 cup of water, covered, for 20 minutes) has been used as a tonic for thousands of years. Like burdock root (see p. 331), it contains inulin, a polysaccharide that doesn't provoke the release of insulin, and is good for people with blood sugar problems.

It also contains the glycoside taraxacin that promotes the flow of bile, reduces inflammation of the bile duct, and helps get rid of gall stones. The herbalists who'd been using the decoction for liver problems for hundreds of years certainly got it right this time. It's also helpful for chronic hepatitis, where it reduces jaundice and liver swelling, and promotes digestion by stimulating the production of bile.

The decoction is also diuretic, so it's used for water retention and kidney problems, although the causes of these conditions must also be addressed.

RECIPE

Dandelion Berbere

This hot Ethiopian seasoning is perfect with dandelions, where the strong flavor of the greens and spices is moderated by tofu. Serve it over clear noodles or brown rice.

¼ cup olive oil

2 14-oz. packages firm tofu, drained

2 cups dandelion greens, chopped

8 cloves garlic

Sauce Ingredients

2 cups almond milk or other nondairy milk

6 tbsp mellow (light-colored) miso

6 tbsp peanut butter

2 tbsp Berbere powder (see below)

2 tbsp arrowroot or kudzu

¼ tsp cayenne pepper, or to taste (optional)

1. Sauté the dandelions and tofu in the olive oil for 5 minutes.
2. Add the garlic and sauté another 5 minutes.
3. Meanwhile, combine all the other ingredients in a food processor, or in a bowl with a whisk.
4. Stir the sauce into the sautéed ingredients. Bring to a boil over medium heat, stirring constantly. Reduce the heat to low and simmer, covered, for 10 minutes.
   Serves: 6
   Preparation/cooking time: 30 minutes

RECIPE

Berbere Powder

Here's my version of a very tasty seasoning that most Americans have never tried.

Ingredients

2 tsp. cumin

17 cloves

1 tbsp. cardamom

2 tsp. black pepper

1 tsp. allspice

4 tsp. fenugreek seeds

2 tsp. coriander seeds

3 tbsp. paprika

2 tsp. powdered ginger

Directions

1. Cook all ingredients except the paprika together in a frying pan, over medium heat, stirring constantly, until fragrant. Remove from the heat to prevent burning.
2. Grind into a powder in a spice- or coffee-grinder.
3. Mix in the paprika.
   Serves: Makes 1/4 cup
   Preparation/cooking time: 15 minutes

Spearmint
(*Mentha spicata*)

Family: Lamiaceae, the mint family

Other names: Garden mint, menthol mint, mint, sage of Bethlehem, silver mint

Everyone's familiar with the flavor of this European plant, but finding it is still special. Like other mints, it's a square stem and opposite leaves, and this has features that distinguish it from its edible relatives, in addition to its fragrance.

Spearmint grows 10–20 inches tall. The stem is branched and purple-tinged, and it spreads via branching rhizomes.

Its leaves are pointed, accounting for the "spear" part of its common name. They're oval to lance shaped, nearly hairless, stalkless of short-stalked, and deeply veined. They grow up to 2 inches or more long, and up to 1 inch wide.

The flowers bloom from late spring through mid-fall, both in tufts, from the leaf axils, and in terminal spikes along the tops of the stems. The many bilaterally symmetrical, five-lobed flowers may be white, pale violet, or purple-pink. The stamens protrude, accounting for the specific name *spicata*, which means furnished with spikes. A small, inconspicuous, dry fruit capsule contains one to four seeds.

Spearmint grows in sunny or partially shaded wet habitats, meadows, fields, disturbed habitats, and near lakes and rivers. It grows throughout most of the United States and southern Canada, and is in season from early spring to late fall.

Cut or break off the aboveground parts for tea, or strip the leaves and tender tops of the stems with your fingers to use as food. You can still save the rest of the stems, and all parts except for the roots, for tea.

Finely chopped, the leaves are superb in virtually any kind of dessert. Leave them whole to use as a garnish. Use them raw in salads and sandwiches, or cook them around 10 minutes in pies, cakes, sauces, puddings, ice cream, jellies, breakfast cereals, and more.

Spearmint supplies you with vitamins A, B1, B2, B3, beta-carotene and other related antioxidant carotenoid A precursors, the flavonoid hesperidin, and tryptophan. It also contains the minerals calcium, phosphorus, and iron.

A major medicinal plant, spearmint contains the essential oil menthol, plus at least twenty-nine additional biologically active compounds and antioxidants, most of which you've probably never heard of.

An infusion of the aboveground parts is excellent for stomachaches and indigestion. Due to its gentleness, it's especially good for children. It's been used for indigestion in children, and colic, for centuries, whereas stronger peppermint is preferred for adult indigestion. Spearmint tea is also good for morning sickness and motion sickness.

It contains antimicrobial compounds, and it's been used for colds, influenza, and fevers, although it should be tested for action against specific pathogens. It's been used for nervous headaches, and research even shows that it's good for mild hirsutism (excessive hairiness) in women, because it reduces androgen levels.

Spearmint is also a mild diuretic. A strong cup of hot tea will promote the flow of urine and relieve swelling due to water retention, although the cause of the condition, which might be dangerous, should be determined.

Macerated spearmint stems are also useful as a poultice for bruises, especially mixed with burdock (see p. 441) leaves, water, and clay.

RECIPE

Spearmint Ice Cream

The only seasoning in this ice cream is spearmint, and lots of it. That's all it needs to show off how well my vegan ice cream formulation works and how good spearmint tastes!

3½ cups soy milk, almond milk or other nondairy milk

1 tsp agar powder or 1 tbsp agar flakes

1 tbsp arrowroot or kudzu

½ cup silken tofu, drained

½ cup raw pine nuts or cashews

¼ cup vegetable glycerin

¼ cup grape seed oil

¼ cup fresh spearmint or other mint leaves, or to taste

1 tbsp clear liquid stevia

½ tsp salt

1. In a small saucepan over medium heat, bring 2 cups of the soy milk to a boil with the agar, arrowroot, and half the spearmint, stirring constantly.
2. Reduce the heat to low and simmer, uncovered, for 5 minutes or until the agar is dissolved.
3. Transfer to a blender and purée with all the remaining ingredients except half the spearmint. Start on low speed, and hold down the blender cover with a towel to prevent eruptions.
4. Add the remaining spearmint leaves and blend briefly until finely chopped.
5. Freeze in an ice cream machine according to the manufacturer's directions.
   Yields: 5½ cups
   Preparation time: 30 minutes
   Freezing time: 2 hours (varies)

Japanese Knotweed (*Fallopia japonica, Polygonum cuspidatum*)

Family: Polygonaceae, the smartweed or buckwheat family
Other names: Fleeceflower, Himalayan fleece vine, monkeyweed, Hancock's curse, elephant ears, pea shooters, donkey rhubarb, sally rhubarb, Japanese bamboo, American bamboo, Mexican bamboo, tiger's walking stick

This widely despised East Asian invasive member of the smartweed or buckwheat family is one of my favorite early spring wild foods. You can often find dense stands of upright, unbranched, green shoots, ½–1¼ inches wide, and dappled with red, pink, and magenta (like psychedelic asparagus) in large quantities. Papery, whitish sheaths grow upward from the regularly spaced joints, characteristic of this perennial's family. These turn into tall, hollow, conspicuous, woody, jointed stems that reach 9–12 feet in height, creating what looks like a thicket of bamboo. The previous year's growth persists through the winter, helping you locate the plant even before the shoots appear.

The alternate leaves look like bulging triangles. Pointed, toothless, and with flat bases and pointed tips, they grow 4–6 inches long and 2¼–2½ inches wide.

The greenish-white flowers bloom in the summer. Hundreds of them grow on showy, long, lacy spikes. Their attractiveness caused gardeners to import them around the world, creating great chagrin. The flowers develop into many tiny, three-sided, smooth, beige, papery fruits in autumn, each with a tiny, hard, brown seed inside. The remaining skeletons of the seeds turn white in the winter.

There are no poisonous look-alikes. Asparagus has green shoots, but no joints or reddish flecks. Giant knotweed (*Fallopia sachalinensis*) is a close relative that's larger than Japanese knotweed, equally edible, but much less common.

A poster child for invasive species, this plant spreads by hardy rhizomes as well as the seeds. You can find it in partial shade or full sunlight and on disturbed soil, where it takes over. It also seizes roadsides, fields, and riverbanks, where flooding destroys existing vegetation and Japanese knotweed can take hold. Although it's supposed to be very bad, there's no more now than there was when I first started foraging, so in the Northeast at least, it's integrated itself into the ecosystems and helps convince me that scientists who want to take a second look at the concept of invasive species are right.

This plant grows throughout most of North America, wherever it escaped cultivation. The shoots are in season in early spring. Break or cut them off near the base, and remove and discard the tough leaves. When more than a foot tall, cut or break off any parts that are still tender near the tip of the shoot. You'll need to peel off the tough cuticle of older shoots. On rare occasions, new shoots come up after stands of knotweed have been cut down in the summer and fall, but I've only seen this happen twice in 34 years, believe it or not!

The shoots have a wonderfully sour flavor, like its relatives, rhubarb and sheep sorrel (see p. 29). You can grill them like asparagus, sauté them, or simmer them in soups, stews, and grain dishes. They cook in about 5–10 minutes.

They're especially good used in small quantities to contrast sweet ingredients (the way rhubarb is used) in desserts, and they're just as good adding zing to bland foods, such as potatoes or tofu.

You can break through the membranes between the segments of large knotweed, using a chopstick, stuff it, and bake it. You can also use the rind, like orange rind, for making marmalade. This plant is also mucilaginous, slightly thickening soups, stews, and sauces. People have also eaten it raw in small without ill effects; however, large portions of raw knotweed might give some people diarrhea and aren't recommended.

This plant is loaded with vitamins A and C, the antioxidant flavonoid ruin, plus the minerals potassium, zinc, and manganese.

It's also a great source of resveratrol, better known as the substance in red grape skins and red wine that lowers bad cholesterol and reduces the risk of cardiovascular disease. It may be helpful in Alzheimer's disease, prostate cancer, Lyme disease, and osteoporosis, but research is still in its early days.

This plant contains oxalic acid, like wood- (see p. 99) and sheep sorrel (see p. 20), lamb's quarters (see p. 127), and spinach, so it's not something people with kidney disease should eat if they can't eat spinach.

RECIPE

Sweet Grilled Knotweed

Because Japanese knotweed is so lemony flavored, grilling it with sweet herbs works perfectly. Once you try this one, you'll be looking forward to knotweed season every year!

8 cups Japanese knotweed shoots

⅓ cup sweetened miso coating (see p. 5)

1. Mix the knotweed with the coating.
2. Place the knotweed on a rack over an oiled cookie sheet.
3. Grill 2–4 minutes in a broiler or until black flecks begin to show on the knotweed.
4. Flip the knotweed with tongs or a fork, then grill until black flecks begin to show on the other side.

   Serves: 4–6

   Preparation time: 5 minutes

   Cooking time: 8 minutes

Shepherd's Purse (*Capsella bursa-pastoris*)

Family: Brassicaceae or Cruciferae, the mustard, crucifer, or cabbage family
Other names: Mother's heart, pickpurse, pickpocket, lady's purse, rattle pouches

This European mustard starts off in early spring as a basal rosette consisting of deeply toothed leaves up to 9 inches across, broader toward the tip. They look like the dandelion leaves, but with blunter teeth that point outward, not toward the leaf's base. Unlike dandelion leaves, there's no white, milky sap. Also, the slender, white taproot differs from the dandelion's stout, beige one.

In mid-spring, a little-branched, slender, erect flower stalk grows up to 2½ feet tall with alternate, stalkless leaves (smaller than the basal ones), clasping the stem with two small, pointed lobes.

The tiny, white, four-petaled flowers—whose petals form a cross like related mustards—alternate around the tip of the stalk on racemes. These give way to long-stemmed, flattened, triangular, two-parted seedpods, ⅛ inch long, that supposedly resemble the purses of ancient shepherds.

This European annual comes up throughout North America. It grows in full sunlight or partial shade, along roadsides and in fields, pastures, lawns, and parks. It's one of the first plants to appear in newly disturbed habitats.

The basal leaves are good to eat in early spring, and a second growth of basal leaves are edible from mid to late fall. The flower buds and flowers are available to eat in mid-spring.

Sever the taproot of the basal rosette with a knife, shake off the debris, and bag the basal leaves. This is more efficient than picking the leaves one by one. Pick bunches of the flower buds and flowers with your fingers.

The basal leaves are the most mild-flavored of all the wild mustards I've ever tasted. They're fine with stronger-tasting ingredients, raw or cooked, in salads, sandwiches, or side dishes and entrées that call for vegetables, but don't contribute much. They cook in 10–15 minutes.

On the other hand, the flowers, flower buds, and the top parts of the stems taste like broccoli, excellent in salads and sandwiches, or as a garnish. They cook in about 5 minutes, but they're so small, they'd probably get lost in recipes with lots of other ingredients.

The seedpods are edible, but they're also small and without flavor. The root is edible, but too small as well, and hard to chew.

The leaves contain vitamins A, C, K, B1, B2, B3, choline, and inositol, plus the minerals calcium, potassium, and phosphorus. The aboveground parts of this plant also have saponins, choline, acetylcholine, and tyramine.

The leaves provide fumaric acid, which has been shown to inhibit the growth of cancer cells in mice, but it hasn't been tested in humans. An infusion of this plant is considered to be an astringent, an anti inflammatory, and a diuretic. It's also supposed to constrict the blood vessels, lower blood pressure, contract the uterus, and stop bleeding. Herbalists recommend its use during or after childbirth and to ease difficult menstruation, but doctors warn pregnant women to avoid this plant because of its possible effects on the blood, and scientific experiments performed with this plant have been inconclusive. I tried it on a paper cut to stop the bleeding, but it didn't help.

Pizza Purse Shepherd's purse leaves are normally pretty bland, but not when roasted into chips with this Italian-style coating.

4 cups shepherd's purse basal (bottom) leaves, the larger the better

½ cup Pizza Coating

1. Gently fold the Pizza Coating onto the shepherd's purse leaves, using your fingers.
2. Spread the leaves onto four oiled non stick baking mats placed over four cookie sheets.
3. Bake for 30 minutes in a preheated 300° F oven, or until dry and crisp, but not black.
   Serves 4 to 6
   Preparation time: 30 minutes
   Cooking time: 30 minutes

Pizza Coating This purée of pizza flavorings is great for roasting wild leafy greens or store-bought vegetables, and goutweed makes it especially tasty.

6 cloves of garlic

½ cup pine nuts

½ cup fresh or frozen basil

¼ cup parsley

2 cups white miso

1 cup olive oil

¼ cup nutritional yeast

2 tbsp tomato paste

4 tsp oregano, ground

1 tsp paprika

1 tsp thyme, ground

1 tsp fennel seeds, ground

1 tsp hot pepper flakes, ground (optional)

¼ tsp black pepper, or to taste, ground

1. Chop the garlic, pine nuts, basil, and goutweed or parsley as finely as possible in a food processor.
2. Add the remaining ingredients and purée.
   Makes 3 cups
   Preparation time: 15 minutes

Ramp
(*Allium tricoccum*)

Family: Liliaceae
Other names: Wild leek, wood leek

This is a dangerous plant, if you're standing between it and a knife-wielding celebrity chef! This is a first-rate wild food, as are so many others covered here; but this species must have a good PR agent, as all the celebrity chefs know about it!

This perennial smells like its close relatives, onions and garlic, when injured. It's basal leaves exclusively, and only two or three of these, but it grows in dense stands.

The smooth, elliptical, pointed, light green leaves, with parallel veins typical of its group, grow 4–12 inches long and 1–3 inches across. Each leaf first emerges from a purple, scallion-like leafstalk wrapped in a sheath. Clusters of leaves up to 10 inches across emerge in early spring, then yellow and die to the ground in mid-spring, when tree leaves block the sun from their forested habitat.

As the leaves die back, the flowers emerge, blooming in early to mid summer, above a smooth, slender, round, erect, unbranched, leafless red stalk that reaches 6–18 inches in height. There's another sheath at the bottom.

Around thrity-five creamy-white, six-tepaled, white-stalked flowers, ⅛ inch across and ¼ inch long, bloom, configured in a dome-shaped cluster 1–2¼inches across. They grow above a short-lived pair of bracts.

Tiny, hard, shiny, spherical black seeds, grouped in threes, replace the flowers, ripening in late summer and fall. Some skeletons of the seed stalk sometimes persist through the winter, marking the locations of the bulbs.

The pear-shaped, onion-like, white bulbs consist of two to six layers. Each bulb grows from ¾ to 2 inches long, wrapped in a light brown, papery covering.

It's largest in the summer and fall after the leaves have died, and smallest in the early spring when the leaves are growing.

Poisonous lily of the valley (*Convallaria magalis*) has leaves that look like ramp's, but they've no odor and grow on a stem, whereas ramp leaves are always basal. The roots, flowers, and seeds are also completely different.

Ramps grow in partially shaded, moist, deciduous woodlands, on slopes, in swamps, and near rivers. It's distributed throughout most of eastern North America, but not Alabama, Georgia, and Florida.

Ramp leaves are in season from early to mid spring, when they die. The bulbs are almost too small to be worth picking in early spring, but they get large when the leaves die and remain edible in the summer and fall. You've to spot the flower head, seed head, or skeleton to locate them when the leaves are gone. Some years, and in some places, the skeletons disappear in autumn and you're out of luck then. Other times, they persist through the winter and into early spring.

Unscrupulous commercial harvesters have wiped out ramps, especially near the edge of their range, but if you collect a small portion of any stand where they're very abundant and leave some bulbs of each cluster you dig up, you'll have a bountiful, sustainable harvest indefinitely. All the stands my very large groups have enjoyed since 1982 are still completely intact!

Use the rightfully prized, strong-flavored leaves and bulbs like scallions or shallots, raw in salads or cooked, using nearly any method in virtually any savory recipe. The bulbs also make excellent pickles, although you've to remove the mature bulb's tough, slender core after splitting the bulb open with a paring knife. The leaves and bulbs cook in about 10–15 minutes.

Ramps are among the best-tasting member of onions, garlic, and their relatives—well worth the bad breath they cause. In the Deep South, gala ramp festivals are held every year, celebrating its appearance in early spring, months before farm crops became available. It saved the lives of pioneers and slaves who were dying of vitamin A deficiency from many months without fresh greens. Nowadays, they close all the schools the day after a ramp festival. They can't pay the teachers enough to stay in a room full of kids who have been eating ramps all weekend!

In addition to vitamin A, ramps provide vitamin C and some vitamin B1, plus the minerals potassium, phosphorus, calcium, and iron.

Not currently in use medicinally, Native Americans ate the leaves as a spring tonic (probably due to its vitamin A content) and to treat colds and croup. They also applied the warm juice of the bulbs and leaves to the ears for earaches.

RECIPE

Red Ramp Curry

Quite easy to make, this Thai recipe will knock your socks off, depending on how much curry paste you decide to use. And the ramps certainly won't get lost among all the other ingredients and flavors. Serve this over clear noodles or brown rice.

3⅓ cups (2 16-oz. cans) of coconut milk

2 cups ramp leaves or chopped shallots

2 cups fresh or canned pineapple, diced

2 carrots, sliced

1 yellow summer squash, peeled and sliced

3 celery stalks, sliced

1 14-oz. package firm tofu, drained and diced

1 cup raw peanuts

2 cloves of garlic, chopped

5 tbsp Thai curry paste (available in Asian grocery stores and some health food stores), or to taste

1. Simmer all ingredients together for 1 hour or until the veggies are tender.
   Serves: 6
   Preparation time: 15 minutes
   Cooking time: 60 minutes

Common Blue Violet (*Viola sororia*, *V. papilionacea*)

Family: Violaceae, the violet and pansy family
Other names: Common meadow violet, purple violet, woolly blue violet, hooded violet, wood violet

Widespread both in gardens and in the wild, this colonial plant propagates itself by means of branched rhizomes, about ½ inch thick.

All the leaves are basal, but there are no rosettes. Tightly curled at first, each leaf grows on top of a single, slender, hairless leafstalk 3–8 inches high. Odorless, heart-shaped, hairless, and shallow-toothed, the leaves grow 3–5 inches long and equally wide.

Hardly taller than the leaves, each bilaterally symmetrical, scentless, violet-colored flower also emerges from the ground on its own slender, hairless flower stalk. There are five-rounded petals and two-bearded lateral ones. Bushy stamens grow near the flower's throat. The three lower petals are deeply veined, and the lowest one is slightly spurred. Although hundreds of these colorful flowers, ¾–1 inch across, cover meadows toward the end of early spring, they're all sterile!

Fertile flowers mature in the fall. Hidden at ground level, these inconspicuous oblong, beige capsules grow to about ½ inch long. They mature and self-fertilize, splitting lengthwise into three long, narrow troughs, releasing a few dozen tiny, spherical seeds that resemble ant eggs, which ants spread. Translucent white at first, they become dark brown when mature.

White violets and intermediate blue-and-while violets are now considered subspecies of the common blue violet, and you use them all the same way. The round-leaf yellow violet (*Viola rotundifolia*), a similar relative that grows in swamps, was formerly thought to be poisonous, but turns out to be edible as well.

The swamp blue violet (*V. cucullata*) is another edible relative. Its flower rises high above the basal leaves, making it easy to distinguish.

Young garlic mustard (see p. 11) leaves resemble violets', but they're rounded, not pointed, with wavy margins. They're very deeply veined, they smell like garlic when crushed, and they form in a basal rosette. Other stages and parts look completely different too.

Common mallow (see p. 33) leaves resemble violets', but they're pleated as well as rounded rather than pointed. Other parts are completely different too.

Wild ginger (see p. 306) also has heart-shaped leaves, but they're entire with no teeth, they're much larger than violet's leaves with very long leafstalks, and they grow in pairs.

Caution: Other plants have violet flowers, but that doesn't make them violets. Larkspur (*Delphinium* spp.) has a long spur extending from the rear of its flower and a five-parted leaf, not a heart-shaped one. Monk's hood (*Aconitum napellus*) has a hooded flower and feathery leaves. Neither plant has basal flowers, the flowers don't have any of the features of violet flowers except for their color, and they're both poisonous.

Violets grow in gardens, meadows, fields, parks, and damp woodland openings; on lawns; along trail edges and roadsides; and near riverbanks. They're native to eastern North America and many of the central states. Gardeners and landscapers plant them everywhere.

The leaves are edible from early through mid spring. After that they get tough and coarse. New tender leaves sometimes come up after mowing in autumn, although not in great quantity. The edible flowers bloom in quantity from the end of early spring into the start of mid-spring, although a few bloom in autumn as well.

Harvest by holding down handfuls of plants with one hand and pulling off as many leaves and flowers as possible, with as few of the relatively tough leaf-stalks and flower stalks as you can. The fruit capsule and their seeds inside aren't edible, and the rhizomes are poisonous, causing vomiting, not that I ever saw anyone on my tours attempting to take a bite out of those (yet!).

Violet leaves and flowers are very tasty, mild at first, then with a slight bite. Use them raw in salad or sandwiches, or cook them for about 10 minutes using virtually any cooking method, in any kind of recipe that calls for greens. You can also freeze the flowers in water inside ice cube trays and serve these in drinks.

The leaves are a good source of vitamins A and C, and the flowers contain vitamin C. The leaves contain genistein, also present in red clover (see p. 118), plus isoflavone, a plant estrogen and antioxidant, which may lower the risk of cancer. Genistein changes the action of the genes that prostate cancer cells use to spread throughout the body, and research is ongoing to find out whether taking genistein helps prostate cancer patients.

RECIPE

Sweet Violets

Cooking onions until translucent brings out their sweetness, and this is just what you want when you're cooking violets seasoned with sweet herbs to make a veggie side dish everyone will love.

¼ cup of vegan butter substitute or peanut oil

2 red onions, diced

8 cups common blue violet leaves and flowers, or other greens

1 tsp salt

¼ tsp cloves, ground

¼ tsp almond extract

1. Gently sauté the onion in the vegan butter substitute for 20 minutes.
2. Add the remaining ingredients and sauté for another 10 minutes.

   Serves: 4–6
   Preparation time: 5 minutes
   Cooking time: 30 minutes

False Solomon's Seal (*Maianthemum racemosum* ssp. *racemosum*, *Smilacina racemosa*)

Family: Asparagaceae, the asparagus family
Other names: Solomon's treacle, Solomon's plume, false spikenard, feathery false lily of the valley

This colonial perennial has an unbranched, gracefully arching, zigzag stem that grows from 1 to 3 feet tall. It arises from a stiff, cylindrical, yellow-brown rhizome that gets up to ¾ inch thick. Circular leaf scars from earlier years' growth form impressions like those of a signet ring at regular intervals.

Toward the end of early spring, undeveloped young leaves tightly wrap themselves around the tops of the erect, pencil-shaped shoots and a grayish sheath covers the shoot's lower part. Within a couple of weeks, the alternate leaves develop on very short leafstalks. They're long, pointed, elliptical, and smooth edged with parallel veins. They grow from 2¾ to 6 inches long and up to 3 inches wide. They turn yellow in autumn.

A flattened, branched, pyramidal panicle, 1–4 inches long and 2 inches wide, grows at the stem's tip in late spring and early summer; and 20–80 tiny, cream white, 6-tepaled, star-shaped flowers, ⅛ in diameter, with stamens longer than the tepals, soon bloom there. The flowers look like tiny lilies, and they're related.

Spherical berries ½ inch across, each containing one to four spherical seeds, ripen on the panicle in the fall. They first change from green with copper spots to cream, then ripen to purple-striped with red.

Related Solomon's Seal, which is also edible, but much less common, looks similar, but its flowers and blue berries grow under the arching stem, not at the tip, and its rhizome is white, not yellow-brown.

Starry false Solomon's seal (*Maianthemum stellatum*), another edible relative, has more narrow leaves than false Solomon's seal. The rhizome lacks prominent seal-like scars, and the plant grows near the seashore as well as in moist meadows. Other edible relatives also have different flowers, fruits, and roots.

False hellebore (*Veratrum viride*) is a swamp plant with an upright green shoot the width of the fat crayons toddlers use, quite unlike a slender pencil. The shoot and mature leaves are deeply pleated, like an accordion, and the flowers and fruit are different from false Solomon's seal's, so you'd have to be very careless to confuse the two plants. Be aware anyway of false hellebore and try to spot it in swamps, as it's deadly, and you never know when the boss might drop in for dinner!

Break or cut off false Solomon's seal shoots when they first appear, before the leaves unfurl about two weeks later and the shoots get too fibrous to eat. The berries on the East Coast are horribly bitter, but they're reportedly delicious on the West Coast, possibly because it's a different subspecies.

The rhizomes are very bitter and poisonous, with a strong laxative effect. While some foragers have tried to counter this by boiling them in lye overnight, this may not work, it isn't worth the effort or the risk, and this is no lye!

This native plant grows in rich, partially shaded woodlands and moist areas, along stream banks, and in clearings and meadows throughout most of eastern North America, and other very similar edible subspecies grow throughout much of the rest of North America.

The shoots taste like asparagus, but better. Add them raw to salads and sandwiches, or cook them for 10–15 minutes. They're superb in recipes that call for cooked vegetables, and they're much more common than Solomon's seal.

This plant hasn't been analyzed nutritionally and herbalists don't use it nowadays, but Native Americans applied a poultice of the roots to sunburns. They also dried and smoked the rhizomes to treat hyperactivity and depression, and to suppress coughs, but this hasn't been tested scientifically, and may not be safe.

RECIPE

Wild Rice Pilaf

Here's a simple and easy recipe, featuring wild rice and false Solomon's seal, that's as tasty as it is filling.

4 cups vegetable stock

1-½cups wild rice

1 red onion, chopped

2 medium carrots, sliced

2 celery stalks, sliced

1 cup false Solomon's seal shoots, chopped

6 cloves of garlic, peeled and left whole

2 tbsp olive oil

2 tsp Vege-sal (a seasoned salt available in health food stores) or seasoned salt, or 1 tsp salt

1 tsp rosemary, ground

1 tsp smoked paprika

1 tsp sage, ground

1 tsp prepared mustard

Simmer all ingredients together for 2½ hours, or until all the liquid has evaporated or been absorbed.

Serves 6

Preparation time: 15 minutes

Cooking time: 150 minutes

Solomon's Seal (*Polygonatum biflorum*)

Family: Asparagaceae, the asparagus family
Other names: True Solomon's seal, smooth Solomon's seal, small Solomon's seal

This colonial native perennial springs from a stout, whitish, knobby, segmented rhizome, which bears scars from previous years' growth at regular intervals, like impressions of a signet ring. In early spring, an unbranched, gracefully arching, zigzag, pencil-like stem grows from 1 to 6 feet long, tightly wrapped around the top by the undeveloped leaves.

The long, pointed, elliptical, smooth-edged, hairless, alternate leaves open in less than two weeks after this shoot appears. Growing up to 6 inches long and 4 inches wide, they turn yellow in autumn. They're stalkless, and the leaf bases clasp the stem.

In late spring or early summer, twelve to twenty tubular, six-parted, bell-shaped, whitish green to pale yellow-green flowers bloom, hanging under the upper portion of the stem. They look like small lily flowers, and the plants are related. The flowers grow in twos or threes, from ½ to ¾ inch long, dangling from long, slender, branched flower stalks that droop from the leaf axils. Later in the summer, groups of two or three dark blue, spherical berries, up to ½ inch across, supersede the flowers.

False Solomon's seal (see p. 74) looks similar, it's true, but you can tell them apart because false Solomon's seal's rhizome is yellow-brown, not white, and its flowers and berries grow at the tip of the stem. Other edible relatives also have different flowers, fruits, and roots.

The deadly false hellebore (*Veratrum viride*) has an upright green shoot, but it's the width of the fat crayons toddlers use, not like a slender pencil. The shoot

and mature leaves of false hellebore are deeply pleated, like an accordion, and the flowers and seeds are different from Solomon's seal's, but you should still be aware of this toxic swamp plant.

Solomon's seal grows in rich soil, in partially shaded woodlands and moist areas, along stream and pond banks and roadsides, in ditches, clearings, meadows, and gardens, where it's sometimes planted as an ornamental. It ranges throughout most of North America east of the Rockies, and foragers in the Pacific Northwest report finding it there too.

The shoot is in season for two weeks or less, toward the second half of early spring, before the leaves unfurl and the stem becomes too tough to eat. Cut or break them off the stems.

The rhizome is in season in fall and early spring, but it shouldn't be uprooted, unless it's grown in a garden, because the plant is rarely plentiful enough for this. Even though the shoot grows back, collect only a small proportion where the plant is abundant and leave it alone entirely in areas where it's legally protected.

The tender, young shoot tastes like asparagus, a relative, but better. Discard the acrid leaves and enjoy the shoots raw in salads or sandwiches (it's a fantastic trail nibble too), or steam or simmer them for 10–15 minutes in any dish that calls for vegetables. The berries are inedible.

The rhizomes are a little sweet and crisp, like water chestnuts. They're good raw, sliced and roasted in a light vegetable oil with sweet spices, or dried and ground into flour. They're also excellent in soups, stews, and casseroles, cooking in 10–15 minutes. If you garden, grow them. If not, get a friend to do so!

A decoction of the root is used for lots of ailments, from indigestion to coughs. It's used for menstrual cramps, PMS, bleeding, high blood pressure, and increasing concentration and mental clarity.

A poultice of the roots has been applied topically on cuts and bruises, acute injuries of tendons, joints, ligaments, muscles, bones, bruises, connective tissues, and cartilage, as well as for osteoarthritis, but this plant hasn't been tested scientifically.

RECIPE

Solomon's Dip

Here's a simple dip you can make in minutes that's better than any expensive versions you may have bought, definitely fit for King Solomon, who'd certainly give it his Solomon's seal of approval!

1¼ cups silken tofu, drained

1 tsp brewer's yeast

1 tsp brown rice vinegar

1 tsp Vege-Sal or seasoned salt

1 tsp hot paprika

1 tsp Tabasco sauce, or to taste

¼ tsp black pepper

2 tsp vegan butter substitute, or corn or olive oil

2 tbsp lecithin granules

1⅓ cups Solomon's seal shoots or drained canned artichoke hearts, chopped

1. Purée all ingredients except the Solomon's seal shoots until smooth in a food processor.
2. Add the shoots and chop until well-integrated but not puréed.
   Yields: 2 cups
   Preparation time: 10 minutes

Ostrich Fern
(*Matteuccia struthiopteris* or *Pteretis pensylvanica*)

Family: Onocleaceae
Other names: Fiddlehead fern, garden fern, hardy fern

This especially delicious colonial fern first forms an emerald-green fiddlehead, tightly rolled up (like the curved, narrow end of a violin) atop a stout, upward-tapering base. Unlike other ferns, a distinctive groove runs along the length of the fiddlehead, on the opposite side of the unrolling leaflets. It's also covered with distinctive, large, brown, papery scales. In addition, it's smooth, not hairy like fiddleheads of many other species.

Underground, a thick, braided rhizome with black roots creeps along, sprouting the new fronds. Throughout the colony, a black, rough, knobby tangle of dead material lies just above ground level.

The ostrich fern gets quite large when mature, growing from 2 to 6 feet tall. Curved, unbranched, and feathery, the infertile (nonreproductive) frond really does look like an ostrich's plume, with one distinct central stem per frond. From twenty to sixty toothed primary leaflets arch away from the main stem on each side. These fronds narrow abruptly toward the tip, with leaflets getting increasingly smaller and tapering toward their bases.

The rigid leafstalk grows to about 1 foot long. It's deeply grooved at the base, but ungrooved above. Curving outward, the fronds form a distinctive vase shape.

From five to seven much smaller fertile (fruiting) fronds, up to 2 feet tall, grow inside the "vase." They bear rounded, pod-like sori, which contain spores. Dark green at first, they become stiff, dense, and leathery, and look a little like bird tails. The woody fertile fronds overwinterv

Poison hemlock has finely divided, fernlike leaves, but never forms fiddleheads. Other fern fiddleheads are hairy or don't have the groove at the base of the stem. These usually aren't tasty, and some are of unknown edibility.

The ostrich fern is a circumpolar species native to eastern North America and southeastern Canada, as well as northern Europe and parts of Scandinavia. You can find it in partially shaded or sunny areas, on rich damp ground, in swamps and moist woods, along riverbanks, on alluvial plains, and in expensive gourmet restaurants! It's one of the few wild foods chefs know about.

It's a short season of about ten days, toward the end of early spring, varies year by year, according to how long winter has lasted, so I often schedule my foraging tours in fiddlehead territory, which I have to do months in advance, too early or too late. Once you know where ostrich ferns grow, check your location frequently as the fiddlehead season comes close.

Snap off "half" the fiddleheads and their stems from each cluster with your fingers, or cut them off with a knife. Fiddleheads don't grow back after you cut them, so leave the rest to provide food for the rhizomes, so you don't kill the plant. Don't gather poisonous unrolled ferns, and collect a small proportion only where the ferns are very abundant. This plant can be harvested sustainably for decades using common sense, or wiped out quite rapidly if selfish commercial harvesters get at it.

Rub off the scaly membranes under room temperature running water in a tall colander set into a shorter bowl. Drain, chop, and then steam, simmer, or sauté the fiddleheads for 5–10 minutes. They taste like a combination of asparagus and snap peas, but can be somewhat dry, so add a light sauce, such as lemon sauce. The contrast will turn the dryness into an asset. Avoid over-seasoning or overcooking fiddleheads, and don't combine them with many other ingredients, or you'll drown out their wonderful but delicate flavor.

Fiddleheads provide vitamin A; niacin; some vitamin C; the minerals potassium, phosphorus, magnesium, and iron; and the trace minerals manganese, zinc, and copper. They're also relatively high in protein. They're not used medicinally.

RECIPE

Ostrich Casserole

I've always found fiddleheads difficult to cook with because it's so easy to drown out their delicate flavor, but baking them over noodles with a mildly seasoned sauce brings out the best of these young ferns.

4 cups whole-grain noodles

4 cups ostrich fern fiddleheads, coarsely chopped

Sauce Ingredients

2 cups vegetable stock or water

3 tbsp arrowroot or kudzu

4 cloves of garlic

¼ cup vegan butter substitute or olive oil

¼ cup white miso

½ cup silken tofu

2 tbsp goutweed or parsley

½ tsp fresh ginger or ¼ tsp powdered ginger

¼ tsp black pepper

1. Cook the noodles a few minutes less than instructed and drain.
2. Meanwhile, purée all the sauce ingredients together in a blender.
3. Layer an oiled casserole dish with half the noodles, ⅓ of the sauce, half the fiddleheads, half the remaining sauce, the remaining noodles, the remaining fiddleheads, and the remaining sauce.
4. Bake in a preheated 350°F oven for 30 minutes or until bubbly.
   Serves: 6
   Preparation time: 30 minutes
   Cooking time: 30 minutes

Common Greenbrier (*Smilax rotundifolia*)

Family: Smilacaceae, the greenbrier family
Other names: Catbrier, Bullbrier, Horsebrier, Blasphemy Vine, Stretchberry

When I was teaching myself to forage, I was surprised to read about what seemed to be a very unusual vegetable and even more astonished when I soon spotted it along the side of a trail a few days later, looking just like it did in the field guide I was using. A very distinct native, it's quite tasty and it's widespread throughout the eastern and south central United States and eastern Canada, so it's a great one for other beginners to look for.

It's a green, high-climbing, zigzag shaped, vine-like shrub—not a true vine because it's woody. Armed with large stiff spines, it sometimes forms a tangled, impenetrable mass, held in place with paired tendrils emerging from the leafstalks.

Growing from 2 to 5 inches long, the smooth, leathery, round to heart-shaped, alternate leaves have pointed tips and parallel veins. The leaves have no teeth, which all the thorns make unnecessary!

The common greenbrier has small, tubular, six-petaled flowers that look like lilies, with which this shrub used to be classified, but they're smaller than most other lilies. They're yellow-green and grouped in small, flat-topped clusters. They bloom in the spring. Male and female flowers grow on separate vines.

The spherical berries, powdered with a waxy, bluish bloom, ripen in autumn. They're small, dry, and rubbery, accounting for the name "stretchberry." Inside are usually two seeds that are too hard to eat.

Other greenbrier species (*Smilax* spp.) that look like common greenbrier are also edible. The only other similar vine, carrion flower, is also edible. It's non-woody and has no thorns, so the two vines are easy to tell apart.

Look for greenbrier in partially shaded habitats. It grows in thickets, old fields, edge habitats, open woodlands, and clearings; along roadsides; and near the seashore. It climbs on trees, fences, and any other stable structure.

The leaves, tendrils, and shoots (the rapidly growing, tender tips) are all edible in mid-spring. After that, the older leaves and tendrils become tough, and by mid-summer, only a few small leaves and the tips of the shoots provide a trail nibble.

Strip off the young leaves and tendrils with your fingers, and break off the tender parts of the shoots. The flowers are too small to be worth the bother. The berries, touted in some foraging books, only make an outstanding food for anyone who enjoys eating the erasers of pencils!

One of my favorite leafy greens, greenbrier has a wonderful, sweet sour flavor, ideal for salads and sandwiches, and great in any dish that calls for veggies, cooking in about 5 minutes. When you find it in the field, it's hard to stop nibbling!

RECIPE

White Beans Supreme

Beans, although very nutritious, are intrinsically unspectacular, but this shortcoming is cured by using piquant greenbrier leaves and plenty of savory seasonings, as you'll find out when you can't resist something a dish that's not at all boring!

1½ cup white beans, soaked overnight or steeped for 1 hour in water just off the boil, rinsed, and drained

5 tbsp olive oil

1 onion, chopped

3 cups greenbrier leaves, shoots, and tendrils, or other greens, chopped

3 cloves of garlic, chopped

2 tbsp dried wakame seaweed, soaked to reconstitute, drained, and chopped

1 tbsp savory, ground

¼ cup fresh basil, chopped

2 tsp tarragon, ground

2 tsp lemon thyme or thyme, ground

1 tsp black pepper, ground, or to taste

3 cups vegetable stock

⅓ cup white (mellow) miso

1. Pressure cook the beans in the stock with the basil, savory, tarragon, thyme, pepper, and 1 tbsp of the olive oil for 20 minutes or simmer, covered, for 3 hours or until the beans are tender.
2. Meanwhile, sauté the onion in the remaining olive oil for 15 minutes.
3. Add the greenbrier and garlic and sauté for another 5 minutes.
4. Add the sautéed veggies to the beans and simmer for 10 minutes.
5. When the beans are tender, add ¼ cup of them to a blender with ½ cup of the liquid and the miso. Purée and then stir into the remaining beans.
   Serves: 4–6
   Preparation time: 30 minutes
   Cooking time: 30 minutes

Watercress (*Nasturtium officinale*)

Family: Brassicaceae or Cruciferae, the mustard, crucifer, or cabbage family
Other names: Brooklime, brown cress, cress, cresson, nasturtium, water cresses, true watercress

This European perennial escaped into the wild of America and became the better for it. Identical-looking to store-bought watercress, it usually floats in dense mats in shallow, cold, flowing, fresh water, first appearing toward the end of early spring.

A hairless, toothless mustard, its fleshy, trailing, hollow stems attach to fibrous, white roots at nodes, growing upright at their ends. If the roots detach, flow downstream, and encounter an obstacle, they take root and form a new colony.

The delicate, shiny, basal leaves, which turn purple in cold weather, grow from 1½ to 6 inches long. The fleshy, wavy-edged, feather-compound leaves divide completely into three to eleven smooth-edged, oblong to oval, opposite leaflets. The terminal leaflet is the largest. The youngest leaflets aren't divided.

In early summer, terminal racemes of tiny, white, four-petaled flowers, ⅛ inch across, grow above a grooved, hollow stem that grows up to 6 inches tall. Other racemes also emerge from the upper leaf axils. Lower down, alternate leaves—similar to but smaller than the basal ones—grow from leafstalks that partially clasp the stem.

In mid-summer, the flowers turn into short, slender, slightly curved, cylindrical seed capsules 1 inch long, growing at the ends of long seed stalks with four rows of tiny, spherical seeds inside.

People confuse this plant with winter cress, but that edible relative has much thicker, glossy leaves and grows near the water, not in it.

Watercress's basal leaves of early spring and fall are the best, similar to store-bought watercress, but more flavorful. When the plant flowers, the leaves become harsh tasting, although still edible. The flowers, young seedpods, and tender parts of the stems are edible in the summer, but they're nowhere nearly as abundant or good as the basal leaves.

The basal leaves are also edible in early winter, if everything isn't frozen, but frosts cut the plant down to the level of the water, and they are entangled with large quantities of dead plant material that take forever to remove.

There are no poisonous look-alikes, but if the water is contaminated with pathogens, don't consume the plant raw. You could get sick even if you rinse it off. The only way to protect yourself is to bring a lawyer with you, then the parasites can attack each other and leave you alone!

Watercress grows in sunny, shallow, fresh, moving water and ditches; on wet ground; in springs; and along the edges of lakes and streams throughout most of North America.

Watercress leaves, flowers, young stems, and young seedpods have a strong, spicy flavor that adults love, but many kids hate. Add it raw to salads and sandwiches, or cook for 5–10 minutes in soups, sauces, casseroles, or other vegetable dishes and entrées. It makes dishes with bland ingredients such as potatoes, tofu, or pasta more interesting, and more than holds its own in dishes with other spices. The seedpods are tiny and hard to collect in quantity, but you can use them to make prepared mustard.

This is one of the most nutritious foods on the earth, with more vitamins A and C, carotenoids, folic acid, iron, and potassium than anything you can buy. It's a great source of flavonoids; vitamins E, B1, and B2; as well as the minerals and trace minerals phosphorus, sodium, iodine, manganese, sulfur, zinc, copper, cobalt, and vanadium. It also provides arginine, aspartic acid, biotin, glutamic acid, glycine, histidine, isoleucine, lysine, methionine, pantothenic acid, phenylalanine, serine, threonine, tryptophan, tyrosine, and valine.

Watercress also contains phenethyl isothiocyanate, which helps prevent cancer and inhibits it once it's present. Hippocrates used an infusion of the plant as a stimulant and expectorant. It's a traditional gentle diuretic, cleansing and toning the urinary tract and promoting the flow of urine. Herbalists gave it to convalescents, who would have benefited from its concentration of nutrients, just like chickweed (see p. 6). They also used it to treat tuberculosis, the best they could do before effective antibiotics were developed.

A poultice of the leaves was applied externally to glandular tumors, lymphatic swellings, and chronic skin irritations and inflammations. This hasn't been tested.

RECIPE

Watercress in Peanut Sauce

Here's a great Indian-style vegetable side dish you can make with wild or store-bought watercress. The plant's strong flavor shines through the spicy sauce. Serve with whole grains, noodles, or bread.

¼ cup peanut oil

2 tsp mustard seed

1 tsp cloves

½ tsp coriander

1½ inch cinnamon stick

2 cloves of garlic

12 cups watercress, chopped

1 package soft tofu, drained and diced

Sauce Ingredients

1 cup water

½ cup peanut butter

Juice of 1 lime

2 tsp salt

1 tbsp nutritional yeast

1 tbsp chili paste, or to taste

2 tsp arrowroot

1 tsp cardamom, powdered

1. Cook the mustard seeds, cloves, coriander, and cinnamon stick in the peanut oil over medium heat for 2 minutes or until the mustard seeds begin to pop.
2. Add the tofu and garlic and sauté for 5 minutes.
3. Add the watercress and sauté for another 2 minutes.
4. Meanwhile, purée the sauce ingredients in a blender.
5. Pour the sauce over the sautéed ingredients and bring to a boil over medium heat, stirring constantly. Reduce the heat to low and simmer, covered, for 10 minutes.
   Serves: 4–6
   Preparation/cooking time: 30 minutes

Poor Man's Pepper (*Lepidium virginicum*)

Family: Brassicaceae or Cruciferae, the mustard, crucifer, or cabbage family
Other names: Virginia pepperweed, peppergrass

Poor man's pepper got its common name because people used this native plant after it became widespread in Europe, during the Age of Exploration. Spices were in demand, to cover up the taste of partially spoiled food in times of need, but imports from Asia were too expensive for most people, who used poor man's pepper instead.

This small- to medium-sized, spicy-flavored annual begins with a basal rosette in early spring, growing above a small, white taproot. The narrow, stalked, lobed basal leaves grow 2–5 inches long. Soon the lobes turn into deep, sharp teeth that point toward the leaf tip.

Dandelion (see p. 44) leaves look similar, but the teeth point to the leaf base, and its leaves—along with those of its edible relatives—contain white, milky sap, which poor man's pepper lacks.

Soon, a long, wiry, branching stem grows from the center of the rosette, reaching around 1½ feet tall where mowing doesn't occur, and the basal leaves vanish. You'll find this form from mid-spring to fall, although some new rosettes reemerge in mid and late fall. The stem bears linear to lance-shaped, toothed, alternate, usually stalkless leaves (smaller than the basal ones) that taper toward the base.

Racemes grow at the tips of the branches from spring to fall, covered with many tiny, short-stalked, white flowers, ⅛ inch wide. The four petals form a cross, like all mustards. The flowers develop into small, flat, short-stalked, circular seedpods, also ⅛ inch wide, with very slightly notched tips in the summer and fall. This form resembles a bottle brush. Subsequently, the plant whitens and dies, leaving a branched skeleton that often persists into the winter.

This common mustard grows in sunny and partially shaded habitats, on lawns, in gardens and parks, along roadsides, and in disturbed habitats, fields, and meadows throughout the United States as well as in eastern and western Canada.

As with other basal rosettes, you can sweep a knife under its center to cut off the root and get the entire rosette in one motion, although picking the leaves one by one works too. Strip the flowers, leaves, and seedpods off the branches, which are too tough to eat. The taproot is sometimes tender enough to eat when the plant is young, but it's so small, I don't find it worth the effort.

Poor man's pepper tastes like radish, horseradish, and wasabi. You can use all aboveground parts except for the wiry stem raw in salads or sandwiches, or in any cooked dish that calls for pungent greens. It cooks in about 10 minutes. You can also purée the green seedpods (the seeds inside are too small to use) in a blender with vinegar, spices, and salt to make prepared mustard.

The leaves supply vitamin C, calcium, iron, and potassium. Herbalists have used infusion of the leaves for diabetes, to expel intestinal worms, as a diuretic, and to reduce the pain of arthritis. An infusion of the seedpods has been used for coughs and asthma, to assist expelling phlegm, and to help with the accumulation of liquid in the chest, although the plant hasn't been tested scientifically.

RECIPE

Beluga Beans with Poor Man's Pepper

Spicy ingredients are great with beans, and poor man's pepper is certainly the right choice for belugas, resulting in a whale of a recipe!

1 cup beluga beans, rinsed and picked free of debris

3 cups vegetable stock

¼ cup poor man's pepper leaves, chopped if large, or seedpods

1 tbsp vegan bacon bits

1 tbsp vegan butter substitute or olive oil

1 tsp marjoram, ground

6 tbsp field garlic leaves or bulbs, or 3 scallions, chopped

2 tbsp white (mellow) miso

1. Pressure cook all ingredients except the miso together for 15 minutes over high pressure, or simmer, covered, for 40 minutes or until the beans are tender.
2. Drain, mix the miso into ¾ cup of the drained liquid with a whisk, and stir this back into the beans.
   Serves: 4–6
   Preparation time: 15 minutes
   Cooking time: 15 or 40 minutes

Curly Dock
(*Rumex crispus*)

Family: Polygonaceae, the knotweed, smartweed, or buckwheat family
Other names: Curled dock, yellow dock, sour dock, narrow dock, narrow-leaved dock, garden patience

This large, common, European perennial is common, easy to recognize, and very tasty and nutritious. It begins with a basal rosette emanating from a large, stiff, yellow, branching taproot in early spring. The long, narrow, smooth, toothless, stalked leaves grow up to 2 feet long and nearly 2½ inches wide. The very wavy margins of these narrow leaves make them quite distinct. A branched stem up to 3 feet tall appears in mid-spring, with alternate leaves similar to but smaller than the basal ones. The base of the short leafstalk wraps around the stem, forming a

sheath. The stems' branches become draped with dense clusters of small, inconspicuous, green flowers in the summer, superseded by reddish-brown seed clusters in summer and fall.

Break or cut off the basal leaves and leafstalks in early spring, before the flower stalk appears, and again in mid and late fall as well. They're edible, cooked, in the summer, but too bitter for many people. The new immature flower stalk is good in mid-spring. Too hard and bitter to eat, you can dig up the taproot for medicinal purposes, in the spring, summer, and fall.

Curly dock grows in sunny and partially shaded habitats throughout the United States, southern Canada, and much of the rest of the temperate world. I even spotted it on the southern tip of South America. It's especially common in disturbed habitats, as well as in fields, along roadsides and riverbanks, and near the seashore.

Bitter dock, also edible, but not as tasty, looks similar to curly dock, but with much broader lacking the very curly edges. On the other hand, beware not to confuse "Curly" dock with Moe Dock or Larry Dock—Nyuk! Nyuk! Nyuk!

The young leaves of early spring and new leaves of autumn are excellent raw in salads and sandwiches, with a wonderful lemony flavor. They're even more lemony cooked for 2–5 minutes. Place the rinsed, chopped leaves in a heavy pot, for example, cover, and cook over low heat for a few minutes, until just wilted. Season with salt, pepper, or any savory or sweet herbs that you like, plus a dash of the oil of your choice, and serve piping hot. Don't sauté, or they'll get mushy. You can also cook the young leafstalks, which I find too tough to eat raw, for 2–3 minutes as well. The peeled immature flower stalks, in season in mid-spring, are great raw (like a lemony celery) and excellent cooked too. The seeds are too tiny to eat, and they're inside hard husks that in turn grow inside a dense cluster of papery bracts. Some authors suggest grinding the "seeds" into flour, but you're really making 99 percent chaff flour, nonpoisonous, and about as tasty and nutritious as eating paper.

Other authors quake in fear from curly dock's oxalic acid content, but the concentration is equivalent to that of spinach, so unless you've such severe kidney disease that spinach is off the menu, there's no danger whatsoever. This highly nutritious "weed" provides vitamins A, B1, B2, B3, and C, plus the minerals iron, potassium, calcium, manganese, and phosphorus. Herbalists used the leaves to treat anemia, effective if the anemia was caused by iron deficiency. It's also been used as a blood purifier or detoxifier for skin conditions, glandular inflammations, and swellings. It contains rumicin, a liver decongestant that stimulates the production of bile, and studies have shown it to help the body expel heavy metals, of no concern to me, as I'm a jazz fan! A decoction is used as stomach tonic. It contains emodin, which stimulates peristalsis and helps with constipation, although an overdose can cause diarrhea. It may slow the growth of cancer, although further research is needed.

The root's tannin makes it an astringent. As such, it's used to stop bleeding—so when an injured Dr. Beverly Crusher spotted it growing on another planet in an episode of *Star Trek: The Next Generation* (I told you it's very widespread!), she had Captain Jean-Luc Picard apply the yellow taproot to her bleeding wound, and it saved her life! Curly dock also contains anthraquinones, used for ringworm and other fungal skin infections. In England, it's used interchangeably with bitter dock and burdock (see p. 310) for nettle stings. You rub the leaves on the affected area and recite, "Dock in, nettle out." However, scientific testing shows it to be no better than placebo, so stick to proven herbal medicines such as jewelweed, common plantain, or long-leaf plantain.

RECIPE

Greens and Beans

Curly dock adds the perfect spark to white beans.

2½ cups vegetable stock

1 cup white beans, soaked overnight or steeped for 1 hour in water just off the boil, rinsed, and drained

¼ cup fresh goutweed, honewort, or parsley, chopped

4 cloves of garlic, chopped

1 tbsp olive oil

1 tbsp vegan bacon bits

1 tsp thyme, ground

1 tsp marjoram, ground

1 tsp oregano, ground

1 tsp sage, ground

¼ tsp black pepper, ground, or to taste

1½ cups curly dock leaves

¼ cup white (mellow) miso

2 tbsp vegan butter substitute or sesame oil

1. Cook the beans along with all the remaining ingredients except for the miso in a pressure cooker over high pressure for 20 minutes, or simmer in a heavy saucepan, covered, for 2–3 hours or until the beans are tender.
2. Drain the beans and reserve the stock.
3. Mash ½ cup of the beans with ½ cup of the stock and the miso, then stir this into the rest of the beans.
   Serves: 4
   Preparation time: 25 minutes
   Cooking time: 20 minutes

Yellow Wood Sorrel
(*Oxalis stricta*)

Family: Oxalidaceae, the wood sorrel family
Other names: Sourgrass, shamrock, pickleplant

This common, widespread, delicious plant is one of the first wild edibles I learned, and it's always been one of my favorites. It's so tasty and easy to recognize, it's one of the best to teach kids too.

This medium-sized plant has a weak, green to pink stem, branched at the base, and grows from 6 to 18 inches tall. It can also creep along the ground. Rhizomes and fibrous roots underlie the stems.

The alternate, palmate-compound leaves, which grow about ¾ inch across, consist of three distinctive, heart-shaped leaflets, each with a seam running down its length. Superficially, it resembles clovers (see p. 118), but clovers have oval leaflets. Therefore, yellow wood sorrel reminds me of my young daughter, who I love, because of the hearts, while clover, which has oval leaflets and no hearts, reminds me of my ex-girlfriend who ran off with another guy on Valentine's Day in 1995. She also has no heart!

The radially symmetrical, yellow, five-petaled flowers, ⅓–¾ inch across, bloom on the stem from late spring to fall. They only open when it's sunny, so people used to think they predicted rain when they were closed.

They develop into banana- or pickle-shaped seedpods. *Stricta* means narrow, and they're slender, as well as upright, pointed, and ridged. Sparsely hairy, they also have flat sides with five sepals at the base. Inside are tiny, spherical, reddish-brown seeds that pop out if you touch it, as the mature pod splits.

Sheep sorrel (see p. 29) sounds and tastes like yellow wood sorrel because the name they share means sour in Old French, but the plants look completely different. Other wood sorrel species (*Oxalis* spp.) with similar leaves and different flowers or seeds are also edible, but they grow in other parts of the country, and I never find them in the Northeast unless they've been planted.

You can find yellow wood sorrel in abundance from the end of early spring to the start of late fall. Sometimes sheltered spots will produce small amounts of tiny plants pre- or postseason.

Yellow wood sorrel grows in sunny or partially shaded habitats; on lawns; in gardens; along edges, trailsides, and roadsides; in fields, meadows, and thickets; on disturbed soil; and in partially sunny spots in the woods. This European plant grows throughout most of the United States and southern Canada, except for the West Coast and Rocky Mountain states.

Strip off the leaves, flowers, seedpods, and any tender parts of the stems with your fingers, holding down the rest of the plant with your other hand, to avoid collecting the tougher parts of the stems.

One of the tastiest ingredients you can add, raw, to salads and sandwiches. It's also quite good in any cooked dish that can benefit from some sourness, although it loses some of its strength cooked, especially in comparison to sheep sorrel. It cooks in 5–10 minutes.

A great source of vitamin C, an infusion of the aboveground parts is supposed to be cooling—a refrigerant, a febrifuge, as well as a diuretic. It's been used for fever, cramps, and nausea, but hasn't been tested scientifically.

Warnings about this plant's oxalic acid content are highly exaggerated. It's the same oxalic acid as spinach and it's just as dangerous. Unless you've kidney disease and can't eat spinach, there's nothing to worry about. We've been eating it in quantity on most of my public tours and on school trips since 1982 and it's never caused any problems.

RECIPE

Wood Sorrel Curry

Wood sorrel adds a sour touch to this simple curry. I used mushrooms I happened to have on hand, but you can substitute any other wild or store-bought species. I use konjak, a little-known plant thickener, here, because it works really well.

¼ cup coconut oil

2¼ cups firm tofu (1 1-lb. package), drained and diced

1 large red onion, diced

½ cup raw cashews, chopped

⅓ cup milky hygrophorus mushrooms (*Lactarius hygrophoroides*) or other mushrooms, chopped

2 tbsp spring agaricus mushrooms (*Agaricus bitorquis*) or other mushrooms, chopped

3 cups coconut milk

3 tbsp red curry paste, or to taste

1 tbsp konjak

2 cups wood sorrel, chopped

1. Sauté the tofu, onion, cashews, and mushrooms in the coconut oil for 10 minutes.
2. Meanwhile, purée the curry paste and konjak with the coconut milk in a blender.
3. Pour the blended ingredients into the sautéed ingredients, add the wood sorrel, and bring to a boil over medium heat, stirring constantly. Reduce the heat to low and simmer, covered, for 10 minutes, stirring occasionally.
   Serves: 6
   Preparation time: 30 minutes
   Cooking time: 20 minutes

Stinging Nettle
(*Urtica dioica*)

Family: Urticaceae, the nettle family
Other names: Burn nettle, burn weed, burn hazel, mountain nettle, nettle, giant creek nettle, hoary nettle

A well-known wild food, medicine, and nuisance plant, this species is covered with tiny hypodermic needles that inject unwary victims with acetylcholine, histamine, serotonin, and formic acid. A colonial perennial and the namesake of its family, its erect, somewhat stout, 4-sided, unbranched, hollow stem grows from 3 to 7 feet tall. It spreads through creeping, branching rhizomes, as well as seeds. Growing 2–6 inches long and 1–2 inches wide, the long-stalked, opposite leaves are oval and dark green, with a rough, papery texture. The long tip is pointed, the base is heart-shaped, and the teeth get larger toward the tip. A pair of stipules grows at the base of each leafstalk. Tiny, green, inconspicuous flowers bloom from late spring to early fall, growing on long, slender, paired panicles suspended from the upper leaf axils. Male and female flowers grow on separate plants. The fruits resemble the flowers, but with tiny seeds inside.

Stinging nettles have no poisonous look-alikes, but there are similar-looking edible and inedible species. Slender nettle (U. gracilis) looks like stinging nettles, but with sparse stingers and none on the leaves' upper surfaces. The leaves are lance-shaped, not oval. Wood nettles (Laportea canadense) leaves are larger and rounded, opposite when young and alternate when mature. They're both edible, and you use all three species the same way.

Clearweed (*Pilea pumila*) is a similar-looking inedible relative with a translucent stem and no stinging hairs. Here's how I know it's nonpoisonous: Back in 1982, when I had just begun leading foraging tours, I encountered a group of Boy Scouts with their adult troop leader collecting clearweed in Forest Park, Queens, NYC.

"What are you gathering?" I asked.

"We're collecting stinging nettles, and we're going to eat them," one of them answered. "We've been collecting and eating them for years."

"It's clearweed, not stinging nettles," I replied. "It has no stinging hairs, and the stem is translucent green. I'm an expert. I know what I'm talking about.

Without stingers, it can't possibly be stinging nettles."

"It's stinging nettles," he replied. "We've been eating it for years, and we're going to keep collecting it and eating it!"

Nothing I could say convinced them. So if you happen to be walking in Forest Park and see a group of middle-aged men and one senior citizen with a long, gray beard, all in tattered scout uniforms, chowing down on clearweed, you'll know why!

Henbit deadnettle (*Lamium amplexicaule*) is a foully, musty-smelling, nonpoisonous, hairy mint with drooping, opposite leaves and a square stem, plus small, conspicuous, 2-sided, pink flowers. A softly hairy plant, it doesn't sting. This European plant tastes quite awful to me, although English foragers tell me it's quite delicious there—in comparison to English food, anything would taste good! Catnip (Nepeta cataria) has a square stem and opposite leaves like stinging nettles, but no stinging hairs, and downy leaves are downy. It smells minty, and it attracts cats!

Stinging nettles grow in partially shaded, moist, rich soil, in disturbed habitats, fields, and open woodlands; along edges of trails; in thickets; and along riverbanks, throughout most of North America and the temperate world.

Harvest wearing work gloves or rubber gloves, or place your hand inside a plastic bag. Long pants and long sleeves also make things easier. Strip or cut off the leaves of plants less than 9 inches tall, plus the small top leaves of larger plants. You can use the tough stems for making tea.

If you get stung, rub the juice of jewelweed (Impatiens spp.) stems or the crushed leaves of common plantain (Plantago major) or long-leaf plantain (*P. lanceolata*) on the affected area for quick relief. After Bite®, which you can get in drug stores, also works. Untreated stings hurt for about 20 minutes in some people, and for many hours in others. In England, it's traditional to rub curly dock leaves on nettle stings, but a control, double blind study done there showed that this herb is no better than a placebo.

Stinging nettle is an excellent potherb, with a rich, earthy flavor. Handle it wearing rubber gloves. Brief cooking stops it from stinging, and it's great cooked for 5–15 minutes in any savory recipe. Just don't boil it in water, as some sources suggest. That ruins the flavor. The plant also makes an excellent tea, where you can use parts that are too tough to eat.

Highly nutritious, it provides more protein than any other green, plus carotenoids, vitamins C, K, and B-complex; as well as chlorophyll, lecithin, choline, linoleic acid, linolenic acid, flavonoids, palmitic acid, pantothenic acid, quercetin, sterols, tannins, and over thirty other biologically active compounds. It's also very high in readily absorbable iron, calcium, chromium, magnesium, potassium, phosphorous, manganese, silica, iodine, sodium, sulfur, and zinc.

Traditional Russian herbalists used juice wrung from lots of nettles using a cloth for what we'd call chronic fatigue today. If the cause was iron-deficiency anemia, the iron would cure it, and this juice also cures nettle stings! Nettle leaf infusion is considered a safe, gentle diuretic, supposedly restorative for the kidneys and bladder, and used for cystitis and nephritis, although the latter can kill you if the remedy doesn't work! People put it in weight loss formulas and it's very effective, only it makes you shed pounds of water, not fat! The infusion is used as an expectorant for asthma, mucus in the lungs, and chronic coughs. It helps blood clot, probably due to its vitamin K, and it's good for excessive menstruation. It's been used for nose bleeds, which is safe to do; and for hemorrhages, bloody coughs, and bloody urine, which, again, are dangerous conditions you shouldn't treat yourself. A whole-plant tincture is used for the flu, colds, bronchitis, pneumonia, and eczema. It supposedly promotes lactation, lessens snoring, and helps regulate blood sugar, but these uses haven't been tested. Studies have shown ground freeze-dried nettle leaves to relieve or reduce the symptoms of hay fever in a third of sufferers, but because you can't patent a plant, this has gotten little notice. People also whip themselves with nettles for severe osteoarthritis, an autoimmune disorder. The plant has anti inflammatory properties, but this still needs scientific testing. Would some arthritic masochists please limp forward! Nettle tea has been used for gout, glandular diseases, poor circulation, enlarged spleen, diarrhea, dysentery, worms, intestinal and colon disorders, and hemorrhoids, as well as for digestive disorders, to stimulate digestion, often with other herbs. German doctors use root extracts for benign enlarged prostate, and Russian scientists are experimenting with nettle leaf tincture for hepatitis and gall bladder inflammation.

RECIPE

Stinging Nettle Risotto

Here's a creamy vegan rice-and-cheese casserole, punctuated by the wonderfully earthy flavor of stinging nettles.

5 cups cooked brown rice

4 cups stinging nettles or other nettle species

1-⅔ cups soy mozzarella cheese, grated

½ cup hazelnut milk or other nondairy milk

¼ cup any mushrooms, sliced

¼ cup roasted, unsalted pistachio nuts

2 tbsp Savory Marinade (see p. 315)

1 tbsp Vege-Sal or seasoned salt

1. Cover and bake all ingredients in an oiled casserole dish for 45 minutes in a preheated 350°F oven.
   Serves: 4–6
   Preparation time: 10 minutes
   Baking time: 45 minutes

Glasswort (*Salicornia* spp.)

Family: Amaranthaceae, the amaranth family
Other names: Samphire, pickleweed, sea bean, sea asparagus, saltwort

This is an unusual-looking upright, leafless, green, branching, jointed plant that consists mostly of a succulent stem, making it easy to spot in its seashore habitat. It grows up to 6 inches tall and turns a translucent pink in the fall.

To stop loss of water from evaporation in an environment lacking fresh water, the leaves are reduced to inconspicuous, opposite scales that you can barely make out. Minute green flowers grow in groups of three to seven. Only ⅛ inch long, they're hidden in the joints of the upper branches.

The seeds are so tiny you usually don't see them either. These features make the species, most of which are annuals (with one perennial), difficult to tell apart, but you use them all the same way. There are no look-alike plants.

Collect glasswort at low tide, wearing footwear appropriate for mud, or going barefoot. Break off the stems with your fingers. There are swarms of mosquitoes, biting sand flies, and midges too small to see, among other vicious insects in this habitat in the summer, so go early in the morning, when it's cool enough to cover yourself up, and spray insect repellant on your clothes if necessary. Sheltered bays are much better for these insects (and worse for you), while areas close to the open ocean and windy days make things more difficult for the insects.

Glasswort grows on mud flats and salt marshes, along shores, where it's sometimes submerged at high tide. You can find it along East Coast, the Gulf Coast except for Utah, and the California coast. It's native to the United States as well as to Europe, South Africa, and South Asia. Wherever it originated, it probably rafted across the ocean with fallen trees, grasses, and mud to have become distributed so widely.

Glasswort is in season from mid-spring to early fall. It tastes best when it first comes up, and later on it develops a tough core that needs to be removed.

This crunchy vegetable tastes like spinach and asparagus to me. It's so good that purveyors of gourmet foods are trying to bring it into the marketplace as an exotic vegetable. However, it's name, glasswort, is a turnoff. "Wort" is simply an old word for plant and because of its silica content, it had been used in the manufacture of glass, but that's not going to help sales, so marketers are selling it as "sea beans," even though it's in the amaranth (see p. 59) family and has nothing whatsoever to do with beans.

I detect a bitter aftertaste when I eat it raw, although some foragers don't, so I cook it for 10–15 minutes in soups, stews, and grain dishes. It also makes great pickles. In seasons when it's a tough core, you can cook it by itself, let it cool, then remove the core with your fingers, and add the glasswort to any dish that calls for vegetables, if desired.

To cope with its salty habitat and to stave off dehydration (salt tends to draw water out of cells that don't contain lots of salt), it takes in salt, so you don't need to add salt to any recipe that contains this plant, which is sometimes used (dried and ground) as a salt substitute.

Glasswort contains the essential fatty acid, linoleic acid, as well as lots of the aforementioned sodium, plus potassium, calcium, iron, iodine, and copper.

Juice pressed out of the plant is a traditional diuretic, but that's because it's salty, making you drink lots of water, and you know what eventually happens after that! Sodium is essential for life, but too much leads to high blood pressure in some people, and when you excrete sodium in the urine, it takes potassium (which is in short supply in the modern food-scape) along with it. So, this is one of the best herbal diuretics to avoid using!

RECIPE

Boston Baked Beans with Glasswort

There are so many great classic recipe concepts with which to experiment with. It took me thirty-three year to get to this one, and only because someone I knew had a craving for this dish. An uncharacteristic sweet bean recipe, burnt sugar extract and caramel extract (available at http://www.bickfordflavors.com/index.html) with my standard sweetener, liquid stevia, provide the sweet flavor of the traditional sugary molasses without refined products; while barbecue seasoning replaces the barbecue sauce; and glasswort adds the saltiness and more flavor.

2 cups cooked red kidney beans

2 cups vegetable stock or water

¼ cup fruit-sweetened ketchup

2 tbsp tomato paste

2 red onions, chopped

1 large red bell pepper, chopped

5 Tofu Pups (vegan hot dogs, available in health food stores), sliced

1 tbsp olive or corn oil

¼ cup glasswort, or 2 tsp Vege-Sal, or 1 tsp salt

2 tsp black peppercorns, ground into 4 tsp, or to taste

2 tsp barbecue seasoning

1 tsp cumin, ground

½ tsp clear liquid stevia

¼ tsp caramel extract

¼ tsp burnt sugar extract

1. Mix together all ingredients and bake, covered, in an oiled casserole dish in a preheated 350°F oven for 2½ hours.
   Serves: 6
   Preparation time: 10 minutes
   Cooking time: 2½ hours

Edible Wildflowers

Some of the wildflowers that bloom at different times during the spring make delicious foods. I don't cover them all in this section, as some species (like the daylily, see p. 23) also have edible shoots and tubers. Here are plants where the main edible parts are the flowers. They're fun to collect, to use in recipes, and to serve to astonished non-foraging friends and family members.

Redbud
(*Cercis canadensis*)

Family: Fabaceae
Other names: American redbud, eastern redbud, Judas tree

This is a wonderfully beautiful, small- to medium-sized tree that landscapers love to plant and foragers delight in eating. This shrubby native has a short main trunk, a rounded crown, and zigzag stems. It grows from 20 to 30 feet tall and 25 to 30 feet wide, beginning with a vase shape. As it matures, it leans toward the sunlight or develops an irregular shape, with an umbrella-shaped crown. The bark begins dark brown and smooth, then becomes scaly and ridged, occasionally with maroon or orange-brown patches where the bark peels off.

The alternate, smooth-edged, pointy-tipped, heart-shaped leaves are quite distinct. They grow from 2 to 6 inches across and of equal length. Red-tinged bright green as they develop, they become dark green when mature and bright yellow in autumn.

While the leaves are first developing in early spring, purple-red buds cover the branches and trunk. They open into showy, dense clusters of rosy-pink, pea-like flowers when early spring gives way to mid-spring, creating a gorgeous display.

The flowers morph into persistent, flattened pods, 2–4 inches long, red when they first appear in mid-spring, next green, and finally brown. Inside are several dark brown, flat, elliptical seeds, around ¼ inch across.

Redbuds grow in sunny to lightly shaded places. They're very common in cultivated parks, but also grow in thickets and ravines, along the borders of streams and edges of woods, and in lightly shaded, moist woodlands. They grow wild in much of eastern North America, and landscapers can plant them anywhere.

The unopened buds are nonpoisonous but unpleasantly astringent, better pickled than eaten raw, but the open flowers are much better. Strip them and the immature seedpods off with your fingers.

The sweet sour, visually appealing flowers taste a little like fresh snap peas and are great in salads, sandwiches, and a large variety of cooked dishes. I add them to oatmeal when it's finished cooking, or cook them in pancake batter to make fritters. They're excellent baked into breads as muffins, and used as sprinkles on ice cream. You can freeze them with water in ice cube trays and serve these in drinks. They're also great for wine-making.

You can use the seedpods like snow peas during the first week of their appearance. Later on, they become too tough to eat. With enough simmering or pressure cooking, you might be able to make the seeds soft enough to eat (Native Americans roasted them), but they're so small, collecting enough to use would be very labor intensive.

They flowers provide vitamin C and anthocyanins, and the young pods and seeds provide proanthocyanidins and linolenic, α-linolenic, oleic, and palmitic acids.

A decoction of the cambium, which is astringent, has been used to treat dysentery and diarrhea, as well as leukemia, chest congestion, and whooping cough, but there's no supporting evidence that it works. Herbalists aren't using it nowadays, and even if it's not harmful, the serious diseases it's been used for could kill you if not treated effectively.

RECIPE

Redbud Blossom Cookies

Here's another example of how to use vegan ingredients to advantage, replacing white flour with whole grain flours, sugar with liquid stevia, and eggs with arrowroot, xanthan gum, flaxseeds, and lecithin granules. The wild redbud flowers, complemented with just the right seasonings, add a final touch to these perfect cookies. Incidentally, I designed them without any crunchy ingredients so my then-eleven-month-old daughter could safely eat them, and she loves these cookies as much as I do!

Dry Ingredients

3 cups sweet brown rice flour + 6 oz. buckwheat flour

¼ cup flaxseeds, ground into ½ cup meal

3 tbsp arrowroot

1 tbsp xanthan gum

1 tsp salt

1 tsp cream of tartar

½ tsp baking soda

1 tsp cinnamon

Ingredients to Blend

1½ cups pear juice

½ cup corn oil

¼ cup lecithin granules

2 tsp liquid stevia

½ cup currants

1 tbsp fresh lemon rind

1 tsp orange rind

1 tsp vanilla

Other Ingredients

1 cup redbud flowers

1. Mix together the dry ingredients.
2. Purée the ingredients to blend in a blender.
3. Mix the wet ingredients into the dry ingredients. Don't overmix.
4. Stir in the redbuds. Don't overmix.
5. Shape into thirty-six cookies and place on three cookie sheets.
6. Bake for 10 minutes or until lightly browned underneath in a preheated 400°F oven. Turn with a spatula and bake for another 5–10 minutes on the other side. Be careful to avoid scorching.
7. Cool on wire racks.
   Yields: 36 cookies
   Preparation time: 40minutes
   Cooking time: 20 minutes

Red Clover
(*Trifolium pratense*)

Family: Fabaceae, Leguminosae, or Papillionaceae, the legume, pea, or bean family
Other names: Beebread, cow clover, cow grass, meadow clover, purple clover, wild clover, meadow honeysuckle, meadow trefoil, trefoil, broad red, cleaver grass, mari grass

This familiar, upright Eurasian perennial, which sometimes also creeps along the ground, grows from 6 to 24 inches tall, with long, slender, downy stem branches and fibrous roots. The alternate, palmate-compound leaves are divided into three oval to elliptical leaflets, ½–1½ inches long, and half as wide as they're long. A dark, conspicuous, V-shaped chevron centered on each leaflet's medial seam makes the plant more noticeable. Tiny magenta florets crowd into rounded flower heads at the tops of the stems, which grows up 1 inch long. There may be up to sixty bilaterally symmetrical florets, each up to ½ inch long, on each flower head. After the flowers dry out, very tiny, brown seeds are released. There are no poisonous look-alikes. White clover (Trifolium repens) is a smaller plant with white flowers, and you use the two plants the same way. However, people confuse wood sorrel (see p. 99), also edible, with clovers, but wood sorrel, with different flowers, has heart-shaped rather than oval leaves, and lacks chevrons.

Young leaves appear in early spring. The flowers are at their best in late spring, right after they bloom and develop their color, although you may still be able to find a few fresh ones in the summer and fall. Clovers like full sunlight, and are especially common in meadows, pastures, open fields, and lawns, as well as in disturbed habitats, trailsides, roadsides, and parklands.

Pull the florets off the most brightly colored flower heads with your fingers. These are much better than faded and dried out flowers. The brown ones are quite awful. You can eat the youngest leaves when they first come up, before they become hard to digest. They taste like raw string beans, but more stringy. I don't care for them, and happily relegate them to those macho wilderness survivalists who haven't bothered to track down the many much tastier plants that this book covers!

The fresh flowers are slightly sweet, with a hint of green peas, great in salads, and any dish that calls for vegetables, cooking in about 15 minutes. Sprinkle on top of ice cream, like, well, sprinkles!

Pour a cup of boiling water over a handful of flower heads to taste (you may include some leaves) and let it steep, covered, for 20 minutes. This traditional tea provides vitamins C, B1, B3, and E, as well as the minerals calcium, chromium, magnesium, phosphorus, and potassium, plus isoflavones—plant estrogens and antioxidants. These include genistein, irilone, and pratensein, which act on cellular estrogen receptors. This is bad for insects, disrupting reproduction, whereas in healthy humans, they block normal estrogen and human-made estrogen-like environmental contaminants from promoting cell division, possibly reducing your risk of cancer, especially breast cancer. It's like having the wrong key in a lock. It won't open the door, and blocks the right key from doing so as well.

Tests are underway to see if these compounds are helpful for prostate cancer. Paradoxically, if you already have cancer, the tea could make it worse, as cancer cells can be triggered to divide by substances that wouldn't affect normal cells. It should also be avoided by people with estrogen-sensitive conditions such as endometriosis, ovarian cancer, uterine cancer, or fibroid tumors. It's also contraindicated for pregnant and lactating women. This tea is also supposed to have a calming effect on some people. It's used for menopause, but research has had mixed results. It may be helpful for osteoporosis, and heart disease but research again has had mixed results.

It's been used for bronchitis, burns, ulcers, and asthma. An ointment, made by boiling the flowers in oil and thickening this with beeswax, has been used for eczema and psoriasis. There have been no mixed results here, but only because there have been no scientific tests!

RECIPE

Peachy Keen Ice Cream with Red Clover Sprinkles

Here's a flavorful, creamy ice cream you can make with wild or store-bought peaches, plus red clover sprinkles, making it even more special.

3 peaches, chopped

2¾ cups soy milk, oat milk, or nut milk

1 tbsp arrowroot or kudzu

1 tsp agar powder or 1 tbsp agar flakes

½ cup pine nuts or cashew nuts, raw

½ cup silken tofu, drained

¼ cup lecithin granules

¼ cup grape seed oil

¼ cup vegetable glycerin

1 tbsp liquid stevia

¼ tsp salt

¼ tsp powdered ginger

¼ tsp nutmeg, ground

¼ cup red clover florets

1. Simmer the peaches in the soy milk with the arrowroot and agar for 5 minutes or until the peaches are tender, stirring often.
2. Strain out the peaches.
3. Purée all ingredients except half the peaches and the clover florets in a blender.
4. Freeze in an ice cream machine according to the manufacturer's directions.
5. Fold in the remaining peaches using a large rubber spatula.
6. Serve sprinkled with the clover florets.

Yields: 5½ cups
Preparation time: 20 minutes
Freezing time: 2–3 hours (varies)

Warm-Weather Herbs, Shoots, and Greens

Some plants don't like the cold and won't appear until the threat of frost is long gone. These plants take many forms, and vary in how long they persist. Some stick around for the remainder of the growing season, while others soon go out of season. Many of these varied warm-weather plants are especially tasty and healthful.

Lady's Thumb (*Persicaria maculosa*)

Family: Polygonaceae, the smartweed or buckwheat family
Other names: Redleg, persicaria, Redshank, spotted lady's thumb, gambetta, Adam's plaster

This is a very common plant everyone has seen, although most people don't know what it is. An erect, herbaceous, European annual, it grows from 1 to 2½ feet tall in dense stands, arising from both fibrous roots and a shallow taproot.

The smooth, pointed, alternate, lance-shaped leaves grow from 1½ to 4½ inches long, without teeth or lobes. A slightly darkened triangular chevron often spots the leaf's center, as though a lady had imprinted her thumb there.

The stem is divided into regular intervals by swollen, reddish-tinged nodes, as do its relatives. A translucent sheath fringed with very short, upward-pointing hairs grows above each node.

Conspicuous, distinct, upright terminal clusters of small, pink (sometimes white) flowers grow on narrow racemes up to 1½ inches long.

Related smartweeds (*Polygonum* spp.) without the fringe of hairs will make you smarter. Eat them and your mouth will smart so much, you'll become smart enough never to eat them again (one of their common names is smartass!).

This very common plant is in season mainly from mid-spring through mid-fall, although you can sometimes find a few survivors in late fall if the weather has been mild. It grows in full or partial sunlight, in disturbed habitats, roadsides, parks, meadows, stream banks, lawns, and meadows, especially if there's

low, wet ground, throughout most of the United States and Canada.

The leaves are edible raw or cooked, and some people like the flowers, although I don't. The leaves are very bland to adults, but sweet to toddlers and very young children, who collect and eat as much as they can. I sometimes use the leaves raw or cooked to tone down recipes with lots of spicy ingredients or to fill up salads, but they're not flavorful enough to be used as a main ingredient.

There's been no nutritional analysis, and the plant isn't used in herbal medicine.

RECIPE

Wild Rice with Wild Veggies

Wild rice is a great grain by itself. With wild greens and seasonings, it's both wilder and better.

3 cups vegetable stock

1 cup wild rice

1 cup lady's thumb or other greens, chopped

¼ cup goutweed or parsley, chopped

¼ cup field garlic or scallions, chopped

4 cloves of garlic, chopped

1 tbsp olive oil

1 tbsp All-Purpose Seasoning (available in health food stores), or other savory spice mix

½ tsp salt, or to taste

¼ tsp black pepper, or to taste

1. Simmer, covered, all ingredients together in a saucepan for 100 minutes or until all the stock has been absorbed.
   Serves: 4–6
   Preparation time: 10 minutes
   Cooking time: 100 minutes

Lamb's Quarters (*Chenopodium album*)

Family: Amaranthaceae, the amaranth family

Other names: Wild spinach, fat-hen, goosefoot, white goosefoot, Good King Henry, nickel greens, pigweed, dungweed, bathua, allgood, baconweed, dirtweed

This common, odorless annual tastes so good, I eat it any time I find it, even though I'm a vegan! It usually grows from 3 to 5 feet tall, although I've seen it grow up to 10 feet under exceptionally favorable circumstances. It takes the shape of a tree, with lots of branches. Where the branches split from the lined stem (the axil), you'll see a distinctive blotch of purple.

The youngest leaves, near the growing tips of the branches, are linear, but they soon become diamond-shaped with some shallow teeth, leading Carl Linnaeus to give it the generic name *Chenopodium*, goose foot. The undersides of the mature leaves and both surfaces of the youngest leaves are covered with a white, waxy powder, preventing desiccation, and letting the plant grow in sandy, water-poor soil. Thus the specific name *album*, which means white. The leaves grow up to 4 inches long. Tiny, green, inconspicuous, spherical flowers bloom on short, dense spikes in the upper leaf axils and at the plant's tip in the summer. In the fall, they eventually become reddish brown fruits containing thousands of tiny, shiny, black seeds.

People have confused lamb's quarters with epazote (Dysphania ambrosioides), but the latter has elliptical rather than diamond-shaped leaves, they're not whitish underneath, and there's a strong resinous smell. Orache, also edible, (Atriplex patula) looks a little like lamb's quarters, but with triangular, not diamond-shaped leaves, no teeth, and, again, they're not whitish underneath. Lamb's quarters is sometimes called pigweed, but so is amaranth (see p. 259), which is quite a different plant. Refer to scientific names to dispel any ambiguity.

Five days before first writing this very page, I was leading a foraging tour in Central Park and recounting an incident from the week before, when I had shown people lamb's quarters and, for the first time in 33 years, someone began putting deadly white snakeroot *(Ageratina altissima)* into her bag, just because it was growing next to the lambs quarters. The plants are completely different. White snakeroot, which doesn't branch, has much larger, long-stalked, triangular, opposite, regularly toothed leaves that aren't white underneath. While I was recounting this, a woman who must have been paying either too much or too little attention to what I was saying was herself putting white snakeroot, which was

again growing right next the lamb's quarters, into her bag! So be very careful about anything that may be growing near your intended dinner, and if you ever teach people to forage yourself, carefully watch in all directions to what everyone's doing at all times!

Lamb's quarters can pick up nitrates from soil contaminated with artificial fertilizers, which will poison you when you eat the plant, so avoid picking on or near fertilized agricultural fields. Some of the leaves are often spotted with red, or have white, dead areas, due to the lamb's quarters' leaf miner (*Chrysoesthia sexguttella*), which is so small that it tunnels between the upper and lower surface of the leaf. Don't eat any of such insect-infested leaves, especially if you're a vegetarian! You may sometimes read that this plant is dangerous because of its oxalic acid content, but it's about as much oxalic acid as spinach, and the two foods are equally threatening!

Lamb's quarters grows in rich soil and sandy soil, in sunny or partially shaded habitats. It's very common in urban parks and in spots where its primary predator fears to attack it: lawn mowers shy away from benches, walls, rocks, or fences. You can find it in disturbed habitats, along roadsides, in fields and agricultural lands, near the seashore, and along the edges of trails and roads. This native plant grows throughout North America, and is native to Eurasia too. Wherever it originated, a migrating bird, blown off course by a storm, probably transported the tiny seeds across the Atlantic on its muddy feet in prehistoric times.

The shoots first appear in mid-spring and the leaves last until late fall, when they're destroyed by frost. The seeds are best collected from the dying or recently deceased plants in late fall. You can pinch or snip off the young shoots in early spring. After that, strip the leaves off the branches with your fingers. Try to get as many leaves and as few pieces of the stems as possible. I find the flowers unpleasantly bitter. Harvest the seeds the same way as you would for amaranth (see p. 259).

A relative of spinach and beets, lamb's quarters tastes like spinach, only better. Enjoy the raw leaves chopped into salads and sandwiches, or cook them like spinach. They're good sautéed, or in soups, stews, casseroles, grain dishes, stir-fries, bean dishes, and virtually anything else. They cook in 5–10 minutes.

Not in the grass family, the seeds (usually quite labor intensive to collect) are a pseudo-grain, as you use them like grains, simmered in stock to cover, with savory seasonings, for about 15–20 minutes, or until tender.

Not used in herbal medicine, the leaves are an excellent source of vitamin A, calcium, potassium, and iron, preventing or treating deficiencies in these nutrients. The leaves also supply some thiamin, riboflavin, and niacin. The seeds contain protein, calcium, phosphorus, potassium, and niacin.

RECIPE

Creamed Lamb's Quarters

Here's my version of a traditional American spinach recipe, using lamb's quarters instead of spinach, and further transformed by vegan alternatives supplanting the cream. After I sketched out the recipe on an index card, it sat on top of my refrigerator for 2 years before I got around to trying it. I'd really kick myself for this if I could. It became one of my favorite methods of preparing a large variety of wild greens. Serve it over pasta or on toast, using the liquid as a sauce.

6 cups lamb's quarters, chopped

6 tbsp silken tofu

6 tbsp water

6 tbsp corn, coconut, or flaxseed oil, or vegan butter substitute

¼ cup lecithin granules (available in health food stores)

1 tbsp arrowroot

⅜ tsp liquid stevia

8 cloves of garlic, peeled and uncut

½ tbsp salt

½ tsp black pepper, ground, or to taste

½ tsp nutmeg, ground

1. Purée the water, tofu, oil, lecithin granules, and stevia in a blender.
2. Combine it with the remaining ingredients in a saucepan, cover, and cook over low for heat for 10–15 minutes or until the greens are just wilted.
3. Remove the garlic, slice it, and return it to the dish.
   Serves: 4–6
   Preparation time: 10 minutes
   Cooking time: 15 minutes

Common Cattail
(*Typha latifolia*)

Family: Typhaceae, the cattail family
Other names: Broad-leaf cattail, cat-o'-nine-tails, bullrush

This is a favorite of mine and other wild food enthusiasts. It's common, easy to recognize, and very tasty, and you can use various parts of the plant. Cattails grow in dense colonies in marshes—sunny wetlands with grasslike plants. The erect, sword-shaped leaves—"always basal," arising from the base of the plant, not from a stem—grow from 3 to 10 feet tall and ⅓–¾ inch wide, tapering toward the top. From twelve to sixteen of them grow on each shoot. The leaves have parallel veins and look spongy when cut cross section. A clear, slimy liquid oozes out from between the leaves, and it makes an excellent hand lotion. Branching rhizomes produce the aboveground parts. These stout subterranean stems usually grow ¼–1 inch across, but about 3–4 inches under mud or sand, and up to 27 inches long. Cylindrical flowers grow at the top of a tapering, upright, leafless stem, ¼–¾ inch wide, that emerges from the center of the leaves. Male and female flowers grow on different parts of an unjointed, terminal spike, 6 inches tall and 1 inch across, with the male, which will eventually shed pollen, above the female. The flowers start off green in late spring, but the male soon becomes coated with golden pollen. After the pollen is gone, the male flower shrivels to the size of a toothpick. The female flower turns brown in the summer, then gets coated with distinctive, fluffy, white seeds in the fall. Some of the seed heads persist into early spring, very useful for distinguishing the cattail stand from other wetland plants at a glance.

You can use the similar narrow-leaf cattail (*Typha angustifolia*) the same as the common cattail. This smaller species has a gap between the male and female

flower spikes. It's tasty too, but provides there's less food. However, both plants are common enough that you should be able to find the larger common cattail easily.

People often confuse cattails with other wetland plants with sword-like leaves, but without bothering to find out about the cattail's features. The common reed (*Phragmites australis*) has alternate, sword-like leaves arising from a tall, upright stem, plus a plumlike flower and seed head, completely unlike the cattail's cigar-shaped one. There's a small amount of bad-tasting food inside the stem in early spring, if you peel long enough. Young cattail shoots look a little like poisonous daffodil (*Narcissus pseudonarcissus*) and iris (*Iris* spp.) shoots, which have similar leaves, but they don't have the cattail shoot's rod-like shape or its tender, white, inner core. Cattail stands also retain at least a few left-over seed heads from the previous year, and neither of these poisonous plants grows more than a few feet tall. Cattails get much taller by mid-spring.

Cattails are easiest to harvest after periods of dry weather, when there's less mud and the plants are more accessible. Collect the shoots in mid- and late spring. You get much more with less effort then, when the shoots are much larger than in early spring, when they first appear. Use only those shoots that haven't developed the stem, or the shoots will be woody all the way through.

Before you pull out a cattail, look around to make sure there are no animal rights activists watching! Then spread a few leaves away from the larger shoots with both hands, grab the inner part, then pull out the central part of the shoot. Peel away the tough outer leaves from the top down, until you're left with a white core tender enough to pinch through with your thumbnail (the rule of thumb!). You can also do this at home. Remove the protective sheath (if it's still present) from the immature green flower heads, and clip off the male flower head with shears or with a knife. The female flower head retains almost no food and isn't worth collecting. Shake the mature flower heads, which are covered with golden pollen, into a paper bag, going from one to another. You'll get the most pollen when there hasn't been much wind for a few days, since the wind blows the pollen away. You can dig up the rhizomes in fall and early spring, or in the winter (if the ground isn't frozen), but this is very hard, messy work, and you get very little food for your effort compared to the other parts.

The peeled shoots are crisp and crunchy, with a flavor like cucumbers. Add raw shoots to salads and sandwiches, cook them using any method whatsoever from stir-fries to soups, or use as a substitute for zucchini. They're incredibly versatile, and there's lots of food in the shoots once they get large. They cook in 10–15 minutes. Cook the green male flower heads like corn on the cob (a distant relative). You can steam them, bake them with seasoned oil, or simmer them for 15–20 minutes. They're dryer than corn, and this makes them superb served with a sauce—another demonstration of the culinary principle of combining contrasts, as in the familiar sweet-and-sour dishes. You can also store the green male flower heads in a paper bag at room temperature for a week or two. They'll mature, and you'll get the pollen you may have missed if the wind blew it away. Sift the pollen to get rid of plant debris, and use the pollen like flour. It doesn't make baked goods rise, so use it with flour that does rise if necessary. It tastes great, a little like sweet cornmeal, and it's excellent in pancakes, waffles, and muffins.

If you've managed to dig up the rhizomes, hose off all the mud or clean it in a sink (which may get clogged). You can then chew on the fibers and swallow the starch, or rub the starch off the fibers with your fingers in a bowl of water. Let the starch settle and pour off the water. Two hours of work yielded enough starch to thicken a soup to serve six when I tried this, although other foragers have reported better results, possibly with rhizomes that contained much more food than the ones I find around NY. Alternatively, you can dehydrate the cleaned rhizomes, pound them with a mallet, and sift out the debris to obtain the starch, again, this too labor intensive for me. The lateral shoots growing on the rhizomes during the cold-weather seasons taste like the shoots, but they're small and muddy, far inferior to the larger shoots that grow when the weather becomes warm. Nevertheless, some foragers love them.

Cattail shoots are good sources of vitamins K and B6, as well as the minerals iron, phosphorus, calcium, sodium, magnesium, potassium and manganese, while the immature and mature flower heads, and the pollen, provide essential fatty acids, calories (highly sought-after by wilderness survival enthusiasts), and protein—all rare in wild plants.

In addition to its use as a hand lotion, the slime between the leaves has been used as an antiseptic for cuts and as a dental anesthetic, but this hasn't been tested. The rhizomes have been pounded into a poultice and applied to skin sores, cuts, wounds, burns, stings, and bruises. The pollen has been used externally and internally for bleeding, but I'd have to see convincing evidence of this plant's effectiveness as a medicine before I'd use it.

RECIPE

Cataroni and Cheese

Here's a vegan variation of macaroni and cheese, enhanced with cattail shoots. It's very easy to make and very good.

3 cups whole-grain macaroni

3 cups cattail shoots or zucchini, sliced

2½ cups almond milk or other nondairy milk

¾ cup vegan mozzarella cheese, grated

½ tbsp Vege-Sal or seasoned salt, or 1 tsp salt, or to taste

½ tsp sage, ground

½ tsp marjoram, ground

½ tsp savory, ground

¼ tsp black pepper, ground

1. Mix all ingredients together and cook for 30–40 minutes in a slow cooker, or simmer, covered, in a saucepan for 10–15 minutes or until the macaroni is al dente, stirring often.
   Serves: 4–6
   Preparation time: 10 minutes
   Cooking time: 15 or 40 minutes

RECIPE

Baked Cattail Flower Heads

You can't get much simpler than this one, only two ingredients, but a perfect combination. Cattail flower heads are flavorful but dry, so Sweet Herb Spread is just right for them.

24 green (immature) cattail flower heads

2 tbsp Sweet Herb Spread, or as needed

1. Toss the cattail flower heads in the Sweet Herb Spread.
2. Bake on a rack over a cookie sheet covered with a nonstick baking sheet, or over an oiled cookie sheet, for 10–15 minutes or until lightly browned.
   Be careful not to let the cattails burn.
   Serves: 6
   Preparation/cooking time: 20 minutes

Sweet Herb Spread

Sweet herbs make this simple spread or dip especially flavorful.

2 tsp allspice, ground

4 tsp fresh ginger, store-bought or wild

½ tsp dried (or ½ tbsp fresh) sassafras cambium or cinnamon, ground

2 tbsp dried (or 6 tbsp fresh) mint leaves, any species

The scrapings of the inside of 2 inches of a vanilla bean, or 2 tsp vanilla extract

2 cups white miso

1 cup sesame oil

½ cup pine nuts or lecithin granules

2 tbsp freshly grated lemon or lime rind

1. Finely chop the ginger and pine nuts in a food processor.
2. Add the remaining ingredients and process to form a paste.
   Makes 2-⅔ cup
   Preparation time: 5 minutes

Sea Rocket
(*Cakile edentula*)

Family: Brassicaceae or Cruciferae, the mustard, crucifer, or cabbage family
Other name: American searocket

Sometimes as wide as it's tall, this native annual mustard has an erect to prostrate, zigzag, branching, succulent stem, ½–20 inches tall.

The oval to spoon-shaped, alternate leaves grow 1–3 inches long and ¼–1 inch across. They're widest along the upper third, making them look wedge-shaped. They're also distinctly fleshy, as well as smooth and wavy-toothed. The lower leaves are larger than the upper ones.

From summer to fall, at the ends of irregular terminal racemes 2–10 inches long, the flowers bloom. Small and short, the flowers have four petals configured like a cross, as do all the related mustards. The petals are purple-pink to lavender, or sometimes white.

The two-parted seedpods grow beneath the flowers. They're ½–¾ inch long and narrowed in the middle. The upper part is beaked and bulbous, while the

cone-shaped base is smaller and more narrow. The pod looks like the cone of a rocket ship, even though the word "rocket" means mustard. The pod's upper part, which contains one seed, detaches and often spreads via the ocean, while the lower segment stays near the parent plant and contains either one seed or none.

Native to the East Coast, the sea rocket also grows along the coast of the western United States, the Great Lakes, and Canada. Look for it in full sunlight, close to open water, on sandy or gravelly beaches, and on dunes.

Collect the leaves from mid-spring to early fall, and the tender young pods and flowers from mid to late summer. Strip off the leaves; the tender, immature seedpods; and the young, tender tops of the stems with your fingers.

The leaves, flowers, and the young seedpods (which get tough when they mature) continuously become more spicy, eventually tasting like wasabi and horseradish. They cook in about 10 minutes. They're great raw or cooked in any dish that needs some fire. You can even pickle the young seedpods or use them to make prepared mustard, as in the recipe below.

This plant hasn't been analyzed for nutrients, but all mustards are nutritive and healthful. Although not commonly used by herbalists, it may have properties similar to horseradish.

RECIPE

Sea Mustard

Here's a hot prepared mustard similar to commercial mustard, but much better, thanks to sea rocket seedpods. If you like your mustard extra spicy, skip the cooking.

⅓ cup young sea rocket seedpods or ground yellow mustard seeds

¼ cup white wine vinegar

½ cup water

1 large clove of garlic, crushed

½ tsp turmeric

½ tsp salt

1. Purée all ingredients in a food processor.
2. Bring this to a boil over medium heat in a heavy saucepan, stirring constantly.
3. Reduce the heat to low and simmer, uncovered, for 5 minutes, stirring often.
4. Add more water if necessary to achieve your desired consistency.
   Yields: 1 cup
   Preparation/cooking time: 10 minutes

Asiatic Dayflower
(*Commelina communis*)

Family: Commelinaceae, the dayflower or the spiderwort family

Other name: Blue Dayflower, Dew Herb, Duckfoot Herb, Mouse Ears, Mouse Flower, Monsoon Flower

This Asian species is the first edible wild green I ever ate. When I was beginning to teach myself foraging, my then-girlfriend and I ventured into a local woodland in early spring, field guide in hand, passing dozens of wild foods I was yet to discover. All we could identify was wild lettuce (Lactuca spp.), but because it didn't have flowers, we weren't sure, and neither of us could convince the other to try it first. That plant is still growing there to this day!

Our next attempt was in mid-spring. Because there aren't many plant with two blue petals, I was able to make a positive ID, enjoyed eating the plant on the spot, and later on, making recipes with it.

This hairless plant usually grows no more than 1 foot tall, with simple, smooth-edged, lance-shaped, pointed, alternate leaves, 3–5 inches long, that look a little like grass leaves. They lack leafstalks, but wrap their bases wrap around the stem instead, forming a distinct sheath.

The flower has two sky-blue petals about ½ inch long, growing above a third, tiny, withered-looking, inconspicuous, translucent-white petal. Therefore, Carl Linnaeus, the great eighteenth-century scientist who established the biological classification system we still use today and didn't lack a sense of humor, called the genus that includes this plant *Commelina*: In his day, there was a family by the name of Commelijn that had three sons. Two became famous, a botanist and an author. They're represented by the two bright blue petals. The third son was a ne'er-do-well and is represented by the puny, inconspicuous, lower petal. His business ventures failed, he could never get out of debt, the woman he loved married someone else, and then he died young.

Each flower on the plant lives but one day, hence the plant's common name. However, the name of the hapless son and his more illustrious brothers live on indefinitely in the form of this plant and its relatives!

Two short, elliptical sepals grow beneath the flowers, often enclosing two small, pale yellow-green seeds, which look and taste like tiny peas. There are no poisonous look-alikes, but deer tongue grass (*Dichanthelium clandestinum*) has

similar leaves, although the flowers and seeds are different. Unlike Asiatic dayflower leaves, it's densely hairy, so you can tell them apart at a glance if you know of that distinction.

Spiderwort (*Tradescantia virginiana*), with edible flowers, looks a little like Asiatic dayflower, but this relative is much larger, with much longer leaves, and you usually find it cultivated in gardens. Happily, all three petals are large and blue. Perhaps it represents a parallel universe, where the third brother had a successful life too!

Asiatic dayflowers are in season from mid-spring to mid-fall. They grow in cultivated and disturbed areas, in full sunlight and partial shade. You can find them on road- and trailsides, in openings in the woods, on lawns, and in parks.

Harvest fresh-looking plants without brown parts. Strip off the leaves, any tender parts of the stems, flowers, and seeds with your fingers. Adults usually find the seeds too small to be worthwhile, whereas kids love seeking them out and eating them.

This plant tastes like string beans. It's excellent raw in salads and sandwiches, and it's amazingly good in soups. Use it in any dish that calls for cooked greens, especially where the flavor of string beans would be welcome. It cooks in about 10 minutes.

There's been no nutritional analysis of this plant, but extracts have shown substances with biological activity: It contains *p*-hydroxycinnamic acid (which has antibacterial activity) and D-mannitol (which is good for coughs). A study using dog kidney cells and live mice found the plant to be protective against the H1N1 influenza A virus.

This parallels some of its uses in traditional Chinese medicine. An infusion of the aboveground parts of the plant is taken internally for fever and diarrhea, and gargled for sore throat and tonsillitis. It's used externally for bleeding, and it's considered to be a diuretic and a detoxifier.

RECIPE

Dayflower Fried Rice

Asiatic dayflowers lend just the right touch along with Chinese five-spice seasoning to turn leftover rice into a fantastic dish.

1½ tbsp sesame oil

1½ tbsp dark (toasted) sesame oil

2½ cups leftover brown rice

1 red onion, sliced

2½ cups Asiatic dayflower leaves, chopped

2 cloves of garlic, chopped

1 tbsp Wild Five-Spice Seasoning (see below) or store-bought five-spice seasoning, or to taste

2 tsp tamari soy sauce

1. Sauté the onions and Asiatic dayflower leaves in the sesame oils for 10 minutes.
2. Add the garlic and five-spice seasoning, and sauté another 5 minutes.
3. Add the rice and sauté another 5 minutes.
4. Stir in the tamari soy sauce.

   Serves: 4–6

   Preparation/cooking time: 20 minutes

RECIPE

Wild Five-Spice Seasoning

This is a traditional Chinese seasoning combination with a wild touch, great in any East Asian dish.

2 tsp dried sassafras (see p. 2) cambium or 2 tbsp cinnamon

2 tbsp dried wild ginger (see p. 306) or powdered, store-bought ginger

2 tbsp star anise

2 tbsp fennel seeds

2 tbsp cloves

¼ tsp black pepper

1. Grind all ingredients together in a spice grinder.
   Yields: 10 tbsp
   Preparation time: 5 minutes

Quickweed
(*Galinsoga parviflora*)

Family: Asteraceae or Compositeae, the aster, daisy, composite, or sunflower family
Other names: Galinsoga, four-pointed galinsoga, gallant soldiers, soldiers of the queen, shaggy soldier, peruvian daisy, potato weed, guascas

This colonial annual grows from 6 inches to 2 feet tall, emerging from fibrous roots. It's a pliable, slender, erect, ridged, branching stems, and the whole plant is covered with soft hairs.

The lance-shaped, oval to triangular, coarsely toothed, opposite leaves are medium to dark green. Densely hairy above, they grow about 3 inches long and 2 inches wide. The leafstalks of the larger leaves reach 1½ inches long. The leaves are smaller and stalkless toward the stem's apex.

Quickweed blooms from early summer to late fall. The flowers grow both in sparse terminal clusters and in clusters coming from the leaf axils. Because the flowers are tiny, only ¼–2/5 inch wide, the plant's species name is *parviflora*, which means small flower.

Each composite flower consists of four or five white, three-toothed, ray flowers, surrounding many tiny, yellow disk flowers. About two outer and several inner green, oval, scale-like bracts surround each flower. The seeds are achenes that look like miniature sunflower seeds, smaller than those of the dandelion, and they disperse with the wind.

Quickweed comes from Central and South America, but has spread throughout most of the United States, parts of Canada, and much of the rest of the world. Look for it in sunny and partially shaded areas with moist soil; in gardens, cultivated areas, parks, and lowland fields; on disturbed soil; and in cracks in the pavement. It's in season from mid-spring through late fall. Strip off the leaves, flowers, and any tender parts of the stems with your fingers. Although the plant tastes like artichokes and it's edible raw or cooked, I find the hairy texture unpleasant and wrote it off as marginally edible for a quarter of a century, until the solution, obvious in hindsight, struck me. Cooked and puréed in a blender into a cream soup or cream sauce, it's delicious, and the hairs are gone! You can also dry the plant, grind it into a powder in a blender, and add it to any vegetable dish that would benefit from the flavor of artichoke. Adding the raw leaves to pesto, where everything is ground together, is also good.

Quickweed contributes some protein and calories, plus beta-carotene, vitamins B1 (thiamin), B2 (riboflavin), B3 (niacin), and C, as well as the minerals calcium, magnesium, potassium, phosphorus, and iron.

Quickweed juice is great for wounds, speeding blood coagulation, and possibly hastening healing. It's good for nettle stings too. Quickweed contains ACE inhibitors that are used in to lower high blood pressure. It also provides phenolic compounds that inhibit high blood pressure in type 2 diabetes. It definitely deserves further testing.

RECIPE

Quick Dip

Quickweed adds an artichoke touch to this olive-flavored dip and spread.

1⅔ cups silken tofu, drained

1 cup slow-sodium green olives, pitted

2 tbsp lecithin granules

2 tbsp olive oil

½ tbsp vegan grated Parmesan cheese

½ tbsp nutritional yeast

1 tsp lemon juice

1 tsp dried, powdered quickweed

1 tsp oregano, ground

½ tsp sage, ground

½ tsp rosemary, ground

½ tsp paprika

Purée all ingredients in a food processor, and do it quickly!
Yields: 2¼ cups
Preparation time: 5 minutes (see, it is quick!)

Purslane (*Portulaca oleracea*)

Family: Portulacaceae, the purslane family
Other names: Pussley, verdolaga, pigweed, little hogweed

This hated garden "weed" becomes a favorite food of nearly everyone who tries it. It's a smooth, sprawling, annual with a small taproot that produces many fibrous secondary roots. A thick, succulent, purple-red stem grows 4–10 inches long and up to 6 inches tall. Its fleshy, opposite (sometimes alternate), stalkless, toothless, paddle-shaped leaves grow ½–2 inches long.

The tiny, yellow flowers grow tucked in the leaf axils. Only 1/5 inch wide, they've five petals and two sepals. They bloom from mid to late summer, opening only on sunny mornings. They develop into ovoid fruit capsules up to ¼ inch long in late summer. These split in half and drop tiny, hard, roundish, black seeds the size of poppy seeds.

Purslane grows in sunny habitats; on very poor soil; on lawns; in gardens, fields, and meadows; and in cracks in the sidewalk. This European invader grows throughout most of North America, and is available from late spring to early autumn.

Break or cut off the stems and bag them with the leaves. Discard any rare woody stems. The seeds are too small to be collected in any meaningful manner.

This is a first-rate vegetable any way you prepare it. With a sweet sour flavor, crunchy texture, and a slight thickening effect, you'll enjoy it raw in salads and sandwiches or cooked by any method. It takes 10–15 minutes to cook.

If there ever was a superfood, purslane it's, providing vitamins A, C, and E; some B-vitamins and carotenoids; the minerals magnesium, calcium, potassium, and iron; and the antioxidant glutathione. It also has more omega-3 fatty acids, especially α-linolenic acid, than any other plant. It's even an excellent source of eicosapentaenoic acid. In addition, it provides reddish betacyanins and the yellow betaxanthins, both with antimutagenic effects, so they may reduce the risk of cancer.

Traditional Chinese herbalists treat infections, urogenital bleeding, and dysentery with purslane. The fresh herb has been applied topically to skin sores, insect stings, and snake bites, although none of these uses have been tested scientifically.

Eating purslane greatly reduces the symptoms of oral lichen planus, an autoimmune disease of unknown cause that effects the mouth's mucus membranes.

RECIPE

Purslane Lover's Salad

This simple salad uses only a few ingredients, but the balance works out perfectly. Serve with Garlic Mustard Salad Dressing (see p. 16)

½ red onion, chopped

4 cups purslane, chopped

4 cups romaine lettuce, chopped

1 cup roasted walnuts, chopped

1 cup grapes, chopped

1. Soak the onion in water for 15 minute to smooth out its bite, drain, and pat dry with a clean towel or with paper towels.
2. Toss with all the remaining ingredients.
   Serves: 6
   Preparation time: 15 minutes

Fruits and Berries

Successively ripening from when summer is about to come until just before winter, the parade of wild fruits and berries you can pick has to be tasted to be believed. Most of these fruits have short seasons, but this is good, as it prevents you from losing your sanity with too much delicious food to gather and eat.

Mulberries (*Morus* spp.)

Family: Moraceae, the mulberry or fig family

This is one of the first wild foods I didn't know about. I thought there was a "blackberry tree" next to my apartment building, before I even thought of foraging, and I ate the delicious berries from the branches. Fortunately, I didn't poison myself. Later, when I began to teach myself foraging, I found out what it really was.

Mulberries comprise a group of two closely related trees that grow wild in New York, and they hybridize and create a third variant. The native red mulberry (*Morus rubra*) has reddish-brown bark and reaches up to 65 feet in height, while the white mulberry (*M. alba*) comes from Asia and has lighter, rough, ochre-gray bark and spreading branches. It reaches just 40 feet. All mulberry trees have distinct vertical cracks or furrows in the bark and sporadic orange-brown streaks between the cracks. They also exude a white, milky sap when any part is injured. The roughly oval, toothed, alternate, long-stalked leaves reach 2–8 inches in length. They can be unlobed, mitten-shaped, or three-lobed. They're shiny, and the red mulberry leaves feel rough underneath, while the white mulberry leaves underside feels smooth. Wind-pollinated flowers appear in mid-spring, while the leaves are still developing. The tiny, yellow-white, male and female flowers hang on separate, small, slender spikes. The longer male cluster is ½ inch long, while the rounder female cluster is ¼ inch long. The female flowers develop into spherical or cylindrical multiple fruits, ½–1½ inches long in total, each conglomeration suspended from a short, slender, fruit stalk. Each individual unit in the cluster has its own seed. The fruit is green at first. White mulberries become soft, sticky, and white. Red mulberries, also sticky when ripe, progress from white to pink, then reddish, purple, and almost black. Hybrids of white and red trees have intermediate characteristics, and wind up soft, sticky, and pink.

Mulberry trees are common on residential streets; in backyards, vacant lots, disturbed habitats, parks, and fields; along edges of woods; in open woods; and near lakes, ponds, and rivers. The red mulberry grows throughout most of eastern North America, while the white mulberry ranges throughout most of the continent. Other mulberry species (*Morus* spp.) grow in other parts of the country, hybridizing where ranges overlap, but these are all edible, and there are no poisonous look-alikes. Blackberries (see p. 181) have fruit that looks like red mulberries', but they grow on thorny canes, not trees, and there's no seed stalk. Sassafras (see p. 2) has three kinds of leaves, but they're smooth, not toothed, toothed, and the fruit is completely different.

Immature mulberry leaves are edible in early spring. The berries come into season in late spring and are usually gone in early summer, although on very rare occasions, individual trees may produce ripe berries in the summer, or even autumn.

Harvest after periods of dry weather or the day before rain, which washes away much of the flavor, is predicted. You can pick the berries one at a time from low-hanging branches and put them in a container, but the best way to harvest is by placing a 9 × 11 inch, medium-gauge drop cloth under the branches of trees you've chosen with the best-tasting berries and plenty of branches you can reach. If it's windy, place rocks or other weights on the corners of the drop cloth to keep it in place. Shake the branches and it'll rain mulberries. Move the drop cloth under successive branches until you've covered them all. Sort out the coarse debris and transfer the delicate berries into food containers. At home, place the berries in a colander and put this in a bowl with a rim lower than that of the colander. Run tepid water through the colander to rinse the berries, which can't overflow. Let the berries drain for a few minutes, then transfer them to a tray and sort out any remaining debris and any unripe fruit. After a modest amount of work, you'll have a huge amount of very tasty fruit.

Store the mulberries in food containers, refrigerated, for a few days. They're perishable, so eat them or cook them soon. Otherwise, you can dehydrate them in a food dehydrator, or freeze them on trays or cookie sheets before packing them into food containers. That way, they won't stick together and you can defrost as many as you want, instead of the whole container.

Mulberries taste sweet, a little like figs, to which they're related, and they're juicy. Since they're not tart, they benefit from the addition of lemon juice, lime juice, or sumac (see p. 213) concentrate. Use them like other berries, raw in fruit salads; baked into pies, muffins, cakes, or pancakes; added to ice cream; turned into jam; or in cobblers, compotes, fruit soups, or beverages. You can also eat the immature leaves in early spring, boiled for 20 minutes. Discard the somewhat toxic water, which some people think is hallucinogenic, but causes such bad headaches no one tries it or the immature berries, with the same reputed properties, twice. The mature raw leaves of the white mulberry tree are edible too, and can comprise 100 percent of your diet, but only if you're a silkworm!

Mulberries are a good source of anthocyanins, vitamin C, and the minerals calcium, potassium, magnesium, iron, and zinc. They even contain some protein. Exotic, imported, dried mulberries from the Himalayas are touted as a superfood, because something from far away commands higher prices, but the common species growing in the United States are just as healthful. The berries aren't used medicinally, but the leaves of the white mulberry contain a phytoalexin substance called chalcomoracin, which shows antibacterial activity against *Staphylococcus aureus* (a potentially deadly antibiotic-resistant bacteria). Research to turn this into a medicine is underway. 1-Deoxynojirimycin, also present in the leaves, might inhibit sugar digestion, so sugar is excreted rather than absorbed. It's being researched for use in blunting the blood sugar spike characteristic of diabetes. Herbalists have used a decoction of the roots or cambium for weakness, difficult urination, dysentery, and tapeworms; and the sap has been applied externally to treat ringworm, but these uses haven't been tested scientifically.

RECIPE

Mulberry Crisp

Like other crisps, this one has a fruit layer baked under a rolled grain and nut layer. However, the mulberries, the right seasonings, and the correct proportions make this one special. Serve hot or cold, topped with Vegan Whipped Creme.

Fruit Layer

8 cups red or other mulberries

¼ cup arrowroot or kudzu

2 tsp liquid stevia

1½ tbsp lemon juice

½ tsp powdered ginger

¼ tsp ginger

Grain Layer

4 cups rolled oats

1 cup raw cashews or other nuts, chopped

¼ cup peanut oil

1 tbsp poppy seeds

1 tsp cinnamon, ground

1 tsp liquid stevia

¼ tsp salt

1. Mix together the fruit layer and transfer to an oiled baking dish.
2. Mix together the grain layer and spread this on top of the fruit layer.
3. Bake for 45 minutes or until lightly browned on top in a preheated 375°F oven.
   Serves: 6–8
   Preparation time: 20 minutes
   Cooking time: 45 minutes

RECIPE

Vegan Whipped Creme

Use this vegan topping on sweet dishes, just like the dairy version. The silken tofu makes it creamy, the dates and stevia provide sweetness, and the sumac supplies a touch of tartness.

2¼ cups of silken tofu, well-drained

½ cup Medjool (soft) dates

2 tbsp lecithin granules

2 tbsp grape seed oil

1 tbsp sumac concentrate or lemon juice

The scrapings of the inside of 2 inches of vanilla bean, or 2 tsp vanilla extract

1 tsp liquid stevia

¼ tsp butterscotch extract or caramel extract

¼ tsp salt

Puree all ingredients together in a food processor until smooth.

Makes 2-½ cups

Preparation time: 10 minutes

Juneberry
(*Amelanchier* spp.)

Family: Rosaceae, the rose family

Other names: Serviceberry, sarvisberry, shadbush, shadblow, shadwood, saskatoon, currant-tree sugarplum, chuckley pear, wild-plum

This group consists of six to thirty-three mostly native species of multistemmed shrubs or small trees, usually 20 feet tall, with a spread of around 10 feet, but sometimes up to 60 feet in height. Hybridization leaves the exact number unknown. They all have smooth to slightly furrowed, tight, ash-gray to blackish bark, patterned with wavy, dark gray to reddish, vertical stripes.

The finely toothed, oval to elliptical, alternate leaves grow 1–2 inches long and half as wide, with a pointed leaf tip and a rounded to slightly heart-shaped base, and the underside is a much lighter green (and often slightly downy) than the upper surface.

The five-petaled, radially symmetrical, white flowers bloom in early spring, before the leaves are fully formed. Around ¾ inch across, the flower has five sepals under the petals. The many protruding stamens make the flower look like the related apple tree's (see p. 219) blossoms, although unlike apples, four to twenty juneberry flowers grow on long, sparse racemes, around 2 inches long.

The spherical berries, ¼–⅓ inch in diameter, go from green to red to blue, although one cultivated English species has red berries. With a five-parted, frilled crown, remnants of the sepals, at the tip, they resemble unrelated blueberries and huckleberries (see p. 186), but those grow on smaller bushes with different flowers, leaves, and bark, and the fruit doesn't grow on the loose racemes like juneberries. Also, unlike the former, juneberries contain several soft, irregularly ellipsoid seeds that taste like almonds.

No additional species resemble juneberries. Some shrubs have blue berries, but they lack the distinctive crown.

You can find juneberries throughout most of the United States and Canada. They grow in full sunlight or partial shade. The various species grow wild in moist and somewhat dry soil, along streams and lakes, on mountains, in thickets, in clearings, and in the vicinity of the seashore. Because of the early blooming showy flowers, landscapers plant them in parks, around shopping malls, on residential streets, and in garden apartment complexes.

The fruit usually ripens in late spring and drops by early summer, although the English species' red fruit ripens in autumn. Pull off the berries with your fingers, eat until you're full, then put additional berries in a container attached to your clothing. A saw-edged scoop also works.

These berries are dangerous. Although there are rare species with bad-tasting fruit, the vast majority are so tasty, when you eat them, you can die of happiness! They're sweet, with the flavor of apples, blueberries, and almonds. Use them like blueberries, raw or cooked, in any fruit dessert whatsoever. They cook in 5–10 minutes.

The Iroquois used a decoction of the roots and cambium to prevent miscarriage and to help recovery after childbirth, and both the Iroquois and traditional Chinese herbalists used it to expel worms, something that certainly merits scientific scrutiny.

RECIPE

Banana Juneberry Ice Cream

My then-seven-year-old daughter, Violet, thought up this combination of fruits, based on an ice cream protocol I'd already developed. We made it together, and it worked perfectly.

3½ cups nondairy milk

1 tbsp arrowroot or kudzu

1 tsp agar powder or 1 tbsp agar flakes

2 bananas

½ cup raw pine nuts or cashews

¼ cup lecithin granules

¼ cup grape seed oil

¼ cup vegetable glycerin or other liquid sweetener

1 tbsp clear liquid stevia

¼ tsp salt

1½ cup juneberries or blueberries

1. Stir the agar and arrowroot into the nondairy milk and bring to a boil over medium heat, stirring constantly. Reduce the heat to low and simmer, uncovered, for 5 minutes or until the agar is dissolved, stirring often.
2. Combine with the remaining ingredients, except the berries, in a blender and purée.
3. Freeze in an ice cream machine according to the manufacturer's directions.
4. Fold in the berries.

Serves: 6
Preparation time: 20 minutes
Freezing time: 2 hours (varies)

Common Strawberry (*Fragaria virginiana*)

Family: Rosaceae, the rose family
Other names: Virginia strawberry, wild strawberry

This trailing, somewhat hairy, colonial perennial arises from slender, horizontal, reddish-tinged runners up to 2 feet long and short, scaly rhizomes.

A three-parted, palmate-compound leaf grows above a long, finely hairy leafstalk about 6 inches long. Pale green underneath, the wedge-shaped leaflets grow 1–3 inches long and about 1½ inches wide, with coarse, sharp, even teeth, and very short leafstalks.

A new, softly hairy, leafless stem 3–4 inches long emerges from the ground in mid-spring, with terminal clusters of 2–15 five-petaled, radially symmetrical, odorless flowers, typical of the rose family, ½–1 inch across.

Familiar red strawberries ½–¾ inch across ripen about five weeks later, toward the end of spring. They're ovate versions of store-bought strawberries, with seeds partially sunken into the flesh and ten tiny green sepals at the base of the fruit.

Although technically a different species, the woodland strawberry (*Fragaria vesca*) is nearly identical to the common strawberry and just as good, although the fruit is larger and more elongated.

Avoid the Indian strawberry (*Duchesnea indica*), which has a small, spherical, red berry, with seeds on the outside. It can be fatal: It looks really good, but when you eat it, it's no flavor whatsoever—as tasteless as my jokes—and you soon die of disappointment!

Common cinquefoil (*Potentilla simplex*) can also kill you. Its leaves look like strawberries', only there are five rather than three, and you die of old age waiting for a strawberry that never appears!

Wild strawberries grow in open, sunny places and partial shade; on moist ground; in dry openings and open woods; along woodland edges; in rocky areas, meadows, and fields; near the seashore; and on hillsides and slopes. The four subspecies grow throughout North America.

The berries ripen at the end of spring or start of summer, although you can use the leaves for tea from spring to fall.

The berries are much tastier, but much smaller than store-bought strawberries, so use them, raw and cooked, as a minor component to any dessert recipe, unless you've enough time to collect them in quantity.

Strawberries supply you with magnesium, potassium, beta-carotene, iron, and malic and citric acids, plus the protein NRF2. This increases antioxidant activity and decreases blood lipids and cholesterol, so eating strawberries may reduce your risk of cardiovascular disease. An infusion of the leaves provides vitamins C and K.

Strawberries are mildly laxative, a good food for mild constipation. They're also supposed to break up calcareous stones from the kidneys, gallbladder, and bladder, although this hasn't been tested.

Strawberry juice is supposed to be good, externally, for oily skin. Crushed strawberries have been used for sunburn too, and strawberry juice does protect skin cells from ultraviolet light, possibly due to the proanthocyanidins they contain.

RECIPE

Almond Strawberry Pudding

Here's a great way to make a sweet, healthful dessert with wild strawberries, as well as any kind of fruit or berry.

4 cups almond milk

¾ cup wild or store-bought strawberries, or other fruit, chopped

3½ tsp agar powder or 3½ tbsp agar flakes

1 tsp liquid stevia

1 inch vanilla bean, scraped, or 1 tsp vanilla extract

¼ tsp almond extract

⅛ tsp amaretto extract (optional)

⅛ tsp salt

½ cup freshly roasted almonds, chopped

1. Simmer, uncovered, all ingredients together (except for the almonds) for 10 minutes or until the agar is dissolved.
2. Place a few drops of the liquid in a metal spoon and place that in a freezer for 5 minutes or until cold. If too thin, add more agar to the pudding and simmer, uncovered, for another 5 minutes or until dissolved. If too thick, stir in more almond milk. Then test again.
3. Chill until set.
4. Serve sprinkled with the almonds.
   Serves: 6
   Preparation time: 20 minutes
   Chill time: 3 hours (varies)

Sweet Cherry
(*Prunus avium*)

Family: Rosaceae, the rose family

Other names: Wild cherry, gean, massard, mazzard

Although this Eurasian tree that people grow in backyards grows from 50 to 70 feet tall, it still managed to escape cultivation and make its way into the wild—quite a feat!

The tree has a symmetrical, conical crown at first, but becomes rounded to irregular in older trees. The shiny, smooth, purplish-brown bark becomes dark silvery-gray and develops fissures as the tree ages. The bark is streaked with whitish, horizontal lines.

The oval, pointed, alternate leaves are shiny and finely toothed, growing from 2¾ to nearly 6 inches long and 1½–2¾ inches wide. They turn orange, pink, or red in the fall.

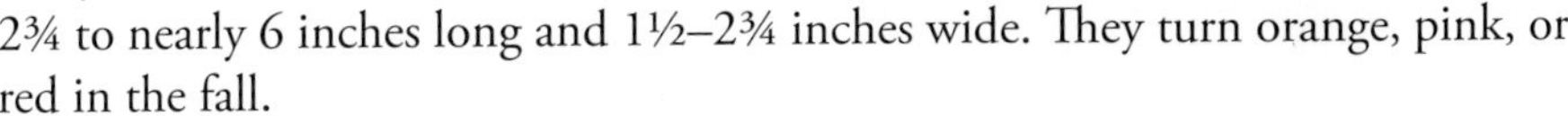

From two to five small, red glands grow on the leafstalk, which gets from under 1 to 1⅓ inches long. These glands are nectaries, which may feed insects that protect the tree from herbivores.

The radially symmetrical white flowers, which bloom in early spring, grow in showy clusters of two to six. Growing at the tips of twigs, on flower stalks 1–2 inches long, they're 1–1½ inches across.

Long-stalked cherries, ½–1 inch across, ripen at the end of spring and the beginning of summer. They're smooth and spherical, usually red or black, but sometimes yellow. Several fruit stalks originate from the same place on the twig. Each cherry contains 1 hard stone, ⅓ inch across.

Collect the cherries with your fingers and put them into a container attached to your backpack or clothing, or strung around your neck. Look for smaller trees, growing along woodland edges, that are getting lots of sunlight. Unless there are low branches, most of the cherries on larger trees will be out of reach. About one out of every three years you'll get a really good crop.

Sweet cherries grow in edge habitats, parks, cultivated areas, and woodlands. This fruit is similar to store-bought cherries, but because it grows from seed rather than cloned from cuttings, the genes aren't uniform and the fruit tends to be more sour and smaller than the uniform domestic variety, although the flavor's more intense. Enjoy these cherries raw, or remove the seeds with a cherry pitter, or by cooking them with a sweetener and a thickener, and passing them

through a food mill. They're superb in any dessert that calls for fruit. Better, in my opinion, than store-bought cherries.

Cherries provide natural sugars, vitamins C, K, and folate. They're rich in the carotenoids beta-carotene, choline, zeaxanthin, and lutein. They're also a good source of the minerals iron, magnesium, and phosphorus.

In European health spas, people go on cherry "cures," where they eat nothing but cherries. Recent research shows that short fasts can actually provide benefits, but hasn't addressed this form of fasting yet.

Traditional herbalists use the fruit stalks of cherries as an astringent, a diuretic, and a tonic. They recommend this for cystitis, edema, bronchitis, diarrhea, and anemia, but the decoction contains amygdalin and prunasin, which could change into cyanide. Small amounts of these natural wannabe medicines have been shown to stimulate respiration, promote digestion, and make people feel well, but their use is controversial, as cyanide can be deadly. It can cause gasping, weakness, excitement, pupil dilation, spasms, convulsions, coma, and respiratory failure.

All parts of the tree contain these substances, even the cherry stones. However, cooking destroys them.

RECIPE

Black Forest Cake

Here's my version of a classic chocolate cake, using whole, unrefined ingredients that tastes even better than the bakery version.

Dry Ingredients

¾ cup + 1 tbsp buckwheat flour

1 cup + 1 tbsp sweet brown rice flour

¾ cup unsweetened cocoa powder

½ cup flaxseeds, ground into ¾ cup meal

1 tsp xanthan gum

½ tsp guar gum

2 tsp cinnamon, ground

1 tsp nutmeg, ground

2 tsp cream of tartar

1 tsp baking soda

¼ tsp cloves, ground

Ingredients to Blend

2 cups soy milk or nut milk

6 tbsp almond oil

¼ cup lecithin granules

6 dates

4 common spicebush berries or ¼ tsp ground allspice

2 tsp vanilla

1 tbsp clear liquid stevia or powered stevia

Cherry Topping

2½ cups pitted wild sweet cherries or commercial cherries

1¼ cups water

1¼ cups cherry juice concentrate

1 tbsp agar

5 tsp arrowroot

1 tsp clear liquid stevia or powdered stevia

1 tsp dried water mint or other mint, ground

½ tsp powdered ginger

⅛ tsp amaretto extract or almond extract

Icing

3 cups silken tofu, drained

¾ cup dates

¼ cup lecithin granules

2 tbsp almond oil

1 tbsp fresh lemon extract

2 tsp vanilla

1 tsp clear liquid stevia or powdered stevia

¼ tsp butterscotch extract or caramel extract

¼ tsp salt

1. Mix together the dry ingredients.
2. Purée the ingredients to blend in a blender.
3. Mix the purée into the dry ingredients. Don't overmix.
4. Transfer to three oiled 9-inch pie tins and bake in a preheated 350°F oven for 30 minutes or until an inserted toothpick emerges dry.
5. Cool on racks.
6. Meanwhile, mix the cherry topping ingredients in a saucepan and bring to a boil over medium heat, stirring constantly. Reduce the heat to low and simmer, uncovered, for 5 minutes, then chill.
7. Purée the icing ingredients in a food processor.
8. Layer the cake, icing, cherry topping, and cake until all ingredients are used up.
   Serves: 8–10
   Preparation time: 45 minutes
   Cooking time: 30 minutes

Black Raspberry
(*Rubus occidentalis*)

Family: Rosaceae, the rose family
Other names: Wild black raspberry, black caps, black cap raspberry, thimbleberry, scotch cap

This arching or erect native bramble, with many rounded canes (woody stems), grows 6–12 feet tall, emerging from woody, branching taproots. Sparsely armed with curved prickles, it takes root where the cane tips touch the ground. The smooth, blue-green stems are coated with a blue-white, waxy powder called a bloom.

Primocanes (first-year stems) only bear leaves, while floricanes (the second-year, lateral branches) bear flowers and fruit, before the canes die to the ground for the winter, to renew the cycle the following year.

Black raspberries have sharply, double-toothed, palmate-compound leaves that are hairy-white underneath. Primocanes have three leaflets, while floricanes have five. Growing around 3 inches long and 2 inches wide, the leaflets are oval to heart-shaped. The leading leaflet has a short leafstalk, which the lateral leaflets lack. So does poison ivy (Toxicodendron radicans), which has few if any teeth and no prickles.

With five to seven elliptical to oblong petals, the white to pink flowers grow ½ inch across and bloom in mid to late spring. They grow above five triangular sepals that spread beyond the edge of both the flowers and the ensuing berries, both of which are arrayed in clusters of three to five on short, flattened, terminal racemes.

The hollow aggregate fruits, ⅓–½ inch across, are ovoid and hemispheric. They begin green, change to red, and mature as black. Each subsection, a fruitlet, encloses one small, hard seed. The fruit ripens in early summer and is gone by mid-summer.

Blackberries (see p. 181) look superficially similar, but they mature later; the fruit isn't hollow; the stems are angled, not round; there's no waxy powder; and the prickles are dense, not sparse.

The black raspberry grows in full sunlight or partially sunny thickets, along trailsides, in overgrown vacant lots and fields, in open deciduous woodlands, along woodland borders and fence rows, and in savannas and disturbed habitats. It ranges throughout most of eastern North America.

Using your fingers, pick only the completely ripe, totally black fruits that detach easily. Wearing work gloves with the fingertips of the dominant hand's

gloves cut off and attaching a container to your clothing or backpack make collecting more efficient. Wearing long pants and sleeves, and planning your foraging for a relatively cool day in early morning also help.

Wild black raspberries are much tastier than their wimpy store-bought descendants. Use them raw or cooked in virtually any recipe that calls for fruit, such as cereals, pancakes, muffins, sauces, pies, fruit salads, compotes, puddings, ice creams, jams, jellies, and smoothies. The hard seeds become annoying in puréed recipes, so pass this through a strainer as part of the procedure.

Black raspberries give you vitamins A, E, K, C, thiamin, riboflavin, niacin, B6, pantothenic acid, and folate, as well as the minerals calcium, iron, manganese, magnesium, phosphorus, potassium, sodium, zinc, copper, manganese, and selenium. They also provide healthful antioxidants such as ellagic acid, the flavonoids quercetin and kaempferol, and the cyanidin-based molecules cyanidin-3-glucosylrutinoside and cyanidin-3-rutinoside.

Anthocyanins, which color this fruit, have been shown to be beneficial to vision, cardiovascular health, and memory retention in old age. They reduce risk of hypertension, and may also lower the risk of cancer. They inhibit pathogens such as *Candida albicans*, which causes yeast infections and could aggravate irritable bowel syndrome.

An infusion of the leaves and roots is a major tonic for the female reproductive system, used for centuries by Native Americans, European, and East Asian herbalists. It's constituents that both stimulate and relax the uterus, and is recommended during the last three months of gestation, for childbirth, to reduce the symptoms of menopause, and for menstrual cramps.

It's also used as an astringent for diarrhea, especially for children, because it's more gentle than other herbs. It's recommended for nausea and to suppress vomiting, as a gargle for tonsillitis and mouth inflammations, as a poultice for sores, and as a wash for conjunctivitis, minor wounds, burns, and varicose ulcers.

Black raspberries are currently being tested in humans to see if compounds they contain could shrink malignant esophageal and colon tumors.

RECIPE

Black Raspberry Ice Pops

Here's a delicious, healthful alternative to the artificially colored, high-fructose, and corn syrup junk kids stuff themselves with in the summer.

3 cups water

3 cups black raspberries or other berries

½ tbsp clear liquid stevia

½ tbsp lemon juice

1. Purée all ingredients in a blender.
2. Remove the seeds using a strainer.
3. Pour into 8 pops mold divisions and freeze.
   Yields: 8 pops
   Preparation time: 5 minutes
   Freezing time: 6 hours (varies)

Wineberry
(*Rubus phoenicolasius*)

Family: Rosaceae, the rose family
Other names: Japanese wineberry, wine raspberry

This common, invasive bramble helped get me hooked on foraging very early on. It's easy to recognize, there are no poisonous look-alikes, and it's incredibly delicious.

Growing 3–9 feet tall, with its bristly, reddish, glandular hairs (*phoenicolasius* means purple hairs), these upright, multistemmed biennial canes arise from perennial roots, with new roots forming when the tips of the arching stems touch the ground.

New stems with leaves only come up the first year. Side branches with flowers and fruits appear the second year, before the branch dies to the ground, and the cycle repeats.

Growing from 4 to 7 inches long, the palmate-compound leaves are composed of three large, broadly oval, pointy-tipped, sharply toothed, papery leaflets. They're green above and matted with very fine, whitish, wooly hairs underneath.

The tiny, white, inconspicuous, five-petaled flowers, 1/5–2/5 inch across, bloom in mid-spring on bristly, many-flowered panicles, emerging from the side shoots. It's five long, narrow, triangular, bristly sepals, which are supported by a densely prickly, red flower stalk and create a star-shaped backdrop for the flower.

These sepals close over the flower after fertilization, then open again in mid-summer, revealing an orange, aggregate fruit that becomes bright red, then dark purple-red. The juicy, spherical, hollow berries reach 1 inch or more in diameter, growing in small clusters. An orange receptacle remains behind after you pick the berry.

Other brambles (*Rubus* spp.), also edible, aren't covered with the distinct red bristles, which makes the wineberry easy to recognize, even in the winter.

Wineberries grow in sunny and partially sunny habitats with moist soil; in thickets, fields, disturbed habitats, wetlands, and open woods; and along trails, forest edges, and roadsides. This invasive Asian plant grows in the Mid-Atlantic states, southern New England, and parts of the Deep South.

The berries ripen at the beginning of the second half of the summer, and are gone before late summer begins, although you can use the leaves for tea from mid-spring to fall.

As with other brambles, plan to forage early in the morning on relatively cool days, wearing long pants and sleeves for protection from the bristles and mosquitoes. Wear work gloves with the fingertips cut off the dominant hand, and attach a collecting food container to your clothing or backpack. Keep additional containers in your backpack. The most darkly colored berries are the best.

More flavorful and tart than store-bought raspberries, you can use wineberries in any berry recipe, with superior results guaranteed. The seeds are hard, so strain them out in any recipe that will be puréed, such as jams and sauces. You can make an infusion with the leaves as well.

This plant isn't used medicinally and hasn't been tested for nutrients, although the chances are that it's highly nutritious.

RECIPE

Wineberry Custard

Wineberries, along with other fruits, make this egg-free custard exceptionally tasty.

2 cups coconut milk or other nondairy milk

2 cups wineberries or raspberries

¾ cup of strawberries, sliced

⅔ cup wild or store-bought blueberries

1 green apple, sliced

1 plum, sliced

1 banana, sliced

3 tbsp lecithin granules

½ cup raisins

½ tbsp liquid or powdered stevia

1 tsp agar powder or 1 tbsp agar flakes

¼ tsp freshly grated orange rind or orange extract

¼ tsp vanilla extract

¼ tsp cinnamon, ground

1. Simmer all ingredients together for 10–15 minutes or until the apple slices are tender, stirring often.
2. Chill until set.
   Serves: 6
   Preparation time: 10 minutes
   Cooking time: 15 minutes

Blackberries (*Rubus* spp.)

Family: Rosaceae, the rose family
Other names: Caneberry, bramble, lawyer

I love blackberries, but they've become very rare in recent years. This is due to too much competition from the iPhone!

Like other similar members of their genus, all of which are edible, blackberries have prickly, arching, woody stems called canes that take root when the tip touches the ground. The canes bear only leaves the first year, then produce flowers that develop into berries the second year. By winter, the aboveground parts all die to the ground, but the perennial roots live on, to renew the cycle the following year. This is an unusual arrangement, but it works, since there are so many species of blackberries and raspberries in so many parts of the world.

People get confused distinguishing blackberries from raspberries, but when you pick a blackberry, a cone-shaped structure at the base of the berry, the receptacle, comes off the stem along with the berry. With raspberries, this is left behind, so raspberries are always hollow, whereas blackberries aren't. Also, raspberries have round stems, while blackberry stems are angled—the surfaces are flat. This lets you tell them apart, even in the winter.

In Shakespeare's day, 500 years ago, people called lawyers "bramble bushes." That's because they both have sharp prickles, they grab on to you, and they don't let go until they've drawn blood—the same as lawyers today!

With the exception of a few cultivars, the bark of blackberries is covered with many short, stiff, sharp spines, so I collect early in the morning, on relatively cool days, wearing long pants and sleeves, plus work gloves with the fingertips of one glove cut off. This, plus a container tied or clipped to my backpack or clothing make collecting much easier.

Blackberries have alternate, palmate-compound leaves with three to seven medium-sized, oval, pointy-tipped, toothed leaflets.

Medium-sized, five-petaled, radially symmetrical, white flowers, with many bushy stamens surrounding the packed central pistils, bloom in the spring, growing on loose, short racemes on the tips of short, new stems.

Each flower has many ovaries, so it creates many of tiny, blackberries called drupes. Each contains one seed, forming an aggregate fruit that's more seedy, but much tastier than the inferior store-bought blackberries. Wild blackberries, which go from green to red to black, grow from ½ to 1½ inches long, with five sepals beneath each fruit.

All blackberry species are edible, and there are no similar-looking poisonous berries. Mulberries (see p. 155) look a little like blackberries to beginners, but they hang on slender, short stems from trees, the leaves are simple, and there are no thorns.

Poison ivy (Toxicodendron radicans) has palmate-compound leaves and often grows along with blackberries. However, the three-parted leaves aren't sharply toothed, there's no thorny cane, and the flowers and fruits are completely different, so as long as you're on the lookout for it, you'll be able to avoid contact.

Different blackberry species can hybridize, and you never know when someone will bring in a new foreign variety. Nevertheless, there are three common species I find over and over again in New York:

1. The common or Allegheny blackberry (*Rubus allegheniensis*) is the most common, for some reason. It grows 2–8 feet tall, upright or arching, with reddish to purple stems. The prickles are especially nasty. It's three- or five-parted palmate-compound leaves that are pale green beneath. The pointed leaflets grow 3–7 inches long. They're double-toothed, so the teeth themselves bear sharp teeth.

   Long clusters of six to fifteen white flowers, each up to 1 inch long, bloom in late spring and early summer. They're replaced by blackberries under 1 inch long that ripen in the second half of the summer. The season can last three weeks or more, and I sometimes find ripe fruit in late summer.

Fortunately, unlike in Europe, blackberries here are gone by fall, since you can't eat them anymore after Michaelmas Day, September 29. That's the day Archangel Michael defeated Lucifer and kicked him out of Heaven. He fell, kicking and screaming, onto a blackberry bush, which scratched him so badly that he cursed it and peed on it, making the berries quite unwholesome from then on!

2. The cut-leaf or evergreen blackberry (*R. laciniatus*) is a cultivated, European species I see planted in parks, and some of these have been bred to lack prickles. Unlike the common blackberry, its sharp-toothed leaves are very deeply lobed, and some leaves persist into the winter. It's as good as the common blackberry and the fruit is larger, over 1 inch long. It also ripens in the second half of the summer.
3. The common or northern dewberry (*R. flagellaris*) has a three-parted leaf and creeps along the ground. Otherwise, it's similar to the common blackberry, but it ripens soon after the start of summer, before the other species.

Blackberries grow in many different habitats, in full sun or partial shade. They tolerate poor soil, and you can find them in thickets and clearings; along roadsides and paths; on hillsides and mountain slopes; in overgrown fields, disturbed habitats, ditches, hedgerows, and empty lots; along fencerows; in pine barrens; in young woodlands; along woodland margins; and in wetlands. My favorite place for them is in bushy fields near the seashore, where, in full sunlight, they're unbelievably abundant and tasty.

Use wild blackberries the same way you use store-bought berries, raw or cooked in pies, cobblers, or any other fruit dishes. The superior flavor more than compensates for the hard seeds, which you hardly notice, unless you purée the berries to make a smoothie or sauce. In that case, pass the purée through a strainer to get rid of the seeds.

The wild blackberry is a superfood, loaded with vitamin C and beta-carotene, plus the minerals potassium, magnesium, calcium, iron, and phosphorous. Blackberries also provide the polyphenol antioxidants ellagic acid, ellagitannins, quercetin, gallic acid, anthocyanins, tannins, and cyanidins, substances shown to reduce the risk of heart disease, diabetes, and cancer.

Due to their tannin content, the roots, cambium, and leaves are astringent. Tannin interferes with mineral absorption, so it's not good to take long term, but a decoction has been used in traditional herbal medicine for diarrhea and bleeding gums (it'll stop the bleeding, but you still need a dentist to treat the underlying infection). Gargling with the decoction lessons the symptoms of sore throat, although it doesn't address the underlying infection.

RECIPE

Blackberry Kasha Breakfast Cereal

Tasty, filling, and nutritious—you can't beat this one any time of the year, and it's simple to make. Serve with the nondairy milk of your choice.

2⅓ cups soy milk, nut milk, or oat milk

1 cup kasha

1 wild apple or small green apple, chopped

½ cup wild or commercial blackberries

¼ cup pine nuts

¼ cup currants

1 tbsp corn oil or vegan butter substitute

1 tbsp lecithin granules

1 tbsp flaxseeds

1 tsp clear liquid stevia or powdered stevia

1 tsp salt

¼ tsp almond extract

¼ tsp mango extract or orange extract

1. Bring all ingredients to a boil in a saucepan over medium heat, stirring constantly.
2. Reduce the heat to low and simmer, covered, for 20 minutes or until all the liquid is absorbed.
   Serves: 4–6
   Preparation time: 10 minutes
   Cooking time: 20 minutes

Blueberries and Huckleberries (*Vaccinium* spp.)

Family: Ericaceae, the heath or heather family

Growing from 1½ to 14 feet tall, these closely related deciduous shrubs have fruit that looks like store-bought blueberries, only smaller. The smooth bark is colored red and green when young, becoming craggy and brown with maturity in blueberries, but staying smooth and dark in huckleberries. The twigs are slender and green. Sometimes leathery, the elliptical leaves grow from ½ to 3 inches long, and from 1/5 to ½ inch wide. Blueberry leaves have fine teeth, while huckleberry leaves have smooth edges, plus tiny but distinctive golden resin dots on their undersides. White, five-parted, bell-shaped flowers—sometimes tinged with pink, red, or green—bloom on terminal clusters in the spring. The spherical, blue or dark blue berries, green and purple when immature, grow from 1/5 to 3/5 inch across, like store-bought blueberries, but smaller. Unlike the similar European or common buckthorn (*Rhamnus cathartica*), which has smooth, undifferentiated fruit, each blueberry and huckleberry has a distinctive, five-parted, flared, star-like crown at the tip. Buckthorns are poisonous, so check for the crown.

Juneberries (see p. 160) look a little like blueberries, and the edible fruit has a crown, but it's a larger shrub or tree, with smooth, gray, vertically striped bark.

Blueberries and huckleberries ripen in mid-summer, sometimes persisting into early autumn. Blueberries are lighter blue than huckleberries, the crown is

more pronounced, and they're powdered with a whitish, waxy bloom you can rub off with your fingers. The flesh is white or greenish, and the seeds are too small to notice. Huckleberries are darker and smaller than blueberries. The flesh is red or purple, and you can detect the ten tiny, crunchy seeds when you eat the berry. They're all delicious.

People take it for granted that the foods you buy have been cultivated for hundreds of years, but this isn't so for blueberries. In the early twentieth century, people who lived in the Pine Barrens, New Jersey (so-named because only cranberries could be cultivated in the sandy soil of terrain that used to be under the Atlantic Ocean), thought that blueberries, which the disparaged "Pineys" collected for personal use, couldn't be cultivated. But a local farmer, Elizabeth Coleman White, advertised in local newspapers for people to send her as many varieties as possible. She succeeded, and first brought blueberries to NYC markets in the 1920s.

For tall people, the highbush blueberry (*Vaccinium corymbosum*) is the most suitable. Growing over 14 feet tall, with large, easy-to-collect berries. Kid will love the lowbush blueberry (*V. angustifolium*), only 1 foot tall, forming dense thickets. The huckleberry (*V. parvifolium*), also very short and forming dense stands, is also good for kids, but not for adults with back problems.

These berries grow in moist, acidic soil, in partly or completely shaded places. Look for them on mountains, in thickets, along roadsides and lakesides, and in swamps and bogs. Some years are much better for these berries than others. Collect with your fingers and transfer to a container attached to your

clothing or backpack, to keep both hands free. For even faster collection, get a blueberry scoop online. Use these fruits like store-bought blueberries in any kind of dessert. Like apples, they contain pectin, a thickener, so you'll need less thickener than for other desserts.

Blueberries received lots of well-publicized scientific scrutiny. I need to find their press agent to promote my tours and books! They're a great source of vitamins B6, C, and K; the mineral manganese; and health-promoting anthocyanins, proanthocyanidins, resveratrol, flavonols, and tannins. They're good for digestion and may kill harmful organisms in the digestive tract. Neomyrtilicine, found in the leaves, reduces blood sugar levels, and an infusion has been used to treat diabetes. Research has shown that the tannin in the infusion is good for urinary tract inflammations. Another substance in blueberry leaves blocks replication of the hepatitis C virus and might lead to a treatment. Pterostilbene, present in the fruit, boosts the innate immune system, like the better-know resveratrol in red wine, which works with vitamin D to increase the expression of the human cathelicidin antimicrobial peptide gene (good for immunity). Eating blueberries reduces stroke damage in lab animals, which also benefit from reduced cholesterol and lowered total blood lipid levels. It even lessens high blood pressure and builds bone mass in lab animals, a possible treatment for osteoporosis, but all this needs to be tested in humans.

RECIPE

Wildest Blueberry Jam

My vegan method for making jam works perfectly with wild blueberries. You'll love this one, and if you can't find wild blueberries, they sell them dried in health food stores and online. In addition to using this as a spread, you can add it to smoothies or use it as a dressing for fruit salad.

1 cup dried or fresh wild (or commercial) blueberries

1 cup blueberry juice concentrate

1⅔ cups water

1¼ tsp agar powder or 1¼ tbsp agar flakes

1 tsp liquid or powdered stevia

½ tsp freshly grated lemon rind

¼ tsp salt

1. Simmer all ingredients for 5 minutes or until the agar has dissolved.
2. Chill until set.
   Yields: 3 cups
   Preparation/cooking time: 15 minutes

Black Cherry (*Prunus serotina*)

Family: Rosaceae, the rose family
Other names: Rum cherry, wild black cherry, mountain black cherry

This very common tree gave me quite a scare as a beginning forager, the first time I identified it, a few blocks from where I lived, on a side street in Queens, New York. The flavor was so unusual, I was afraid I might have misidentified it and, too late, had second thoughts about eating the fruit. I was greatly relieved when I woke up the next morning and noticed that I was still alive!

This very common, medium-sized native tree usually reaches 40–60 feet in height, but can grow up to 125 feet tall. The trunk can extend up to 2⅓ feet in diameter. In the forest, it's a straight and narrow tree. In the open, its crown is broad and irregular.

Young trees have shiny, silver bark, streaked with horizontal, whitish lenticels. The mature tree has blocky, cracked bark, upturned in parts, and broken with dark brown, almost black, fissures.

Broken twigs and crushed leaves smell like bitter almond, the same as the inside of the stones of related apricots and peaches. The black birch (Betula lenta) has similar bark, but the broken twigs smell like wintergreen. There are no poisonous look-alikes.

The elliptical, finely toothed, alternate leaves are glossy and sharp pointed. Thick and leathery, they're lighter underneath. They grow 2–5 inches long and 1–1½ inches wide, and turn yellow, orange, or red in the fall. Tiny, orange-brown glands that look like tiny hairs grow along the midrib of the leaf's underside.

After the leaves have appeared in early spring, dense clusters of oblong cylindrical, green, drooping racemes, 4–6 inches long and ¾–1 inch across, appear at the tips of the twigs' new growth, with about forty small, radially symmetrical, white, five-petaled flowers, under ¼ inch across. They smell foul and attract flies for pollination.

Starting in mid-summer, the racemes turn red and bear many spherical, short-stalked, shiny, spherical fruits—red at first, then black. They reach up to ½ inch in diameter. Each cherry contains a hard stone ⅓ inch across.

The closely related and similar edible choke cherry (*Prunus virginiana*, see p. 196) leaves lack the black cherry leaf's orange glands, and the fruit's awful raw, way too astringent to eat, but great cooked.

The sweet cherry (see p. 196) tree is a feral descendent of European cherries, with a reddish bark, but each fruit, which may be red or black, hangs from a single, long fruit stalk emerging from the branches, with no racemes. Also, they ripen at the beginning of the summer. Other edible cherry species similar to the black cherry grow in the Northeast, but I only found one of these. It was in Connecticut, and it looked more like the European species.

Black cherry trees grow in full sunlight and partially shaded habitats. The best ones grow in fields near the seashore, but they can also bear excellent fruit in cultivated parks, backyards, thickets, fields, and along residential streets and roadsides. You can find them in mixed hardwood forests, along forest edges, in residential streets, and along trail and field edges.

To collect black cherries, clip a container to your clothing or backpack, or tie it around your neck or to your belt with a string, and strip the ripe cherries off the racemes with your fingers. When the collecting container is full, transfer your harvest to another container and resume collecting.

The quality of this fruit varies greatly from tree to tree, and from year to year. Look for trees growing in full sunlight with an abundance of relatively large, soft fruit. These are usually the best. Some years you'll find many such trees, other years there will be nothing worth harvesting.

The intense flavor of black cherries is complex. They taste somewhat like store-bought cherries, but bittersweet, with an overtone of grapefruit. If you get good ones, they're great raw or cooked. Simmer them in fruit juice, such as cherry juice, with a thickener and sweetener, then pass through a food mill to remove the stones. Use the purée to make jams, jellies, pie fillings, sauces, puddings, fruit leather, smoothies, or anything else that strikes your fancy. They're especially good in chocolate desserts. Use sparingly with other fruits, or the cherries will overpower them.

The fruit is very nutritious, providing vitamins A, B1, C, folate, and pantothenic acid, plus the minerals calcium, magnesium, iron, sodium, phosphorus, potassium, copper, selenium, and zinc.

It's also an important traditional medicine that has received some scientific scrutiny. Native Americans used an infusion of the cambium for coughs. European settlers took this up, so that when people started selling cough medicines, no one would buy them unless they contained black cherry, a tradition that accounts for cherry flavor in over-the-counter cough medicines today.

Black cherry cambium infusion contains prunasin, which is destroyed by boiling, so you don't make a decoction with it. Although this substance is a chemical precursor of cyanide, low doses are safe. It's excreted mainly through the lungs, where it stimulates respiration and suppresses the cough reflex. High doses, on the other hand, are dangerous. If cyanide is formed, it can be deadly.

It's used as a decongestant and expectorant in traditional herbal medicine, plus a sedative and disinfectant. It's also been used for infections, asthma, ulcers, hysteria, mucus congestion, diarrhea, and inflamed gums. It certainly deserves more research to realize its full potential and to rule out uses that don't work.

RECIPE

Black Cherry Chocolate Cookies

Chocolate is one of the best complementary flavors for cherries, and wild black cherries are no exception. These cookies feature a tantalizing balance of both flavors.

Dry Ingredients

2 cups buckwheat flour + 1⅓ cups oat flour

1¼ cups almonds, ground into meal

2 tbsp flaxseeds, ground into ¼ cup

¼ cup arrowroot or kudzu

¼ cup unsweetened cocoa powder

1 tsp dried mint, ground

½ tsp salt

Wet Ingredients

1 cup black cherry purée

½ cup apple juice

2 tbsp almond oil

1 tbsp clear liquid stevia

½ cup dark, unsweetened chocolate, melted in a double boiler

½ tsp amaretto extract or almond extract

1. Mix together the dry ingredients.
2. Mix together the wet ingredients.
3. Mix the wet ingredients into the dry ingredients.
4. Roll the dough into a circle ⅜ inch thick on a floured pastry sheet, using a rolling pin enclosed in a floured sleeve.
5. Cut into cookies with cookie cutters and transfer to two nonstick baking sheets or onto two oiled cookie sheets.
6. Bake for 20–30 minutes or until lightly browned underneath in a preheated 375°F oven.
   Yields: 2 dozen cookies
   Preparation time: 30 minutes
   Cooking time: 30 minutes

Choke Cherry
(*Prunus virginiana*)

Family: Rosaceae, the rose family

Other names: Common chokecherry, black chokecherry, red chokecherry, California chokecherry, Virginia chokecherry, eastern chokecherry, western chokecherry, rum chokecherry, whiskey chokecherry, wild cherry, wild blackcherry, bird cherry, jamcherry, chokeberry, cabinet cherry, chuckley plum, sloe tree, bitter-berry, caupulin

This small native tree or an erect to straggling shrub grows from 20 to 30 feet tall, with a short, irregular trunk, 2–6 inches across. The branches either ascend or spread widely. The brown bark, covered with small, raised, horizontal lenticels, is smooth when young, then somewhat scaly or wrinkled when mature. Broken twigs smell like bitter almond. The root system can sometimes spread, to create dense thickets. The finely toothed, pointy-tipped, oval to elliptical, alternate leaves grow from 2 to 4 inches long and ¾–2 inches wide. The upper surface is bright green and hairless. The underside is paler and may be matted with very short hairs. From one to two purplish-red glands grow near the leaf base. The leaves turn yellow in autumn. The leafstalks grow from ½ to 1 inch long. Blooming from mid to late spring, the white, five-petaled, sweetly almond-scented flowers hang from long, crowded racemes, 3½–6 inches long and about 1 inch across. From ten to twenty-five flowers grow on each raceme. Each flower

is ¼–¾ inch across, with fifteen to twenty conspicuous stamens as long as the petals, plus one pistil. The nearly round petals grow to around 1/5 inch long. The flower stalks grow 1/5–⅓ inch long, and the five green sepals are shorter than the petals. Hanging from the same racemes in late summer, ripe, shiny, spherical cherries, dark red, purple, or blackish, grow from from ¼ to ⅜ inch across, and all contain one hard stone. The edible black cherry (see p. 191) looks like the choke cherry, but it's a larger tree, the ripe fruit is always black, and tiny, orange-brown hairs grow along the underside of its leaf's midrib.

People confuse the chokeberry (*Aronia* spp.) with chokecherries because the names are similar, but the two species have very different features. For example, the chokeberry bush's fruit has a crown, which cherries lack, and the astringency of the marginally edible fruit is only removed by juicing the otherwise-awful fruit.

Chokecherries grow in full sunlight and partial shade, on rich, moist soil. You'll find them in thickets, in and along the edges of woods, and near shores. They grow throughout the United States and Canada, except for some Gulf Coast and Southeast states. In New York State, they're very common in some regions, such as in the Adirondacks, but I've only spotted them growing wild twice in the NYC area, both times in Central Park.

Strip the ripe cherries off the racemes with your fingers and transfer them to containers. Clipping a container to your clothing or backpack makes this easier. They're awful raw, way too astringent and sour. Also, the raw seeds are poisonous if eaten in quantity, but the fruit is great cooked for 5–10 minutes in fruit juice, with a sweetener and thickener. Strain out the seeds using a food mill, and use the very tasty cooked fruit in jams, sauces, pies, puddings, smoothies, ice cream, and other desserts.

Chokecherries provide vitamins A, B6, C, E, K, thiamine, riboflavin, niacin, and pantothenic acid, as well as the minerals calcium, iron, magnesium, phosphorus, potassium, zinc, copper, and manganese. Native Americans and immigrant settlers used a decoction of the cambium as a sedative, detoxifier, tonic, and appetite stimulant, as well as for coughs, tuberculosis, malaria, stomachaches, and intestinal worms. However, the tree contains hydrogen cyanide. This stimulates respiration and improves digestion in small quantities, and there have been claims that it helps with cancer, although research didn't bear this out. Nevertheless, in large quantities, some of this substance is converted into cyanide, causing respiratory failure and death. Children who ate lots of raw berries and swallowed the seeds died this way, so it is not a safe home remedy.

RECIPE

Choke Cherry Jello

This fruit is as delicious cooked as it's awful raw. Quite tart, it's balanced here with pear juice, raisins, a sweetener, flavorful blueberries, and appropriate seasonings. Agar, as always, is a great jelling substance.

4 cups pear juice

3 cups choke cherries

3 tbsp + 1 tsp agar powder

4 tsp liquid stevia

2 inches vanilla bean or 2 tsp vanilla extract

1 tsp cinnamon, ground

1 tsp almond extract

1 cup blueberries

1 cup raisins

1. Simmer, uncovered, the pear juice, choke cherries, agar, stevia, vanilla bean, cinnamon, and almond extract for 5 minutes. or until the agar is dissolved.
2. Remove the cherry stones and vanilla bean using a food mill.
3. Return the purée to a boil, with the blueberries and raisins, and simmer for another 5 minutes.
4. Chill until set.
   Serves: 6
   Preparation time: 15 minutes
   Cooking time: 10 minutes

Wild Raspberry (*Rubus strigosus*)

Family: Rosaceae, the rose family
Other names: American red raspberry

My mother, who was born in Europe, where foraging is more common than here, taught me to recognize this berry along with blackberries (see p. 181) and blueberries (see p. 186) when I was a young child, on vacation in the Catskills, New York. She didn't know any other edible species, but the berries were so good, with this in mind, I was very happy to discover that I could learn foraging myself as an adult, as an outgrowth of my interest in cooking, health, and nutrition.

This bramble grows many canes, arching or erect, thorny, rounded woody stems and arising from perennial roots. First-year primocanes have leaves only, while second-year floricanes (lateral branches) bear flowers and fruit, before dying back to the ground.

The alternate, palmate-compound leaves are bright green and consist of three to five (sometimes seven) pointed, toothed, oval leaflets, whitish underneath. They grow 1½–2½ inches long and about half as wide. They turn red and purple in autumn.

The small, white to greenish, five-petaled flowers grow on short, loose, terminal racemes in the second year. They develop into round, downy, red raspberries, each with five triangular sepals at the fruit's base, ripening in mid-summer.

You can find this native fruit throughout North America, except for parts of the Southeast. Look for it in moist, sunny or partially shady habitats, in thickets, along hedges, in overgrown fields, along edges of woods, in openings in the woods, and along trail- and roadsides.

Collect the berries the same as you would black raspberries (see p. 173) and use them in any dessert that calls for berries, straining out the annoyingly hard seeds in any recipe that's puréed. The fruit tastes way better than store-bought raspberries.

This fruit is highly nutritious, providing vitamins A, B1, B2, B6, C, E, K, pantothenic acid, and folate, as well as the minerals and trace minerals calcium, iron, magnesium, phosphorus, potassium, sodium, zinc, copper, manganese, and selenium. It's loaded with healthful antioxidants, such as ellagic acid; the flavonoids quercetin and kaempferol; and the cyanidin-based molecules cyanidin-3-glucosylrutinoside and cyanidin-3-rutinoside.

These phytochemicals show antimicrobial properties, inhibiting pathogens such as *Candida albicans*, which causes yeast infections and could aggravate irritable bowel syndrome. The fruit may also reduce the risk of cancer.

An infusion of the leaves and roots is used as an astringent for diarrhea, especially for children, as it's more mild than other herbal astringents. It's used the same way as black raspberry (see p. 173) for the female reproductive system.

It's also used for nausea and to suppress vomiting, as a gargle for tonsillitis and mouth inflammations, and as a poultice or wash for sores, conjunctivitis, minor wounds, burns, and varicose ulcers. Scientific testing is called for.

RECIPE

Wild Raspberry Jam

Here's a simple, delicious jam you can make with any species of bramble, and it tastes like the berry itself, rather than of the generic jam flavor of store-bought spreads.

4 cups wild raspberries

6 tbsp pear juice

½ tsp agar powder or ½ tbsp agar flakes

1 tbsp clear liquid stevia

1 tbsp red wine (optional)

1 tsp raspberry extract (optional)

¼ tsp orange extract

1. Simmer all ingredients together for 5 minutes or until the agar is dissolved.
2. Purée in a blender, holding down the cover with a dish towel and beginning at low speed at first, to prevent an eruption.
3. Strain out the seeds using a fine-mesh strainer.
4. Test a spoonful in a freezer for 2 minutes. Add water if too thick, or simmer with more agar for 5 minutes if too thin.
5. Chill until set.
   Yields: 4 cups
   Preparation/cooking time: 15 minutes
   Setting time: 90 minutes (varies)

Mayapple
(*Podophyllum peltatum*)

Family: Berberidaceae, the barberry family

Other names: American mandrake, wild mandrake, hogapple, Indian apple, mayflower, umbrella plant, wild lemon, devil's apple

With a single, long, smooth, erect stem reaching 8–20 inches tall, this weird-looking, native colonial perennial spreads via dark brown, fibrous, jointed rhizomes. One large, long-stalked leaf grows from the top of the stem when the plant's young, joined by a second, opposite leaf when the plant gets older.

From 4 to 14 inches across, the spreading, shiny leaves are roughly circular, deeply palmate-lobed, and coarsely toothed toward the five to nine lobes' tips. The lobes themselves are also often partially divided at their tips, making the leaves look like ragged umbrellas that have seen one too many rainstorms.

In mid-spring, only plants with the twin leaves bloom. Only 1 nodding, fragrant, showy, waxy, white, stalked flower, ¾–2 inches across, grows from the axil, where the two leafstalks diverge. The yellow-orange stamens and the fused pistils are encompassed by six sepals and six to nine petals.

Later on, the flower develops into a solitary, lemon-scented, nodding, ovoid fruit, 1¼–2 inches in diameter. It appears just as the leaves are dying, growing from the leaf axil that hosted the flower. The thick skin is green at first, then turns yellow as the fruit ripens, after it falls to the ground. Inside, it's white flesh and a few hard seeds.

Nothing else resembles the mayapple, but some of the common names are misleading. The mayapple is called the American mandrake, but it's not related to the European mandrake (*Mandragora officinarum*), and doesn't look like it. Other unrelated and different-looking plants that also bloom in May are also called mayflowers.

The mayapple grows in dappled, light shade; in moist, open woods; in thickets; and in fields and pastures throughout eastern North America. The fruits ripen in mid-summer and is gone by late summer.

Collect the fruit from the ground. It continues to ripen after you pick it. Store the unripe fruit in a bowl at room temperature until it's ripe, and refrigerate any ripe fruit. Storing it with apples, which give off ethylene gas, hastens ripening.

Of all the wild fruits, this one provides the worst harvests. Full sunlight will give it the energy to make lots of fruit, but it grows in shady places, so it's only once in very many years that you'll get more than a handful of fruits.

The pulp of this fruit, after you discard the skin and seeds, tastes like lemon custard. It's great raw and makes superb puddings, pie fillings, custards, cake toppings, jellies, or marmalades. It cooks in about 15 minutes. It freezes well too.

Caution: The roots and seeds are poisonous, as is the unripe, green fruit. Eat only the pulp of the soft, ripe, yellow fruit.

Native Americans and traditional American herbalists used the roots as a cathartic, in the days when "cleansing" the foul, sinful human body was considered beneficial. Nowadays, for some reason, giving yourself explosive diarrhea is considered a sign of insanity!

On the other hand, beneficial substances have been extracted from the rhizomes: The resinous podophyllin, although highly allergenic, inhibits cell growth, so doctors apply it topically to treat venereal warts. Another, etoposide, is used, along with other substances, in cancer chemotherapy for Ewing's sarcoma, lung cancer, testicular cancer, lymphoma, nonlymphocytic leukemia, and glioblastoma multiforme. However, the rhizomes themselves are way too poisonous to use in home remedies.

The mayapple can increase longevity, by forcing you to adapt a healthful lifestyle, so you may live long enough to get a good harvest of the fruit!

RECIPE

Sweet Mayapple Smoothie

Here's a healthful beverage that's as simple to make as it's tasty.

3 cups soy milk, nut milk, or oat milk

1¼ cup mayapple pulp or the flesh of 1 mango, coarsely chopped

2 tbsp lemon juice

¼ cup silken tofu

¼ cup raw cashews

1 tbsp clear liquid stevia

1 tsp grape seed oil, almond oil, sunflower oil, apricot kernel oil, or other light oil

1. Purée all ingredients in a blender.
   Yields: 5 cup
   Preparation time: 5 minutes

Common Elderberry (*Sambucus canadensis*)

Family: Adoxaceae, the moschatel family

Other names: Elderblow, American elderberry, American elder, common elder, elder, elderberry

This large, common shrub, native to eastern North America, often grows in dense stands. It reaches from 5 to 15 feet tall and becomes just as wide. The crown is broad and rounded, and the arching branches are slender. The smooth, gray bark is marred by corky bumps, lenticels, which allow exchange of gasses with the atmosphere. There's a white, spongy pith inside the branches and twigs. The feather-compound leaves, which can grow over 3 feet long, are divided into five to eleven opposite, saw-toothed, short-stalked, pointed, elliptical, dark green leaflets, 2–7 inches long and half as wide. The single leading leaflet is longer than the rest. They smell foul when bruised or cut, and turn yellow, orange, and red in autumn. The large, showy, slightly rounded to flat-topped flower heads consist of lacy panicles of many tiny, branched, five-feet-petaled, star-shaped flowers. Fragrant and white when young, they become musty and yellowish and with age. They bloom in late spring and early summer. Many tiny, spherical, shiny, purple-black, juicy berries weigh down the panicles from the middle of the summer through early autumn. Each berry grows ⅛–¼ inch in diameter and contains 3–5 tiny, hard seeds.

Caution: Extremely inattentive people have confused the very deadly water hemlock (*Cicuta maculata*) with elderberries, even though the latter is non-woody and not a shrub. It does have umbrella-like clusters of white flowers and feather-compound leaves, but, unlike the elderberry, the leaves are twice or thrice compound, and nothing else is similar. Devil's walkingstick (Aralia spinosa) is a shrub or small tree with alternate feather-compound leaves a little like the elderberries', but it's fiercely prickly; the leaves are alternate, not opposite; and the poisonous flowers and toxic berries (the peeled shoots are edible) are arranged in small circles. Other elderberry species (*Sambucus* spp.), some better to eat than others, grow in different parts of North America.

Look for elderberry bushes in partial shade and in moist and dry places. It grows in thickets, along trail- and roadsides, and in edge habitats, open woods, marshes, and cultivated parks. You can harvest the flowers or berries by breaking off the flower- or fruit heads and taking them home. This takes almost no time, but separating the flowers or berries from the stalks is more labor intensive. Freezing the berries on a tray or cookie sheet beforehand makes this faster. Throw out all the mildly toxic stems.

The fresh flowers taste like vanilla. The old flowers are awful. Inedible raw, the young flowers are great dipped in pancake batter and fried into fritters, or cooked in oatmeal or other hot cereals. You may also soak the flowers in vinegar for a few weeks, refrigerated, before straining them out, to flavor the vinegar. They also make a great wine, which is also a superb vehicle for hiding arsenic, as in the classic movie, *Arsenic and Old Lace.* The crunchy, flavorful berries are great in any fruit dish, but unlike other berries, they're not sweet, so add a sweetener. They taste much better cooked than raw, and some people experience gastric distress from eating raw elderberries, so this isn't the best fruit for raw food enthusiasts.

The berries provide vitamin C, beta-carotene, sugar, and fruit acids, plus the minerals potassium, calcium, and phosphorous. The flowers haven't been analyzed for nutrients. This species is used medicinally by Native Americans, and Hippocrates used a European species in 400 BC, but only the flowers and berries are suitable for home remedies. The rest of the plant is loaded with cyanide, a point dramatically driven home when my then 10-year-old daughter and I were hired to lead a private tour on a farm in 2014. Two of their goats had died, and the vet didn't know what plant could be killing them. During the two-hour tour, we looked at plant after plant without finding the culprit. I love animals and was becoming dismayed, when, at the literal last minute of the tour, we came across an elderberry bush stripped of its leaves, while the surviving goats, who had been following us, were clamoring for more. Fortunately, the second I denounced the guilty party, the farmers collectively yanked this large shrub out of the ground and replanted it behind a fence, in a goat-free area. The cyanide-deprived goats had nothing better to do than to try to clamber on top of my daughter to feast on black birch (Betula lenta) leaves, as she bent down the branches for them.

Distilled elderflower water is used to clean the skin, lighten freckles, and treat sunburn. An infusion or tincture of the flowers is used as an astringent, an expectorant, and a diaphoretic. Along with yarrow and peppermint, it's recommended by herbalists for colds, flu, and asthma. An increasing body of research supports this, indicating that extracts do help the immune system combat influenza. They'll shorten the time you're sick with either virus by around four days. The research was done with various species, but it's likely our native species works too. An infusion of the flowers is also used to soothe children's upset stomachs, and for flatulence. It's applied externally for swellings, rashes, and chilblains, and used as an eyewash for conjunctivitis and eye inflammations. Herbalists steep the flowers in oil to make a massage lotion and to apply to burns and rashes. However, there's also evidence that applying oil to burns is counterproductive.

RECIPE

Elderberry Pancakes

The inclusion of elderberries here brings out the best of my basic pancake formulation.

Dry Ingredients

1½ cups buckwheat flour + 1½ cups sweet brown rice flour

2 tbsp flaxseeds, ground into 5 tbsp of meal

½ tbsp cream of tartar

1 tsp baking soda

1 tsp ground wild ginger or 1 tsp powdered ginger

½ tsp salt

Ingredients to Blend

3¾ cups soy milk, oat milk, or nut milk

¼ cup corn oil, vegan butter substitute, or sesame oil

¼ cup lecithin granules

2 tsp clear liquid stevia

Other Ingredient

1 cup fresh elderberries

1. Mix together the dry ingredients.
2. Purée the ingredients to blend in a blender.
3. Mix the blended ingredients into the dry ingredients. Don't overmix.
4. Stir in the berries.
5. Pour a ladle full of the batter onto a hot, oiled griddle and cook until lightly browned underneath.
6. Flip with a spatula and cook until lightly browned underneath again.
7. Repeat steps 5 and 6 until all the batter are used up.
   Yields: 20 pancakes
   Preparation/cooking time: 45 minutes

Sumac (*Rhus* spp.)

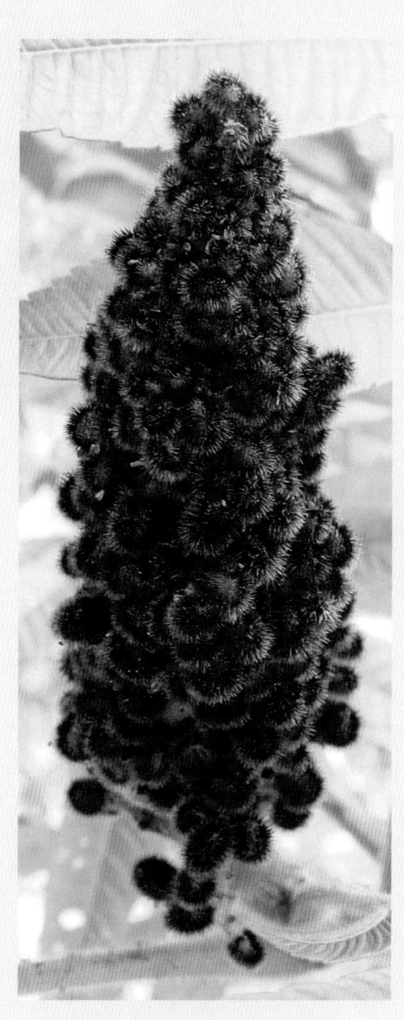

Family: Anacardiaceae, the cashew or sumac family

These shrubs or small trees grow 4–30 feet tall, often forming dense stands and spreading by underground runners. The stocky twigs exude a sticky, white latex sap when injured.

The alternate, feather- (sometimes palmate-) compound leaves may grow more than 2 feet long, with a lemony fragrance and many paired, elliptical to lance-shaped leaflets, which turn scarlet in autumn. They are pointed at both ends.

The many, tiny, yellow-green, five-petaled, fragrant flowers bloom on terminal spikes or panicles, 2 inches to 1 foot long, in mid-summer. They develop into dense clusters of small, hard, dry, sticky, spherical red fruits called drupes, each containing a tiny hard seed inside. They become rust-colored as they age, fading more if they persist on their stiff, brown, branching stems in the winter. Many species, all good to use, grow throughout North America. Here are the four I find in New York and vicinity:

1. Staghorn sumac or red sumac (*Rhus typhina*), a shrub or small tree, grows mostly from 4 to 15 (sometimes 30) feet tall. Usually lacking a trunk, the spreading branches form a wide crown. It's distinctly covered with furry velvet, so the bare forked branches look like antlers in the winter.
   Each feather-compound leaf comes with eleven to thirty-one sharply toothed, lance-shaped leaflets. The leafstalks are densely covered with rust-colored hairs. Dense, cone-shaped, male and female flower clusters, each 8 inches long, may grow on the same, or on separate, shrubs. In late summer or early fall, the female flowers develop into furry, scarlet drupes, ⅛ inch across.
2. Smooth sumac or red sumac *(R. glabra)* is another shrub or small tree. This one grows up to 20 feet tall, with feather-compound leaves 12–18 inches long. Its eleven to thirty-one lance-shaped leaflets, whitish

underneath, grow from 2 to 4 inches long.

A smooth, reddish midrib grows between the leaflets. Dense, cone-shaped clusters of male and female flowers, 8 inches long, bloom on separate plants. This species isn't hairy. Its fruit clusters, looser than staghorn sumac's, are shaped like a Christmas tree.

3. Winged, dwarf, or shining sumac (*R. copallina*) is a small tree growing up to 30 feet tall, with a short trunk and spreading branches. Its feather-compound leaves may reach up to 12 inches long, with seven to fifteen shiny, mostly toothless leaflets. Distinct pairs of thin, flat membranes, called "wings," grow on both sides of the midrib. The flowers bloom on pyramidal panicles 3–5 inches wide. The short-hairy fruit clusters aren't as dense as the other species.
4. Skunkbush, sourberry, three-leaf sumac, or squawbush's (*R. trilobata*) densely, hairy twigs produce an intense, skunk-like odor when broken. The three-parted, palmate-compound leaves grows 2–3 inches long, with very coarsely toothed or lobed leaflets that are dark green and shiny above. Small, white to creamy, yellow flowers grow in spikelike terminal clusters. The clusters of drupes that follow are much smaller than the other species, but the berries are a little larger.

Poison sumac (*Toxicodendron vernix*) is a rare species that grows in sandy swamps; has white berries, not red ones; and the panicles droop, rather than growing upright. People don't like it, but it has one redeeming quality—it makes you appreciate poison ivy (Toxicodendron radicans): Poison ivy gives you a very bad, itchy rash that lasts around a week and goes away. Poison sumac's rash is much worse. It lasts a month or longer, and after it goes away, it comes back again. Give me poison ivy any time!

Other trees have feather-compound leaves, such as black walnut (see p. 279), Kentucky coffee tree (Gymnocladus dioica), and ailanthus (*Ailanthus altissima*), but they're large trees. Devil's walkingstick (Aralia spinosa) has feather-compound

leaves and it's smaller than the others, but it's fiercely prickly. Also, only sumac twigs release white latex when broken.

Smooth sumac is native to most of North America. Staghorn and winged sumac are native throughout most of eastern and much of central North America. Skunkbush is native to the western half of North America, but landscapers plant it widely in parks and cultivated places. Otherwise, look for sumac in full or partial sunlight, in old fields and thickets, along the edges of woods, in disturbed areas, along stream banks and roadsides, near the seashore, and on dry, sandy, or rocky soil. Smooth sumac and squawbush berries ripen in late summer. Staghorn sumac fruit ripens in early fall, and winged sumac ripens in mid-fall. Collect as soon as you can after the fruit ripens, before rain washes the flavor away. On rare occasions, when a dry fall is followed by a very cold winter, some flavor persists into early spring. Sumac is at its best when the fruit is spotted with whitish deposits of acid. Pinch the fruit, then touch a finger to your tongue, to determine the degree of sourness. Or have someone else do this, and determine the sourness by how much their face twists and contorts!

Don't rinse this fruit before use, or you'll wash away the water-soluble flavor, but shake off any bugs. Submerge the fruit clusters in a bowl of room temperature or warm water, then squeeze and twist it vigorously with your hands for 1–2 minute (you can also steep the clusters in hot water). Strain out the fruit with a fine sieve or cheesecloth-lined colander, sweeten to taste, and enjoy the best pink lemonade you've ever tasted.

People in the Mideast use their species of sumac dried, powdered, mixed with herbs (such as thyme, oregano, savory, salt, and sesame seeds) to make a seasoning called za'atar. You can rub sumac berries that haven't been moistened in a strainer, collect what comes out, and mix it with those flavorings in proportions you like, but I discovered that the best way to use our species as a seasoning is to make sumac concentrate:

Successively rub five batches of sumac in the same water, straining and discarding the sumac each time, until you attain the acidity of lemon juice, and use that with the other za'atar herbs, or use it without other seasonings (in place of lemon juice) in other kinds of recipes. You can freeze the concentrate in ice cube trays, then transfer to a freezer container, and defrost cubes as needed, to make pink lemonade, or as a lemon juice alternative.

You can peel the young growth at the tips of the branches (the shoots) in the spring and use them, raw or cooked, in any vegetable recipe. I find them somewhat bland, but other foragers love them, and some species may be better than others.

Sumac is a great source of vitamin C and may provide healthful proanthocyanidins, as do other brightly colored fruits, but no analysis has been undertaken. Sumac is an astringent, so Native Americans used a compress, externally, on wounds, to slow or stop bleeding. It's also been used as an antiseptic and a tonic. Cold sumac pink lemonade was also used for fever. If it doesn't have antimicrobial properties, the cooling effects would be palliative. A decoction of the cambium, or an infusion of the leaves, was given for diarrhea, dysentery, asthma, urinary tract infections, sore throat, chronic gum problems, and cold sores. Native Americans chewed the root to ease swollen or infected gums and to stop children's bed-wetting, but the plant hasn't been tested scientifically.

RECIPE

Sumac Ice cream

This light, flavorful ice cream imparts the lemony flavor of sumac into every bite.

3½ cups almond milk, coconut milk, soy milk, or any nondairy milk

1 tbsp arrowroot or kudzu

1 tsp agar

¼ cup sumac concentrate

¼ raw cup pine nuts or cashews

¼ cup coconut oil or grape seed oil

¼ cup lecithin granules

¼ cup vegetable glycerin

2 tsp liquid stevia

½ tbsp freshly grated lemon rind

1 tsp wild or commercial mint

½ tsp salt

1. Mix the arrowroot and agar into 2 cups of the nondairy milk, using a whisk.
2. Bring to a boil over medium heat in a heavy saucepan, stirring constantly.
3. Reduce the heat to low and simmer, uncovered, for 5 minutes or until the agar is dissolved and the mixture is thickened, stirring often.
4. Purée with the remaining ingredients in a blender.
5. Freeze in an ice cream machine according to the manufacturer's directions.
   Yields: 4½ cups
   Preparation time: 25 minutes
   Freezing time: 2 hours (varies)

Apples and Crab Apples (*Malus* spp.)

Family: Rosaceae, the rose family

What can be easier than recognizing an apple? Apples that resemble store-bought ones are easy to recognize, but small, apple-like fruits may or may not be apples. Nevertheless, all apple varieties have clear and distinct identifying characteristics: They're small- to medium-sized trees, growing from 12 to 36 feet tall. Unless very young, they've scaly, gray, brown, or reddish-brown bark, and dense, twiggy crown. The thirty to fifty-five species are nearly always thornless, unlike the similar hawthorn (see p. 224). The coarse, elliptical, pointed, stalked, slightly toothed, alternate leaves are slightly fuzzy underneath. Medium to dark green, they grow from 1 to 4 inches long. The short-lived, fragrant flowers bloom in early spring and grow up to ¾ inch across. The five radially symmetrical petals may be white, pink, or red.

Apples usually ripen in late summer and autumn, although I've found one tree with ripe fruit in early summer. The red, yellow, or green fruit looks like an imperfect store-bought apple. Crab apples are smaller. The brown, teardrop-shaped seeds grow in sets of five around the core's circumference, a surefire way to distinguish crab apples from other, similar-looking fruit. Cut an apple in half across its "equator," and you'll see the seeds arranged in a five-parted star. This pentagram made this fruit especially important in witches' ceremonies. It's no coincidence that Snow White's evil stepmother chose an apple to poison her enemy.

Apples that have fallen by themselves, "windfalls," are the best. Bring strong bags to collect them. They're heavy. If there's insect damage on the skin, ignore it. It's only cosmetic. An insect has taken a bite off the surface and moved on, and the skin has healed. If other bugs have penetrated into the fruit, cut away the "wormy" parts, if there aren't too many. Do this soon after collecting, or the larvae will ruin the fruit. Refrigerate wild apples after collecting and separate any fruit showing signs of damage. Use the damaged ones ASAP. The intact ones may last, refrigerated, for weeks.

Wild apples are usually more tart and flavorful than store-bought ones. You can certainly eat them raw if, like Thoreau, you enjoy eating sour fruit in the field. Their more intense flavor makes them much better for cooking, in all the same recipes for which you use store-bought fruit. The latter are clones bred for appearance and durability, at the expense of flavor. You won't believe how good the wild apple recipes will taste until you try them. Trees with fruit less than 2 inches across are defined as crab apples. There are many varieties. Some are similar to larger apples, and you can use them the same way. Others seem to be too hard and bitter to eat, but these often transmute in late fall, changing from red or yellow to amber-brown, and becoming very soft. They develop a very sour flavor, similar to tamarind, which most people have tasted in the form of a brown sauce in Indian restaurants. Strain out the seeds, using a food mill or strainer.

Sweeten, and use as a sweet-sour condiment. Unsweetened, you can use the sour pulp in recipes that call for lemon or vinegar.

Caution: Apple seeds contain enough cyanide to kill you if you eat enough of them at once. You can core the apples and discard the cores, or strain out the seeds after cooking. Fortunately, cooking also destroys cyanide, so some people make applesauce by simmering chopped up apples, including the cores, plus a sweetener and seasonings, then puréeing everything in a blender. Apple blossoms are nonpoisonous. Some foragers enjoy eating them, although I don't find them at all tasty.

Apples are an excellent source of vitamins A and C, beta-carotene, and folate, plus the minerals calcium, phosphorus, potassium, magnesium, and iron. They contain malic (*Malus* means apple) and tartaric acids, which are supposed to aid in digestion. Their pectin slowly removes heavy metals from the body, but not quickly enough to prevent acute poisoning. For this, you need prompt medical treatment. On the other hand, the pectin helps prevent slow accumulation of such toxins. It also decreases absorption of fat and cholesterol through the small intestine, helpful for preventing heart disease. It does the same with sugars, making it good for diabetics and hypoglycemics.

However, the myth that an apple a day keeps the doctor away is false: While leading a private foraging tour for a group of medical doctors, we came across a magnificent wild apple tree loaded with fruit, but instead of fleeing in disarray, the physicians all ran toward the tree and filled their backpacks with the delicious wild fruit!

RECIPE

Wild Apple Crumble

Wild apples' flavor is far superior to that of commercial apples in desserts, and adding other wild ingredients such as black walnuts, acorn flour, and water mint, if available, makes an already excellent recipe so much better.

Fruit Layer

10 cups wild or Granny Smith apples, sliced

1½ cups pear juice

1 cup raisins

1 tsp cinnamon, ground

2 tsp liquid stevia

Crumble Layer

2½ cup rolled oats

½ cup acorn flour or any whole-grain flour

¼ cup black walnuts, commercial walnuts, or other nuts

⅓ cup walnut oil or other light oil

1 tsp powdered or liquid stevia

¼ tsp nutmeg, ground

¼ tsp salt

1. Mix the fruit layer ingredients together.
2. Mix the crumble layer ingredients together.
3. Transfer the fruit layer mixture into an oiled baking dish.
4. Press the crumble layer onto the fruit layer.
5. Bake for 1 hour or until the crumble layer is lightly browned and the fruit layer is bubbly in a preheated 350°F oven.
   Serves: 6–8
   Preparation time: 30 minutes
   Cooking time: 60 minutes

Hawthorn
(*Crataegus* spp.)

Family: Rosaceae, the rose family

Other names: Thornapple, hagedorn, haw, hazels, gazels, ladies meat, bread and cheese tree, mayblossom, hedgethorn, maybush, mayflower, whitethorn

The trees and shrubs of this large, varying group include native and Eurasian species. They grow from 15 to 45 feet tall. The branches are bedecked with distinctive, straight, sharp spines 1–5 inches long, making it easy to recognize, even in the winter (although some Florida species that don't grow in the north are spineless). The bark is smooth and gray at first, but develops vertical cracks when the tree gets older.

The leaves are so extremely variable that when a botanist was given two leaves and determined that they were from two different species, it was revealed that they were both from opposite sides of the same tree. The leaves are roughly oval, with a ragged appearance due to uneven teeth and occasional lobes. These medium-sized leaves are deeply veined, and they may spiral around long shoots or grow clustered on small spur shoots that stick out of the branches or twigs.

The showy, white, five-petaled, radially symmetrical flowers bloom in early spring. Before the modern calendar was instituted in 1582, this was at the start of May, not in April, so May 1, Mayday, was the pagan holiday celebrating the start of spring and this tree was the official one to be used as the maypole.

The fly-pollinated flowers, which grow from ½ to ¾ inch across, smell befittingly foul, so in past centuries, it was forbidden to bring them into a house, as the smell of death would portend the death of someone living in the house.

The fruits are round to heart-shaped. They're usually red, but can be dark purple or yellowish. They grow from ¼ to 1 inch across and form loose clusters. Unlike similar-looking crab apples (which don't have thorns), there are one to five large, hard nutlets inside, but no core. No other apple-like fruit has thorns that look like knitting needles.

You can harvest the developing leaves with your fingers toward the end of early spring. The berries of some species ripen in late summer. Autumn is the peak of the season, but some fruits ripen in late fall and persist into the winter.

Hawthorns are commonly planted as street trees and in parks. They used to be planted as thorny hedges. In fact, the word "haw" is an obsolete word for hedge. You can also find hawthorns in thickets and fields, and along forest edges and streams. They grow throughout North America.

Enjoy the fruit raw and spit out the seeds, or cut the flesh away from the seeds with a paring knife and discard the seeds. You can also cook the fruit with the seeds in fruit juice, plus a sweetener and sweet herbs, then strain out the seeds using a food mill. Like apples, hawthorns contain pectin, a natural thickener. You can also steep the fruit in water just off the boil, covered, for 20 minutes to make tea.

However, you do need to be careful with this fruit. Once, an aspiring nutrition student named Madeleine attended my foraging tours. Her university didn't

Harvest them with your fingers, from the tree or from the ground, and put them into containers. They taste more like apples than like any other fruits, but with a tart flavor all their own. The best species, with the largest fruit (red and the size of a grape), is the Washington hawthorn (*Crataegus phaenopyrum*) and it's a favorite of landscapers.

teach the use of herbs, so she used books to study them. She was thrilled when we found ripe hawthorn berries she was able to eat and collect in Prospect Park, New York.

Soon thereafter, she found more on her own in Central Park, New York, near the Alice in Wonderland statue. She looked so happy eating them that after a while, a whole crowd of people had joined her, all except for one man, who stood aside. When Madeleine offered him a berry, he refused. When she asked him why, he told her that he had opened one up and there was a "worm" (actually, the apple maggot) inside.

"There's a worm in mine too," someone else exclaimed.

"Mine as well," shouted someone else.

"They're all full of worms," screamed a third person.

There are two morals to this story:

1. Look before you eat.
2. Never accept a hawthorn from Madeleine! (Fortunately for Madeleine, she's not a vegetarian!)

Some hawthorn trees, such as the ones by the statue, have maggoty fruit every year. Others have them only rarely.

The young leaves are edible in early spring. They're pretty bland, so I occasionally add them to cooked vegetable dishes as a minor ingredient.

The fruit provides vitamins C, B1, B2, B3, B5, B6, B9, and B12, plus PABA, choline, and inositol, as well as flavonoids.

Herbalists have been using hawthorn for heart disease for centuries, and research demonstrates that the fruit's flavonoids can dilate the peripheral blood vessels, lowering blood pressure and reducing the burden on the heart. It slightly dilates the coronary vessels, increases enzymatic activity in the heart muscle, and helps the heart muscle use oxygen. Nevertheless, way more research money went into studying different herbs, such as foxglove (*Digitalis purpurea*) and patentable drugs that effect the heart. There are no pharmaceuticals made from hawthorn, and heart disease is too serious a condition to treat yourself, even if this herb is safe.

Herbalists use hawthorn berry decoction for high and low blood pressure, angina, irregular heartbeat, and the arterial spasms of Reynaud's disease; but it takes about six weeks before the herb takes effect; and since heart disease can be dangerous, it's best to use in conjunction with the care of a cardiologist.

Herbalists also use a decoction of unripe hawthorn berries for diarrhea. Hawthorn flower infusion has been used as a diuretic, and a decoction of the ripe berries has been used for sore throats, skin diseases, diarrhea, and abdominal distention. None of these uses has been studied scientifically.

RECIPE

Lemony Hawthorn Pudding

Here's an improved version of a traditional pudding, enhanced with whole, vegan ingredients and an especially tasty wild fruit.

3½ cups soy milk or other nondairy milk

2 cups large hawthorn berries

½ cup walnut oil or almond oil

¼ cup lecithin granules

¼ cup pine nuts or cashews

¼ cup vegetable glycerin

1 tbsp arrowroot

1 tbsp clear liquid stevia

2 tsp agar powder

2 tbsp lemon juice

½ tsp vanilla extract

¼ tsp almond extract

¼ tsp salt

⅓ cup raisins

1. Cut the flesh away from the seeds of the hawthorns with a paring knife and discard the seeds.
2. Purée all ingredients except the hawthorns and raisins in a blender.
3. Transfer this to a heavy saucepan with the remaining ingredients and bring to a boil over medium heat, stirring constantly.
4. Reduce the heat to low and simmer, uncovered, for 10 minutes or until the agar is dissolved and the pudding has thickened, stirring often.
5. Chill.

Serves: 6
Preparation time: 30 minutes
Cooking time: 20 minutes

American Hackberry
(*Celtis occidentalis*)

Family: Cannabaceae, the hemp family
Other names: Common hackberry, nettletree, beaverwood, northern hackberry

This small native tree usually grows from 30 to 60 feet tall, but can reach 100 feet in height under optimal conditions. The crown is rounded. The branches can spread or droop slightly. The trunk can reach 1–2 feet in diameter, and the gray bark is corky-looking.

The simple, rough, oval, stalked, dull green, finely toothed, alternate leaves grow from 2 to 5 inches long and 1–2 inches wide. Three long veins run the length of the leaf, but what makes their shape striking is the long, pointed tip, and the asymmetrical, rounded base, which is always larger on one side of the midrib than on the other.

Horticulturalists, who care much more about appearance than flavor, are galled by this tree, because it's subject to two nonfatal deformities:

1. An insect-transmitted fungal infection twists the twigs so they point in all directions, a condition called witch's broom.
2. In addition, the female American hackberry gall wasp stings the leaves, lays its eggs, and inserts its own DNA. This forces the leaf to form distinctive, nipple-shaped galls, in which the larvae feed and develop in safety. When mature, each young wasp drills a hole through the underside of the leaf, escapes, and renews the cycle.

How can you account for such genetically modified organisms in our ecosystems? There can be only one explanation: Monsanto must have been around way longer than they let us know, and released these Franken-bugs millions of years ago to promulgate their evil agenda!

The tiny, light green, bilaterally symmetrical, wind-pollinated flowers are the least conspicuous parts of the tree. With four or five lobes, they bloom soon after the leaves have begun to grow.

The small, spherical, solitary berries grow from ¼ to ⅓ inch in diameter. They're often orange-brown when ripe, but may be dark purple as well. They grow suspended from the twigs on slender stalks, around ⅓ inch long. Inside the thin, dry flesh is a large, spherical, hard, cream-colored seed. Partially decomposed berries often cling to the tree through the winter, making it easy to recognize even then. No other tree in the Northeast looks like the hackberry, although it's relatives in other parts of the country and may hybridize with these where their ranges overlap. It grows throughout most of eastern and central North America and most of southeastern Canada, but not in Vermont or Louisiana.

This tree grows in full sun or partial shade. Look for it in rich, moist soil, gravelly or rocky hillsides, woodlands, parks, backyards, empty lots, riverbanks, rocky barrens, and floodplains.

You can pick the berries with your fingers, but they're small, making collecting them labor-intensive. However, Eugene Dubois, the first scientist to search for fossil evidence of human ancestors, excavated fossils of Java Man (*Homo erectus*) in a cave in Java, Indonesia, in 1891, along with piles of the seeds of an Asian species of hackberries. These close relatives of modern humans had collected hackberries (probably using my app!) and brought them to their dwellings, something apes never do. So if you don't have the patience to collect these berries yourself, ask a *H. erectus* (the surviving individuals are all public officials) for help!

The berries are sweet, and one of my favorite trail nibbles. To me, they taste like the candy coating of M&Ms. Unfortunately, they're too small for making recipes.

I'd always found the seeds to be as hard as rocks and spit them out. However, foragers in other parts of the country reported the seeds to be edible and crunchy. For decades, I assumed they still had the teeth of *H. erectus* to be able to chew such seeds; but after 31 years, I tested the seeds of a hackberry tree I'd been foraging from in Central Park for decades; and, to my surprise, they were crunchy and tasty. So far, that's the only tree I've found with edible seeds, so this variety must be rare in the Greater New York Region.

The berries haven't been analyzed for nutrients and the plant isn't used medicinally, although in the past, a decoction of the cambium was used as a gargle for sore throats and for pain. The berries were also used for dysentery, but there's no evidence that they really work.

Wild Grapes (*Vitis* spp.)

Family: Vitaceae, the grape family
Other Names: Beach Plum Bush, Seaside Plum

People are surprised that grapes grow wild throughout North America, but when Leif Erikson landed in Newfoundland around AD 1000, there were so many native grapes, he called the region Vineland. Grapes are high-climbing woody vines that shed bark in distinctive vertical strips, making identification easy all year. Grapes can grow close to the ground and form thickets, or reach from 60 to 100 feet in height. Although the alternate leaves range from broadly triangular to nearly heart-shaped, or oval, and are partially divided into three or lobed, they usually look like maple leaves. They grow from 2 to 8 inches long, and just as wide. Growing opposite to the leaves, persistent forked tendrils shaped like the letter "Y" cling onto trees and fences. They become dark brown and brittle with age. Long clusters of inconspicuous, tiny, fragrant, five-petaled, yellow-green flowers bloom in mid-spring, hanging from the leaf axils. Sometimes tinged with green or red, they mature into dark purple, thick-skinned grapes in autumn.

Growing in long clusters of close to twenty, the grapes reach from ½ to ¾ inch across, with two to six small, hard seeds inside. The largest and best species is the fox grape (*Vitis labrusca*), which was interbred with European grapes to create the Concorde grape. Because wild grapes hybridize with each other and with European cultivars, it's hard to tell which species you've, but they're all good to eat, although some varieties are more sour than others.

Grapes are easy to tell apart from poisonouss look-alikes if you check for the distinguishing characteristics. If not, you may poison yourself. Canada moonseed (*Menispermum canadense*) is a rare vine with leaves and fruit similar to grapes, but the fruit contains one crescent-shaped seed, not many seeds like grapes, and it lacks tendrils, twining around its support structure. Also, the leafstalk perforates the leaf, near the base, something grapes never do. Poisoning may be fatal, so there's one good thing to do with Canada moonseed berries: Send them back to Canada! Likewise, you can send Virginia creeper (*Parthenocissus quinquefolia*) back to Virginia! This very common, low-climbing toxic vine has spherical fruits that look enough like grapes that people have eaten them, sickened themselves, and sometimes died. However, the leaf is completely different from the grape's maple-like leaf. It's a palmate-compound leaf, with five-toothed leaflets, spreading out from the base like a fan. Porcelainberry or Amur pepperoni (*Ampelopsis brevipedunculata*) has leaves similar to grape leaves, but the vine is non woody, and doesn't peel in long strips like grape vines. It has a white pith, whereas grape vines have a brown pith. The decorative berries may be blue, purple, turquoise, or white, nothing like grapes, so people have poisoned themselves with leaves. On the upside, this is the best of any poisonous plant to eat, if you must do so: it gives you a stomachache, you throw up, and recover quickly!

The fruits of various grape species ripen from early to late fall, and rarely at the end of summer. Grape leaves and tendrils are in season from mid-spring through early summer. Here's how I learned that the medium-sized leaves are the best ones to harvest: One day in May, around 1980, while bicycling past Cunningham Park in Queens, New York, for exercise, at a time when I was exploring the culinary possibilities of ethnic foods in local markets and bringing concepts of nutrition into my culinary experiments, I passed a group of ethnic Greek women, garbed in traditional black, harvesting food in the woods. I asked them what they were doing, but couldn't understand a word: it was all Greek to me! Nevertheless, I came home with a bagful of grape leaves. They even showed me that the medium-sized leaves were the best. You can't stuff the tiny ones, and the largest ones are too tough and coarse. I stuffed they leaves, they were delicious, then I returned in the fall and found the woodlands festooned with fox grapes. That's how I began foraging. A year later, foraging in the same park, it struck me that other people might enjoy wild foods as much as me, and decided to try leading foraging tours, which I began in 1982.

Grapes grow in partially shaded habitats, such as thickets, open woodlands, parks, edges habitats, and fields; along streams and riverbanks; in wetlands; and near the seashore. Usually only a fraction of grape vines produce grapes, and you sometimes have to look closely under the mass of leaves to spot them. Grape harvests vary from year to year, dry years being the best. Gather the leaves and tendrils by stripping them off with your fingers. Break off clusters of grapes and pull off the individual grapes, either before placing them in food containers or after you get home. Young grape tendrils make a flavorful, lemony trail nibble or garnish. Young wild grape leaves are quite delicious, cooked until soft enough to chew. Cut off the stems and simmer the leaves in lightly salted water, with a dash of olive oil or vinegar if desired, for about 1 minute, or until tender enough to chew, but not mushy. Drain in a colander and plunge this into cold water to halt the cooking. Place a dollop of any kind of stuffing you like (traditional or original), fold the left and right sides of the leaf over the stuffing, then roll up the rest of the leaf from the bottom. Wild grapes are sour and seedy, and have tough skins, but they're much more flavorful than store-bought grapes. They're fine raw if you like sour fruit, and superb cooked with a sweetener and thickener, then passed through a food mill to remove the seeds. You can use them in any recipe that calls for fruit. Of course, wild grapes are also superb for wine-making.

Grape leaves are an excellent source of beta-carotene and vitamin B3. The fruit provides beta-carotene, potassium, fructose, tartaric acid, flavonols, caffeic acid, ellagic acid, quercetin, tannin, malic acid, plus resveratrol, the substance in red wine that accounts for its health benefits. It reduces blood platelets' stickiness (lowering the chance of clots) and raises levels of the good cholesterol reducing the risk of cardiovascular disease. It also can sensitize prostate cancer cells to radiation, making radiotherapy more effective. Grapes contain adiponectin too. This works with resveratrol to combat obesity, insulin resistance, and aging. Rapamycin, another constituent, will extends your life if you're a mouse, but hasn't been tested on humans. Grapes are important in traditional herbal medicine, something you'd know if you were attuned to the traditional herbal grape vine! Considered diuretic, they've been eaten to relieve urinary tract irritations and decrease the urine's acidity. They're supposed to sooth inflamed tissues and promote healing. Some European health spas promote grape "cures." Clients eat only grapes for days. This is definitely beneficial to the owners of the spas and the grape industry, but hasn't been tested in humans. The grape vine's white sap is a home remedy for weak eyes and floaters, but hasn't been tested for safety or effectiveness. The crushed leaves have been used as a poultice, along with common plantain, for various skin sores. Infusions of the leaves and seeds are astringent, and have been used for bleeding and diarrhea. Native Americans used it for hepatitis and stomachaches.

RECIPE

Fox Grape Jam

Using my standard jam-making method with these especially tasty wild fruits leads to an outstanding result. The water successfully tones down the intensity and sourness of this fruit. If you make this recipe with less flavorful commercial grapes, use grape juice instead.

7 cups fox grapes or other grape species

1 cup water

¼ cup vegetable glycerin

1 tbsp liquid stevia

2 tsp agar flakes or 2 tsp agar powder

1. Simmer all ingredients together for 5 minutes or until the agar dissolves.
2. Test by putting a spoonful in the freezer for a couple of minutes or until chilled. If the texture is too watery, add more agar, cook until dissolved, and test again. If too thick, add more water and test again.
3. Strain out the seeds using a food mill and chill until set.
   Yields: 4½ cups
   Preparation time: 15 minutes
   Cooking time: 10 minutes

Beach Plum
(*Prunus maritima*)

Family: Rosaceae, the rose family

This much sought-after shrub (at least, for anyone who forages) is native to the Northeast and a member of the very large rose family. To no one's surprise, it grows in thickets near coastal beaches and bays, usually in dense stands.

A thornless shrub has many branches, it grows from 3 to 12 feet tall, although around 8 feet is most usual, and its spread equals its height. The reddish-brown bark, streaked with horizontal white lines, has a rough appearance. Growing 1–2 inches long, the dark green, stalked, finely toothed, oval, alternate leaves are from ½ to 1 inch broad.

In the spring, showy, white, fragrant, long-stalked flowers, each about ½ inch across, bloom in clusters of two to five. The flower has five radially symmetrical petals, plus lots of long red, pink, and white filaments that end in yellow anthers.

The plums ripen in the fall, the thin skin changing from green, red, and purple to blue-black. They're about the size of grape and dusted with a faint, white bloom, a powder you can rub off with your fingers. The dull orange flesh contains a single, large, flattened stone.

For fast collecting, clip or tie a food container to your belt or backpack, or tie it around your neck. When the collecting container is full, transfer the plums to a storage container and gather more plums.

If mosquitoes, which are more common around bays and marshes than near the open seashore, are still around, plan your collecting on a relatively cool, windy day (the wind blows away the mosquitoes) and cover yourself with long pants and sleeves.

Sweet and tart, beach plums are great tasting, raw or cooked. They cook in about 10–15 minutes. Remove the stones with a food mill after cooking, and use the fruit in any kind of dessert.

Beach plums provide vitamins A, C, and potassium, plus various antioxidants, typical of brightly colored fruit, so they may lower your risk of heart disease and cancer. Experiments have shown that eating dried plums will reduce your risk of osteoporosis, but, so far, only if you happen to be a lab animal.

RECIPE

Beach Plum Supreme

A sweet, creamy substrate makes a perfect setting for this delicious fruit.

6 cups silken tofu, drained

¼ cup lecithin granules

8 Medjool (soft) dates, pits removed

2 tbsp walnut oil

4 tsp clear liquid stevia

½ tsp salt

3 cups beach plums or other plums, seeds removed

1. Purée all the ingredients except the plums in a food processor.
2. Stir in the plums.
   Serves: 6
   Preparation time: 10 minutes

Roses
(*Rosa* spp.)

Family: Rosaceae, the rose family

This large group of plants with familiar flowers and less conspicuous edible fruits that includes trailing, woody canes, shrubs, and climbing vines. They hybridize readily, keeping the botanists busy trying to define species. Armed with curved barbed prickles, they've alternate, feather-compound leaves consisting of three to eleven small, toothed, elliptical leaflets. Most people recognize the radially symmetrical flowers, with five petals, five sepals, lots of stamens and pistils in the center, and the familiar fragrance, no matter the size and color. The oval to round fruit or hip grows up to 1 inch across, beginning hard and green, then softening and turning red-orange, with many tiny, hard, white seeds shaped like teardrops inside.

Here are the two most common and distinct wild species in New York:

1. The multiflora rose (*Rosa multiflora*) is an invasive Japanese species growing 9–15 feet tall. Its leaves consist of seven to nine oval, toothed leaflets, ½–1 inch long. Dense clusters of small, white flowers, ½–1 inch across, have a center with protruding stamens. The abundant hips are small with hardly any flesh, so they're only good as a trail nibble or for making tea. They ripen from mid to late fall and persist into the winter.

   It's very common, growing in sunny and partially shaded habitats, in thickets, along road- and trailsides, in edge habitats and fields, in disturbed soil,

and near the seashore. It grows throughout eastern North America, the West Coast states, and British Columbia.

2. The wrinkled rose or beach rose (*R. rugosa*), another East Asian species, is the much better. Coated with dense bristles and thorns, it grows from 4 to 6 feet tall. The dark green leaves consist of five to nine strongly wrinkled leaflets.
The flower's narrow, spoon-shaped, rose-purple or white petals grow from 3 to 4 inches across, larger than most wild species. The spherical, fleshy fruit, also relatively large, grows up to 1 inch across. Ripening in the fall, it's crowned with sepals, and there's a smooth, green, floral tube underneath. This species grows in shrub-like thickets and sandy places, along roadsides, and in fields near the seashore. Landscapers love planting it. It grows wild in northeastern North America and Washington State.

Other rose species have been planted in cultivated places and may escape into the wild, but I've found their fruits bitter and sometimes prickly, not worth eating. Heavy-duty work gloves are good for harvesting from these thorny shrubs. Wrinkled rose hips ripen throughout the fall, while the multiflora rose's fruit ripens toward late fall. The flowers bloom in quantity in late spring, although some wrinkled rose flowers bloom in the summer and fall too.

Rose petals are edible (the center of the flower is bitter). You can add them to salads or dessert dishes. I've never found them to be tasty, perhaps because they're traditionally prepared with white sugar, which I avoid because it's unhealthful. On the other hand, the petals are a major ingredient in Bulgarian cuisine. You should try them and judge for yourself. The fruit of the multiflora rose is ripe when the berries turn deep red and feel soft. They're too small and seedy (rose seeds aren't poisonous, but they're hard and bitter) for recipes, but they make a good trail nibble and tea, with a sweet, fruity flavor, a little like raspberries. The best way to eat them is to wait until early winter, when they're all ripe. Grab a big handful of the fruit, remove any stems, and stuff the whole mass of fruit into your mouth. The flavor is so good, it's worth having to spit out dozens of seeds after you've swallowed the fruit! Wrinkled rose hips, also ripe when they feel soft, taste like apricots, and they're sweet. They contain pectin, the thickener apples contain, so cooked and puréed, they create the texture of applesauce. They're so good that I spent many an hour splitting them open with a paring knife and laboriously scraping out all the seeds with a grapefruit spoon. It took me only three decades to discover the right way to process them: Steep them in water to cover, just off the boil, for 20 minutes, to make a healthful, delicious tea. (I normally avoid herb teas because they're all diuretics for me, and if ever I try to duck into the bushes, thirty people will follow me to see what I'm going to find!) Once the hips are cool, splitting them open and removing the seeds takes seconds, and the delicious fruit is ready for any kind of sweet recipe—puddings, cakes, cookies, sauces, compotes, jam, fruit soups, ice cream, breads, etc.

Rose hips are a great source of vitamins A, B3, C, E, and K, plus the minerals calcium, manganese, and zinc, as well as pectin, malic and citric acids, fructose, sucrose, bioflavonoids, carotenoids, anthocyanins, catechins, and other polyphenolics. Rose hips' vitamin C was used to cure scurvy long before vitamins were discovered. Herbalists also used rose hips for infections, chest congestion, and bladder problems. Due to the pectin, like applesauce, eating rose hips is good for diarrhea. The fruit has been used to help people digest rich foods. It's also been used to treat arthritis, and it's being researched to combat triple negative breast cancer, which it may also help prevent. Traditional Chinese herbalist use an infusion of the flowers for poor circulation, stomachaches, liver pains, mastitis, dysentery, vaginal yeast infections, and pregnancy. These medical applications haven't been tested scientifically yet.

RECIPE

Hip Jello

Making healthful Jell-O using the rose hips from the wrinkled rose is definitely a hip way to cook!

3 cups wrinkled rose hips

3 cups apple juice

1 tsp agar powder or 1 tbsp agar flakes

1 tsp liquid stevia

4 tsp lemon juice

½ tsp dried peppermint or other mint, ground

1. Place the rose hips in the boiling water, remove from the heat, allow to steep, covered, for 20 minutes.
2. Strain out the fruit and reserve the tea.
3. When cool, remove the flesh from the seeds with your fingers and discard the seeds.
4. Add the fruit and all the remaining ingredients to the apple juice and bring to a boil over high heat. Reduce the heat to low and simmer, uncovered, for 5 minutes or until the agar is dissolved.
5. Purée in a blender if desired, holding down the cover with a dish towel and beginning on low speed, to prevent eruptions.
6. Chill until set
   Serves: 4–6
   Preparation time: 30 minutes
   Cooking/steeping time: 25 minutes

Autumn Olive
(*Eleagnus umbellata*)

Family: Elaeagnaceae, the oleaster family
Other names: Autumn berry, Japanese silverberry, umbellate oleaster

When I first found this invasive East Asian shrub, I was quite suspicious of it. It wasn't in any wild food guides, and although a botanist friend told me the berries were edible, they were astringent and awful tasting.

This all changed when I was hired to lead a private tour in Fort Tilden Park, an abandoned World War II military base in Rockaway, Queens, New York. This was my first year leading foraging tours. I didn't know one-tenth as many species as my daughter did when she was nine, and the seashore habitat in November, when many of warm-weather plants with which I was familiar were gone, was very challenging.

Right away, I spotted dozens of autumn olive bushes, a virtual wild orchard, and figured there'd be no harm in letting people taste them. The berries were a sensation—sweet and juicy, with a flavor like that of raspberries, currants, and pomegranates! The ones I'd tried previously had simply been unripe, hence their awful flavor.

Now my problem was stopping tour participants from coming to blows over which bush had the best berries. Some people simply prefer sweeter berries, others favor more tart fruit. The moral: before serious collecting autumn olives, try different bushes to see which one has an abundance of fruit that you prefer.

This large, twiggy bush grows from 12 to 20 feet tall, but it's not a tree, as there's no trunk. The bush has a serious case of freckles: The smooth, gray bark, the leaves, and the berries are speckled. Sometimes some of the bushes have thorns.

Lance-shaped to oval, the speckled leaves grow from 2 to 4 inches long and from ¾ to 1½ inches wide. They're dull green above, with wavy, smooth-edged, toothless margins. They're covered with shiny, silvery-white scales beneath. This distinctive lustrous sheen makes the shrub easy to spot from a distance.

The radially symmetrical flowers are very fragrant, as well as tubular, and tipped with four lobes, like the related honeysuckles. About ½ inch long, pale yellow and scaly, they grow clustered in groups of two to five, arising from the leaf axils. They bloom in early spring, after the leaves have appeared.

The flowers slowly morph into dense clusters of spherical, stalked, red berries, around ½ inch across and distinctly dotted with silver. They ripen in autumn, when they become soft and juicy (hard, dry fruits are unripe). Inside are several small, soft, oblong, ribbed, yellowish seeds. The seeds aren't poisonous, and some people swallow them, but I find them unpleasant and spit them out or strain them out when making recipes using a food mill.

The sweet, juicy, fully ripe berries are wonderful raw. Cooked 5–10 minutes with a sweetener and thickener, then passed through a food mill, they're superb in sherbets, sauces, puddings, pie fillings, or virtually any dessert, and you can dehydrate the sweetened pulp to make an outstanding fruit leather.

Look for autumn olives in sandy fields. Like legumes, they can incorporate nitrogen, an essential constituent of protein, from thin air (which is 78 percent nitrogen), so they can thrive in poor, sandy soil, or depleted former agricultural fields, where their competitors are at a big disadvantage, since you need nitrogen to make protein. They can grow in full sun or partial shade. I find endless bushes near the seashore, but you can also find them in disturbed habitats, thickets, cultivated parks, hay fields, and pastures, as well as along roadsides.

This superfood has close to seventeen times as much of lycopene as tomatoes. There are strong indications that this carotenoid helps fight prostate cancer, and may be good for combating and preventing other cancers as well. Beta-carotene, phytoene, and beta-cryptoxanthin are some of the other healthful carotenoids the berries provide. If this weren't enough, eating these berries also give you vitamins A, C, and E, as well as essential fatty acids, which are very rare in fruits.

Chinese traditional herbalists used a tea of the seeds for lung problems and coughs, although this hasn't been tested by Western medicine yet.

RECIPE

Autumn Olive Purée

Here's how to prepare autumn olives for any recipe. You cook them briefly, then strain out the seeds using a food mill (an inexpensive mechanism that pushes food through a strainer), which holds back the unwanted seeds. Use the purée, which you may thicken and sweeten, in any kind of dessert.

8 cups autumn olive berries

1. Bring the berries to a boil in a heavy saucepan over medium heat, stirring often.
2. Reduce the heat to low and simmer, covered, for 5 minutes, stirring often.
3. Pass this through a food mill to remove the seeds.
   Makes 3½ cups
   Preparation/cooking time: 20 minutes

RECIPE

Autumn Olive Sherbet

This fruit is so tasty, it's no wonder it makes an outstanding sherbet, frozen with a few complementary ingredients, such as strawberries, which go especially well with autumn olives.

¾ cup apple juice

¾ cup pomegranate juice

½ cup autumn olive puree (see above)

6 tbsp raw pine nuts or cashews

¼ cup vegetable glycerin

¼ cup lecithin granules

¼ cup grape seed oil

1 tbsp liquid stevia

¼ tsp salt

¼ tsp orange extract

⅛ tsp cinnamon

1¾ cups strawberries

1. Purée all ingredients except the strawberries in a blender.
2. Add the strawberries and blend on low speed until the strawberries are just chopped.
3. Freeze in an ice cream machine according to the manufacturer's directions.
   Yields: 4 cups
   Preparation time: 10 minutes
   Freezing time: 2–3 hours (varies)

American Persimmon
(*Diospyros virginiana*)

Family: Ebenaceae, the ebony family or the persimmon family
Other names: Common persimmon, date plum, simmon

This tree may be as small as 15 feet tall, or as tall as 100 feet in height. The slender trunk often grows spreading droopy branches and sometimes forms a narrow, rounded crown. The thick, blocky, dark gray bark, divided into mosaic-like squares 1½ inches across, is characteristic of the ebony family, of which this is the northernmost member.

The simple, toothless, elliptical, alternate leaves grow up to 6 inches long and 3 inches wide. The tips and bases are pointed, the upper surfaces are shiny, and the undersides are light green.

Fertile flowers grow on female trees only. They're bell-shaped, pale yellow, short-stalked, and fragrant. About ¾ inch long, these solitary flowers produce both male and female parts, with four petals and eight stamens. Male trees grow only sterile but similar flowers, around ⅓ inch long, in clusters of two or three, with sixteen long stamens—the male parts.

The spherical fruit, 1–2 inches across, grows on female trees only and is orange throughout, but discolors to yellowish-brown. Brown and leathery, four sepals surround the fruit's base. Inside are one to eight large, flattened, hard, brown seeds.

Wild persimmons grow in upland forests and piney woods, on rocky hillsides, in bottomland swamps, along stream banks, in fields, on dry scrublands, along the edges of fields, and in parks. This native tree grows wild in southeastern North America up to Long Island, New York, but it's planted in parks and botanical gardens further north.

Collect the persimmons from the ground or shake the smaller trees. Pack the delicate fruit into food containers, keeping the ripe ones, which you store in the refrigerator, separate from the unripe ones, which ripen at room temperature. You can speed this up by storing them with apples, which give off the ripening hormone—ethylene gas.

You can gather the leaves for tea from when they first appear, in the spring, until they turn color and fall to the ground. The fruit ripens in early fall on very few trees and from mid to late fall on most.

When it's soft, discolored, blotchy, and ugly, this is an especially delicious, sweet, pulpy, and filling fruit. Carl Linnaeus wasn't kidding when he named the genus *Diospyros*, fruit of the gods. Store-bought Asian persimmons are quite good, but they're insipid compared to our native species.

Don't eat unripe or partially ripe fruit, which is so astringent, you'll feel like you've a mouthful of talcum powder. Amazingly, eating a ripe persimmon right away will cure you completely!

Enjoy the fruit raw or cooked in any dessert, from smoothies to ice creams, and in cakes, pies, breads, puddings, or pancakes. Use a food mill to strain out the seeds, or remove them by hand. Orange and lemon juices, or their freshly grated rinds, are perfect complementary flavors for this divine fruit, which you can also dehydrate or freeze. You can steep the leaves to make a tasty herb tea as well.

American persimmons are high in the calories. They're a great source of vitamins C and D, plus the minerals calcium, phosphorous, and potassium. Persimmon leaf tea is very high in vitamin C as well.

Because of its astringency, Native Americans applied the cut, unripe fruit, which may also be slightly antiseptic, to burns, to stop them from oozing, and to wounds, to stop bleeding. The fruit provides the digestive enzymes papain and bromelain, also found in pineapple, papaya, and digestive enzyme pills, so eating it'll aid digestion.

RECIPE

Simmonola

Wild persimmons cooked into the roasted oats turns this granola into something special. Serve with fresh fruit or raisins.

5 cups rolled oats

¼ cup sesame oil

4 cups American persimmons, or 2 cups store-bought persimmons

14 Medjool (soft) dates, pitted

2 tsp cinnamon, ground

1 tsp powdered ginger

½ tsp nutmeg, ground

¼ tsp salt

5 cups mixed, roasted nuts of your choice

1. Roast the oats in the sesame oil with the salt for 1 hour in a preheated 350°F oven.
2. Meanwhile, remove all the seeds from the persimmons and purée them in a food processor with all the remaining ingredients except the nuts.
3. Thoroughly mix the purée with the roasted oats and continue baking for another 30 more minutes.
4. Stir in the nuts.
   Yields: 10 cups
   Preparation time: 45 minutes
   Cooking time: 90 minutes

Wintergreen (*Gaultheria procumbens*)

Family: Ericaceae, the heath or heather family

Other names: Teaberry, tea leaf, American wintergreen, checkerberry, boxberry, deerberry

This well-known species is technically a shrub, even though it grows only 3–6 inches tall, because the unbranched, upright, reddish-brown stem is slightly woody. Creeping runners allow this colonial evergreen to form mats, and all parts of the shrub produce its familiar fragrance when injured.

Thick, wavy-edged or slightly toothed, shiny, elliptical to oval, leathery, evergreen, alternate leaves grow clustered at the top of the stems. They're 1–2 inches long and ⅓–¾ inch wide. Although the younger, softer leaves are yellowish-green, the remainder are dark green above and lighter below. Winter weather tinges them with red.

The small, white, five-lobed, bell-shaped flowers grow in twos or threes, ¼–½ inch long, hanging from the upper leaf axils on drooping stalks. They bloom from summer to early fall. Five sepals encircle the flower's base.

Bright red, spherical berries, ¼–½ inch across, supersede the flowers on the drooping stalks. They ripen in autumn and can persist through the winter. Use your fingers to pick the berries or strip off the leaves.

The berries' familiar, refreshing flavor makes them perfect for vegetable and fruit salads, and in fruit dishes, cereals, puddings, jellies, pies, cakes, and sauces, but they take so long to collect, you'll only have enough to use as a minor ingredient or garnish.

You can steep handfuls of the fresh or dried leaves, or berries, in water to cover to make a mild, pleasant-tasting, refreshing tea. Fermenting the leaves and berries in warm water for a few days increases their strength.

Wintergreen berries are a good source of vitamin C, but nutritional analysis is incomplete. However, an infusion of any of the aboveground parts of this plant contains oil of wintergreen, with the same medicinal uses for pain, inflammation, and reducing the risk of heart attacks.

The tea is also considered an analgesic, an astringent, a carminative, a diuretic, a stimulant, a tonic, and an emmenagogue—used internally for delayed, irregular, or painful menstruation and to ease the pain of childbirth. The tea is used as a mouth rinse and gargle. Chewing the leaves or eating the berries has been used for bad breath, to soothe irritated gums, and for canker sores.

Concentrated oil of wintergreen, which you'd have to buy, has been used for a variety of ailments, but it hasn't been tested scientifically. It's dangerous and can cause death if used internally, and rarely even kills people when used externally! That's why Bayer experimented with chemically similar willow extracts in the 1800s and invented aspirin.

RECIPE

Wintergreen Curry

Wintergreen berries make this Thai curry even more exotic tasting.

4 cups soy milk or other nondairy milk

3⅓ cups (2 16 oz. cans) of coconut milk

2 cups veggie beef (available in Chinese speciality stores) or firm tofu, diced

1¼ cup bamboo shoots

1 cup long-grain brown rice

4 celery stalks, sliced

2 carrots, sliced

1 large red onion, chopped

1 mango, chopped

¼ cup Thai curry paste, or to taste

½ tbsp salt, or to taste

¼ tsp clear liquid stevia

1 cup wintergreen berries

1. Bring all ingredients except the wintergreen berries to a boil over medium heat, stirring constantly.
2. Reduce the heat to low and simmer, covered, for 1 hour or until the rice is tender.
3. Serve garnished with the wintergreen berries.
   Serves: 8–10
   Preparation time: 15 minutes
   Cooking time: 60 minutes

Nuts and Seeds

There aren't a huge number of nut and seed species compared to some other wild food types, but there are certainly enough to keep you busy from late summer to fall (and occasionally beyond). They are all very tasty, highly nutritious, and well worth the effort it takes to process them.

Amaranth (*Amaranthus* spp.)

Family: Amaranthaceae, the amaranth family
Other name: Pigweed

These common annuals have leaves you can eat from late spring to mid-fall and edible seeds that ripen in autumn. Native to the Americas and Eurasia, they commonly grow in full sunlight and partial shade. You'll find them in fields, disturbed habitats, edge habitats, and in cultivated places such as parks.

These coarse-looking, leafy plants bear oval to lance-shaped, long-stalked, alternate, toothless leaves that grow from 1 to 2 inches long. There's no odor. The various species can grow from 2 to 8 feet tall.

Conspicuous, dense masses of tiny, green, inconspicuous flowers, surrounded by hair-like bracts, bloom on cymes in the summer. *Amaranthus* means everlasting flower. They give way to thousands of tiny, round, black seeds, in the same configuration, in autumn.

Two species commonly grow wild in New York, although similar, edible relatives grow throughout North and South Americas, and a cultivated species with purple-red flower and seed heads, also edible, grows in gardens:

1. Mature common amaranth, tumbleweed, or redroot amaranth (*Amaranthus retroflexus*) has oval, smooth-edged, alternate, long-stalked, medium-sized leaves. *Retroflexus* means bent backward. The tall cymes are densely covered with flowers or seeds. This is an excellent species for harvesting the seeds, and the leaves are great too.

Common amaranth has alternate, oval, stalked leaves and can get several feet tall.

2. Low amaranth, careless weed, or Palmer's amaranth (*A. palmieri*) can creep along the ground or grow upright. It's irregular, alternate, elliptical, long-stalked, smooth-edged, medium-sized, distinctly notched leaves. The spikes of tiny seeds are too small for an effective harvest, but the cooked leaves are especially tasty.

To harvest the leaves, simply strip them off the stems with your fingers. To collect the seeds most effectively, clip off the seed heads and let them dry in paper supermarket shopping bags for a couple of weeks, then release the seeds by rubbing the seed heads over a tray. Blow away the chaff and store the seeds in a jar at room temperature, until you're ready to use them.

The leaves taste like a combination of spinach and string beans. I find them too strong-flavored and bitter to enjoy raw, although other foragers disagree. I like them cooked, using virtually any method, similar to the way people cook spinach or other greens. They're tender after about 10 minutes of cooking. The flavor is like a combination of green beans and spinach.

Although not technically a grain (because it's not in the grass family), you can use the seeds of this pseudo grain like true grains. They're great cooked with real grains or beans. I especially like adding them to oats when I make oatmeal. They cook in about 15–20 minutes.

The leaves are high in beta-carotene, vitamin C, calcium, and iron. The seeds provide vitamins A, K, B2, B6, C, and folate, as well as palmitic, oleic, and linoleum acids, plus the minerals calcium, iron, magnesium, phosphorus, potassium,

The leaves of low amaranth, which grows to less than one foot tall, are oval, but with a notch at the tip.

zinc, copper, and manganese. They're also high in protein, and form complete proteins when combined with grains.

Herbalists use the leaves as an astringent. A tea has been used as a gargle for hoarseness, and for diarrhea, excessive menstruation, and intestinal bleeding, although the plant hasn't been tested scientifically.

Cautions: The leaves slightly resemble the poisonous leaves of black nightshade (Solanum nigrum), although amaranth leaves are much more coarse, and the flowers and berries are completely different. Avoid eating these plants where the soil is contaminated by poisonous nitrates, caused by misuse of agricultural fertilizers.

When Hernán Cortez conquered Mexico, he outlawed the cultivation and use of amaranth. Because it makes so many seeds, the Aztecs considered it as an herb for fertility and used it in ritual human sacrifices. Cortez didn't like this, although at the same time, back in Spain, people were being burned at the stake by the Spanish Inquisition for crimes as innocuous as being Jewish.

So Cortez made amaranth a Schedule II controlled substance, then burned the amaranth fields for good measure, since the resulting starvation made it easier to steal the Aztecs' gold. So before picking amaranth, look around first, and make sure Cortez isn't watching!

Lamb's quarters (see p. 127), which also has edible leaves, looks a little like amaranth, but the leaves are diamond-shaped and their undersides are whitish. Confusingly, both plants are sometimes called pigweed.

RECIPE

Mulberry and Amaranth Porridge

Here's an update version of the classic Scottish breakfast dish, with the addition of wild berries and wild seeds—which would make The Three Bears so proud that they'd be willing to share their cereal with Goldilocks!

2 tbsp grape seed oil or other light oil

1 cup steel-cut oats

¼ cup amaranth seeds

1 quart soy milk, nut milk, or other vegan milk

2 tsp clear liquid stevia

1 tsp cinnamon

1 tsp vanilla extract

¼ tsp orange extract

¼ tsp almond extract

¼ tsp salt

1 large green apple, chopped

1½ cups red mulberries (see p. 155) or other berries

⅔ cup raisins

¼ cup lecithin granules (optional)

¼ cup oat bran (optional)

1. In a saucepan, cook the oats and amaranth in the oil over medium heat for 5 minutes or until fragrant, stirring often.
2. Add all the remaining ingredients except for the lecithin and bran. Bring to a boil over medium heat, stirring constantly.
3. Reduce the heat to low and simmer, uncovered, 30–45 minutes or until the porridge is thickened and soft.
4. Remove from the heat and allow to set, uncovered, for 15 minutes.
   Serves: 6
   Preparation time: 15 minutes
   Cooking time: 35–50 minutes

Hickories (*Carya* spp.)

Family: Juglandaceae, the walnut family

This is a group of common woodland trees that's mainly native to eastern North America, although one of the twenty-five species grows in China. Many species produce great-tasting nuts, some drop awful-tasting ones, but none is poisonous. With the exception is the pecan (*Carya illinoensis*), which grows only in the Deep South, they don't produce good crops every year, so no one can afford to grow them commercially. Hickories grow from 60 to 180 feet tall. They have fragrant, alternate, feather-compound leaves consisting of five to seven opposite, lance-shaped to elliptical, toothed leaflets that get from 8 to 30 inches long. They turn yellow in autumn.Tiny, green male flowers hang from long catkins in spring-time in the spring, when small spikes of female flowers bloom, concealed at the branches' tips. In the fall, the trees drop nuts that are packed inside distinctive, spherical, four-parted, green husks, which grow ½–1½ inches across.

Here are the species you're likely to find in New York State:

The shagbark hickory (*C. ovata*), a common species, is a favorite among foragers. It usually grows from 60 to 120 feet tall, but may reach a height of 180 feet, with a straight, cylindrical outline. The light gray bark looks distinctively shaggy when mature, with long, flat, vertical slabs curling off the trunk, forming long strips, easily recognizable even in the winter. The leaves grow from 8 to 14 inches long, usually with five to seven apple-scented leaflets, each 4–6 inches

long and about 2 inches wide. The toward the leaf base are the smallest. The catkins reach from 4 to 6 inches long, while the female flowers grow on short spikes ⅓ inch long. The nuts grow singly or in clusters of two or three, in a thick, spherical husk 2 inches across. The husk turns from green to yellow-green, then to black. A thin-shelled, light tan, ovate nutshell, 1–1½ inches across, surrounds a sweet, especially tasty nut that's not exceptionally difficult to crack or to extract from the shell. Less common is the similar shellbark hickory (*C. laciniosa*). It's less curly bark and nine to seventeen leaflets per leaf. The mockernut hickory (*C. tomentosa*) usually reaches 50–60 feet in height, but sometimes gets 100 feet tall. The trunk is straight and the crown is rounded. The dark-gray, tight, furrowed bark creates a diamond pattern, and there's dense hair under the twigs. The leaves grow 6–12 inches long. The leaf axis is hairy underneath, as are the five to nine leaflets, which grow up to 8 inches long. The ovoid to ellipsoid nut grows 1½–2 inches long, with a thinner husk than the shagbark's, but with a thick, light tan, four-ribbed, hard shell. In fact, *mockernut* means heavy-hammer nut in Dutch. The nutmeat tastes good, but is hard to remove from the labyrinthine shell. The pignut (*C. glabra*) is also delicious, but only if you're a pig. It usually grows from 60 to 80 (sometimes 100) feet tall and 10 to 40 inches wide. The cylindrical crown is 25–35 feet wide. The gray-brown, shallow-ridged, furrowed bark forms a distinctive diamond pattern, making the tree easy to identify at once. The leaves, which grow 8–12 inches long, have five to seven finely toothed, hairless, lance-shaped leaflets. The terminal leaflet is the biggest, 2½–5 inches long and

1–2 inches wide. The male catkins grow in groups of threes, from short spurs near the young twigs' tips. The thin, dark brown, pear-shaped husk gets 1–2 inches long and close to ¾ inch across. The nut grows about 1 inch across, with a thick, flattened shell. Other foragers claimed to have found pignuts that taste good. The ones I've found have always been even worse than my middle school's hot lunch! The bitternut or yellowbud hickory (*C. cordiformis*) is just as bad, and very common. It grows from 60 to 100 feet tall, with a cylindrical, irregular crown up to 25 feet wide. The trunk grows from 1½ to 3 feet across, with shallowly ridged, gray bark. The powdery, sulfur-yellow leaf buds make this species distinct. The 3–5 inch long catkins cluster in threes. The leaf is 7–14 inches long, with five to nine sharply toothed, stalkless leaflets. The four narrow ridges of the husk extend from the outer tip inward, between ½ and ⅓ of the fruit's length, so only the bottom half of the thin husk, which grows from 1 to 1½ inches across, splits open. The rounded, beaked, cream-colored, smooth, thin-shelled nutshell is 1 inch in diameter. Inside you'll find a reddish-coated kernel. The best thing to do with it after you've shelled it is to throw it away!

Hickory trees grow in full sunlight or partial shade, in a wide variety of woodland habitats. The nuts ripen from early to mid fall, but you may still find a few fresh ones in late autumn. They only produce a good harvest about one out of every two or three years, so stock up when you can. Just bag the nuts from the ground (unless you care to climb up a 100 foot tall tree!). Nuts with green husks are least likely to have insect damage as you approach the end of the season. You can remove the husks using a screwdriver. Crack the shells open with a heavy-duty nutcracker that you can buy online, the best implement. Otherwise, use a vise or a large rock. A nutpick (also called a lobster pick) makes removing the nutmeat much easier. You can store hickory nuts in paper bags until the husks dry and open, releasing the mature nuts. Unshelled nuts keep indefinitely in this state. Once shelled, you can store them refrigerated in closed containers for a few weeks, or freeze them. Use them like any other nuts, raw or roasted. They're great in pies, cakes, puddings, granola, ice cream, salads, or stuffing. People have also tapped shagbark hickory trees, like maple trees, in late winter, boiling down the sap to 1/40th its volume and making syrup with a smoked hickory flavor, although this is too much unhealthful processing for me.

Hickory nuts score high in nutrition, even compared to other wild foods. Two thirds of the nut's dry weight is a high-quality, easily digestible oil that includes heart-healthy essential fatty acids. The nuts are high in calories, important to wilderness survivalists, but not for people trying to lose weight. They also provide protein, carbohydrates, vitamins A and C, iron, phosphorus, potassium, and trace minerals. This tree isn't currently used in herbal medicine. In the past, though, the new growth of young leaves was steamed to make an inhalant for headaches, and the cambium was been used for arthritis, internally as a decoction, and externally as a poultice, but there's no evidence showing that any of this works.

RECIPE

Pineapple Hickory Bake

Hickory nuts topping a cream-covered pineapple layer and baked over bean-thread noodles are as tasty and decadent as it's unusual.

Bottom Layer

2 cups bean thread noodles, boiled for 5 minutes in lightly salted water with a dash of sesame oil

Middle Layer

2 cups fresh pineapple, diced

½ tsp liquid stevia

½ cup Chocolate Coating

Ingredients to Blend

3 cups silken tofu, drained

8 Medjool (soft) dates, pitted

4 tsp grape seed oil or any other light oil

1 tsp cinnamon, ground

1 tsp lemon extract

½ tsp fresh ginger or ¼ tsp powdered ginger

Top Layer

1 cup hickory nuts or chopped pecans

1. Place the noodles in an oiled casserole dish or baking dish.
2. Mix the middle layer ingredients together and place over the noodles.
3. Purée the ingredients to blend together in a food processor and spread this over the middle layer.
4. Sprinkle the hickory nuts on top.
5. Bake for 45 minutes in a preheated 375°F oven.
   Serves: 6–8
   Preparation time: 20 minutes
   Cooking time: 45 minutes

RECIPE

Chocolate Coating

Here's a great way to add an exotic chocolate flavor to any recipe, from desserts, to roasted chips made with large, edible wild leaves.

2 cups white (mellow) miso

1 cup sesame oil or peanut oil

½ cup pine nuts

6 oz. unsweetened baker's chocolate, melted in a double boiler

2 tbsp liquid stevia

8 pitted Medjool (soft) dates

½ tsp coffee extract

1 tsp common spicebush berries, or ½ tsp allspice, ground

Purée all ingredients together in a food processor.

Makes 4 cups

Preparation time: 10 minutes

Hazelnuts (*Corylus* spp.)

Family: Betulaceae, the birch family
Other name: Filbert

American hazelnut (*Corylus americana*) and beaked hazelnut (*C. cornuta*) are two similar species, and their spreading, smooth-barked gray shrubs reach a height of 10–20 feet, with a spread of 8–13 feet. They often grow in dense stands. The native species has rough hairs on the twigs and leafstalks that the European species lacks.

Growing from 2 to 6 inches long, the simple, alternate, toothed or double-toothed leaves may be rounded or nearly heart-shaped.

Considered one of the first harbingers of spring, the catkins mature close to the end of winter. Yellow brown and 1–4 inches long, these male flowers grow, evenly spaced, in clusters of twos or threes along the branches, dispersing their pollen into the wind. The crimson female flowers are less than ¼ inch across. Their bright red pistils spread in all directions, from the tip of the ovate ovary.

The nuts ripen in late summer. Inside shells are enclosed by paired husks that grow from 1 to 2 inches long. The native species' husks are blunt and open-ended. The beaked hazelnut's husks are long and pointed.

Inside each husk is a spherical, thin-shelled, white nut, growing up to ½ inch across, and lies wrapped in brown, papery coating.

Hazelnuts grow in thickets, dry to moist woodlands, forest margins, roadsides, fence rows, under power lines, and in other disturbed areas. The American hazelnut ranges throughout temperate eastern North America, while the beaked hazelnut sticks mostly to the northern part of those parameters.

Harvest these nuts by hand, wearing work gloves for protection from the bristles, in late summer and early autumn, and try to get them before the squirrels and other critters who also bought this book do so! You can gather them somewhat underripe and let them mature in a paper bag.

Use these nuts like store-bought ones. Crack them with a nutcracker and add them, raw or roasted, to any dish that calls for nuts. You can also grind them into meal and use them, along with whole-grain flour, in baking. They make a great nut butter too, ground in a food processor with oil and some salt.

Hazelnuts provide vitamins A, B1, B2, B3, B6, C, E, and K, as well as alpha-carotene, beta-carotene, folate, pantothenic acid, and choline. They're rich in the minerals calcium, copper, iron, manganese, phosphorus, potassium, selenium, and zinc.

The shrub is also medicinal. The leaves and cambium contain the phytochemicals hamamelitannin and proanthocyanidins. The nuts contain 3-caffeoylquinic acid, 5-caffeoylquinic acid, *p*-coumaroyl tartaric acid, myricetin, quercetin, gallic acid, and kaempferol. Extracts have been shown to have a beneficial effect on the heart, and another constituent, doxorubicin, is protective against cataracts.

Herbalists apply extracts of the cambium and leaves to skin irritations, sunburn, diaper rash, scalds, bedsores, eczema, and insect bites. They give it internally for sore throat and diarrhea.

RECIPE

Harzipan

Here's a hazelnut confection analogous to a German almond paste confection called marzipan, but with healthful ingredients instead of refined sugar, and the additional flavors of hazelnuts and common spicebush berries.

1¾ cups raw hazelnuts

½ cup silken tofu, drained

1 tbsp almond oil

1 tsp clear liquid stevia

1 tsp hazelnut extract (optional)

½ tsp vanilla extract

½ tsp common spicebush berries, ground, or ½ tsp allspice, ground

¼ tsp salt

3 tbsp carob powder

1. Grind the hazelnuts into a fine meal in a food processor.
2. Add all remaining ingredients except for the carob powder and grind into a paste.
3. Roll into balls 1 inch across and roll the balls in carob powder.
   Yields: 24 balls
   Preparation time: 30 minutes

Oaks
(*Quercus* spp.)

Family: Fagaceae, the beech family

Most of us take these familiar trees for granted, but they've been an important food source for all traditional First Nations people for millennia. Their acorns are quite good and very enjoyable, if somewhat time-consuming to prepare. Oak trees, which grow from 12 to 120 feet tall, have long, simple, alternate, lobed leaves and distinct, ovate, thin-shelled, cupped acorns. The leaves are blunt-edged in the white oak group, the easiest ones to prepare. Long, narrow, drooping catkins with tiny, yellow male flowers hang from the twigs in early spring, before the leaves mature, releasing pollen into the air. Then the catkins all fall to the ground. The female flowers, which grow on much smaller spikes, usually escape notice. White oak acorns take one year to mature, and the insides of the nutshells are hairless. Red oak acorns' nutshells are hairy inside, they take two years to mature, and the leaf tips are pointy.

The white oak tree (*Quercus alba*) is the flagship species of the white oak group. It grows from 60 to 120 feet tall. The bark is light gray, a little furrowed, slightly scaly, and flat ridged. The crown is rounded and the branches spread horizontally. The leaves grow from 5 to 9 inches long and from 2 to 4 inches wide. They have seven to ten shallow or deep, even, rounded lobes. The leaves are dark green and glossy above, and sometimes slightly downy underneath. Male catkins grow 2–4 inches long. The female flower is a single, short, reddish-green spike. The long-ovate, stemless acorns, which become light brown when mature, usually grow less than 2 inches long. The bowl-shaped cup covers around ⅓ of

the acorn. This species can hybridize with its relatives, which can make exact identification difficult, but they're all good edibles. Occasionally, other members of the white oak group that don't grow wild are planted in parks. These are usually relatively easy to process as well.

The chestnut oak or rock oak (*Q. prinus* or *Q. montana*) is a medium-sized member or the white oak group that often grows from 60 to 70 feet tall, with a spread as wide as its height. The thick, reddish to dark brown bark is deeply furrowed, like alligator hide, with long, tight ridges. The coarsely toothed, elliptical to oblong leaves have wavy margins, like chestnut trees' (*Castaneus* spp.), 5–10 inches long and 3–4½ inches wide. They're dark green above and light green, with a slight fuzz, below. The acorns grow individually or in pairs, reaching 1–1½ inches long. The cup covers ⅓ of their length. Like the white oak, they require little leaching. Members of the red oak group (*Quercus* spp.), unlike those in the white oak group, have lobes with pointed tips. They usually take much more time and effort to process.

Oak trees grow throughout most of eastern North America, in forests, thickets, cultivated parks, and along neighborhood streets. White oak nuts are in season at the very end of the summer and in early autumn. Sometimes red oak acorns, usually too high in tannin for practical use, are good to go at the end of the winter, leached of most of their tannin under the snow. You can gather the immature leaves or white oaks for wine-making in mid-spring. To harvest, just pick up the acorns from the ground soon after they've fallen. Discard any with insect holes, especially if you're a vegetarian (insect-infested nuts also float in water)! Some years produce much better harvests than others.

Boil the acorns for 1 minute to loosen their shells. You can buy acorn shellers online. Otherwise, split the acorns with a paring knife, and either peel them using your fingers or remove the nutmeat with a nutpick or grapefruit spoon. The tannin, which is water soluble and bitter, and can cause health problems, must be removed. Chop the nutmeat in a blender with water to the size of rice grains, then soak the nutmeat in room temperature water, changing the water occasionally, until the nutmeat no longer tastes bitter. This can take from one to many days.

For red oak acorns, this can take many weeks. Native Americans dropped these acorns, in sacks weighted by rocks, into streams, or buried them, then retrieved them weeks later. A mesh bag in the top tank of a flush toilet, where the water is clean, will do the same thing. If the tannin turns the toilet brown, you can always say you forgot to flush! A faster way is boiling the acorns for hours in successive changes of water. However, this removes the oils, and the gelling quality of cold-leached acorns, alright if you're going to dry the nutmeat and grind it into flour, but inferior for most other uses. Another method is to grind the nutmeat with water in a blender, at high speed, for 1–2 minutes, pouring the pulp into a dishtowel-lined colander and running water through this, while stirring with a wooden spoon, for about 5 minutes, or until the water runs clear and the acorns no longer taste bitter. Then wring out the excess water.

Leached acorns have a mild, nutty flavor, a little like chestnuts, but not as sweet. Native Americans added them to soups and stews, or dried them and ground them into a non-rising flour. Korean people use their gelling properties to make a jelly called dotorimuk, which they serve in Korean restaurants. You can also roast leached acorns like other nuts, in oil, with salt or seasonings. They're great in mock meat loaf too. You can also dehydrate them, then grind them into flour. Roasted until black, acorns have also been used as a coffee. You can also use immature white oak leaves to make an outstanding wild wine.

Acorns are a good source of protein, fat, vitamins B3 and B6, folate, and pantothenic acid, plus the minerals calcium, magnesium, potassium, zinc, copper, and manganese. They usually contain the bitter polyphenolic compound, tannin, plus gallic acid and ellagitannin. Astringent, antiseptic, and antiviral, tannin has both anti tumor and anti carcinogenic activities. Although it's present in commercial Chinese tea, long-term intake is harmful, causing constipation and blocking calcium absorption. Prolonged high doses can cause kidney damage. Be sure you've removed it from the acorns you're going to eat.Native Americans and Europeans drank a decoction of the white oak cambium for diarrhea. They used it as a gargle for sore throat and as a douche for yeast infections. It's supposed to make a good wash for skin ulcers, ringworm, and other fungal skin infections. A cold compress is used for cuts and burns. People also inhaled the dried, powered cambium, like snuff, for nosebleeds.

RECIPE

Acorn Burgers

Here's a great-tasting, high-protein veggie burger, courtesy of common white oak acorns.

10 tbsp olive oil

1 bell pepper, chopped

3 celery stalks, chopped

5 scallions, chopped

4 cloves of garlic, chopped

¾ cup acorn flour (made from leached, dried, ground acorns, and available from Korean food websites)

2 cups oat flour

¾ cup lecithin granules

¼ cup flaxseeds, ground

¼ cup arrowroot

¼ cup white (mellow) miso

2 tbsp fresh basil, chopped

1 tbsp brewer's yeast

2 tsp oregano, ground

1 tsp celery seed, ground

¼ tsp black pepper, ground

1. Sauté the bell pepper, celery, scallions, and garlic in 2 tbsp of the olive oil for 10 minutes.
2. Mix this together with the remaining ingredients, except for the remaining olive oil.
3. Shape into 12 patties.
4. Fry for 5–10 minutes or until the undersides are lightly browned in the remaining olive oil.
5. Flip and fry the other sides until lightly browned.
6. Drain on paper towels.
   Yields: 12 burgers
   Preparation time: 30 minutes
   Cooking time: 20 minutes

Black Walnut
(*Juglans nigra*)

Family: Juglandaceae, the walnut family
Other name: Eastern black walnut

This large tree is one you won't want to miss. It's large and hard, so if you do miss it and walk into it, you'll injure yourself! Also, it produces large crops of exceptionally good nuts.

It grows 50–130 feet tall, with a trunk 1–4 feet in diameter, a crown spread of 70 feet, and no branches near the bottom. The dark brown, deeply furrowed, ropey-looking, ridged bark creates diamond patterns. Wooly, whitish buds, from ⅓ to ½ inch long and rounded at the tips, develop at the tips of the stout, smooth, greenish-brown to gray twigs in late summer.

Alternate, feather-compound leaves, 1–2 feet long, open in mid to late spring. They consist of ten to twenty-four lance-shaped, narrow, finely toothed, distinctly lemon-scented, unevenly paired leaflets. They're 3–5 inches long and about 1 inch broad, and they've pointed tips and uneven bases. Pale green above and downy below, they become yellow in autumn. The largest leaflets grow near the leaf's center, and unlike the related butternut (*J. cinerea,* an edible relative with spindle-shaped nuts), there's usually no terminal leaflet.

Inconspicuous male flowers grow on long, slender, green catkins, 3–4 inches long, in the spring. They dangle from the branches and release pollen into the air before the immature leaves become large enough to block this. At the tips of the branches at the same time also grow small, inconspicuous, green, pear-shaped, Y-tipped female flowers, in terminal clusters of two to five.

Ripening mainly in mid-autumn (a few nuts usually fall early, and you can sometimes find nuts that haven't rotted inside in late fall), the spherical,

lemony-scented, semi-fleshy fruits, 2–2½ inches across, grow singly or in tight groups of up to four. Don't mistake these delicious foods for tennis balls!

As autumn progresses, the thick husk turns yellow, then blackens as it decomposes and gets consumed by maggots. Inside the husk, a hard, furrowed black nutshell, 1½ inches across, encloses the bilaterally symmetrical nutmeat. It resembles the nutmeat of the store-bought English walnut (*Juglans regia*). Walnut shell fragments persist on the ground under the tree all year, making identification certain.

You can find black walnut trees on rich, well-drained soil, in deciduous woods, on bottom lands and floodplains, sometimes along residential streets, and in urban and suburban parks. It's native to the eastern half of North America and Utah, and similar edible relatives grow in the Southwest and on the West Coast.

Remove the husks by stomping on them with your shoes, or insect larvae in the husks will eat through the nutshell and consume the nutmeat.

Caution: Wear rubber gloves if you don't want a dye in the husks to stain your hands, and never touch the husks bare-handed if you're a public official. They contain substances that kill parasites.

In the field, you can crack the shell with a heavy rock. Do this on a level pavement or use a flat rock as an anvil, or the nut will roll away. You can also buy a heavy-duty nutcracker online to use at home. A nutpick or lobster pick makes removing the nutmeat easier.

You can air-dry the de husked nuts in a paper shopping bag. After a couple of weeks, they won't stain your fingers, and the nutmeat, which tastes like

walnuts and wine, matures and gets even better. The nuts last indefinitely in the shells, but become rancid in a few weeks if you don't freeze them after they've been shelled.

You can use black walnuts like other nuts, raw or roasted, but they're so strong-tasting, they're best used sparingly in recipes, lest they drown out all the other ingredients. I use one part black walnuts with three parts store-bought walnuts when I cook or bake with them.

People have allegedly pickled the small, immature nuts that fall from the trees in the summer, but I've never gotten this to work. They've also tapped the trees, like maple trees, in the winter to make syrup, but you've to boil the sap, outdoors, to ¼th its volume to make the sugary end-product.

Black walnuts provide protein and carbohydrates; the fatty acids linolenic, linoleic, palmitic, stearic, and oleic acids; vitamins B1, B2, B3, and E; and the minerals iron, magnesium, and potassium.

They also contain alkaloids with anticancer properties, but research is incomplete. A decoction of boiled husks, which contain tannin, juglandin, juglone, and juglandic acid, has been used internally to kill parasites. A compress of the decoction has been used for athlete's foot, ringworm. and other fungal infections of the skin. It's also been used to treat herpes and eczema, although there's no convincing evidence that it's effective.

A decoction of the cambium has been used for diarrhea and to stop milk production, but it can cause vomiting, and isn't safe. And an infusion of the leaves has been used to lower high blood pressure, something that should be tested scientifically with a blood pressure cuff.

RECIPE

Black Walnut Ambrosia

This creamy fruit pudding is all the better with the inclusion of black walnuts.

2 small wild apples or 1 Granny Smith apple, grated

1 peach, chopped

¼ cup black walnuts, English walnuts, or other nuts, chopped

¼ cup raisins

Ingredients to Blend

½ cup (or 6) pitted Medjool (soft) dates

3½ cups silken tofu, drained

10 strawberries, sliced

¼ cup lecithin granules

1 tbsp white (mellow) miso

1 tbsp clear liquid stevia

1 tbsp sunflower oil or any light vegetable oil

¼ tsp salt

¼ inch vanilla bean, scraped, or 1 tsp vanilla extract

1. Chop the dates in a food processor with the chopping blade or chop by hand.
2. Purée the ingredients to blend in a blender.
3. Stir in the fruits and nuts.
   Serves: 4–6
   Preparation time: 10 minutes

Ginkgo
(*Ginkgo biloba*)

Family: Ginkgophyta, the ginkgo family
Other name: Maidenhair tree

This is one of the most unusual and spectacular edibles of all. The only extant member of its phylum (one of the twelve top-level subdivisions of the plant kingdom), it's native to Laurasia, a supercontinent that included all present-day Northern Hemisphere continents before it split into today's continents. The ultimate survivor on this planet, the oldest fossils were found from 270 million years ago, preceding the dinosaurs by 39 million years. Some trees alive today are thought to be 2,500 years old, and six of them withstood the atomic bombing of Hiroshima! The tree even survived the asteroid impact that wiped out the dinosaurs, probably in the form of seeds that lay dormant until conditions improved, but it was thought to have finally met its end at the hands of Ice Age glaciers. Scientists, who knew the tree only through its fossils, were astonished when, in 1690, German botanist Engelbert Kaempfer found the tree in Japanese temple gardens, cultivated by the monks who'd rescued the tree from extinction in China in ancient times. This is speculative, but I'm willing to bet that it may even survive the presidency of Donald Trump! The botanical sensation of the eighteenth century, this living fossil was planted all over the world, and Johann Wolfgang von Goethe even wrote a poem about it. Having outlived all its diseases, it thrives, planted as a street tree and in parks, throughout the temperate world. It needs full or nearly full sunlight.

With furrowed, gray bark, this straight, slender, sparsely branched, columnar tree grows from 65 to 115 feet tall. Distinctive short, knobby spur shoots make the tree look like it's bullet-shaped twigs, making even winter identification a snap. The fan-shaped leaves, which are alternate and grow clustered on the spur shoots, are also unique. Many are notched or lobed, accounting for the specific name *biloba.* They grow from 2 to 4 inches across and turn saffron yellow in autumn. Raised, nearly parallel veins fan out from the leaf base, repeatedly branching, but never reconnecting. Other broad leaves evolved from ancestral needles that expanded. Only the ginkgoes and its extinct relatives formed broad leaves from needles that knit together, like the webbed feet of ducks. The wind-pollinated flowers are tiny and inconspicuous, hanging from the spur branches in short, slender clusters. They appear in early spring. The orange, spherical, fleshy, long-stalked, fruit ripens in autumn, growing to nearly 1 inch across. It contains butyric acid, first chemically characterized from rancid butter and also present in decaying flesh and vomit. It may have made herbivorous dinosaurs think there'd been a kill and predators could still be around, repelling the plant eaters; or perhaps some scavengers liked the rotten smell, as vultures do today, eating the fruit and dispersing the seeds through their droppings. What kind of animal would be content eating such awful food? It must have been an English dinosaur! A single, thin, light brown, woody, seamed, almond-sized nutshell inside the fruit encompasses a soft, greenish, almond-sized, ovate kernel, itself wrapped in a brown, papery membrane. This seed is the part you eat. Most modern trees are hermaphrodites, with male and female organs on the same tree, making pollination more efficient. But this primitive species has separate male trees, which are taller and more slender, and female trees, which are shorter and wider. Unlike more familiar beings, it's the female of this species that has the nuts!

Ginkgoes begin to ripen and fall to the ground in mid-autumn, although many trees don't drop fruit until late fall—the peak of the season. The crop diminishes, but you can still gather nuts from under some trees in the winter. If there's a cold winter, the nuts freeze, the smelly fruit vanishes, and the nuts remain good into early, or even mid-spring, when you find nothing under most trees, and a bumper crop under a few. The fruit is poisonous, and a very small minority of people get a rash from handling it, as it contains minute amounts of the same toxin as is in poison ivy (Toxicodendron radicans), so wearing rubber gloves, which also keep your hands from stinking, is an option to consider. Gather fruits or nuts from the ground. Those clinging to the branches are unripe). Remove and iscard the fruit as you gather. One of my friends, in an unsuccessful effort to hurry to the NYC subway before rush hour, didn't bother removing the fruit. Not only did she get a seat in a fully packed train, but by the time she reached her destination, she had the whole subway car to herself. Even the homeless had fled!

The raw nuts are poisonous. Rinse off the nuts in a colander, then bake them (Asian people boil them, but I think baking is better) in a preheated 300°F oven for 35 minutes, stirring occasionally. Be prepared for a smelly kitchen. Place the cooked nuts on a towel or rag, and gently hit the shells with an empty water glass or mallet, with just enough force to crack the shells without shattering them. Enjoy the shelled nuts as is, or add them to soups, casseroles, stir-fry dishes, grains, beans, casseroles, or any savory recipe. Soft and chewy, they taste like a combination of green peas and limburger cheese. Traditional Japanese cooks will tell you not to eat more than seven ginkgoes at a serving. You should only eat small amounts of ginkgoes the first time, and slowly increase the serving, in case you've a sensitivity to this food. Eating huge quantities, especially in children, has been documented to cause poisoning by 4-*O*-methylpyridoxine. I've never seen this happen, and the convulsions it causes are cured by vitamin B6, but the best approach is to enjoy this food in moderation.

Ginkgoes provide vitamins C, B1, B3, B6, and folate, plus the minerals copper, iron, magnesium, phosphorus, potassium, sodium, as well as calories, protein, and flavonoids. A traditional medicinal plant, an alcohol extract of the leaves contains antioxidant and anti inflammatory ginkgolides, heterosides, and vasodilators. Reputedly good for memory, it's prescribed by doctors in Germany, but a recent mathematical compilation of many studies convincingly shows that it doesn't work for healthy people, or for victims of Alzheimer's disease. This contradicts my own experiment, showing that it does work: One whiff of the fruit and you'll never forget the awful smell! Some research shows that the extract is good for headaches, tinnitus, intermittent claudication, and depression, possibly because it improves blood flow in the arteries and capillaries. It's also used for circulatory problems, asthma, toxic shock syndrome, bleeding, bruising, heart and kidney disorders, glucose intolerance, and edema. The extract contains an analog of platelet-activating factor, intervening in the formation of arterial plaques. It also is supposed to destroy free radicals, which might make it lower the risk of cancer. However, other research shows that it doesn't work for anything, and that using it medicinally can have bad results. Obviously, the final word isn't in yet. In Chinese folk medicine, the fruit is applied as a dressing for wounds. An infusion of the fruit is used for indigestion and as an expectorant for asthma, bronchitis, and tuberculosis. But the fruit is poisonous, both internally and externally, and it's quite repulsive, so I think you'll get even more benefits by avoiding it! Eating ginkgo nuts is considered very healthful in China and Japan (as well as on my foraging tours). It's supposed to assist digestion and reduce the effects of excessive alcohol. The nuts could have similar benefits to the leaf extract (or none), but this hasn't been tested.

RECIPE

Ginkgo Stir-Fry

Ginkgo nuts add their unique flavor to what could otherwise be a standard Chinese stir-fry. Serve over brown rice or noodles.

⅓ cup sesame oil, or as needed

2 tbsp dark sesame oil, or as needed

3 cups lettuce or other greens, chopped

1 19-oz. package of firm tofu, drained and diced

2 tsp fresh ginger, chopped

4 cloves of garlic, chopped

¾ cup cooked, shelled ginkgo nuts

3 celery stalks, sliced

2 bell peppers, sliced

1 small onion, chopped

Sauce Ingredients

1 cup vegetable stock

1 tbsp arrowroot or kudzu

3 tbsp dark miso

1 tsp salt

1. Purée the sauce ingredients in a blender.
2. Meanwhile, mix the oils and heat 1½ tbsp of this in a wok or frying pan.
3. Stir-fry the ginkgoes for 3 or 4 minutes or until the brown, papery membranes begin to separate from the nuts, and set aside.
4. Add more oil as needed, stir-fry the lettuce for 2 minutes, and set aside in a bowl separate from the ginkgoes.
5. Add another 2 tbsp of the oils and stir-fry the tofu with the ginger for 3 minutes.
6. Add the garlic, stir-fry for another 2 minutes, and set aside with the lettuce.

7. Stir-fry the celery for 3 minutes with more oil and add to the lettuce mixture.
8. Stir-fry the bell peppers for 3 minutes with more oil and add this to the lettuce mixture as well.
9. Stir-fry the onion for 3 minutes with still more oil and also add this to the lettuce mixture.
10. Remove and discard the brown membranes from the now-cooled ginkgoes.
11. Return all ingredients to the wok, stir in the sauce, and bring to a boil over high heat, stirring constantly.
12. Simmer, covered, over low heat for another 10 minutes, stirring occasionally.

Serves: 6
Preparation time: 30 minutes
Cooking time: 20 minutes

Root Veggies

Roots are often plants' storage organs, so food is stored underground in autumn and released to growing aboveground parts in mid-spring. With some exceptions, the time to dig them up is from fall through early spring, with a hiatus during the winter when the ground is covered with snow and frozen, and aboveground foliage has been destroyed. However, global warming is shortening winters and thereby increasing the root season, although each year is different.

Common Evening Primrose (*Oenothera biennis*)

Family: Onagraceae, the willowherb or evening primrose family

Other names: Weedy evening primrose, German rampion, hog weed, King's cure-all, fever-plant, evening star

This native biennial, widespread throughout the NE, first appears in early spring, emerging from a white, fleshy taproot, noticeably pink toward the top, and grows from 2 inches to over 1 foot long. It produces a tight basal rosette of elliptical to lance-shaped leaves the first year. From 2 inches to 1 foot long with ragged edges, they're light green, hairy, and sometimes slightly toothed. Each leaf has a distinct, white midrib, and frosty weather adds reddish tints to the leaves. The rosette is finally destroyed by lots of very icy weather at the end of autumn, but rebounds in early spring of the second year. In mid-spring, it then produces a stout, hairy, erect, light green to reddish stem that reaches 4–7 feet in height. It may be unbranched, or branched near the base. The alternate leaves are similar to the basal leaves, but smaller, and grow in a spiral pattern. The long-stemmed, four-petaled, yellow, radially symmetric flowers grow 1–2 inches across. They're long stemmed, pale yellow, and faintly lemon scented. They grow in terminal panicles from the tops of the branches and open in the evening, attracting moths, then close by noon. The petal bases fuse, forming a long, narrow tube, and the distinctive, four-parted stigma forms an X shape in the center of the flower. Green sepals droop beneath the flowers. Each flower develops into a hard, woody, cylindrical, flat-topped seed capsule, green at first, growing up to 1½ inches long. It's full of tiny, elongated, hard, reddish-black seeds. This capsule persists through the winter, splitting into four sections.

Common evening primrose grows in sunny places. It's quite at home in poor, sandy soil and does great in fields and dunes near the seashore. You can also find it in parks, empty lots, disturbed sites, prairies, glades, thickets, and along roadsides. The root is in season in early spring, before the stored food is depleted by rapid mid-spring growth of the aboveground parts, and in autumn, when food is stored underground again. The root is good to use all winter, but once the aboveground parts are obliterated by the cold, you can't locate it anymore. Dig it up with a shovel or any other digging implement. In loose sand, you can sometimes just pull it up with your hands. The immature stem of the second-year plant is good to use in mid-spring while it's flexible and the center is tender. Harvest it with a knife or clippers. The leaves are best in early spring and late fall, although you can roast them in the summer too. Just strip them off the rosette.

The flowers are in season in the summer and fall, when you can pinch them off with your fingers. The seeds are usable when they turn blackish and harden in the fall. Break open the woody fruit capsule and pour them into a bag.

The taproot is the best part to use, with the most food for your effort, and a complex flavor, like black pepper, and radish, but with sweet overtones, and a mucilaginous, okra-like texture. It slightly thickens soups, stews, and sauces. It may cause loose bowels in some people, if eaten raw in quantity, and it's spicy nature can make the throats of susceptible individuals burn when eaten raw, so it's much better to cook it in any vegetable dish that needs a touch of heat and will benefit from being thickened. It cooks in 15–20 minutes. It can overpower milder ingredients if used in quantity, but easily holds its own in curries, chili, and salsas. I find the tender, young leaves in the center of the young rosette too hairy to enjoy raw, or even cooked in most dishes, but they're fine cooked and puréed in cream soups and cream sauces, my preferred treatment for hairy wild greens, and you also can roast them like kale chips too. The peeled young stem, after it's been parboiled 1 minute to make peeling the rind easier, is like spicy celery, excellent in salads, or cooked in a wide range of vegetable dishes. Use it before it becomes too fibrous. The mild-flavored flowers are insubstantial and take a bit of time to collect, but if you've the patience to harvest them, they'll add color to salads, and they make a fine, exotic garnish. You can also grind the roasted seeds and use them as a peppery seasoning.

The roots haven't been analyzed nutritionally, but the leaves contain quercetin, a bioflavonoid that keeps blood vessels healthy. A poultice of the root is used for bruises and to speed wound healing, but hasn't been tested. A tea made of the dried roots has been used for menstrual cramps, but I haven't had a chance to try it yet! Oil pressed from the seeds, which you must buy, contains gamma-linolenic acid, gamma-linoleic acid (an anticlotting agent), and vitamin F (essential fatty acids). Gamma-linoleic acid is turned into the prostaglandin PGE1 in the body. This short-lived, fatty hormone regulates many metabolic functions. It's used for menopause, rheumatoid arthritis, memory loss, alcoholism, weight loss, bronchitis, eczema, chronic fatigue, multiple sclerosis, attention deficit disorder, and to prevent heart disease. There are indications that it's beneficial for some of these conditions, but research is incomplete.

Caution: Don't use this plant if you suffer from epilepsy. It can also cause headaches, skin rashes, and nausea in sensitive individuals.

RECIPE

Primrose Quinoa Soup

North American peppery common evening primrose and South American nutty quinoa complement each other perfectly, so with a few other vegetables and appropriate seasonings, they lead to a wonderful, filling soup.

¼ cup olive oil

2 cups common evening primrose root, sliced

2 carrots, sliced

2 celery stalks, sliced

4 scallions, sliced

2 garlic cloves, chopped

4 cups vegetable stock

2 tbsp arrowroot or kudzu

2 tbsp white (mellow) miso

½ cup quinoa

½ cup beluga beans

¼ cup parsley

1 tsp oregano, ground

1 tsp tarragon, ground

½ tsp rosemary, ground

¼ tsp black pepper, or to taste, ground

1. Sauté the common evening primrose, carrots, celery, scallions, and garlic in the olive oil for 10 minutes.
2. Meanwhile, mix the arrowroot and miso into the stock.
3. Rinse the quinoa in a strainer with cold, running water for 1 minute, to remove the bitter saponins.
4. Combine all ingredients in a saucepan and bring to a boil over medium heat, stirring often.
5. Reduce the heat to low and simmer, covered, for 20 minutes or until the quinoa is tender.
   Serves: 6
   Preparation time: 30 minutes
   Cooking time: 20 minutes

Wild Carrot
(*Daucus carota*)

Family: Apiaceae or Umbelliferae, the umbelliferous, celery, carrot, or parsley family
Other name: Queen Anne's lace, bird's nest, bishop's lace

This is one of my favorite root vegetables. It's quite common, and there are habitats where the roots are quite large. Its deadly look-alike that's not hard to differentiate, if you pay attention to the salient distinguishing carrot-teristics! This European biennial is the same species as the store-bought carrot, only it went feral and reverted to the subspecies that's the ancestor of the familiar orange variant. The first year carrot produces a basal rosette only. This consists of long-stalked, oblong, lacy, feather-compound leaves growing up to 10 inches long and 4 inches wide. These divide two or three times, and arise from hairy leafstalks. It appears very early in the spring. Under the center of the rosette, you'll find a taproot, 2–8 inches long, that smells strongly of carrot and usually produces side branches. The plant dies to the ground when winter comes, but the rosette returns early the following spring. Then, in mid-spring, the second-year plant grows an upright, branched, hairy stem, 2–3 feet tall. The alternate leaves look just like the basal leaves, only smaller. Twice-branched, flat-topped, terminal flower clusters, 3 inches wide (configured like the spokes of an umbrella), appear on tops of the stems in the summer and early autumn. At the tip of the umbrella spokes, you'll see tiny, white, five-petaled flowers called florets, ⅛ inch across. Many flowers mean more pollination and lots of seeds, and because so many flowers are clustered together, they're as visible to the pollinating insects as they're to us. This flower head is what people recognize as Queen Anne's lace. Often, in the center of the cluster of white florets, there's 1 purple floret, symbolizing a drop of blood that fell when Queen Anne pricked her finger with a needle while

stitching her lace. In mid-summer and fall, the florets fall off, then the flower head contracts and becomes concave (like a cup or bird's nest), and umbels of tiny, bristly, ovoid, ribbed seeds, about ⅛ inch long, develop. They go from reddish purple to green, and finally become brown. The skeleton of the stems and seed heads persist into early spring.

Botanical manuals list wild carrots as growing in sunny, dry, sandy soil, open fields, meadows, roadsides, disturbed habitats, and pastures, but the roots vary in size. The best places to collect them are dry, sandy fields, especially near the seashore, where the plants get lots of sunlight and little competition from grass or other plants, which do poorly under such conditions. The other place for big carrots is in pastures, where they take advantage of the extra nutrients released into the soil by the manure. Dig up the roots of plants in the basal rosette form in early spring and fall (you can't find them in the winter), when they store food. In mid-spring, the food disappears from the root and is distributed to the aboveground parts. A shovel is the best implement for harvesting, but smaller hand tools, and even pointed sticks, will work too, especially in sandy soil. The seeds ripen in late summer. I used to think they perished in the winter, but my then-ten-year-old foraging expert daughter, Violet (who knows all the plants and co leads many of my foraging tours), took a closer look and found completely good, fragrant seeds in what I thought were dead seed heads in early spring, meaning that you can collect them throughout the winter too! Break off the seed heads while the seeds are still somewhat green, or brown, and use them fresh or dried. It's easy to pull the seeds off the seed head, and a small amount goes a long way.

Wild carrots are tougher, stronger tasting, and less sweet than store-bought carrots. Unless you like to chew a lot, they're not as good in salads, but way better in cooked recipes, from soups to carrot cakes, where their texture becomes chewy rather than mushy. They cook in about 15–20 minutes. Some people eat the flowers, but I don't care for their somewhat bitter flavor. The leaves are non-poisonous, but, again, too tough for most people to eat, unless you like eating the carrot tops of store-bought carrots. However, if you make your own soup stock, where you boil strong-tasting veggies with herbs, then strain them all out in the end, they're a wonderful addition. Carrot seeds, on the other hand, have become one of my favorite savory seasonings, excellent in sauces, soups, stews, and a large variety of savory dishes. They're a little like caraway and celery seeds, but more versatile, and they also enhance the flavor of wild carrots. The raw seeds are much stronger tasting than dried ones.

Because they're not orange, wild carrots lack the beta-carotene of store-bought carrots, but they do contain vitamins C, D, E, K, B1, B6, and biotin; the minerals potassium, calcium, magnesium, phosphorus, and sodium; and some trace minerals such as lithium, as well as acetylcholine, gamma-linolenic acid, histidine, lycopene, quercetin, tryptophan, tyrosine, and close to fifty other biologically active substances. Various parts of this plant have been used as home remedies for thousands of years. They haven't been tested scientifically, but they're safe for conditions that aren't serious. An infusion of the leaves, flowers, and stems is considered to be a gentle diuretic, stimulating the flow of urine and the excretion of waste by the kidneys. It's also good for bladder problems. It's supposedly a carminative, as is a tea of the seeds, soothing the digestive tract and useful for digestive disorders and gas. The leaves contain porphyrins, which stimulate the pituitary gland to signal the gonads to increase sex hormone levels. It also stimulates the uterus and brings on delayed menstruation, so don't drink this tea if you're pregnant. On the other hand, the increase in sex hormone levels is supposed to make this tea an aphrodisiac. Unfortunately, this isn't true. A girlfriend and I disproved it: We made ten cups of carrot leaf tea, and only the first six worked! Eating a teaspoon of crushed seeds has been used for birth control, and was used by Hippocrates (who never became pregnant). It does interfere with implantation of the embryo into the uterus of mice, and it blocks progesterone synthesis in humans, so it could reduce the risk of pregnancy in humans, but it's only completely effective when you also hold one carrot seed firmly between the knees!

Caution: Poison hemlock (*Conium maculatum*) looks so much like wild carrots at all stages that some foraging teachers won't include wild carrots in their foraging classes or books, although they're not hard to tell apart. The leafstalks of wild carrot are hairy. You just have to look at them closely to see the hairs. Remember, Queen Anne had hairy legs! Poison hemlock and, its somewhat less deadly similar relative, fool's parsley (*Aethusa cynapium*) have as much hair as the top of my head (none)! The roots of wild carrots smell strongly of carrots. Its poisonous relatives smell musty and unpleasant. If the root doesn't have a clear and distinct carrot smell or the plant has no hairs on the leafstalks, don't eat it. Poison hemlock stops the brain from communicating with the heart and lungs, causing paralysis and death. The ancient Greek philosopher, Socrates, considered the wisest man in the world, was executed with poison hemlock at the age of seventy for "corrupting the youth," by teaching independent and critical thinking, something no educator has ever dared to do again in the intervening 3,000 years: It's called No Child Left Behind!

Fortunately, poison hemlock isn't always fatal. In fact, there's a famous American who wouldn't be harmed by this plant: Donald Trump — he has no brain and no heart!

RECIPE

Beluga Dal

Beluga beans cooked with Indian spices and wild carrots are filling, tasty, and satisfying. (Note: No whales were harmed in the production of this recipe!)

6 cups vegetable stock

2 cup beluga beans

6 tbsp vegan butter substitute or olive oil

1 cup wild or store-bought carrots, grated

1 4-inch stick of sassafras root, or 1 cinnamon stick

⅓ cup field garlic or 2 scallions, chopped

½ tsp coriander seed, ground

¼ tsp cayenne hot pepper, or to taste (optional)

¼ cup white (mellow) miso

1. Simmer all ingredients together except the miso for 40 minutes or until the beans are tender.
2. Drain and stir the miso into the liquid.
3. Remove the sassafras or cinnamon.
4. Pour the liquid with the miso back into the mixture.
   Serves: 6–8
   Preparation time: 10 minutes
   Cooking time: 40 minutes

Wild Parsnip
(*Pastinaca sativa*)

Family: Apiaceae or Umbelliferae, the umbelliferous, celery, carrot, or parsley family

This feral European vegetable escaped cultivation to become both uglier and tastier, with a single, thick, whitish taproot that can grow over 1 foot long that smells like store-bought parsnips. A biennial, it starts growing in early spring as a basal rosette, 6 inches high. Its large, stalked, unbranched, feather-compound leaves get close to 1 foot long and 4 inches wide. From five to fifteen, variable, coarse, ovate to oblong, deeply lobed, saw-toothed leaflets extend from both sides of a midrib. The basal rosette reappears at the same time the second year, followed by a stout, deeply grooved, hollow, branching, hairless stem in mid-spring. This grows from 3 to 5 feet tall. Long-stalked, flat-topped, terminal, umbrella-like flower clusters appear at the top of the stems, without bracts. The stems divide twice, ending with fifteen to twenty-five umbrella-like clusters of twelve to thirty-five long-stalked, yellow flowers—hundreds of five-petaled flowers, ⅛ inch across, in total. The flowers develop into long-stalked seeds in late summer and fall, which may persist into the winter. Growing ¼ inch long, they're flat, oval, ribbed, and fragrant.

As with many edible biennials, the taproot under the basal rosette is good to eat from fall through early spring, although you can't find it in the winter, when there's no foliage. Once the flower stalk appears, the root becomes as tough as wood. You can still cook it, but it'll taste like cooked wood!

Water hemlock (*Cicuta maculata*) has basal leaves that may look like wild parsnip's, but some are divided twice instead of once, the flowers are white instead of yellow, and instead of a single taproot, its fleshy roots grow in bundles. Beware!

The two plants can grow side by side, and one bite of water hemlock, North America's deadliest plant, can kill. Poison hemlock's (*Conium maculatum*) leaves are much more finely divided than wild parsnip's. The flowers are white, not yellow. The stem has purple blotches, and the roots smell musty, not like parsnips. Nevertheless, people who have taken no heed of the identifying characteristics of either plant have confused the two and poisoned themselves. On the plus side, unlike water hemlock, it takes several bites to bring on death! Giant hogweed or giant cow parsley (*Heracleum mantegazzianum*) has feather-compound leaves and umbrella-like flowers, like the wild parsnip, but it's much larger, from 6 to 15 feet (sometimes 21 feet) tall, with a stout, bumpy, bristly, dark reddish-purple stem and hollow, spotted leafstalks. The leaves get 3–5 feet long. Contact causes such a severe rash that public officials, terrified of equally awful lawsuits, assiduously have it eradicated whenever it's spotted, so I have yet to see it myself.

Except for a few southern states, wild parsnips grow throughout North America, in sunny spots on damp, disturbed soil. You'll find them in empty lots, wetlands, fields, and edge habitats, along roadsides, and near the seashore. Dig up the taproots with a shovel or trowel. Don't touch the leaves without gloves (or put your hands inside a plastic bag) if your skin is sweaty and you're subsequently exposed to sunlight, or you might get a severe, blistering rash. Use the root like store-bought parsnips, cooked about 20 minutes, in soups, stews, casseroles, or any dish that calls for cooked root vegetables. They're good steamed too, but don't be shocked by how much sweeter and flavorful it is than parsnips you buy. The roots are marginally edible raw, but tough and stringy, and eating too much raw may have a laxative effect.

Don't eat other parts of this plant: Back in the early 1980s, at the very onset of my career, I appeared on a Manhattan public access cable-TV show, when cable-TV was new, called *The Coca Crystal Show*. As indicated by the title, the people running the show (who were very friendly and supportive of my work) were all refugees from the 1960s, but after demonstrating wild plants, including wild parsnips, through a choking haze of marijuana and tobacco smoke, I got to meet an aged man named Vincent Titus, who regularly read his poetry on the show. He'd been Ernest Hemingway's drinking buddy and served with him in the Abraham Lincoln Brigade during the Spanish Civil War in the 1930s, fighting with the Communists against the Fascists. Hemingway supposedly modeled Robert Jordan, the hero of his masterpiece *For Whom the Bells Toll*, after Titus! Titus, who passed away the following year, told me that European medieval monks, living in monasteries, had to be self-sufficient, so they ate everything they grew, including parsnip leaves, and this poisoned them! His knowledge of history was convincing (and he was so old that he might have seen this first-hand!), and no traditional culture uses parsnip leaves or seeds for food, so use only the roots.

Parsnips provide vitamin C, and the minerals calcium, potassium, and phosphorus, plus fiber. They have more calories than most wild foods, something wilderness survivalists always covet. An infusion of parsnip leaves has been recommended for diabetes and for kidney and urinary problems, but they can also lower the blood sugar too much, consistent with their toxicity, and should be avoided.

RECIPE

Wild Turkish Casserole

Slightly thickened with rice and lentils, this mixture of wild and store-bought vegetables melds into a wonderful veggie casserole, prepared in the style of Turkish cuisine.

2 cups curly dock (see p. 94) leaves, or beet greens, chopped

1½ cups wild or store-bought parsnips, sliced

3 tomatoes, chopped

1 red onion, chopped

½ cup burdock root or daikon, thinly sliced

2 celery stalks, sliced

¼ cup fresh dill weed, chopped

¼ cup cilantro or parsley, chopped

¼ cup lentils

2 tbsp long-grain brown rice

2 tbsp za'atar (a blend of seasonings available in Mideast stores and websites)

2 tbsp olive oil

1 tbsp Vege-Sal or ½ tbsp salt, or to taste

2 cloves of garlic, chopped

1. Mix all ingredients together in an oiled casserole dish and bake, covered, in a preheated 350°F oven for 1 hour or until the rice is soft.
   Serves: 6
   Preparation time: 10 minutes
   Cooking time: 1 hour

Wild Ginger
(*Asarum canadense*)

Family: Aristolochiaceae, the birthwort family
Other names: Indian ginger, Canada snakeroot, coltsfoot

This stemless perennial trails the ground, growing from 4 to 12 inches long. A shallow, fleshy, branched rhizome, under 1/2 inch thick, unites the aboveground parts to form colony, and the whole plant smells like ginger. It has but two leaves. Basal, smooth edged, long stalked, and heart shaped, they grow from 3 to 6 inches across. Growing from the crotch of the two hairy leafstalks and obscured by the leaves, hangs a solitary, slender-stemmed, dark brown-purple flower, blooming from early to mid spring. Three reddish, petal-like sepals fuse to create a protective layer surrounding a cream colored ovary. After ants pollinate it, it develops into a small, leathery, six-parted fruit capsule that ripens in the summer.

Wild ginger grows in partially or fully shaded, undisturbed forests, often near rivers. Violets (see p. 66), which are edible, have heart-shaped leaves, but they're toothed, unpaired, and odorless, although this didn't stop someone on one of my tours, who wanted wild ginger very badly, from asking whether violets were wild ginger. There are other similar species of wild ginger (*Asarum acuminatum* and *A. reflexum*) that grow in the Northeast, but I haven't found them yet in New York or anywhere else yet. On the other hand, I occasionally see European wild ginger (*A. europaeum*), an introduced plant, with leaves and flowers that are much larger than the native species, escaped from cultivation and spreading in New York and other parts of the Northeast. You can use all these relatives the same way.

One of the common names of wild ginger is coltsfoot, but there's a totally different, unrelated, wild medicinal plant (*Tussilago farfara*) with that name, another reason to check scientific names. A lack of scientific names kept me confused for over three decades: George Washington Carver, a great scientist, called wild ginger leaves "the acme of wild plants," but they're awful. Then, in 2014, leading a foraging event in Duke University in North Carolina, I was introduced to a Deep South species of wild ginger (*A. arifolia*), with arrow shaped leaves. Carver lived in the Deep South, so he must have been using the southern species!

Although wild ginger's rhizomes are good all year, and the leaves sometimes persist into the winter, you usually can't find or dig it up then, so the end of early spring through fall are the best times to harvest them. A shovel or trowel makes the rhizomes easy to dig up, although you can sometimes get them with your fingers. Dig only where the plant is very abundant. Use the rhizome, without the roots, fresh, finely chopped, or dried and ground into a powder in a spice grinder, the same as store-bought ginger. The plants are unrelated, but the flavor is quite similar. Wild ginger is superb in fruit dishes, baked recipes, curries, ice cream, pies, pudding, or any other traditional recipe that calls for ginger. It's a great herb tea, steeped for 20 minutes in water just off the boil.

There's no info about wild ginger's nutritional content, but it's an important traditional medicinal plant. Surprisingly, Native Americans independently discovered that it's medicinal uses are similar to unrelated store-bought ginger. They used a decoction of the rhizomes for gastric conditions and nausea, as well as for fever, menstrual cramps, and coughs. They also used it to prevent food spoilage, and it does contain aristolochic acid, which kills bacteria, and a related Asian species is used the same way in traditional Chinese medicine. Native Americans and colonists used the powdered rhizomes like snuff, inhaling it for sinus congestion and headaches. They also applied the crushed rhizomes externally onto inflamed or infected cuts, and onto wounds. They even poured the cooled decoction into infected ears. This has not been tested, but unchecked ear infections can lead to permanent hearing loss. Herbalists also use the rhizome as part of herbal formulas for circulatory system stimulation. However, even though this herb and its relatives have been used for centuries, recent research has shown that the aristolochic acid has caused kidney damage and urinary tract cancer when herbs containing it were used for weight loss, and the FDA has issued warnings about the use of this herb. What to make about this contradictory info? Everyone needs to make their own choice, but personally, I still use small amounts of wild ginger on rare occasions as a seasoning. I wouldn't use it in quantity, and I don't drink wild ginger tea (I'm not a tea drinker.)

RECIPE

Wild Teriyaki Sauce

With wild ginger replacing commercial ginger and stevia replacing sugar, you can make an authentic, healthful, and very tasty traditional Japanese sauce. Use it in stir-fried dishes and on vegetables. Because the tamari soy sauce is salty, you can eliminate any salt from the recipe you're seasoning with this sauce, or add salt at the table as needed.

1 cup tamari soy sauce

½ cup water

¼ cup mirin (Japanese rice wine) or white wine

2 tbsp arrowroot

4 cloves of garlic

1 tbsp wild ginger or fresh commercial ginger

1 tsp liquid or powdered stevia

1. Purée all ingredients in a blender.
2. Transfer to a saucepan and bring to a boil over medium heat, stirring constantly.
3. Reduce the heat to low and simmer, uncovered, for 5 minutes, stirring occasionally.
   Yields: 1½ cups
   Preparation/cooking time: 15 minutes

Burdock (*Arctium minus* and *A. lappa*)

Family: Asteraceae, the aster or composite family
Other names: Love leaves, beggar's buttons, cockle buttons, harebur, gobo, thorny bur, clothbur, gobo

Here's another very tasty common plant—actually two very similar species—that you'll love, once you learn how to harvest and use it. Burdock is a biennial, forming a basal rosette in its first year. The huge, wedge-shaped leaves grow up to 2 feet long and 1 foot across. The leaf's undersurface is whitish, due to a mat of very short, fine hairs. Bitter dock (Rumex obtusifolia), with different food uses, lacks these hairs, and the two plants may grow side by side. Burdock's purple-green leafstalks reach 1½ feet long and ¾ inch across. Common burdock's (*Arctium minus*) are hollow, not furrowed. Greater burdock's (*A. lappa*) are solid, with a groove on the upper surface, and this is the larger of the two species. This Eurasian plant has such a long, deep, stout taproot that as you dig and pull, it feels like there's a hungry Asian person on the other end pulling in the opposite direction! The root can grow up to 4 feet long and 3 inches wide. With an outer rind and inner core, it's whitish after you scrub off the soil, and smells like potatoes.

The second year, it develops a basal rosette again in early spring, then bolts in mid-spring, growing an erect stem from the center of the rosette. This reaches 2–5 feet in height in common burdock, and up to 9 feet tall in greater burdock. The stem's alternate leaves are smaller than but similar to the basal leaves, getting progressively smaller toward the top. Tiny, purple-pink flowers coat the spherical, composite flower heads, which which look like purple shaving brushes, extending from spherical, green bases. Common burdock's flower heads

are short-stemmed and ¾ inch across. Greater burdock's are long-stemmed and 1½ inches across. The light brown burrs are also spherical and the same size as the flowers. They're coated with tiny hooks, so after they stuck to the dog of Swiss electrical engineer, George Mestal, in 1941, they inspired him to invent Velcro. Many small, hard, curved, inedible brown seeds grow inside. People have confused cocklebur (*Xanthium* spp.) with burdock because it also has burrs, but they're arranged in spirals, and the rest of the plant is completely different from burdock. You'd have to be very careless to poison yourself with this plant.

Burdock can grow in full sun or partial shade. It's especially common on disturbed soil, and also grows in backyards, untended gardens, empty lots, overgrown fields, meadows, edge habitats, and urban parks. You can eat the root of the first-year plant from early spring until the leaves disappear in late fall. It's deep, so look for it where the soil is loose, not rocky. Use a shovel if possible. A trowel is harder work. Harvest after it's rained, when the soil is loose. The Japanese remove and discard the outer layer of the root for cosmetic reasons. This is unnecessary, and you're throwing away half your work. Scrub the root with a metal scouring brush under running water to remove the soil. Slice as thinly as possible, using the finest blade of a food processor, or a sharp knife and diagonal cuts. Cook in moist heat (in soups, stews, rice, or casseroles) for at least part of the preparation, to tenderize the otherwise-tough root. Burdock root has an earthy, potato–artichoke flavor, great in a wide variety of recipes that call for roots. After only 32 years, it occurred to me that the tough texture could be used to advantage, so I steamed, marinated, and baked the slices, resulting in vegan beef jerky (see the accompanying recipe), which everyone on my tours loves.

Once the stem of the second-year plant appears, in mid-spring, the root becomes too tough to eat, but these young stems, up to 1½ feet tall, are delicious too. For 31 years, I laboriously peeled the stems, parboiled them for 1–2 minutes to get rid of the bitterness, and used them like artichoke hearts. They're delicious, but I finally realized I was wrong. You parboil the stems first, let them cool, then peel them in a fraction of the time it takes to peel them raw. The parboiled stems are great in nearly any vegetable, bean, or grain dish, but they're only in season for a couple of weeks, around the end of mid-spring and the beginning of late spring. Fortunately, they freeze well after they're cooked. Some foragers use the leafstalks in the spring, summer, and fall, the same way as the immature stems. It's more work for less food, but it's doable, especially with greater burdock. The leaves are so bitter, no matter how you prepare them, that, unless you're a goat or iguana, they taste as bad as English food!

Burdock root is a good source of vitamins B6 and C, plus the minerals magnesium, phosphorus, potassium, manganese, and sodium. It's an excellent source of inulin, a polysaccharide that doesn't provoke an insulin response and isn't absorbed through the digestive tract. It's great for people with diabetes or low blood sugar. A decoction is considered to be a blood purifier or detoxifier in traditional European and East Asian herbal medicine, and burdock root is sold to use as a tea in health food stores for skin, liver, and kidney problems. It hasn't been tested scientifically, and drinking the tea makes no sense to me, since you can eat the delicious root and get any medicinal benefits it may convey that way. A poultice made with the chopped leaves, clay (you can substitute fresh kitty litter), and water (sometimes along with spearmint leaves) is the best home remedy for bruises, and I've seen it work more than once. Burn care workers have used the leaves to inhibit bacterial growth, speed healing, and ease the changing of dressings for burn victims, but I'm not aflame to try this out on myself!

RECIPE

Vegan Beef Jerky

Burdock root isn't as soft as commercial root vegetables. In fact, it can have a chewy texture. You can turn this into an advantage by marinating slices with the kinds of ingredients traditionally used for making jerky, then slowly baking it to create something similar, but more healthful, human, and environmentally sound than the original.

2 cups vegetable stock

4 cups of burdock root, thinly sliced

3½ cups Savory Marinade (see below)

1. Pressure cook the roots in a steamer rack over the stock for 5 minutes, or steam them for 30 minutes. Reserve the stock for other recipes or use it as a tea.
2. Combine the burdock with the Savory Marinade and marinate overnight, stirring occasionally if possible.
3. Drain (you can use the marinade repeatedly) and allow to cool.
4. Spread the burdock strips onto 3 nonstick baking pads placed on 3 cookie sheets, or onto 3 oiled cookie sheets.
5. Bake in a preheated 300°F oven for 30–40 minutes or until chewy, but not crisp.
   Yields: 3 cups
   Preparation time: 30 minutes
   Marination time: 6 hours to overnight
   Cooking time: 30 + 40 minutes

RECIPE

Savory Marinade

Here's a simple basic marinade you can use to add additional flavor to everything from mushrooms to tofu. Just soak the food in the marinade from 6 hours to overnight, refrigerated. Then drain and bake. Foods cooked in this way come out fantastically flavored, even if they're bland beforehand.

1 cup apple cider vinegar

1 cup apple juice

1 cup sesame oil

½ cup olive oil

½ cup wine vinegar

½ cup tamari soy sauce

5 peeled, uncut cloves of garlic

1 tbsp bayberry leaves or ½ tsp bay leaves

½ tbsp of fresh wild or commercial ginger, chopped

1 tsp liquid stevia

1 tsp smoked paprika

1 tsp chili paste or hot sauce, or to taste

½ tsp black peppercorns

¼ tsp whole cloves

1. Place the peppercorns, cloves, and bayberry leaves in a mesh bag or tea ball, so they don't get mixed up with the foods to be marinated (optional).
2. Combine all ingredients.
   Yields: 4½ cups
   Preparation time: 5 minutes

RECIPE

Burdock Stem Casserole

This is a like a typical casserole, with layers of pasta and sautéed vegetables, plus a sauce, and some "cheese." The difference is an especially delicious sauce, plus wild burdock's especially tasty stems.

¼ cup olive oil

1 large red onion, chopped

1 yellow or red bell pepper, chopped

2½ cups parboiled, peeled, immature burdock stems, coarsely sliced

½ tsp Vege-Sal or ¼ tsp salt, or to taste

2 tomatoes, chopped

3½ cups slightly undercooked, whole-grain fusilli, or other pasta

3½ cups Garlic Sauce (see below)

¼ cup vegan Parmesan cheese

1. Sauté the onion in the olive oil for 10 minutes.
2. Add the bell pepper, burdock stem, and Vege-Sal, and sauté for another 10 minutes.
3. Pour half the Garlic Sauce into an oiled baking dish.
4. Spread the pasta onto the sauce.
5. Spread the tomatoes onto the pasta.
6. Spread the sautéed vegetables on top of the tomatoes and pasta.
7. Pour the rest of the Garlic Sauce on top of the vegetables.
8. Sprinkle the vegan Parmesan on top of the sauce.
9. Bake in a preheated 350°F oven for 40 minutes or until bubbly.

   Serves 6–8

   Preparation time: 40 minutes

   Cooking time: 40 minutes

RECIPE

Garlic Sauce

This creamy sauce is great to pour on vegetables or to use in casseroles. Garlic that's peeled but not cut has a much more mellow flavor than cut garlic.

¾ cup silken tofu

2 cups almond milk, soy milk, or other nondairy milk

⅓ cup olive oil

½ cup lecithin granules

16 cloves of garlic, peeled but not cut

2 tbsp arrowroot

1 tsp nutmeg, ground

1 tsp oregano, ground

½ tsp liquid stevia

½ tsp black pepper, ground

¼ tsp Vege-Sal or ⅛ tsp salt, or to taste

1. Combine all ingredients in a saucepan and bring to a boil over medium heat, stirring constantly.
2. Reduce the heat to low and simmer, covered, for 10 minutes, stirring often.
3. Purée in a blender.
4. Add more Vege-Sal or salt to taste, if desired.
   Yields: 3½ cups
   Preparation/cooking time: 20 minutes

Seaweeds

You can collect seaweeds all year, although it's certainly more difficult under winter conditions. The edible seaweeds, again, are delicious, and thanks to the popularity of Japanese cuisine. They're a familiar food nowadays, unlike when I first began foraging, when eating seaweeds was considered weird.

Japanese cuisine, naturally, uses Pacific seaweeds. We have some Atlantic species available with great culinary potential that haven't been explored by chefs. I'm happy to have experimented with them and discovered some great ways of using them.

Irish Moss
(*Chondrus crispus*)

Family: Gigartinaceae, a red algae family

Other names: Sea moss, blancmange, jelly moss, pearl moss, carrageen moss, seamuisin, curly moss, curly gristle moss, dorset weed, sea moss, white wrack, pioka

This is a short, frilly, fan-shaped, perennial seaweed that grows on both sides of the Atlantic. It reaches up to 6 inches in length and feels soft and cartilaginous. Tough and elastic when wet, it gets brittle when dry. It's more colors than any plant in this book. Usually dark purple-brown or blackish, it may also be greenish-yellow or red. It's iridescent-blue underwater, and the sun can bleach it white.

It grows from a disk-shaped holdfast, and its short stalk branches four or five times, creating a variable, fan-like shape, with subsections up to ¾ inch across. It ends in crowded, frilled-looking tips. No other seaweeds look like it.

It's in season all year. Look for it at low tide. If it's been detached from its anchorage by storms and the currents are right, you can find enough washed up on the beach to last for years, and it's easy to dehydrate. You can also find it in tidal pools, and in lower intertidal and shallow subtidal zones.

Irish moss is too tough to eat, so you simmer it for 20 minutes or more enclosed in a mesh bag or cheesecloth, then remove and discard it. It contains carrageenan, a traditional thickener for puddings that's also used in many commercial products. Carrageenan dissolves into your recipe: 1½ cups fresh Irish moss, or ½ cup of dried seaweed, thickens about 3½ cups of liquid. The Irish use it to thicken milk (as a vegan, I use nondairy milk) and make a pudding called blancmange.

Irish moss is a good source of vitamin B1, beta-carotene, and the minerals iodine, sulfur, potassium, calcium, phosphorus, iron, sodium, manganese, and bromine. It also contains mucins, protein, and a little fat.

Irish moss is nutritious and easy to digest, so puddings made with it are traditionally given to convalescents, especially people recovering from tuberculosis and pneumonia. Carrageenan is considered an anticoagulant, an anti inflammatory, a demulcent, an emollient, an expectorant, and a tonic. Because it coats the digestive tract, it's used to sooth peptic and duodenal ulcers, and given for gastritis and colon disorders.

It's a traditional remedy for thyroid problems such as goiter, and if the cause is an iodine deficiency, it'll work. It's also used for obesity, although there's no evidence showing that this works.

It's used to relieve diarrhea and help form bulky stools, and there's evidence that it can lower high blood pressure. Research has demonstrated antiviral properties, supporting its traditional use for irritating coughs, bronchitis, and other lung problems, some of which are caused by viruses.

A syrup of Irish moss, rose hips, honey, and lemon has been used for sore throat. A decoction helps heal chapped hands. Irish moss is also supposed to be help treat radiation contamination, but it needs to be tested. Anyone here interested in a trip to Fukushima?

Reports warn that Irish moss is dangerous because processed extracts are toxic, but carrageenan doesn't get into the bloodstream, no toxins get absorbed, and people have been using this food for thousands of years without problems.

RECIPE

Seaweed Pudding

A pudding made with seaweed sounds strange, but Irish moss has been used as a thickener for pudding for centuries, and it works perfectly here with chocolate and fruit.

3 cups coconut milk or other nondairy milk

½ cup dried Irish moss or 1½ cups fresh Irish moss

1 banana, sliced

¾ cup raspberries

1 orange, sliced, seeds removed

1 tsp liquid or powdered stevia

½ tsp cinnamon

½ tsp freshly grated lemon rind or lemon extract

¼ tsp salt

½ cup pecans, chopped

1. Tie the Irish moss into a bag of cheesecloth, or use a small mesh bag with a draw string.
2. Place this in a saucepan with all the remaining ingredients except the chocolate and pecans. Bring to a boil over medium heat, stirring often.
3. Reduce the heat to low and simmer, uncovered, for 15 minutes, stirring occasionally.
4. Remove the bag with the Irish moss and wring out any leftover material into the pudding when cool enough to handle (or wear rubber gloves if you don't have the patience to wait).
5. Stir in the chocolate until it's melted.
6. Chill until set.
7. Serve topped with the pecans.
   Serves: 6
   Preparation time: 30 minutes
   Cooking time: 15 minutes

Rockweed
(*Fucus vesiculosus*)

Family: Fucaceae, a brown algae family
Other names: Bladderwrack, bladder fucus, sea wrack, kelp ware, black-tang, cutweed, sea oak, dyers fucus, red fucus, rock wrack

Rockweed is so good, I love it even though I'm a jazz fan! This olive-brown seaweed grows up to 3 feet long and ½ inch wide. Yellowish when young, it's composed of many wavy, flat, fan-shaped, ribbon-like strips that repeatedly bifurcate, like the letter Y.

A midrib divides each strip, and distinctive, paired, ovoid air vessels, ½–¾ inch long, grow at regular intervals. These are the bladders, whereas "wrack" means seaweed. Similar white-tipped bumps, up to 1 inch long, grow at the seaweed's tips. Filled with jelly, they're the seaweed's reproductive organs. A woody, branched, discoid holdfast anchors the alga to the rocks—hence the other common name, "rockweed."

It grows in the North Atlantic, and similar relatives you can use the same way inhabit the North Pacific. Pick it off the rocks at low tide (or gather from beaches if a storm has washed it onto the shore), but walk very carefully or wear hiking shoes with cleats, as the wet rocks are very slippery, especially in the winter, when they can be icy as well.

It's an Atlantic seaweed, so it's not used in Japanese cuisine. Therefore, restaurant chefs don't know about it. You won't find it in restaurants, health food stores, or Japanese markets—where you can find better-known Pacific seaweeds.

Nevertheless, this is a very tasty seaweed, somewhat similar to hiziki and kelp, with a fishy overtone that makes it outstanding in vegan mock seaweed recipes. Because it contains sodium, don't add any salt to recipes

that include rockweed until the recipe is done and you've tasted it, in case it's already salty enough.

You can simmer rockweed in soups, stews, grain dishes, and bean recipes (where it reduces gas) for 15 minutes or until it's tender. The air bladders are especially good. They taste like pickles, so superb when sliced and added raw to salads and in sandwiches, in place of pickles. Rockweed can overpower other ingredients, but preboiling it in water for 2 minutes makes it more mild.

You can also dehydrate rockweed, then roast it in a slow oven with a tiny amount of oil, and spices, to make chips. Parboiling it briefly and roasting it with a flavored coating works especially well too.

Rockweed provides sodium, iodine, bromine, sodium, potassium, and chlorine, as well as alginic acid and many trace minerals.

This is a major tradition medicinal plant, and many of its uses have been verified by modern science. It's been used for thyroid problems and goiter for centuries. If the cause is iodine deficiency, it would solve the problem, although it's not as good as using carefully measured dosages of iodine.

It's used in weight loss products, none of which really works, unless, again, the weight gain is caused by iodine deficiency–related thyroid problems.

Rockweed reduces cholesterol levels and acts as a weak blood thinner, upholding its tradition use for heart disease. It contains mannite, an osmotic diuretic agent and a weak renal vasodilator, justifying its traditional use for kidney and bladder inflammation.

Only its external use for arthritis, rheumatism, enlarged or hardened glands, burns, and scalds haven't been tested, nor whether chewing it works for bleeding gums, something usually caused by infection.

RECIPE

Rockweed Trail Mix

This is the best compact food to take with you when foraging. It doesn't weigh much. It's very filling, extremely simple to make, provides sustained energy, and tastes great.

2 cups Chocolate Rockweed (see below)

2 cups roasted cashews, chopped

2 cups vegan, sugar-free carob chips, or chocolate chips

2 cups raisins or currants

½ tsp powdered stevia (optional)

1. Mix together all ingredients.
   Makes 8 cups
   Preparation time: 5 minutes

RECIPE

Chocolate Rockweed

These chocolate-flavored, candied seaweed chips are a great snack food, a wonderful addition to trail mix, and a superb addition to salads. You can even sprinkle them on vegetable dishes. They take a long time to bake, but make them on a day when you're going to be home anyway, and it'll be well worth the wait!

10 cups rockweed

1 cup Chocolate Coating (see p. 269)

1 tsp cinnamon

1 tsp powdered or liquid stevia

1 tsp chocolate extract

1. Boil the rockweed in water for 2 minutes.
2. Drain and mix it with the remaining ingredients.
3. Bake in a roasting pan in a preheated 325°F oven for 5 hours or until crisp, stirring occasionally.
   Yields: 6 cups
   Preparation time: 15 minutes
   Cooking time: 5 hours

Sea Lettuce (*Ulva lactuca*)

Family: Ulvaecea, the sea lettuce family

This common seaweed looks like bright or dark green, plastic, shrink wrap. Soft, translucent, and filmy, it's sometimes rounded, wrinkled, and perforated with holes. The sheets grow from 6 inches to 3 feet across, undivided and without lobes. It's often torn before being washed up onto beaches. Lying on the beach, it may get bleached white by the sun, or discolor black as it dries out or decomposes. The discoid holdfast that anchors it to rocks rarely gets washed ashore. No other seaweed looks like this one.

Although it's an annual, it can grow all year, although I find it in abundance from early summer to early winter around the New York shores. You can find it along the seashore, on submerged rocks and shells, or in the intertidal zone. It's often washed up on beaches. Avoid collecting it in polluted waters, where it thrives.

Pick up this member of the sea lettuce family, which grows worldwide, from the shore or from the ocean; bag it; and refrigerate it until you're ready to use it.

Rinse it thoroughly under running water in a colander set into a low bowl to get rid of all the sand. Change the water in the bowl several times and make sure all the grit is gone.

It's edible raw, but somewhat tough. Sautéed with garlic in olive oil and sprinkled with tamari soy sauce at the end, it's fantastic. It's also great in soups or stews, or stir-fried. It cooks in 10–15 minutes, and you can freeze it afterward.

Like other seaweeds, it tastes a little fishy, so it's superb in vegan mock seafood dishes.

Sea lettuce isn't used medicinally, but it's an excellent source of iron, protein, iodine, aluminum, manganese, and nickel. It also provides beta-carotene, B-complex vitamins, vitamin C, starch, fat, and sugar.

RECIPE

Sautéed Sea Lettuce

Sautéing sea lettuce like a land vegetable, with garlic and other seasonings, is simple but effective.

3 tbsp olive oil

4 cups sea lettuce, thoroughly rinsed and chopped

2 cloves of garlic, finely chopped

1 tbsp fresh dill weed, chopped, or 1 tsp dried dill weed, ground

¼ tsp oregano, ground

¼ tsp savory, ground

¼ tsp black pepper, ground

1 tsp tamari soy sauce, or to taste

1. Sauté all ingredients except the tamari soy sauce in the olive oil for 10 minutes.
2. Stir in the tamari soy sauce.
   Serves: 4–6
   Preparation/cooking time: 15 minutes

GLOSSARY

Achene: A small, dry, one-seeded fruit that doesn't open to release its seed

Agar: A gelatinous substance extracted from various kinds of red seaweed (class Rhodophyceae) that's used in biological culture media and as a thickener in foods, such as traditional Japanese puddings called kanten; also an excellent vegan alternative to gelatin, with the additional advantage of remaining solid at room temperature

Aggregate Fruit: A compound fruit in which one flower contains several ovaries, each of which develops into a small fruit, joined together tightly with its neighbors to make a larger fruit

Alterative: A treatment or medication that restores health

Alternate Leaves: Leaf attachments are singular at nodes and leaves alternate direction, to a greater or lesser degree, along the stem

Anodyne: A painkiller

Anthelmintic: A substance used to kill parasitic worms

Anther: The part of a stamen (male floral reproductive organ) that contains the pollen

Aperient: A substance that's good for constipation

Axillary: Arising from the leaf axil, where the leafstalk or leaf emerges from the stem

Basal Leaves: Leaves at a plant's base

Basal Rosette: A circular arrangement of leaves with all the leaves at the base of the plant, near the soil

Bilaterally Symmetrical Flowers: Flowers with identical right and left sides that are like mirror images

Bract: A modified or specialized leaf, especially one associated with a reproductive structure such as a flower—often different from other leaves

Bramble: Plants of the genus *Rubus*, in the rose (Rosaceae) family, usually prickly

Bundle Scar: The markings within a leaf scar where circulatory bundles were broken as the leafstalk broke off from the twig

Calyx: The set of a flower's sepals that encircle the petals in the bud stage

Cambium: A layer or layers of tissue, also known as lateral meristem, that are the source of cells for secondary growth, such as the layer just under the bark of a tree—sometimes called "inner bark," though it's not the bark

Cane: A flexible, hollow or woody, usually slender stem

Carminative: An herb that prevents or relieves flatulence

Celtic Salt: A very coarse salt that allows you to taste more salt in recipes where the salt doesn't dissolve, thereby letting you enjoy the flavor of salt while taking in way less sodium than you would using table salt

Chevron: A symbol consisting of stripes meeting at an angle, often worn on uniforms, and sometimes present as a dark triangle on leaves, especially of plants of high rank

Cholagogue: A medicinal substance that promotes the elimination of bile from the system

Composite Flower: A member of the aster family with a flower head usually composed of many tiny, central disk flowers surrounded by many, strap-shaped, ray flowers

Compound Fruit: A fruit that develops from several ovaries of either a single flower or multiple flowers

Compound Leaf: A leaf with a fully subdivided blade, each leaflet of the blade separated along a main or secondary vein

Corm: A short, rounded, underground, swollen stem base that serves as a storage organ

Corolla: The petals of a flower, usually forming a whorl within the sepals and enclosing the pistils and stamens

Counterirritant: A substance used to produce surface irritation of the skin, to counteract underlying pain or irritation

Cyme: A usually flat-topped or convex flower cluster where the main axis and each branch end with a flower that opens before those below or next to it

Deciduous: A tree, shrub, or vine that sheds its leaves annually

Decoction: A method of extraction of herbal or plant material that may include stems, roots, cambiums, or rhizomes by boiling

Demulcent: A substance that relieves irritations or inflammations of the mucous membranes, especially in the mouth, by forming a protective film

Deobstruent: A substance with the power to clear or open the natural ducts of the fluids and secretions of the body

Diaphoretic: A medicine or other agent that produces perspiration

Dioecious: A plant with male and female reproductive organs on different individuals

Disk Flower: Any of the tiny tubular florets, usually fertile, in the central part of the flower head of many members of the aster or composite family

Diuretic: Any substance that elevates the rate of urination

Drupe: A one-seeded fruit with a hard, bony seed cover that doesn't split open, surrounded by a fleshy layer that's inside a thin, flexible skin

Entire: Leaves with no teeth, lobes, or other divisions

Expectorant: A substance that helps bring up mucus and other material from the lungs, bronchi, and trachea

Feather-compound Leaf: A leaf divided into segments (leaflets) arranged on either side of the stem, typically in pairs opposite each other; also called a pinnate leaf

Febrifuge: A medicine used to lower fever

Fibrous Roots: Thin, moderately branching roots growing from the stem

Fiddlehead: The young, curled, edible frond of some fern species

Filament: The slender part of a stamen (the male part of a flower) that supports the anther

Floret: One of the small flowers that make up a flower head

Flower Head: A compact mass of flowers at the top of a stem

Follicle: A dry fruit that's derived from a single female flower and releases its seeds by opening on one side

Food Mill: A device consisting of a bowl, a bottom plate with holes like those in a colander, and a crank fitted with a bent metal blade, to force food through the holes in the bottom plate as the crank is turned and very useful for foragers who need to separate fruit from hard seeds

Fritter: Food coated in batter and fried

Holdfast: A stalked organ that a seaweed or other organism uses to attach itself to its substrate

Infusion: A beverage or remedy made by soaking plant parts in liquid, usually water just off the boil

Konjac: *Amorphophallus konjac*, a little-known Far Eastern plant, used as a thickener for hundreds of years, and available in powdered form in health food stores and online.

Leaf Axil: The upper angle between a leafstalk and the stem that bears it

Leaflet: Each of the leaflike structures that together make up a compound leaf, or a part of a compound (segmented) leaf that may resemble an entire leaf, but doesn't grow on a stem like a real leaf, rather on a vein of the whole leaf

Lecithin: A fat essential found in the cells of the human body and an excellent vegan substitute for egg yolks, available in health food stores and online

Lenticel: One of many raised pores in the stem of a woody plant that allows gas exchange between the atmosphere and the internal tissues

Marmite: A sticky, dark brown, flavorful, salty, British, yeast-based food paste, available in health food stores and online

Multiple Fruit: A compound fruit in which several flowers, each with an ovary, develop into small fruits clustered or fused together to form a larger fruit

Nutlet: A seed covered by a stony layer

Opposite Leaves: Leaf attachments that are paired at each node

Palmate-compound Leaves: Leaves consisting of leaflets or lobes radiating from the base of the leaf

Panicle: A loose, branching flower or seed cluster

Parasiticide: A medicine or agent that kills parasites

Parboil: Cook partially by boiling

Pectoral: A medicine for relieving disorders of the chest or respiratory tract

Perennial Herbaceous Plant: A perennial is a plant that lives many years, and an herbaceous species has no woody parts, so nonwoody plants such as common milkweed, which has underground stems (rhizomes), can die to the ground in the winter, but come back the following year

Phytochemical: A biologically active chemical found in plants

Poultice: A soft, moist mass of material, typically of plant matter, mixed with clay or flour, applied to the body to relieve soreness and inflammation, and tied or bandaged in place with a cloth

Purgative: A strong laxative

Raceme: An unbranched, specialized stem of short-stalked flowers

Radially Symmetrical Flowers: Flowers that can be divided into three or more identical sectors that look the same when you rotate the flower

Ray Flower: A strap-shaped, usually sterile floret that grows toward the periphery of a composite flower, closer to the edge than any central disk flowers if they're present

Receptacle: An enlarged area at the tip of a stem that bears the organs of a flower or a fruit

Reflexed: Bent or turned backward

Rhizome: A characteristically horizontal stem usually found underground, often sending out roots and shoots from its nodes; also called creeping rootstocks or rootstocks

Runner: A usually leafless shoot growing along the surface of the ground from the base of a plant that takes root at points along its length

Samara: A winged nut containing one seed, as in a maple tree

Scape: A long, leafless flower stalk arising directly from the root

Seedpod: An elongated seed container of a member of the legume family that splits open on both sides when ripe

Sepals: Modified leaves, usually green, that lie under the more conspicuous petals of a flower

Shoot: New plant growth, which can include stems, flowering stems with flower buds, or leaves

Simple Leaf: A leaf that's not divided into segments, as in a compound leaf or a lobed leaf

Spike: A type of raceme with flowers that don't have individual flower stalks

Sporophyll: A leaf that bears sporangia, an enclosure in which spores are formed

Spring Ephemeral: A wildflower, usually growing in woodlands, that blooms for only a few weeks in early spring and disappears

Spur: A short flower- and fruit-bearing side shoot

Stamen: The male fertilizing organ of a flower, typically consisting of a pollen-containing anther and a filament

Stevia: *Stevia rebaudiana*, a member of the aster or composite family native to Paraguay, with a sweet flavor but no calories and a great substitute for sugar, sold in health food stores and online

Stigma: The part of a pistil (the female flower parts) that receives the pollen during pollination

Stimulant: A substance that functions as an "upper" and raises levels of physiological or nervous activity in the body

Stipules: Outgrowths borne on either side of the base of a leafstalk

Stomachic: A medicine that stimulates the appetite and aids digestion

Tamari Soy Sauce: A less salty, more flavorful Japanese soy sauce, and an alternative to the more familiar Chinese soy sauce

Taproot: A straight tapering root growing downward vertically and forming the center from which subsidiary rootlets spring

Tepals: Petals and sepals that can't be distinguished from each other

Terminal: At the end or tip

Tincture: A medicine made by dissolving a plant in alcohol, usually vodka

Tonic: A plant or medicine that creates a feeling of vigor or well-being

Umbel: An umbrella-like flower cluster where stalks of nearly equal length arise from a common center and form a flat or curved surface

Vegan Butter Substitute: Products made with vegetable oils and without saturated fats or partially hydrogenated oils that replace butter, such as Earth Balance products, available in health food stores and online

Vege-Sal: A seasoned salt that makes dishes taste salty with half the sodium of table salt, available in health food stores and online

Vegetable Glycerin: A clear, odorless liquid produced from plant oils that makes an excellent sweetener, without the unhealthful effects of sugar and related refined or concentrated carbohydrate sweeteners; also used in cosmetics

Vulnerary: A substance of use in the healing of wounds

Whorled: Three or more leaves attached at each point or node on the stem, often circling the stem

INDEX

ABOUT THE AUTHOR

"Wildman" Steve Brill has been leading public foraging tours in parks throughout the Greater New York Region since 1982. He works with schools, day camps, environmental organizations, museums, parks departments, nature centers, scouts, garden clubs, and educational farms, in addition to having published numerous books and released an app on foraging (http://www.wildmanstevebrill.com/). But he's still best-known for having been arrested and handcuffed by undercover park rangers for eating a dandelion in Central Park!